ENCYCLOPAEDIA OF
CYBER LAWS AND CRIME

ENCYCLOPAEDIA OF CYBER LAWS AND CRIME

Vol. 1

The Nature of Cyber Laws

Edited by

S.R. Sharma

ANMOL PUBLICATIONS PVT. LTD.
NEW DELHI - 110 002 (INDIA)

ANMOL PUBLICATIONS PVT. LTD.
4374/4B, Ansari Road, Daryaganj
New Delhi - 110 002
Ph.: 23261597, 23278000
Visit us at: www.anmolpublications.com

Encyclopaedia of Cyber Laws and Crime

First Edition, 2003

ISBN 81-261-1432-0 (Set)

[The responsibility for the facts stated, conclusions reached and plagiarism, if any, in this work is entirely that of the Editor. And the Publisher bears no responsibility for them, whatsoever.]

PRINTED IN INDIA

Published by J.L. Kumar for Anmol Publications Pvt. Ltd., New Delhi - 110 002 and Printed at Mehra Offset Press, Delhi.

CONTENTS

PREFACE

In the last years of the twentieth century a phenomenon has been witnessed which is likely to change the shape of human civilization. This is the explosion which has taken place in electronics and as a result of which there has been infinite expansion of knowledge that is commonly described as information explosion. The most astounding development in this area has been the geometric expansion of trade commerce entertainment and information jointly known as the internet or the web. The web accepts no restrictions of the country, race religion or country and has been totally responsible as a decisive factor in taking the world into what is now known as globalisation.

It is generally believed that a website is created every minute and along with its positive aspect it also brings about a new sense of responsibility. The free trade and commerce available through website in what is known as cyber space has also given birth to a mobile population where intent may be basically criminal. Thus we have hachers, virus carriers, sleepers and moles, who may constitute a real threat to the creativity of the web. There is, therefore, the eternal question of intellectual copyright and the policing of vast cyber space to protect and maintain what manhood can truly achieve.

Consequently the TRAI Act 1997 has been enacted by the Indian parliament in the 48th year of Republic of India on 28th March 1997 to provide for the establishment of the Telecom Regulatory Authority of India (TRAI) to regulate the telecommunication services and for matters connected therewith are incidental thereto.

As per Section 11 (2) of the TRAI Act TRAI is empowered to fix/revise tariff for various telecom services provided in India and service providers including the Department service provisions have to implement the tariffs, notified by the TRAI as per provisions of law.

The TRAI has been mandated to fix/revise tariff for various telecom services by virtue of section 11 (2) of TRAI Act.

The Encyclopaedia tries to cover as many laws as possible, promulgated by various countries and unions of countries like the European Union in this area to give a comprehensive and comparative view of CYBER Law.

The editor has no claims to originality and has simply compiled and edited the material collected from various sources. In view of the English language being the medium most of the material has been collected from American, British and Indian sources.

The editor is grateful to the Librarians of the library of the Supreme Court, the Indian Law Institute and the Ministry of Law, Justice and Company Affairs, for their kind assistance in locating the material from various sources.

The editor is specifically grateful to Shri Jawahar Lal Kumar, Managing Director, Anmol Publications Pvt. Ltd., New Delhi for venturing to publish the Encyclopaedia on Cyber Laws.

—Dr. S.R. Sharma

1 INTELLECTUAL PROPERTY RIGHTS: AN INTRODUCTION

'Intellectual property' is the name given to legal rights which protect creative works, inventions and commercial goodwill. Basically, intellectual property rights are designed to provide remedies against those who steal the fruits of another person's ideas or work. For example, if a person writes a novel, a piece of music or a computer program, he will be able to take legal action to obtain an injunction and/or damages against anyone who copies the novel, music or program without his permission. In view of the large investment required to finance research, design and development in respect of computer hardware and software, these intellectual property rights are of crucial importance to the computer world. Without such protection, there would be little incentive to invest in the development of new products.

What are these intellectual property rights? Some will sound familiar — for example, *copyright*, *patents* and *trade marks* — while others will be less familiar — for example, the *law of confidence, design rights* and *passing off*. The scope of these rights differs but sometimes overlaps. Different rights may be appropriate at different times during the lifespan of a product from inception through development to marketing and subsequent modification and updating. Sometimes infringement of intellectual property rights gives rise to criminal penalties but, primarily, this area of law falls within the bounds of civil law. At the stage, by way of introduction, it will be useful to describe briefly the various intellectual property rights.

Copyright Law

As its name suggests, copyright protects works from being copied without permission. Copyright goes beyond mere copying, however, and extends to other activities such as making the adaptation of the work in question, performing or showing the work in public, broadcasting the work and dealing with infringing copies of the work. The types of works protected by copyright are literary works (including computer programs, preparatory design material for computer programs and databases), dramatic, musical and artistic works, sound recordings, films, broadcasts, cable programmes and typographical arrangements of published editions. Copyright protection has a long duration, the general yardstick being the life of the author (creator) plus 70 years or, depending on the type of work, 50 or 70 years from the end of the year during which the work was created or published. The major attractions of copyright as form of protection are that it is free and that no formalities are required; it is automatic upon the creation of the work in question. Additionally, copyright law is practical in nature and has developed to take account of technological changes and advances. In short, most things, if they have been recorded in some tangible form (for example, by writing or printing or by storing the work on a magnetic disk), are protected by copyright, subject to some basic requirements being satisfied. Copyright law is of vital importance to the computer software industry and to people who prepare, record or transmit all sorts of works (for example, literary works such as books, reports, letters, or musical works) using computer technology. Copyright law is governed by the Copyright, Designs and Patents Act 1988, the main provisions of which came into force on 1 August 1989, and subsequent amendments, together with a wealth of case law.

Until the Copyright and Rights on Database Regulations 1997 came into force on 1 January 1998, databases were protected as compilations, being a form of literary work. Now, there are two forms of protection, for databases. Those that are 'intellectual creations' have copyright investment are protected by a 'database right' which is of shorter duration than copyright. In many cases, databases will be subject to both rights.

Patent Law

Patent law is concerned with new inventions such as a new type of computer hardware, or a new process for use in the manufacture of integrated circuits. For an invention to be protected by a patent, an application must be made to the Patent Office, an expensive and lengthy process and, if granted, the patent can be renewed for a total period of up to 20 years. Three routes are open to the potential patentee: a United Kingdom patent; a European Patent Convention (EPC) patent applying in respect of three or more of the member states; or a Patent Cooperation Treaty (PCT) patent designating some or all of the countries covered by the treaty. The choice of countries in which to obtain protection is obviously of fundamental importance and requires careful planning and timing. The relevant statute dealing with patent law is the Patents Act 1977. To be patentable, an invention must be new, involve an inventive step, be capable of industrial application and not be excluded. Most things which are protected directly by copyright law such as a literary work are excluded from patentability; therefore, a new computer program cannot normally be protected by a patent. If there is an associated technical effect, however, a patent may be a possibility. For example, a new computer controlled industrial process may be patentable even though the inventive step resides in the computer program. A patent is the form of intellectual property *par excellence* giving the nearest thing to an outright monopoly although there are provisions in United Kingdom law and European Community law (and United States law) to prevent abuse of patents and other intellectual property rights.

The Law of Confidence

The law of confidence protects information. Unlike copyright and patent law, the law of confidence is not defined by statute and derives almost entirely from case law. The scope of this branch of intellectual property is considerable and it protects trade secrets, business know how and information such as lists of clients and contacts, information of a personal nature and even ideas which have not yet been expressed in a tangible form (for example, an idea for a new dramatic play or an idea for a new computer program). The contents of many databases will be protected by the law of confidence. However, the major limitation is that the information concerned must be of a confidential nature and the effectiveness of the law of confidence is largely or completely destroyed if the information concerned falls into the public domain; that is, if it becomes available to the public at large or becomes common knowledge to a particular group of the public such as computer software companies. Nevertheless, the law of confidence can be a useful supplement to copyright and patent law as it can protect ideas before they are sufficiently developed to attract copyright protection or to enable an application for a patent to be made. Being rooted in equity, the law of confidence is very flexible and has proved capable of taking new technological developments in its stride.

TABLE 1.1

Intellectual Property Rights — Summary

Right	*Types or works protected*	*Examples with respect to computers*	*Duration*	*Formalities (UK only)*
Copyright	* Original literary, dramatic, musical or artistic works * Sound recordings, films, broadcasts or cable programmes * Typographical arrangement of published editions a computer-aided design or (Computer programs and preparatory design material for computer programs are literary works)	Computer programs and preparatory design material. Databases, other types of work made using a computer or generated by a computer, e.g. a weather forecast automatically made by a computer linked to weather satellites or years music made using a computer. Almost any form of work stored digitally	Generally 70 years after the death of the 'author for the original works For most of the other works the period is 50	None Copyright is automatic upon the work being created
Patent	New inventions including products and industrial processes	New type of printer or computer, new method of making computer'chips', software controlled industrial process	Renewable up to a maximum of 20 years	Application to the Patent Office to be placed on the register of patents

cont...

Right	*Types or works protected*	*Examples with respect to computers*	*Duration*	*Formalities (UK only)*
Confidence	Almost anything of a confidential nature (whether or not stored on computer)	Idea for a new computer program or for a new invention (prior to patent), secret algorithm, lists of customers, business methods.	Until subject matter falls into the 'public' domain'	None
Designs				
* Registered design	New designs, being feature of shape, configuration, pattern or ornament applied to an article by an industrial process and having 'eye-appeal'	Aesthetically pleasing designs for computer hardware including surface decoration, e.g. notebook computer, mouse, computer accessories	Initially 5 years renewable by 5-for periods up to a maximum of 25 years	Registration by application to the Design Registry
* Design right	Original designs, being any aspect of shape or configuration (external or internal) of the whole or part of an article. Applies to functional and aesthetic designs. Spare parts and surface decoration excluded	Diskette case (partly), template for drawing computer symbols, keyboard design, mouse, internal components if not commonplace	15 years from creation or 10 years from first marketing	None-automatic at with copyright

Registered trade marks	Any sign capable of being represented graphically which is capable of distinguishing goods or from those of other under-taking from those of other undertakings	'IBM' 'Microsoft', 'Oracle'. the Apple logo	Initially for 10 years and renewable in 10 years periods indefintely	Application to the Trade Marks Registry
Passing off	Trade names and marks, product 'get-up' or style	Software names which have not been registered as trade marks but a around which a reputation associated with goodwill has been acquired	Indefinite as long as the name, get-up or style still associ-ated with goodwill, e.g. by continued use	None
Semiconductor Regulations (modified design right)	Topography (patterns or arrangements of layers in 'chips')	New design of integrated circuit	15 years been creation or 10 years from commercial exploitation	None

Note: As far as periods for protection are concerned, for copyright, the design right and the semiconductor regulations, these periods are measured from the end of the calendar year during which the relevant event occured, e.g the creation of the work or the death of the author.

The Law Relating to Designs

The statutory provisions covering rights in new designs are complicated. Essentially, there are tow types of right: *registered designs* and a *design right* which is not registrable. The former is available for features of articles which appeal to the eye while the latter is intended to protect any aspect of the shape or configuration of articles without any requirement for visual attractiveness. The complexity of this area of law is compounded by the fact that the distinction between the rights is not easy to draw as there is considerable overlap as regards the rights *inter se* and with respect to copyright law.

COPYRIGHT BASICS

Fundamentals

Copyright protects a wide range of works and has developed enormously since its early beginnings as form of controlling printing in the early sixteenth century. Copyright has a pragmatic approach and it extends to all manner of works regardless of quality, subject to some basic requirements, which are usually easily satisfied. Since the end of the nineteenth century, tables, compilations and even codebooks have been the subject matter of copyright law. During the twentieth century, copyright has flourished and now includes under its umbrella the following: photographs, films, broadcasts, sound recordings, cable programmes as well as computer programs, preparatory deign material for computer programs, databases and works stored in or produced by or with the aid of a computer. The practical development of copyright has been supported by the judges who have usually been sympathetic to the principle of protecting the results of a person's skill, effort of judgment. As Mr Justice Peterson said in *University of London Press Ltd v University Tutorial Press Ltd* [1916] 2 Ch 601:

> ...what is worth copying is *prima facie* worth protecting.

Copyright is declared to subsist (that is, 'exist') in the following works by virtue of section 1 of the Copyright, Designs and Patents Act 1988:

(a) original literary, dramatic, musical or artistic works,
(b) sound recordings, films, broadcasts or cable programmes, and
(c) the typographical arrangement of published editions

proving that the requirements for qualification are met: for example, that the author of an original literary work is a British citizen or has certain other nationality or residential qualifications, or that the work was first published on the United Kingdom.

The owner of the copyright in a work is then given the exclusive right to do certain specified *restricted acts* in relation to the work, described below. It is important to appreciate that copyright is a property right and it can be dealt with just as any other form of property. The owner of a copyright is usually the author of the work (the person creating it), except when the work is made by an employee in the course of his employment, in which case his employer will be the first owner unless otherwise agreed (section 11). There are other exceptions to the basic rule, such as in the case of Crown copyright. The Copyright, Designs and Patents Act 1988 usually refers to the creator of a work as the 'author' of the work, thus a person writing a piece of music is the author of the music and a photographer is the author of his photographs. For sound recordings and computer-generated works, the author is the person who makes the arrangements necessary of the making or creation of the work (section 9), so the author of a report produced automatically by a computer will normally be the person who operates the computer or who manages the computer facilities. In many cases, ownership, as distinct from authorship, will reside with an employer.

The identity of the author is important because the duration of copyright in original literary, dramatic, musical or artistic works (not being computer-generated) is determined by the life of the author, irrespective of ownership. The copyright in such works lasts for 70 years from the end of the calendar year during which the author dies (recently increased from the life of the author plus 50 years as a result of a European Community Directive on the term of copyright, OJ [1993] L290/9).

If the work is one of joint authorship (a collaborative work in which the contribution of each author is not distinct from that of the other authors), as many computer programs and other computer works will be, the 70-year period starts to run from the end of the calendar year during which the last surviving author dies. This generosity in terms of duration of copyright might seem disproportionate in a fast-moving technology but can be justified on the basis that copyright does not give a true monopoly; it does not protect ideas, merely the expression of an idea. For other works, except films where the 70-year period is used, the duration is set a 50 years from the end of the calendar year during which the work was created, broadcast, included in a cable programme service or released, as appropriate. There are exceptions and copyright in typographical arrangements and certain commercially exploited artistic works lasts for 25 years only. The author's identity may also be important for determining whether a work qualifies for protection. It should be noted, however that there are tow international conventions affording reciprocal protection to foreign works of copyright and which also protect United Kingdom works in other countries.

The acts restricted by copyright, and which only the owner of the copyright has the right to do or authorise, are set out section 16. They are:

(a) to copy the work;
(b) to issue copies of the work to the public;
(ba) to rent or lend the work to the public;
(c) to perform, show or play the work in public;
(d) to broadcast the work or include it in cable programme; service;
(e) to make an adaptation of the work or do any of the above in relation to an adaptation.

Section 16(ba) was inserted by the Copyright and Related Rights Regulations 1996 to comply with a European Community Directive on rental right and lending right (OJ [1992] L 346/61. Section 16(b) was also modified to cover all forms of copyright work.

Infringement

A person infringes the copyright in a work if he does not of these restricted acts or authorises another to do one of the acts in relation to a substantial part of the work without the permission of the copyright owner and such a person may be sued by the copyright owner (or an exclusive licensee of the owner) for the infringement. There are certain exceptions to infringement contained in sections 28-77. Copyright is not infringed by 'fair dealing' with a work for the purposes of research or private study or for criticism, review or news reporting or any of the other limited exceptions concerning, *inter alia,* educational and library use. There are also some important exceptions relating to computer programs introduced by the Copyright

(Computer Programs) Regulations 1992. These allow for a 'decompilation exception', making back up copies of computer programs and use of program including error correction. Further specific exceptions relate to databases. There are additional ways of infringing copyright, some of which also carry criminal penalties, known as secondary infringements. In broad terms, these apply where the infringer has been dealing commercially with infringing copies, such as by importing, distributing or selling them, and, unlike the infringing acts described above, some form of knowledge is required, that is, that the person involved knew or had reason to believe that he was dealing with infringing copies. The equivalent criminal offences under copyright law are dealt with separately in Part Three of this book.

Remedies or Infringement

If the owner of copyright successfully sues a person for infringment of that copyright, there are several remedies available. In particular, an injunction, damages or an account of profits might be appropriate and these are provided for by section 96. Copyright damages may be assessed as the estimated loss resulting from the infringment: for example, the licence fee or royalties that the copyright owner would have expected to receive had he given permission for the acts complained of. For example, if a computer software pirate makes and sells 100 copies of a computer program, and associated documentation, each valued at £500, the copyright owner might expect damages equivalent to a 10 per cent royalty: that is, 10% x 100 x £500 = £5000. Damages are not available if the defendant did not know or had no reason to believe that the work was protected by copyright. The meaning of 'having no reason to believe that copyright subsisted in a work' requires an objective test; that is, whether tne reasonable man, having knowledge of the facts knows to the defendant, would have believed that copyright subsisted in the work (see *LA Gear Inc v HI-Tec Sports plc* [1992] FSR 121). An infringer of computer software copyright cannot escape an award of damages merely by turning a blind eye to the question of whether the software is protected by copyright or being indifferent to the possibility. In any case, an account of profits, as an alternative to damages, may be available regardless of the defendant's knowledge and could be awarded even where the person infringing copyright has done so innocently. Of course software piracy can attract similar penalities also.

Injunctions are very important because they prevent continued or anticipated infringement of copyright. An injunction is a count order requiring the defendant to do something or to refrain from doing something. For example, an injunction would be appropriate to stop a computer software pirate continuing to sell unauthorised copies of computer programs. A particularly useful type of injunction is an interlocutory injunction. If a person is used for infringing copyright, it may be a considerable time before the case comes to trial and, in the meantime, considerable damage can be done to the copyright owner's business. This is very relevant in the context of a fast-moving technology like computer technology and, to deal with this problem, the court may be willing to accede to a request for an interlocutory injunction (that is, an interim injunction) pending the full trial. However, an interlocutory injunction will be granted to a plaintiff only if there is serious question to be tried and the claim does not appear to the court to be frivolous or vexatious. Additionally, the balance of convenience must be satisfied, meaning that the damage likely to be done to be plaintiff if the alleged infringement continues is greater than the harm that will be done to the defendant if the injunction is granted (see *NWL Ltd v Woods* [1979] 1 WLR 1294). This balance of convenience is of particular importance if the granting or refusal of an interlocutory injunction would have very serious consequences for either party. In any case, an interlocutory injunction will not be granted if the payment of damages by the defendant at the full trial would be an adequate remedy.

For an interlocutory injunction to be a possibility, the courts used to require that the plaintiff showed a serious issue. However, since the case of *Series 5 Software Ltd v Clarke* [1996] FSR 273, the courts have been more willing to consider the relative strengths of the parties' cases as they appear at that stage. In *Series 5 Software,* the defendant removed software belonging to the plaintiff allegedly in order to encourage that latter to make payment owing to the defendant. The injunctions sought were refused but the judge continued an order for the defendant to deliver up any materials he had which belonged to the plaintiff. If the defendant had any such materials in his possession and failed to deliver them, he would be in contempt of court.

The courts also have a discretion to award additional damages under section 97(2), having regard to the flagrancy of the infringement and the benefit accruing to the defendant. This is akin to punitive damages. Additional damages are suitable in cases where normal damages would not be appropriate: for example, where the defendant has blatantly infringed copyright thinking that he can make a profit far in excess of any normal damages he might have to pay. Another possible use for additional damages is where the plaintiff has not suffered purely economic loss. This might be the case if the infringement concerned some material which the plaintiff did not want to publish such as the contents of his diary. In *Willims v Settle* [1960] WLR 1072, additional damages were considered suitable when a professional photographer, without permission of the copyright, owner, supplied the press with a wedding photograph showing a man who had been murdered.

Recently, plaintiffs seem more prepared to ask for additional damages. In relation to computer software, such damages may be relevant in the case of blatant infringement, for example, by deliberately using someone else's specialised computer software to gain a competitive edge over that other person. Another example is where a person deliberately makes use of another person's database of highly sensitive information. It has been confirmed that additional damages may only be awarded alongside ordinary damages and not an account of profits. A plaintiff has to elect between damages and an account of profits and cannot ask for both.

In addition to the remedies mentioned above, the plaintiff may apply to the court for an order for the infringing copies to be delivered up to him or for those copies to be destroyed.

Moral Rights

Moral rights ar a relatively new concept in the United Kingdom, and were introduced by sections 77-89 of the Copyright, Designs and Patents Act 1988. These rights, which have long been recognised in some European countries, are independent and distinct from ownership of copyright and give the author of a literary, dramatic, musical or artistic work and the director of a film the right:

- to be identified as the author (or director) of the work.
- to object to a derogatory treatment of the work (for example, if someone rewrites a serious play in the form of a farce without the author's permission), and

- to not have a work falsely attributed to him (this right previously existed under the Copyright Act 1956).

There is also a right to privacy with respect to photographs and films made for private and domestic purposes.

These moral rights last as long as the copyright in the work, with the exception of the false attribution right which lasts for 20 years after the death of the person falsely attributed. The rights are designed to give the creator of the work, who may no longer be the owner of the copyright itself, a degree of control and recognition in respect of the work. By section 103, infringements of moral rights are treated as a breach of statutory duty, injunctions and damages being appropriate remedies. Strangely, there is no provision for additional damages and, presumably, damages will be based on economic loss only. However, the plaintiff may also have a claim in defamation, particularly in respect of a derogatory treatment of his work or the false attribution of a work.

As computer programs are considered to be literary works, it is surprising that the first to be the moral rights mentioned above are stated not to apply to computer programs. Less surprisingly, nor do they apply to computer-generated works. These exceptions may be justified because of the commercial nature of most computer programs and other software and because of the need to prevent ex-employees attempting to interfere with any future changes to the software they had previously developed. Problems could arise if computer programmers and systems analysts demanded to be recognised as authors, as many computer programs are the result of teamwork, involving many individuals, both in the development of the original program and in subsequent alterations and upgrades.

Moral rights will exist in relation to other forms of original works created using a computer, such as a report or computer-aided design, and in respect of many other types of work stored in a computer in digital form, for example, in a database of artistic works. However, employee-created works are excepted in relation to things done by or with the licence of the copyright owner and the author must positively assert his moral right to be identified. Furthermore, an author may waive his moral rights.

Dealing with Copyright

We have already seen that authorship and ownership of copyright are two distinct concepts and that, normally, an employee writing a computer program will be the author if that program but his employer will own the copyright unless they agree otherwise. Frequently, the owner of a copyright will want to use a third party to exploit that copyright for him. It might be more attractive financially to use a publisher to market and sell copies of the work, because the latter will have the marketing expense and distribution facilities necessary to sell the work in large numbers. The usual way is for the copyright owner to grant a licence to the publisher. In terms of copyright, a licence is a permission to do one or more of the acts restricted by copyright and licences are usually contractual in nature; that is, the publisher will pay a licence fee or royalties in return for the permission. In may cases, the licence will be exclusive, which means that permission will be granted to one publisher only. In the case of marketing computer programs, the copyright owner might grant an exclusive licence to a software publisher who will then grant non-exclusive user licences to 'purchasers' of copies of the program. The users will need licences because loading a program onto a hard disk or into computer memory involves making a copy or adaptation of the program, acts restricted by the copyright. By section 92(1), an exclusive licence must be in writing and signed by or on behalf of the owner of the copyright. No formalities are required for non-exclusive licences but it is sensible to make a written record of the agreement.

Non-exclusive software licences are very commor and are used where the copyright owner wishes to retain ownership but wants to allow several or many other persons to use the software. This is the way a great deal of 'off-the shelf' software is made available. Each person acquiring a copy of the software obtains a licenced permitting certain uses. Of course, a licence is only required in as much as the use of software is controlled by copyright but the agreement will include additional terms dealing with other issues such as liability for defects.

Alternatively, the owner of a copyright may *assign* the copyright (that is, transfer ownership of the copyright) to another person and an assignment must be distinguished from a licence. With an assignment, the copyright owner transfers all or part of his rights to another person, whereas a licence is a permission given to another person authorising him to do certain specified things in relation to the copyright work. Furthermore, ownership in copyright can pass under a will or by way of intestacy or as a result of the bankruptcy of the copyright owner. Moral rights cannot be assigned (section 94) but may pass under a will or intestacy (by section 95).

Assignments and exclusive licences, to be effective at law, must be in writing and signed by or on behalf of the assignor (person making the assignment) or licensor (person granting the licence) as the case may be. If these requirements are not complied with the courts may be prepared to use the concept of beneficial ownership or to imply a licence giving the acquirer the right to do what, in the view of the court, was intended by the parties. Nevertheless, it is obviously more satisfactory to make sure that the formalities are complied with.

It is possible to deal with a future copyright; that is, copyright in a work yet to be created (section 91). The prospective owner can assign the future copyright or grant licences in respect of it. These provisions are useful where a self-employed consultant is engaged to create a new item of software. The agreement under which he is engaged should contain a term to the effect that he assigns the future copyright in any work created under the agreement to the person engaging him. This agreement must then be signed by or on behalf of the consultant, and, on the work coming into existence, the assignment will automatically take effect. This simple expedient is very important in the software industry, where many persons ar self-employed or freelance, and can prevent a bitter dispute later as to ownership of copyright.

2 COMPUTER SOFTWARE AND COPYRIGHT

Now that the basic principles of copyright law have been described the relevance of copyright to computer software can be examined. There are two main areas; the first concerns the protection of computer software and, in particular, computer programs and databases from unauthorised copying; the second area concerns works of various types which have been created *by* or *with the aid of* a computer or are stored and accessed or made available electronically. This chapter concentrates on computer programs and the following chapters are concerned with databases, computer-generated works and electronic publishing.

Copyright law protects computer software, whether it be programs, databases, computer files or printed documentation, whereas patent law protects new and inventive forms of computer hardware hearing in mind, of course, that items of hardware often incorporate software. The distinction between hardware and software is sometimes difficult to determine. For example, does a 'dongle' contain a computer program? A dongle is a device which is inserted into a computer port enabling certain programs to be used and is employed as a form of copy protection, limiting the use of program to one computer at any given time. In the Australian use of *Dyason* v *Autodeks Inc* (1990) 96 ALR 57 it was held that the dongle together with the program used to write digital information into it were, in combination, a computer program for copyright purposes. Some confusion as to whether a single word in a computer program was itself a program was resolved in the Federal Court of Australia which held that a single statement in a high-level programming language was not a program but was merely the cipher or key to access a set of instructions. *Powerflux* v *Data Access Corp* [1997] FCA 490. In the United Kingdom there has been some judicial confusion as to whether 'hard-wiring' a computer program in a ROM chip allows the algorithm it represents to be patented (see *Gale's Application* [1996] RPC 305).

Although it is clear that computer software is protected by copyright, current issues concern the scope of that protection and the need to preserve a balance between the rights of the copyright owner and the interests of competitors and what should constitute fair use of existing software. It has steady been felt necessary to amend the 1988 Act to achieve that balance (as part of the wider goal of harmonising copyright protection for computer programs throughout the European Community.) Although the legal protection of computer software has been radically improved in recent years, there remain areas of doubt and uncertainty even now that there have been two important High Court cases on the infringement of copyright in computer programs. An awareness of these areas will be important for those developing, using and exploiting computer software.

Computer Programs

The term computer software includes computer programs, databases, computer files, preparatory design materials, all manner of works stored digitally to be accessed by computer and a associated printed documentation such as manuals for users. There has never been any difficulty with regard to printed materials as these have been and continue to be protected by copyright. The protection of computer programs has been less certain and before 1985 it was unclear whether they were protected by copyright. One view was that listings of source code programs were protected as literary works by analogy with codebooks or because they resembled written English to some extent. On the whole, the courts appeared to be sympathetic, towards the notion that computer programs were protected. For example, in *Sega Enterprises Ltd* v *Richgards* [1983] FSR 73, which concerned alleged copies of the computer game 'FROGGER' (the object of which was to get a frog across a busy road without in being sqashed by a lorry), the trial judge was of the opinion that the source code program was protected by copyright and the object code program was protected indirectly as an adaptation of the source code version. However, this was an interlocutory hearing only and the case did not go to a full trial, so the point was not finally decided. Indeed, cases involving copying of computer programs did not seem to get beyond the interim stage, probably because the relief granted by the court at that stage, usually an interlocutory injunction, was sufficient to satisfy the plaintiff.

There remained serious doubts about computer programs in object code form and these doubts were brought to a head by the Australian case of *Apple Computer Inc* v *Computer Edge Pty Ltd* [1994] FSR 481. In that case, the defendant imported clones of the Apple II personal computer into Australia. His initial claim that his computers, appropriately called 'Wombats', did not contain the Apple operating system and start-up programs was rejected when it was discovered that the programs in the 'Wombat' chips had the names of the Apple programmers embedded within them. The defendants' second line of defence was that the programs were not literary works in the copyright sense, being object code programs. This was accepted by the trial judge but rejected by a 2:1 majority in the Federal Court of New South Wales. However, this decision was unsatisfactory in many respects and the Australian Parliament acted very quickly, passing amending legislation (the Australian Copyright Amendment Act 1984) to put the matter beyond doubt; This did little to assuage concerns in The United Kingdom it merely highlighted the uncertainty concerning object code programs.

Following considerable pressure from the computer industry, notably from the lobby group FAST (the Federation Against Software Theft), the Copyright [Computer Software) Amendment Act 1985 was passed which made it clear that computer programs were protected as literary works. The Copyright, Designs and Patents Act 1988 follows the approach and places computer programs firmly within the literary work category for the purposes of copyright 9section 3). It also protects implicitly other forms of works created using a computer or stored in or on computer media. Neither the word 'computer' nor the phrase 'computer program' is defined in the Act. This is sensible in view of the rapid rate of change in the computer industry as attempts to offer precise definitions would probably prove to be unduly restrictive in the light of technological development. It is better to allow the judges to use their discretion sensibly, permitting a degree of flexibility in this respect. There should be no difficulty n a court deciding that copyright subsists in a program written in assembler language or in a computer program in object code form.

On a European Community scale, it has proved necessary to spell out in detail the scope of exceptions to copyright infringement in relation to computer programs and, to this end, the 1988 Act has been amended by the Copyright (Computer Programs) Regulations 1992, as described later in this chapter. The regulations also specifically place preparatory design material for computer programs in the literary work category. Concerns about the protection of databases by copyright law led to another European initiative, resulting in the Directive on the legal protection of databases (OJ [1996] L77/20. This was implemented in the United Kingdom by the Copyright and Rights in Databases Regulations 1997 which further modified the 1988 Act, adding databases to the literary works category. Databases are considered in more depth in the following chapter.

Originality and Storage

By section 3 of the Copyright, Designs and Patents, Act 1988, for copyright to subsist in computer program it must be 'original' and it must be 'recorded'. For the meaning of 'original', we must turn to case law prior to the Act and section 172(3) confirms that this practice is permissible (this is standard procedure unless it is clear that previous cases no longer represent the law). The requirement of originality is not an onerous one and does not mean that the computer program must be novel or unique in some respect. It merely means that the program has been the result of a modest amount of skill, labour or judgment and that it 'originates from the author' (Peterson J in *University of London Press Ltd* v *University Tutorial Press Ltd* [1916] 2 Ch 601). Compilations of existing information as in a street directory have been afforded copyright protection. In *Macmillan & Co Ltd* v *K & J Cooper* (1923) 40 TLR 186, it was held that, although many compilations have nothing original in their parts, the sum total of a compilation may be original for the purposes of copyright. however, the courts will draw a line somewhere and in *G.A Cramp & Sons Ltd* v *Frank Smythson Ltd* [1944] AC 329, a diary which contained the usual information contained in diaries, such as a calendar, tables of weights and measures, postal information and the like, failed to attract copyright protection. The reason given was that the commonplace nature of the information left no room for taste or judgment in the selection and organisation of the material. In the right of these cases, virtually all computer programs will meet the requirement of originality, even if the program comprises little more than an arrangement of commonly used sub-routines, because the selection and arrangement of those sub-routines requires a reasonable amount of skill and expertise.

In the United States, the expenditure of labour alone is unlikely, without more, to confer copyright protection on a work (the 'sweat of the brow' doctrine put to rest in *Feist publications Inc* v *Rural Telephone Service Co Inc* (1991) 111 S Ct 1282). It is difficult to conceive of a computer program which does not involve skill and judgment in its creation, in addition to effort. However, standards vary internationally and in Germany it was said that a computer program, to be protected by copyright, must be the result of creative achievement exceeding the average skills used in the development of computer programs (*Sudwestdeutsche Inkasse KG* v *Bappert and Burker Computer GmbH* (1985) Case 5483, BGHZ94, 276). In other words, a computer program which simply automated an existing process would be unlikely to be the subject of copyright. In the light of the European Community Directive on the legal protection of computer programs, this case must now be viewed as laying down too stringent a test, and, indeed, this was confirmed by the Federal Supreme Court of Germany in the *Buchhaltungsprogram* case (unreported) 14 July 1993 which concerned an accounts program.

In the United Kingdom, another requirement for computer programs, and other literary, dramatic and musical works, is that they must be recorded in writing or otherwise (section 3(2). This has a very wide meaning and 'writing' is defined by section 178 as including:

> ....any form of notation or code, whether by hand or otherwise and regardless of the method by which, or medium in or on which, it is recorded.

Storage of a computer program in a computer memory or on computer storage media such as magnetic disks should present no problems as the above definition in section 178 is sufficiently wide to cover any existing form of storage and any new forms which might be invented in the future. Furthermore, given the spirit of the Act, it is unlikely that the courts will attempt to narrow the concept of 'recording'. It must be noted, however, that the House of Lords has decided that a password held transiently in a computer system was not recorded for the purposes of the Forgery and Counterfeiting Act 1981. If the only form of existence of a computer program is in a computer's volatile memory, there may be a possibility that, following: the *Gold* case, the program will not be considered to be 'recorded.' Nevertheless, because the program will be saved on to a disk or tape before very long, this is unlikely to cause problems in practice. Of course, the program may have been written down by the programmer before entry into the computer or a printout of the program listing may have been taken, in which case the program will be protected anyway. As a matter of interest, the scope of the Copyright (Computer Software) Amendment Act 1985 (now repealed) was possibly wider in that it specifically covered storage in a computer memory.

Preparatory and Ancillary Materials

Copyright protection extends beyond the computer program itself and will cover written or printed listings of programs flowcharts, specifications and notes. Section 3(1)

(c) includes preparatory design material for a computer program in the literary work category. Prior to the Copyright (Computer Programs) Regulations 1992, these materials would generally be protected as literary works although flow charts and diagrams would have been protected as artistic works. The artistic work category of copyright includes paintings, drawings, diagrams, maps, charts and plans which are all protected irrespective of artistic quality. As a result of the regulations, however, preparatory design materials are deemed to be literary works, irrespective of whether they would have qualified previously as graphic works and, hence, artistic works. In practice, this should not be of any significance although there are some differences in the provisions for literary and artistic works. All these preparatory and other ancillary materials must be original in the sense already discussed. Because copying includes copying by indirect means it is possible that making an unauthorised copy of a computer program (or screen display) infringes the copyright infringes the copyright subsisting in ancillary or preparatory materials in addition to any question of infringement of the program itself or of the screen display.

Of course, manuals and other documentation distributed with computer programs will be protected by copyright, independently of the program itself, as original literary or artistic works, as appropriate.

Restricted acts for Computer Programs

Of the acts restricted by copyright, three are worthy of special mention as far as computer programs are concerned. These are:

- copying,
- issuing copies to the public, and
- making an adaptation.

All of these restricted acts have a particular meaning which is only partly explained by the language of the Act. Copying and making an adaptation have fairly technical meanings and both of these acts have been extended to take account of computer technology. Copyright now has to include electronic copying and also has to countenance the situation where a person copies a computer program but uses a different programming language with the results that the original and the copy bear little, if any, literal similarity when the program listings are compared. If copyright law as unable to control such 'non-literal' copying, it would be too easy to circumvent the protection afforded by copyright. The restricted act of making an adaptation, concerned originally with translations of literary works and arrangements of musical works, now has to deal with the process of converting source code into object code and vice versa.

Copying

Copying a relation to a literary, dramatic, musical or artistic work means, by section 17(2) reproducing the work in any material form which includes storage in any medium by electronic means - for example, by making a copy of a computer program on a magnetic disk. Additionally, in relation to all forms of copyright work, copying includes making copies which are transient or incidental to some other use of the work (section 17(6). This implies that the act of loading a computer program into a computer only for the purpose of ruing the program will be considered to be making a copy of the program, even though this 'copy' will be lost as soon as the computer is switched off. In this way, any unauthorised use of a computer program will infringe the copyright in that program. This is why a license is required in order to use another person's computer program or database.

Literal Copying

An unauthorised copy of a computer program may be an exact duplicate of such where a disk-to-disk copy is made. The original and copy will be identical. The question of infringment of copyright will be an easy open to deal with and will be limited to an inquiry as to whether the first program is protected by copyright. Almost all computer programs will be subject to copyright as the basic requirements for copyright subsistence usually will be present. As long as the first program is original in the sense that it originates from its author and is non-trivial and the qualification provisions are satisfied (or reciprocal protection is afforded through the international conventions) then the program will be protected. Identical copies of computer programs made without the permission of the copyright owner are, apart from difficulties associated with dejection, fairly easy to deal with in terms of the law, both civil and criminal. Software piracy usually falls into this category of copying as does making working copies of computer programs by a licensee in excess of the number permitted by the license agreement.

Sometimes a person copying a computer program will do further work on the program. This might be to disguise the origin of the program or to improve it, or both. Where this happens, proving copying may be more difficult and requires a consideration of three questions.

- Does copyright subsist in the plaintiff's program?
- Has the defendant copied parts of the plaintiff's program?
- Do the parts copied represent a substantial part of plaintiff's program?

In Practice, the answer to the first question will rarely be in the negative. The second question is more difficult and depends, *inter alia,* on objective similarities and inferences that can be drawn from them. It is further complicated if the same person has been involved in the writing of both programs. The third question, as we have seen, is concerned with the quality of the part taken rather than its overall size relative to the whole. A small but important part of a program will be deemed to be substantial. Indeed, it is arguable that even a tiny part of a computer program could be significant as the program may 'crash' without it! However, in *Cantor Fitzgerald International* v *Tradition (UK) Ltd, The Times,* 19 May 1999, the court held that substantiality must be judged against the program or progams as a whole in the light of the skill and labour expended in the design and coding which went into the piece of code in respect of which the allegation of copying was made. In that case, the defendant admitted copying some 2952 lines of code from the plaintiff's programs which comprised 77 000 lines of code. The judge found the plaintiff's case made out in part but Mr Justice Pumfrey went on to say that substantiality was not to be determined by whether the system would work without the part copied nor by the amount of use made of the code in question. These and other issues are considered further in the following important case.

In *IBCOS Computers Ltd* v *Barclays Mercantile Highland Finance Ltd* [1994] FSR 275, one of the defendants, a programmer, wrote a suite of programs and files to handle accounts and payroll for agricultural machinery dealers. he further developed this software for the plaintiff and when he left the plaintiff's company, the programmer signed a note agreeing to the fact the company owned the copyright in the software and agreeing not to write computing software for two years. The programmer then wrote another software package, which performed similar functions, for other defendant. This was not marketed until the two-year period in restraint of trade had expired. Nevertheless, the plaintiff sued for copyright infringement and breach of confidence. Both suites of programs were written in similar programming languages, being variants of COBOL.

When the code of the two suites of programs was examined, common errors were noticed. These were primarily to do with spelling, and punctuation in the comment lines in the programs. The same mistakes tended to occur in the same places. The same piece of redundant code was also present in both suites of programs. The judge, therefore, had little difficulty in finding that there had been copying, showing the usefulness of including deliberate mistakes or redundant elements in copyright works. he also held that copyright subsisted not only in the individual programs but in the whole suite of programs as a compilation because the selection and arrangement of a the programs required skill and judgment. On this latter point the judge, Mr Justice Jacob, disagreed with Judge paul Baker who said, *Total Information Processing Systems Ltd* v *Daman Ltd* [1992] FSR 171, that linking several programs together could not constitute an original compilation. In view of the increasing structural complexity of software products, Jacob J's approach should be welcomed by the software industry as strengthening the copyright protection of computer programs.

In the *IBCOS* case, it was held that the defendant had infringed copyright in a number of individual programs in addition to an infringement of the copyright subsisting in the overall structure of the software comprising 335 programs, 171 record layout files and 46 screen layouts. The defendant had argued that similarities were the result of programming style and the reuse of well-know" routines but was unable convince the judge on these points. In other words, the defendant was unable to offer a satisfactory explanation for the similarities. It was also held that the defendant programmer was guilty of a breach of confidence in respect of the plaintiff's source code programs.

In his judgement, Mr Justice Jacob discussed previous case law and was critical of some aspects of it (see the section on non-literal copying later on this chapter). Some other important points made by Jacob J included.

- Modifying a computer program could give rise to a fresh copyright.
- The fact that the program, or parts of it, were constrained by the program's function did not weaken or compromise copyright protection.
- The data division of a COBOL program (being the part defining the variables and database structures) can be a substantial part of a program and a file record, though not a program, could be a compilation.
- Where the evidence clearly indicates copying but this is denied by the defendant, the court should infer that similarities are the result of copying and not due to programming style unless independent evidence suggests otherwise.

The IBCOS case is a important step in the application of copyright law to computer programs. Bearing in mind that preparatory design material is now expressly (and independently) subject to copyright, the width of protection afforded to software is quite strong. Figure 2.1 shows this in relation to a typical software package including a suite of programs and data files.

The concept of non-literal copying can strengthen copyright even more. Whether copying is literal or non-literal, however, it should be remembered that infringement

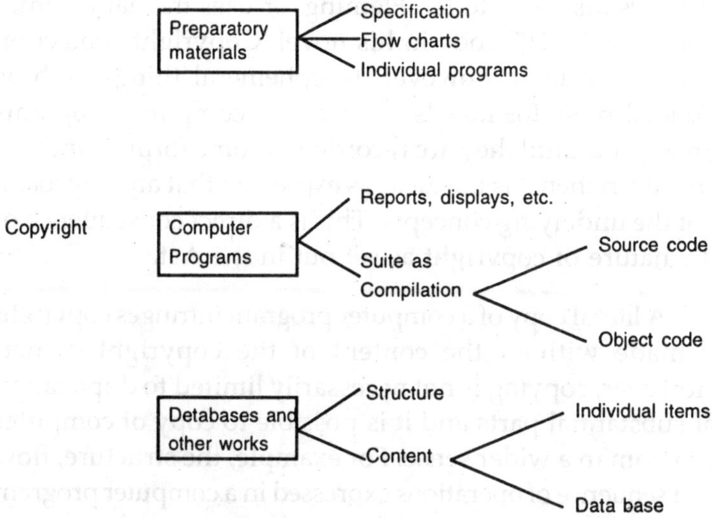

Fig 2.1. Copyright protection of software package

of copyright requires use of the first work and creating a similar work independently will not infringe. Writing new accounts software will not infringe any copyrights in existing software packages provided they have not been used in a way that falls within the restricted acts.

Non-literal Copying

Copyright does not give a monpoly in ideas; what it does is to prevent a person from copying or otherwise using the tangible expressions of ideas made by others in accordance with the acts restricted by copyright. In this way, copyright protects expression not idea. Therefore, in principle, it is quite acceptable to write a novel about a secret agent in the style of Ian Fleming as long as it dos not contain copies of parts of James Bond novels. The late Ian Fleming did not have a monopoly in tongue-in-cheek, humorous adventures about secret agents licensed to kill, but a novelist might commit the tort of passing off if he changes his name to Ian Fleming or uses the name James Bond or the 007 code in his novel. Copyright protection does not extend, however, to ephemeral things such as skeletal plots for novels or ideas for computer programs unless and until they are recorded in some form or another and, even then it is the ideas as expressed that are protected, not the undelying concepts. This is a direct consequence of the nature of copyright as set out in the Act.

A literal copy of a computer program infringes copyright if made without the content of the copyright owner. However, copying is not necessarily limited to duplication of substantial parts and it is possible to copy of computer program in a wider sense. For example, the structure, flow and sequence of operations expressed in a computer program may be copied and, if a different computer programming language is used, a printout of the second program will look dissimilar to a printout of the first program. Should the use of one program to assist with the writing of second program in such a way be within the ambit of copyright protection even though the codes of the two programs look similar? In other words, should copyright extend to non-literal elements which are not directly perceivable? This question is of such fundamental importance, because, if answered in the negative, copyright protection for computer programs would be considerably weakened.

The United States of America progressed much faster than the United Kingdom in determining this question but the basic legal principles are broadly similar: copyright protects expression but not idea Nevertheless, expression goes beyond the immediate literal form. For example, in the united Kingdom Case of *Glyn* v *Weston Feature Film Co* [1916] 1 Ch 261, in which it was argued (unsuccessfully) that a film infringed the copyright in a novel, it was acknowledged that copyright can extend beyond the literal text of a book to the dramatic scenes and incidents contained within it.

Because expression may exist at various levels of abstraction (for example, in the program's structure) the courts have to be able to distinguish between idea and expression. This has not proved easy and the following United States cases give an indication of the development of tests that may be appropriate. (United States law has no binding effect on the United Kingdom courts but it may be of persuasive authority, particularly in the field of computer technology.)

In *Whelan Associates Inc* v *Jaslow Dental Laboratory Inc* [1987] FSR 1, the programs being compared were designed to assist with the administration of dental laboratories. The same person was involved in the development of each program but they were written in different computer languages: the first was written in EDL and the second, attempting to infiltrate the microcomputer market, was was written in BASIC. Thus, there was no substantial literal similarity between the listings of the two programs. The united States Court of Appeals (3rd Circuit) distinguished between idea and expression by references to the purpose of the program. The purpose of a utilitarian work is the idea of the work whereas every thing pertaining to the work which is not necessary to the purpose is expression. If there are several ways of achieving the desired purpose, none of which is necessary to the purpose, then the way chosen is expression and, consequently, protected by copyright.

The purpose of the original program in *Whelan* v *jaslow* was to assist in the running of dental laboratories. There were several different method which could be employed to achieve that same purpose, and therefore the structure of that original program was not essential to the purpose and hence, the structure was expression and not idea. The purpose itself, being the idea, was not protected by coyright, it is quite acceptable for others to write programs to help with the running of dental laboratories. In this case the structures of the two programs were similar, the programs had a similar look and feel even though written in different computer programming languages and this, coupled with the fact that the same person had been involved in the two programs, raised a strong presumption that there had been copying and, thence an infringment of copyright. The distinction between idea and expression has been applied in the context of screen displays. In the 'Pac Man' computer games the maze and dots were deemed to be idea, being necessarily dictated by the program function, but the 'Pac-man' and 'ghost monsters' characters were considered to be expression as different graphical representations could have been used.

Another important case involved the spreadsheet program Lotus 1-2-3 and a compatible spreadsheet program called VP-Planner. In *Lotus Development Corp* v *Paperback Software International* 740 F Supp 37 (D Mass 1990), the defendant claimed that he had not copied the Lotus program code but had used a similar menu system to achieve compatibility (especially with respect to spreadsheet files and macros) and to enable people to change to VP Planner from Lotus 1-2-3 without requiring retraining. The similarities between the programs were the menu command system (two-line moving cursor menu) and the grid system (letters and numbers arranged in a 'rotated L'). It was held by judge Keeton that the defendant had infringed copyright by copying the two-line moving cursor menu. Various spreadsheet programs used different menu systems showing that the system used by Lotus was expression and not idea. He confirmed, however, that there was no infringement of the rotated 'L' grid as this was idea, it being almost inevitable that a spreadsheet program would use such a system.

In a later spreadsheet case, *Lotus Development Corp* v *Borland International Inc* [1997] FSR 61, the 1st Circuit Court of Appeals, the decision of Judge Keeton along the lines of his *Lotus* v *Paperback* judgment was reversed by the Court of Appeals which found that the menu command hierarchy in the Lotus 1-2-3 spreadsheet was not a work of copyright. Therefore, by using the 1-2-3 menu command system in its Quattro spreadsheet, Borland had not infringed copyright. The rationale was that the menu command system was a method of operation which is excluded from copyright protection by section 102(b) of the United States Copyright Act. The court likened the menu system to the buttons on a video recorder. The distinction in *Whelan* between idea and expression was considered unhelpful by the court which confirmed that the fact that the Lotus designers could have designed the system differently was immaterial to the question of whether it was a method of operation. The case was then appealed to the Supreme Court but there was no susbtantive judgment as the court reached a split decision, and the finding of the Court of Appeals stands.

The *Lotus* v *Borland* case can be seen as a further weakening of copyright protection for interfaces (in this case, the interface with the user) and facilitates the pursuit of compatibility in software from an operational point of view. However, it could discourage investment in novel forms of software and major software companies may be encouraged to allow someone else to make the investment in developing innovative software in the knowledge that they can copy the ideas and interfaces to produce similar competing software providing that they do not copy the program code or other protected non-literal elements.

Prior to the *Lotus* v *Borland* case, the authority of *Whelan* v *Jaslow* was already looking shaky and that case had been strongly disapproved of by the United States Court of Appeals, 2nd Circuit, in *Computer Associates International Inc* v *Altai* (1992) 20 USPQ 2nd 1641. The defendant had produced a program called 'Oscar', a job-scheduling program for controlling the order in which tasks are carried out by a computer. it incorporated a common interface component allowing he use of different operating systems and this part had been added by a former employee of the plaintiff who had a similar program and interface. The plaintiff's former employee was very familiar with the interface element (known as 'Adapter') which was part of the plaintiff's 'CA-Scheduler' program and hand even been allowed to take a copy of the 'Adapter' source code home while working on it. When the plaintiff issued a summons and complaint, the defendant rewrote 'Oscar', using different programmers in an effort to avoid infringing the plaintiff's copyright in 'Adapter'. The plaintiff still proceeded even though the defendant had agreed not to challenge an award of $364 444 damages in respect of the earlier version of 'Oscar'. The trail judge held that the later version of 'Oscar' did not infringe the 'Adapter' copyright and the plaintiff appealed to the Court of Appeals which confirmed the decision of the trial judge.

In a far-reaching judgment, the Court of Appeals laid down a new test for the determination of the question of non-literal copyright infringement, that is, whether there has been an infringement of copyright in non-literal elements such as program structure. The test requires a three-step procedure as follows:

- *Abstraction* - discovering the non-literal elements by a process akin to reverse engineering, beginning with the code and ending with the program's ultimate function. The designer's steps are retraced and mapped. This produces structures of different detail at varying levels of abstraction.

- *Filtration* - the separation of protectable expression from non-protectable material. Some elements will be unprotected being idea, dictated by considerations of efficiency (therefore necessarily incidental to idea), required by external factors (*scenes a faire* doctrine), or taken from the public domain. These elements are filtered out leaving a core of protectable materials (this is the program's 'golden nugget').
- *Comparison* - a d termination of whether the defendant has copied a substantial part of the protected expression, that is, ascertaining, whether any aspect has been copied and, so, assessing the copied portion's relative importance in respect of the plaintiff's overall program.

Of course, this test only applies to non-literal copying and the actual code remains fully protected against direct (literal) copying. However, this test is likely to reduce significantly the strength of protection for program structure, menu command systems and interfaces. In many cases, it is possible that, after the process of filtration, there will be no 'golden nuggets' left, that is, no protectable expression, to take forward to the process of comparison. It remains to be seen what effect this case will have on copyright litigation in the united States (the judges in the Court of Appeals recognised that their test would be difficult to apply and would need further case law before its application could be predicted with any certainty). Even more interesting is its effect on copyright law in the United Kingdom, discussed below, althogh it should be noted that the previous test in *Whelan* v *Jaslow* did not achieve any notable successes in the United Kingdom even though it was used in argument on a number of occasions.

Non-literal Copying in the United Kingdom

It was not too long after the *Computer Associates* case that a suitable example of alleged non-literal copying came before the High Court. The fact of *John Richardson Computers Ltd* v *Flanders* [1993] FSR 497 are difficult and provide an object lesson in how not to manage the development of computer software, with scant regard being paid to record-keeping and ownership of copyright. Essentially, the plaintiff had a computer program for use by pharmacists to print labels for drug prescriptions and to monitor stock levels. The driving force behind the plaintiff company was Mr Richardson who had originally written a rudimentary program in BASIC and had later engaged computer programmers, both on an employee and consultancy basis and including the defendant, to refine and enhance the program. Eventually it was rewritten in assembly language for the BBC computer (and is referred to below as the BBC program).

The defendant wrote a program called 'Chemtec' to perform the same functions written in QUICK-BASIC for the IBM personal computer. The plaintiff sued for copyright infringement and breach of confidence though the latter claim was not pursued at the trial. The judge, Mr Justic Ferris, had to consider the claim for copyright infringement in the context of two computer programs written in different languages and bearing no significant literal similarities and with very little English case law to assist him. He identified the following issues raised by the case:

- Does copyright subsist in a computer program?
- If it does, does the copyright in the BBC program belong to the plaintiff?

- If the above questions are answered in the affirmative, when the court's approach be to a claim of 'non-literal' copying?
- Are there any objective similarities between the BBC program and the Chemtec program enabling the Chemtec program to be regarded in any respect as a copy of the BBC program?
- Were any such similarities in fact copied from the BBC program?
- Is any copying thus found copying of a substantial part of the BBC program?

The issue of copyright subsistence was easily dealt with by the judge and ownership of copyright in the BBC program was resolved in favour of the plaintiff. Althogh the defendant may have been the legal owner of part of the program he had written as a self-employed consultant, the plaintiff was the owner in equity and, as the plaintiff had joined the legal owner in the action (by suing him), the full range of remedies was available to the plaintiff should infringement be proved.

After reviewing the English and United States authorities on non-literal copying and discussing the *Computer Associates* case at length, Mr Justice Ferris said that there was nothing in any English decision which conflicted with the general approach adopted in that case. However, he said that in preference to seeking the 'core of protectable expression' in the plaintiff program, an English court will:

- decide whether the plaintiff's program as a whole entitled to copyright protection, and then
- decide whether any similarity in the defendant's program resulting from copying amounts to copying a substantial part of the plaintiff's program.

Ferris J went on to say that the approach to separation of idea and expression as expounded in *Computer Associates* was appropriate and a similar approach should be adopted in England. This would be relevant to issues of substantiality of copying and originality. Thus, the non-literal elements of a computer program are to be taken into account. In testing for infringement, the judge concentrated on objective similarities in the non-literal elements of the programs and he classified them in four ways:

- similarities that were the result of copying a substantial part of the plaintiff's program, being the line editor, amendment routines and dose codes,
- similarities that were the result of copying but not in relation to a substantial part of the plaintiff's program - for example, the date option. operation successful, message, etc.;
- similarities which may have been the result of copying but which, in any case, did not involve copying substantial parts of the plaintiff's program for example, the vertical arrangement of entry prompts;
- similarities that were not the result of copying including the use of the escape key, position of label on screen, etc.

It was held that defendant had infringed copyright in respect of three non-literal elements. This would mean that it might be a relatively simple matter for the defendant to rewrite the offending parts of his program, notwithstanding any award in damages in respect of the infringement.

The judgment in *Richardson* v *Flanders* attracted a fair amount of criticism. In particular, Mr Justice Jacob in his judgment in *IRCOS* v *Barclays* (a case on literal copying) was particularly critical of a blind allegiance to the United States approach, pointing out that United Kingdom copyright law is different, being based on a different statute. He said that the United States approach was not helpful. It must be noted, however, that Jacon J was dealing with a more straightforward case of copying and the two cases are distinguishable, one being on literal copying (*IBCOS*), the other on non-literal copying (*Richardson*), Consequently, it is possible to reconcile the two cases and the judgments can be seen as complementary. *Where Richardson* is weak is, arguably, in the abstraction to non-literal expression. Furthermore, there was no serious attempt to filter out unprotected elements but this is more likely to be due to differences between united Kingdom and United States law than a failure on the part of the judge.

Finally, it should be noted that the defendant in *Richardson* v *Flanders* had made significant additions and enhancements to his program, which was substantially larger than the plaintiff's program and had more features. Nevertheless, when comparing programs for copyright infringement it was confirmed that more attention should be paid to the parts claimed to be the same or similar than the other parts of the program. As a result of the *Richardson* and *IBCOS* cases, it would appear that copyright protection for computer programs is at least adequate and there is a reasonable balance between strength of protection and the development of competing programs by others, as is investigated below.

Copying in Practice

Has copyright law been developed by the courts to prevent the marketing of looklike computer programs? Obviously, if a company makes a new type of computer program which proves to be very successful, other companies will want to bring out their own versions in order to gain a share in the market created or stimulated by the first program. Essentially, copyright law does not prevent this as long as the first program is not copied or adapted. Although copying now extends to the structure and other non-literal elements of a program this should not prevent competitors bringing out programs to perform similar functions. A line must be drawn somewhere and the following hypothetical examples, involving two software companies Acme and Zenith, indicate where it might be drawn. Acme developed a program to record and monitor drug dosages to hospital patients and Zenith, shortly afterwards, brought out a similar program.

1. Zenith did not know of the existence of Acme's program. (*No infringement of copyright.*)
2. Zenith knew of the existence of Acme's program but had not see it in use, (*No infringement of copyright; the function of the program is idea, not expression.*)
3. Zenith had seen Acme's program in use and decided to write a program to fulfill the same purpose, that is, in monitor drug dosages. Zenith did not refer to Acme's program further than this and Zenith developed its own methods of performing the purpose. The structures of the two programs are different in many respects and where they are similar this is the result of coincidence only for because they are constrained by the function. (*No infringement of copyright.*)
4. Zenith buys a copy of Acme's program. Zenith cannot see the source code because the copy is compiled (in object code), but by using the program extensively, Zenith gets a good insight into the workings and structure of Acme's

program and, based on this insight, Zenith writes its program (obviously without and, based on this insight, Zenith writes its program (obviously without using a source code listing of Acme's program. Zenith's knowledge of Acme's program is no more than a competent user would achieve. (*Possible infringement of copyright because the structure of Zenith's program is determined by Zenith's familiarity with the structure of Acme's program which Zenith copies indirectly. Copying menu systems, screen displays and other non-literal elements may also infringe Acme's copyright.*)

5. Zenith decompiles Acme's program and rewrites parts of it to make its program, perhaps using a different computer language. (*Definite infringement of copyright; the act of decompilation itself with constitute an infringement of copyright. The 'decompilation' exception to infringement is unlikely to apply here (see later).*)
6. Zenith employs an ex-programmer of Acme who is familiar with the program; this person writes a program for Zenith using copies of listings and flowcharts that he retained. Qualitatively substantial parts of the program code are incorporated in the new program. (*Definite infringement of copyright and possible breach of confidence.*)
7. As 6 above but the ex-programmer of Acme has not retained any materials from his previous employment; he simply uses what he can remember, (*Possible infringement of copyright.*)

The last example lies in a difficult area and is tied up with questions relating to the law of confidence and restraint of trade. Ex-employees frequently cause problems because of the difficulty to reconciling their continuing duty to their ex-employer with the need to be able to obtain other employment. If the ex-employee is not allowed to make use of anything at all from his part experience, he may well be virtually unemployable because what he has done previously is an integral part of his skill and expertise. This question will be considered further on the law of confidence; at this stage it needs to be noted that an ex-employee will be able to make use of his skills and what he remembers as ling as these are not genuine trade secrets. In terms of writing computer software, a program to automate an existing manual process probably will not be considered a track secret.

If company B writes a program independently and, by chance, it turns out to be very similar to a program written ny company A, there is no infringement of copyright because there has been neither copying not the making of an adaptation of A's program and both A and B will be have a copyright in their respective programs. A substantial similarity between programs, however, can suggest that one has been copied from the other and this can shift the burden of proof to the defendant, especially if there is something else to support the view that copying may have taken place, such as access to the original by the defendant (see *LB Plastics Ltd* v *Swish Products Ltd* [1979] RPC 551). This means that instead of requiring the plaintiff to show the copyright has taken place, the defendant will have to show that he did not, in fact, copy the plaintiff's work and such a shift in the burden of proof can be exceedingly onerous to the defendant.

One approach to the question of copying was suggested by the Court of Appeal in *Francis, Day & Hunter Ltd* v *Bron* [1963] Ch 587, a case concerning an alleged infringement of an old song entitled 'In a Little Spanish Town'. For copying to be proved, the rest is as follows.

- there must be sufficient objective similarity between the two works (an objective issue - would be 'reasonable man' consider the two works sufficiently similar?), and
- there must also be some causal connection between the two works (a subjective question but not to be presumed as a matter of law merely upon proof of access).

It is possible to infringe copyright by subconsciously copying a work, although this is probably more relevant to the music industry than the computer industry. Thus George Harrison's song. 'My Sweet Lord' was alleged to have infringed an earlier song 'He's So Fine'. but it is thought that the evidence required to support this proposition would have to be quite strong. Taken to its logical conclusion this might encourage software developers to adopt a 'clean-room' approach, denying access to existing software by the programmers and analysts in an effort to try to prevent accusations of copying. In most cases, this would not be realistic, given the likelihood that any skilled programmer would already have a wide knowledge of other software products. Even it it is feasible, there is no guarantee that this would provide a defence to an infringement action. In the New Zealand case of *Plix Products ltd* v *Frank W Shinstone (Merchants)* [1986] FSR 63, the defendant asked his designer to design a kiwifruit pack without talking to others in this field and without looking at existing packs. Although there was no direct copying it was held that the copyright in the plaintiff's packs had been infringed through the medium of the New Zealand Kiwifruit Authority's specification for packs, and the court also seemed to accept the possibility that copyright can be infringed through a verbal description. New Zealand copyright law is very similar to United Kingdom law; but, in the united States, it would be likely that the design features indicated in the United States, it would be likely that the design features indicated in the specification would be considered to be an unprotectable idea.

The implications in indirect copying (expressly covered by the Copyright, Designs and Patents Act 1988, section 16) are serious for the software industry and are must be taken to avoid such a claim. There is even a case for deliberately making elements in a computer program (including non-literal elements different from the equivalent part of competing programs if this does not compromise the functionality, usability and attractiveness of the program.

If copyright protection of computer programs is developed by the courts to become too strong, the Act contains safeguards. By section 144(1), as a result of a report of the Monopolies and Mergers Commission (renamed the Competition Commission by the Competition Act 1998), the Secretary of State may grant a license as of right if the public interest would be prejudiced; for example, if the owner of the copyright in a unique computer program refuses to grant licenses on reasonable terms. Therefore, if a company has a virtual monopoly in a particular type of computer system, charges an exorbitant price for it and the Commission prepares a report to the effect that this situation is against the public interest, anyone will be able to apply for a compulsory license to use the software. The license fee and other terms of the licence will be decided by the Copyright Tribunal, a body set up to administer licensing schemes. under section 66, the secretary of State may order that lending of copies to the public shall be treated as licensed subject to payment of a reasonable royalty of other payments as may be agreed or, failing agreement, as determined by the Copyright Tribunal. Section 66 was amended by the Copyright and Related Rights Regulations 1996. Previously, it was framed in terms of rental rather than lending.

Issuing Copies to the Public

Under section 18, issuing copies of a work to the public is a restricted act and will infringe copyright if done without the permission of the owner of the copyright. However, the right to control the issue of copies to the public only applies to the first issue of individual copies. Thus, once a particular copy of a computer program has bene issued to the public by or with the consent of the copyright owner, he can no longer use that right to control subsequent dealings with that particular copy, apart from rental. The right still applies in relation to unissued copies. This principle accords with the doctrine of exhaustion of rights in European Community law. Exhaustion would apply where, for example, a software company has sold copies of its programs to one dealer in Germany and, at a lower price, to another dealer in France. A third party would be able to buy copies in France and import them into Germany in order to resell them, undercutting the German dealer. The software company would not be able to use its public issue right to prevent this.

Rental or Lending Copies to the Public

By virtue of section 18A (which was inserted by the Copyright and Related Rights Regulations 1996) the rental or lending of copies of work to the public is an restricted by the copyright. This provision applies to literary, dramatic and musical works, to artistic works (except works of architecture and works of applied art) and films and sound recordings.

Making an Adaptation

Making an adaptation of a literary, dramatic or musical work is at restricted act. In terms of a musical work, a new arrangement of a song is an adaptation of the original. Changing a cartoon strip into a story told by words only is also an adaptation, as is a translation of a literary or dramatic work. Additionally, for a computer program, making an arrangement or altered version comes within this restricted act. 'Translation' has a special meaning for computer programs, by section 21(4), and includes:

If a high-level, source code computer program is compiled (converted) into an object code program, this will be an adaptation of the source code program and, therefore, a restricted act. This provision is aimed at controlling the compilation, decompilation, assembly and dissembly of computer programs - that is, the conversion of source code programs into object code and vice versa as shown in Fig. 2.2. This would seem to be a reasonable activity to be controlled by copyright, especially as reverse-engineering an object code program will make the techniques, ideas and principles underlying a computer program more accessible. As we shall see later, however, under certain circumstances this is expressly permitted under copyright law.

Source code programs are protected by copyright provided they are 'original'- that is, they are the result of skill, labour or judgment. The position is less clear as far as object code programs are concerned because they may not be original in the sense described above. In most cases, an object code program will have been created by submitting the source code program to a compiler program or assembler program. This process may require little effort or skill on the part of the person creating the object code unless there are several errors detected which need correction before a suitable executable version of the object code is obtained. Even if an object code program is not an original literary work, it will be protected by copyright as an adaptation of such work and the restricted acts extend to an adaptation as they do to the original work. Thus, it is an infringement of copyright to copy an adaptation of a program or even to make an adaptation of an adaptation.

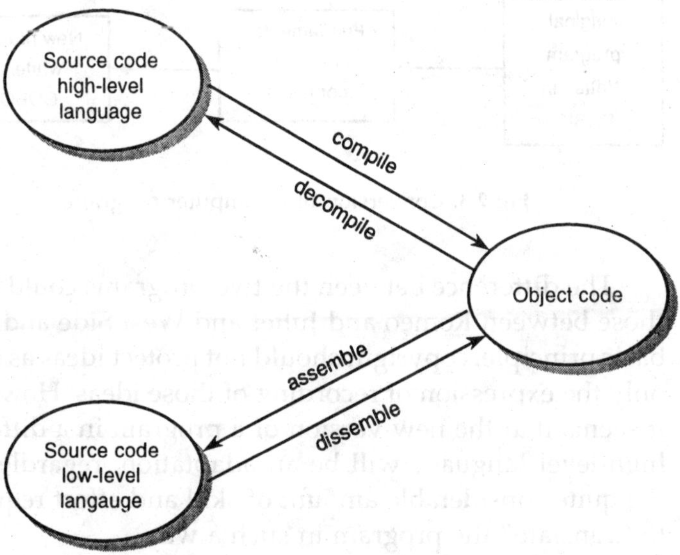

Fig. 2.2. Making an adaptation of a computer programe

It could be argued that the meaning of translation is too wide as it seems to catch a version of a source code program written in a different high level language from that used for the original program, that is, a manual conversion. If a computer program is written using BASIC and someone then rewrites the program in COBOL, the latter will be an adaptation of the BASIC program because it has been converted into a different computer language. To produce a program in a different high-level language, however, is not merely a question of translating the program instructions from one language to another as with spoken languages. The programmer would have to reduce the original program to its underlying concepts and ideas and from those concepts and ideas (not from the computer program itself) develop a new version of the program in another high-level language, as shown in Figure. 2.3

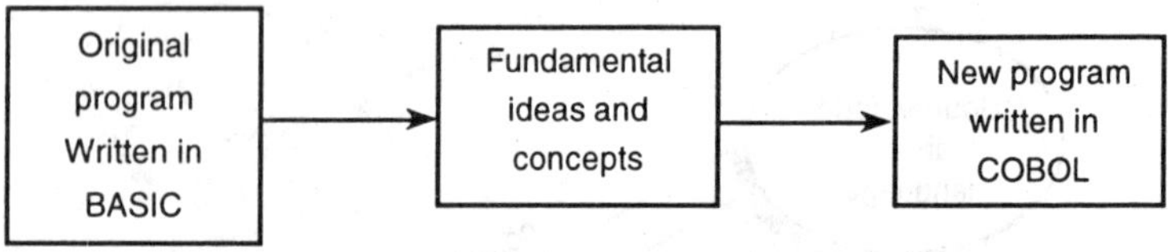

Fig 2.3. Conversion of a computer program

The difference between the two programs could be as those between Romeo and Juliet and West Side and, as a basic principle, copyright should not protect ideas as such, only the expression of recording of those ideas. However, it seems that the new version of a program in a different high-level language will be an adaptation, regardless of the quite considerable amount of skill and effort required to 'translate" the program in such a way.

Restricted acts apply to a work as a whole or to any substantial part of a (section 16(3)). What is substantial is a matter of fact and the courts will look to quality as well as quantity (see *Hawkes & Sons (London) Ltd* v *Paramount Film Service Ltd* [1934] Ch 593). Therefore, a computer program which includes parts (such as sub-routines) copied from another program will infringe the copyright in that other program if the copied parts represent a substantial part of the original program and they may be substantial if they go to the root of the other program or capture its essence, even though they are small in terms of quantity. Theoretically, it is possible to increase copyright protection by modularising a single program into a number of separate sub-programs which, if each individually is the result of skill, labour and effort, will all be independently protected in addition to any copyright in the suite of programs as a compilation. Substantiality, in terms of infringement, will be measured by comparison with a sub-program rather than the unified whole.

Exceptions to Copyright Infringement

When it was decided to classify computer programs as literary works for copyright purposes, the usual exceptions to copyright infringement applied. The Act contains a great many exceptions, called the 'permitted acts'; for example, fair dealing for research or private study or for criticism, review of news reporting. In order to provide for uniform protection of computer programs throughout the European Community a Council Directive on the legal protection of computer programs was published in 1991 (91/250/EEC, OJ [1991] L122/42. United Kingdom law was already well developed and compiled with most of the Directive's provisions. However, because some aspects of united Kingdom law were somewhat vague and ill-defined (for example, the meaning of fair dealing) it was decided to tighten up some of the exceptions to copyright infringement, the necessary changes to the 1988 Act being made by the Copyright (Computer Programs) Regulations 1992. In terms of the permitted acts, three particular issues were addressed:

- 'decompiling' an existing computer program for interoperability;
- making necessary back-up copies;
- copying and adapting including error correction.

These three important exceptions to copyright infringement are described and examined below. It should be pointed out that the previous law probably covered the above acts in most circumstances. For example, fair dealing for research purposes might have allowed decompilation to achieve interoperability and implied licences might have been appropriate in some cases involving error correction and back-up copies. One further point is that, in addition to statutory defences to copyright infringement, there is a defence of public interest - for example, if it is in the public interest that a program listing in published. This might apply to code used by 'hackers' to penetrate computer systems because publication would assist managers of computer installations in their attempts to combat computer backing.

Decompilation of Computer Programs

'Decompilation' is used in wide sense and defined in section 50B as converting a copy of a computer program expressed in a low-level language into a version expressed in a higher-level language and extends to copying incidental to such conversion. The restricted act of making an adaptation includes decompilation and infringes copyright unless allowed by the new decompilation permitted act. The normal fair-dealing provisions apply otherwise. By section 50B(1), a lawful user (being a person having a right under a licence or otherwise to use the program: section 50A(2)) may decompile the program if necessary to obtain the information necessary to achieve the interoperability of any independently created program with the decompiled program or other program. In other words,it is permissible for a lawful user to decompile or disassemble a computer program to determine its interfaces if this is a necessary step in creating a new program which will interoperate (interact) with that or some other program.

Typically, a software developed might want to write a word processing program which will be compatible with another company's spreadsheet program so that data and files can be passed between the two programs (see Fig. 2.4). This form of compatibility is certainly desirable and should not cause any great concerns, unless the spreadsheet company was hoping to make its own compatible word processor in the future. Once the compatible interoperable program has been created there seems no reason why the interface details cannot be used subsequently to create competing, replacement programs as long as there is not a substantial copy made of the code in the original program, as indicated in the figure.

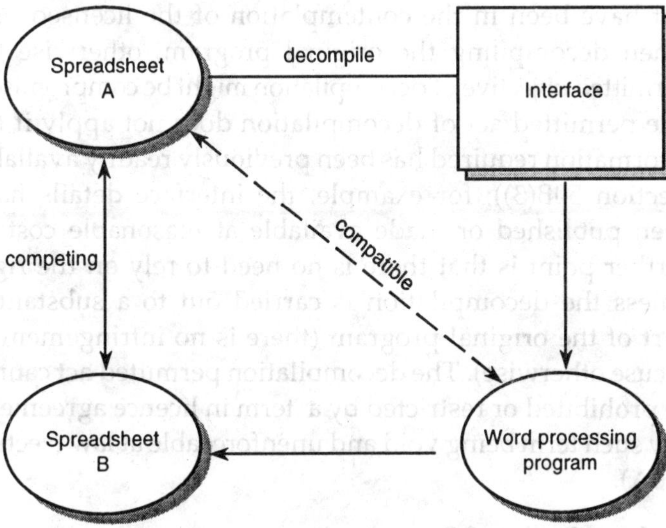

Fig. 2.4. Decompilation of a computer program

The Act, as amended, attempts to deal with this situation by making the use or supply of the information for any other objective, or in the development, production or marketing of any computer program substantially similar in its expression to the original program, an infringement of copyright (section 50B(2)). However, reuse of interface details will not necessarily result in a substantially similar expression and, in the example in Fig. 2.4 the expression 9program listings and structure) may be quite different. Interface details may be qualitatively insubstantial after all the program is a spread-sheet program, not an interface program, and may be written in different code to achieve the same purpose. In practice, these provisions will be very difficult to apply but the preamble to the Directive may give some assistance as it talks about the European

Community being fully committed to the promotion of international standardisation. The only other proviso is that the creation of the second spreadsheet program should not have been in the contemplation of the licensed user when decompiling the original program, otherwise the permitted objective of decompilation might be compromised. The permitted act of decompilation does not apply if the information required has been previously readily available (section 50B(3)); for example, the interface details have been published or made available at reasonable cost. A further point is that there is no need to rely on the right unless the decompilation is carried out to a substantial part of the original program (there is no infringement to excuse otherwise). The decompilation permitted act cannot be prohibited or restricted by a term in licence agreement, any such term being void and unenforceable at law (section 296A).

Back-up Copies of Computer Programs

It is essential that back-up copies of computer programs are made. A back-up copy will be needed if the original copy of the computer program becomes damaged or corrupted in any way. The original may be physically damaged if a cup of coffee is spilt over it, or the magnetic impulses on the disk representing the program may be destroyed or altered by exposure to a strong magnetic field. The original may become contaminated with a computer 'virus'. If a computer program has been obtained for use in a commercial environment, whether it is a word processing package, accounts system or spreadshseet, the chances are that the original will fail at the worst possible moment. If a back-up copy is available, a potential disaster can be averted and the urgent report or whatever can still be completed on time.

The Act, as amended, makes specific provision for the

making of back-up copies of computer programs. Before the amendments made by the Copyright (computer Programs) Regulations 1992, there was no such provision although the court may have been prepared to imply an appropriate term into a software licence where the making of a back-up copy was reasonably necessary to the use of the program in question. Of course, many software companies make express provision for the user to make a back-up copy. It is common for the installation instructions to ask the licensed user to make a copy of the program first and use this as the working copy, placing the original disks in a safe place in case the working disks become damaged or corrupted in some way.

Section 50A states that copyright is not infringed by a lawful user making an additional copy of a computer program for back-up purposes if doing so is necessary to the lawful use. This right cannot be taken away by any terms in a licence agreement but there may be some difficulty with deciding when making a back-up copy is truly necessary. It might not be so if a licence agreement includes terms to the effect that the licensor will himself make a further copy available to the licensee in the e vent of failure of the original copy.

The Act recognises the possibility that back-up copies may have been made. Section 56 deals with transfers of works in electronic from and the position with respect to copies which are not transferred along with the original software. This is best described by way of an example. A business, Acme Ltd, obtains a word processing package (WORDY); the licence agreement allows the making of one back-up copy. Acme uses WORDY and makes two copies of it, one as a back-up and one for use on another computer. Two years later, Acme decides to obtain some new computers and a more powerful word processing program. It looks at the WORDY license and sees that the license does not prevent the transfer of the package to someone else. Acme assigns its licence to use WORDY to Zenith Co and transfers the original copy of the program plus the single back-up copy. By section 56, Acme was permitted to transfer the software because there were no express terms in the licence agreement prohibiting this, but it should have transferred all copies of WORDY. By section 56(2), the copy it has retained is treated as an infringing copy and leaves Acme liable to the owner of the copyright in the word processing programs. additionally, because Acme made two copies instead of the one permitted under the licence agreement, it was in breach of that agreement and, depending on the terms in the licence dealing with breach, it may find that the licence was brought to an end and that the purported transfer to Zenith is void.

Miscellaneous Exceptions and Error Correction

By section 50C, a lawful user is permitted to copy on adapt a computer program providing that it is necessary for his lawful use and not prohibited by the agreement regulating the use (for example, a licence agreement). Section 30C(2) provides a specific example of when this may be necessary, that is, where it is for the purpose of error correction. A licence agreement may specifically prohibit error correction so that all this provision does is to raise a presumption in favour of the lawful user. For example, if disassembling a computer program in order to correct errors is necessary to the lawful use and there are no express terms prohibiting this, then it can be done without infringing copyright. Again, the meaning of 'necessary' may be at issue but the important factor is that the presumption can be and, in many cases in practice, will be cancelled out by express terms. A number of software companies are reluctant to allow licensees or third parties to modify programs. Any such modifications could be carried out badly, resulting in unfavourable publicity for the software company through no fault of its own.

Even though a licence agreement may prohibit error correction by the licencee or a third party, it is possible that other areas of law may apply to defeat the prohibition. The common law principle of non-derogation from grant was used in *British Leyland Motor Corp Ltd* v *Armstrong patents Co Ltd* [1986] 2 WLR 400 to stop British Leyland enforcing its copyright in drawings of exhaust systems for cars to prevent a free market in spare parts. The same argument holds true for computer programs. A licensee should have access to a free market in maintaining the programs and there are signs that judges are likely to accept this possibility in least some situations.

European Community competition law may also impinge on terms prohibiting error correction by anyone other than the licensee on the basis that this is restrictive of trade between member states under Article 81(1) of the Treaty of Rome. Alternatively, where the licensor is a major software company, a restriction on third party maintenance could be seen as an abuse of a dominant position under Article 82.

Section 296(1) of the Copyright, Designs and Patents Act 198 makes any term of condition in an agreement void in so far as it purports to prohibit or restrict the use of any device or means to observe, study or test the functioning of a computer program in order to understand the ideas and principles underlying any element of the program. This reinforces the idea/expression dichotomy but is unlikely to be welcomed by software produces. It would, for example, excuse the form of reverse engineering used in the *Dyason* v *Autodesk* case (measuring the electrical signals passing between the dongle and the computer program).

The exceptions apply to new programs and programs in existence at 1 January 1993 (the commencement date for the new regulations). Agreements and terms or conditions in agreements entered into before 1 January 1993 are unaffected, however. For example a term prohibiting making a back up copy in a pre-1993 agreement will not be made invalid by reason of the changes brought about by the regulations even if the making of a back-up copy is deemed to be necessary to the lawful use of the program.

Employees and Freelance Programmers

The author of a work is the first owner of the copyright in the work. An exception which applies to literary, dramatic, musical or artistic works is where the work is made by an employee in the course of his employment, in which case the employer becomes the first owner of the copyright in the work, subject to a contrary intention (section 11(2)). This raises the following questions.

- Who is employee?
- What is the position regarding freelance computer programmers and consultants?
- What is the meaning of 'in the course of employment'?

The Copyright, Designs and Patents Act 1988 does not specifically define these terms but states that 'employed', 'employee', 'employer' and 'employment' refer to employment under a contract of service or apprenticeship (section 178). The question of ownership of computer programs written by freelance staff will be considered first.

Freelance Staff

It is not always easy to identify when a person is an employee and when he is not; various tests have evolved and some concern questions of 'control'. These tests include whether the 'employer' can tell the person what to do when to do it and how to do it. Does the 'employer' provide the person with time off for holidays, sick pay or a pension? Does the person have to correct unsatisfactory work in his own time and at his own expense? How is income tax paid? In many cases the question will be answered by looking at the terms of the contract between the parties although a description of the parties as 'employer' and 'employee' is not conclusive. In many cases, freelance staff, hired to perform a particular task such as writing or modifying a specific computer program, will be deemed to be self-employed. The consequence of this is that the copyright in any program so written will, *prima facie* and in the absence of any agreement otherwise, belong to the freelance programmer.

It is essential, therefore, when employing freelance staff, or anyone else who is not employed under a permanent contract of employment, to make contractual provision for determining ownership of copyright. The organisation hiring the programmer or consultant may want to own the copyright so that it can exploit the resultant program itself, or it may simply want to prevent its competitors from obtaining a copy of it. In either of these situations the contract should specifically state that the ownership of the copyright belongs to the organisation and not to the programmer and furthermore, there should be a written assignment of copyright, signed by the freelance programmer. Of course, the fee charged will probably be greater as a result because the freelance programmer might have envisaged making use of the program elsewhere; he may know of other businesses which would be interested in what he produces. On the other hand, if the commissioning organisation does not itself contemplate commercially exploiting the software or preventing others from using it, then it is important that a term is included in the contract granting a licence for the continued use of the program.

If the contract is silent on such matters, the freelance programmer may later decide to test his ownership of the program by offering it to others or, worse still, claim that, as owner, he will permit the continued use of the program only on payment of a licence fee. These difficulties may arise especially when the program in question turns out to be more useful and successful than the parties originally envisaged. There is a danger that a freelance programmer will try to hold his client to ransom if he later realises that the value of the software he has produced in out of all proportion to the payment he received for writing it.

Unfortunately, not all 'freelance staff' are self-employed and some are employed by an agency. In this case the same precautions apply and it is even more important to deal with ownership of copyright, otherwise the agency (as employer) could turn out to be the first owner of the copyright.

The Employee and the Course of Employment

As regards persons who can safely be classified as employees, their employers cannot safely assume that they will own the copyright in everything produced by those employees. For example, if an employee writes a computer program to help with his work but he is not employed as a computer programmer, his job is not to write computer programs and an employer cannot necessarily assume that he owns the copyright in that particular program. A lecturer normally owns the copyright in any book or article he writes because he is primarily employed as a teacher and not as a writer of books and articles, even though his employer may encourage this. A person employed as an accountant who writes a computer program to help with the production of financial accounts will own the copyright in that program if he wrote it in his own time, using his own equipment. Initially, this may create no problems because the accountant may have been motivated by interest and a desire to improve his own efficiency at work but problems could arise later if the accountant moves to another fir or discovers that his program is commercially viable. If an employer is faced with the situation where an employee has in his own time and using his own equipment, developed a useful computer program, then the employer should immediately try to reach agreement as regards questions of ownership and use of the program with the employee concerned; rather than allowing the program to be used without such agreement.

If an employee has produced a computer program outside the normal course of his duties, but has used his employer's equipment or done it during the hours of his employment, the ownership of copyright is more difficult to predict, although it is more likely that the employer will be treated as owner. Even here, however, it is wiser to seek agreement at the outset rather than leave matters until there is some disagreement about the continued use or exploitation of the program. Employers should consider the introduction of, or extension of, a 'suggestions' scheme to include computer programs or systems written by staff who are not employed to do this, with effective rewards and suitable provisions as regards ultimate ownership.

Programming Languages and Instruction Sets

A computer program is written using a specific computer programming language. Languages vary enormously from the basic instruction set of the central processing unit to 'fourth-generation' languages and languages used for programming logic. A great deal of skill, imagination and effort goes into the design of a new programming language and the development of new languages will be encouraged if some form of protection is afforded to them. However, the exercise of rights in languages could seriously interfere with the licensing and distribution of computer programs databases. In principle, there is a strong argument for saying that programming languages are ideas and, as such, cannot be protected by copyright. Therefore a person who writes an original program in COBOL infringes no copyright in the process of writing the program. There is an analogy with natural language and it would be ridiculous to suggest that writing n article or report using 'Esperanto' infringed any copyright subsisting in the language. Of course, making an unauthorised copy of an Esperanto-English dictionary would infringe copyright, if only that subsisting in the typographical arrangement.

The European Council Directive on the legal protection of computer programs recognises that programming languages, at least to the extent that they comprise ideas and principles, should not be protected by copyright. Given that this is so one might wonder where in lies the incentive to create a new language. The answer lies in the fact that, usually, the program, once written, can only be run on a computer if it is converted into object code whether temporarily, using an interpreter program or permanently, using a compiler program. The licensing of these interpreter and compiler programs, together with appropriate documentation describing the syntax, semantics and use of the language, is the method by which financial reward is usually sought. These programs are of course, protected by copyright. However, the observation in the United States of withholding copyright protection from ideas including features of programs dictated by function might have the drastic effect, if taken to its logical conclusion, of robbing interpreter and compiler programs of copyright protection.

Some languages and program development tools (languages in wide sense including expert system shells) require 'run-time' licences to be acquired before application programs and systems may is distributed. These generally permit the copying and distribution of cut-down version of the language, tool or shell sufficient to run the application.

A computer's instruction set represents a language at its most basic level and, at this level, it is nearest to idea and, when used to write small programs, it has been argued that there is a merger of idea and expression - in which case protection will be denied. This happened in the United States case of *NEC Corp* v *Intel Corp* (1989) 10 USPQ 2d where it was held that Intel's microcode programs were dictated by the instruction set of the microprocessors and, as there were no alternative ways of expressing the ideas incorporated, reverse analysis of the mocrocode programs did not infringe copyright. However, it was also accepted that such programs could be protected if not dictated by idea.

In the United Kingdom, the question of copyright protection for an instruction set was considered in *Microsense Systems Ltd* v *Control Systems Technology Ltd* (unreported) 17 June 1991, Chancery Division. The plaintiff made traffic control systems and controllers for Pelican crossings, which were programmed using a set of mnemonics (a set of three - letter symbols) which were in turn used to monitor the controllers. The defendant made similar controllers and used total of 49 of the plaintiff's mnemonics arguing that there was no copyright in them because, once the functions had been decided, there was no room for skill and labour in devising the mnemonics. This was an interlocutory hearing so no final decision was taken but the judge thought that there was an arguable case that the list of mnemonics was protected by copyright because of the work in designing the controller in the first place. This seems to contradict the *NEC* v *Intel* case although, being an American case, it is not binding on the United Kingdom courts. However, the defendants, argument that the list was effectively idea reflects the desirability of standardisation in traffic controllers as, otherwise, there could be catastrophic mistakes.

Devices to Overcome Copy-Protection

Some computer programs were marketed in a form that makes them difficult to copy. Almost inevitably, devices and software designed to overcome these attempts at copy-protection soon appeared on the market, to the intense irritation of the software industry. A distinction must be made at this stage between things that can be used to make unauthorised copies of programs, but which also have legitimate uses (for example, computers with disk drives and cassette players with twin tape decks) and things specifically designed to overcome copy-protection, such as software to be used to copy other software which has been copy protected. Where a device or software has lawful uses, it would obviously be unsatisfactory to ban its sale. The music industry tried to interfere with the sale of twin-cassette music centers in *CBS Songs Ltd* v *Amstrad Consumer Electronics Plc* [1988] AC 1013, on the basis that, by the sale and advertising of these machines, Amstrad was inciting the public to infringe copyright. The fact that the machines made by Amstrad had other legitimate uses, such as making copies of the purchasers' own music or of works not protected by copyright, was important, even though it was obvious that the largest use would involve copyright infringement. Not was Amstrad authorising infringement.

There can be little sympathy, however, for firms who make devices or software deliberately designed to permit the copying of works which are copy-protected. The sole purpose of these devices and software is to enable copy-protection to be overcome. By section 296 of the Copyright. Designs and Patents Act, devices or means specifically designed or adapted to circumvent copy-protection of works issued to the public in electronic form are controlled by treating the making, importation, sale or hire, possession in the course of business, etc, of the devices or means as an infringement of copy-right. Furthermore, publishing information to enable or assist the circumvention of copy-protection is similarly treated. The use of the phrase 'devices or means' should be wide enough to cover both hardware devices and software methods designed to overcome copy-protection. Computers with dual disk drives and twin tape cassette machines are not caught by these provisions because they are not 'specifically designed or adapted to circumvent copy-protection'. Similarly, normal copying programs which come with a computer operating system are within the law because they are designed to be used legitimately, to take back-up copies of programs and data files. Indeed, such programs will usually fail to copy computer programs that are copy-protected. A difficulty with this provision is that it is enforceable only by the person issuing copies of the copy-protected work in question to the public, and if the person making, importing, selling or hiring , etc. the device, means or information knows or has reason to believe that it will be used to make infringing copies.

It is arguable that the opportunity should have been taken to deal with this matter by way of criminal penalities as the making, importing, selling or hiring of unauthorised decoders for encrypted broadcasts or cable programmes has been criminalised by section 297A of the Copyright, Designs and Patents Act 1988 (inserted by section 197 of the Broadcasting Act 1990). However, there has been a move away from copy-protection because it is troublesome to customers who, not unreasonably, wish to take back-up copies of important programs. Indeed, the Copyright Designs and Patents Act 1988 now contains a specific right to make a back-up copy if necessary for the lawful use of the program concerned (section 50A).

Implications of Software Copyright Law

The scope of copyright law in relation to computer software in general and computer programs in particular has become more certain in the last couple of years or so. Consequently, a number of practical recommendations can be made to software developers.

- Do not copy screen displays, menus, program structure, database structure or other non literal elements of software.
- Even if some element of new software is likely to be 'dictated by function', create it independently and retain all the preparatory materials in respect of it.
- Prepare, date and keep preparatory materials for items of software.
- Insert deliberate mistakes or redundant code or entries into programs, databases and other works.
- Be aware that copyright extends to a compilation of individual programs and/or data files.
- Make sure employees do not use materials or confidential information belonging to previous employers.
- Obtain a signed written assignment of copyright in respect of works to be created by self-employed programmes or consultants.

- Check licence agreements for void terms in respect of decompilation and making back-up copies.
- Make sensible arrangements for error correction of computer programs.

In general terms, copyright law does not protect the function of a program. It will be perfectly legal to write a program that performs the same function as an existing program provided the function itself is not protected by the law of breach of confidence and the first program is not used in a manner which falls within the acts restricted by the copyright. However, where the same person is involved in writing the first and second programs a great deal of care must be taken to be rebut any presumption of copying that is likely to be raised in any action for infringement of copyright.

3 COPYRIGHT AND DATABASES

Until recently, it was generally accepted that computer databases were protected by copyright as literary works as they could be considered to be compilations. This was,of course, without prejudice to any individual copyrights subsisting in the individual items or works contained within the database. For example, consider a database of modern romantic poems. Each poem would be protected by copyright as an original literary work and, providing sufficient skill, labour or judgment was expended in selecting and arranging, indexing or annotating the poems there would be a separate copyright in the database as a whole. There could be other copyrights also, such as in respect of any index, cross-referencing system or annotations. Some of these elements could be protected as non-literal elements such as, for example, any hypertext links or the indexing system itself.

There was some doubt about whether a database of artistic works could be a compilation as literary works are defined in section 3(1) in terms of works which are written, spoken or sung. It is arguable that this does not apply to most forms of artistic works. An exception is a circuit diagram which, according to Mr Justic Jacon in *Anacon Corp Ltd* v *Environmental Research Technology Ltd* [1994] FSR 656, was also a literary work because it was intended to be read by the person making a circuit board in accordance with thc diagram. Mr Justic Laddie agreed with this in *Electronic Techniques (Anglia) Ltd* v *Critchley Components Ltd* [1997] FSR 401. However, he said that, when considering a circuit diagram as a literary work, the graphic elements must be ignored and, that being so, the work could not be a literary work as it was little more than a list of five or six components. In other words, the circuit diagram was not sufficiently substantial for copyright as a literary work.

The legal protection of databases was significantly changed by the Copyright and Rights in Databases Regulations 1997 which came into force on 1 January 1998. The Regulations were made in order to comply with a European Directive on the legal protection of databases (OJ [1996] L77/20). A particular concern, following developments in the United States in the *Feist* v *Rural Telephone* case (discussed below), was that some databases that might be commercially valuable would fail to attract copyright protection in some member states of the European Community. Thus, a dual approach to protection was taken in the Directive. First, providing a database can be regarded as an intellectual creation, it will have copyright protection. If the database can be regarded as the result of substantial investment, it will attract a new right, referred to in the Regulations as a 'database right'. Of course, in many cases, databases will enjoy both a copyright and a database right (as well as separate rights in the constituent parts in some cases) but the database right was designed specifically for valuable databases which failed to reach the requirements for copyright protection.

In this chapter, the new provisions for databases are described. However, first it will be useful to look at the basic position before the changes brought about by the Regulations and the position in the United States.

Copyright in a Database Before 1 January 1998

Databases were not expressly mentioned in the Copyright, Designs and Patents Act 1988 but were potentially protected by copyright as compilations, provided they were original. Copyright might have subsisted at two levels if the database was a collection of individual works, as mentioned earlier. Each work may be subject to copyright but, on a higher level, there may be a separate copyright in the database as a whole if the selection and arrangement of materials contained within it is the result of a modicum of skill or judgment. This is similar to the copyrights found in the *IBCOS* case. It appeared that most databases would have had copyright protection providing they were the result of a minimum amount of skill, labour or judgment. Traditionally, the threshold for copyright protection in the United Kingdom has been relatively low in comparison, for example, to German copyright law which requires a work to be a personal intellectual creation (German Copyright Act 1963, section 2(2), as amended). This appeared to be a higher standard than that required in the united Kingdom where copyright developed in a very pragmatic manner.

Consider a database comprising details of a company's customers. Say that the information stored includes names and addresses of existing and potential customers together with details of the customers' operations and views on the customers' creditworthiness, payment facilities, discounts, etc. This database would have been protected by copyright in the United Kingdom because it required skill and judgment in the design of the structure of the database (that is, the design of the number and type of fields and heir length) and in the selection of the information to be entered. Thus the structure and the information would have been forms of expression for copyright purposes.

This should be contrasted with a database containing simply the names and addresses of all a company's customers because there is no selectivity or judgment (or very little) in the decision as to what should be included and relatively little skill in designing the structure of the database. This would be similar in principle to *G A Cramp & Sons Ltd* v *Frank Smythson Ltd* [1944] AC 329, in which copyright was denied to a simple diary because the commonplace nature of the information left little room for judgment in the selection and organisation of the information. If the creation of a database was the result of a great deal of effort alone, with little judgment in the design of the databases or in the selection of material (for example, a telephone directory stored in a computer database or a directory of postcodes), it was debatable whether it would attract copyright protection. However, the United Kingdom law traditionally has been generous and compilations of non-original matter have been protected providing that some judgment at least has been expended in their making (see *Macmillan & Co Ltd* v *K & J Cooper* (1923) 40 TLR 186). In reported cases on copyright and databases, including some on the copyright in a database of lawyers, the question of whether the databases were protected by copyright was not put into issue; see for example, *Waterlow Directories Ltd* v *Reed Information Services Ltd* [1992] FSR 409.

The United States and the Sweat of the Brow Principle

The 'sweat of the brow' principle, affording copyright protection to works which are the result of labour only, was roundly rejected in the United States Supreme Court in *Feist Publications Inc* v *Rural Telephone Service Co Inc* [1991] 111 S Ct 1282. In that case, it was held that the 'white pages' in a typical telephone directory were not protected by copyright because of a lack of creativity, as they did not owe their origin to an act of authorship. The court did recognise, however, that a compilation of facts could be the subject of copyright because the author has to choose which facts to include and in what order to place them. The court went on to suggest that the 'yellow pages' section of a telephone directory was protected because of the presence of original material such as drawings in advertisements. There is also some skill in devising the classification system used. Subsequently, however, it was held in the United States that taking a large amount of data from a classified directory did not infringe copyright (see *Bell South Advertising & Publishing Corp* v *Donnelley Information Publishing Inc* (unreported) 2 September 1993, 11th Cir. It is fair to say that the position in the United Kingdom has probably been more generous to database compilers and it has been accepted that headings in a trade catalogue are protected by copyright. The United States Constitution gives a clue to the more rigorous approach there as it states he object of copyright is 'to promote the progress of science and the useful arts' (Article 1, Section 8, clause 8). This would appear to be incompatible with rewarding acts of labour only.

Protection of Databases on or after 1 January 1998

In view of problems such as that highlighted in *Feist* v *Rural Telephone* and bearing in mind even telephone directories and directories of postcodes can be commercially valuable — for example, by being sold on CD-ROM - it was considered important to improve the protection of databases on a European scale. Another factor was that standards of protection varied throughout Europe and there was a need for harmonisation of national laws. The model of protection adopted was to provide for a standard copyright treatment for database requiring skill or judgment in their making but, in addition, to introduce a new *sui generis* right specifically aimed at providing shorter-term protection for databases that might not meet this standard but which were, nevertheless, the result of a substantial investment which would be prejudiced if such databases had no protection.

The new copyright and the database right apply equally to both electronic and non-electronic databases, in line with the general approach of the European Commission not to distinguish between electronic and manual databases. Both of the new rights are without prejudice to copyright in the contents. Thus, where a database contains individual works of copyright, those works will retain their own copyright in addition to any copyright or database right in the database as a whole. For example, consider a database of recipes. If a person copies one of the recipes without permission, he will infringe the copyright in it. If he copies several recipes without permission, he will infringe he copyright in each individual recipe, as well as infringing the copyright in the database and/or the database right, depending on whether one or both subsist.

It should also be noted the moral rights have not been affected by the changes and, consequently, an author of a copyright database may have moral rights in respect of it although there are no moral rights in respect of a database only protected by the database right (ignoring any copyrights in the constituent parts) and music collections on CD-ROM are expressly excluded from these new provisions. They will continue to be treated as compilations for copyright purposes.

First, the copyright protection of databases is considered, followed by an examination of the new database right.

Copyright in Databases

Section 3(1) of the Copyright, Designs and Patents Act 1988 is amended and 'database' is added to the non-exhaustive list of works that are literary works. Databases are then excluded from compilations and there are now some differences as to how databases and compilations are treated by copy-right law. Of course, many of the provisions are the same for both but it should be noted that there is a difference in the fair dealing provisions and there is a special non-derogation from, grant provision, preventive undue interference with the rights of lawful users of databases.

The precise nature of the original works of copyright are not expressly defined in the Act but there is now a detailed definition of 'database', following that in the Directive. A new section 3A is inserted into the Act which defines 'database' as a collection of independent works, data or other materials which (a) are arranged in a systematic or methodical way, and (b) are individually accessible by electronic or other means. The use of the phrase 'other means' shows that the provisions apply equally to non-electronic data-bases and this is confirmed in the recitals to the Directive. A card index will be a database for copyright purposes. Although the Act, as modified, is silent on the point, the Directive makes it clear that the copyright protection for a database dos not extend to any program used in the making or operation of an electronic database. Of course, computer programs are separately protected as another form of literary work.

Unlike the other original works, a gloss is added to the test of originality and a database is original for copyright purposes if and only if, by reason of the selection or arrangement of its contents, the database constitutes the author's own intellectual creation. This is equivalent to the German approach to copyright and seems to be a much stricter requirement than that which existed before 1 January 1998. However, this is not to prejudice pre-existing databases and, where a database was created on or before 27 March 1996 (which was the date on which the Directive as adopted was published) and was protected by copyright immediately before 1 January 1998, that copyright will continue for its full term (that is, 'life plus 70 years'), even if it does not qualify for copyright protection under this new test for originality.

The usual restricted acts apply to databases as they do for literary works generally except that the restricted act of making an adaptation is redefined for databases in terms of an adaptation being an arrangement or altered version or a translation of the database. Examples of these acts are:

- a version in which the information contained in the database has been sorted into a different order (arrangement);
- a version in which some of the information is suppressed (either records or fields or both) (arrangement or altered version);
- the database is converted to be used with a different program to access the contents or it is a converted from 8-bit to 7-bit code or it is imported into a word processing or spreadsheet program (altered version or translation).

The Directive left member states with some discretion as to which permitted acts they applied to copyright databases. The approach in the United Kingdom was to apply the traditional permitted acts that apply to literary works, with the exception of fair dealing for research and private study where tow specific changes were implemented for databases. A new subsection (1A) was inserted into section 29 which, in respect of fair dealing for research or private study, requires the source to be indicated. Furthermore, under section 29(5), it is not fair dealing to do anything in relation to a database for a commercial purpose.

Section 50D was inserted into the Copyright, Designs and Patents Act 1988. This applies to any person having a right to use a database or part of a database. Such a person dos not infringe, copyright if, in the exercise of that right, he does anything which is necessary for the purposes of his access to sand use of the contents of the database (or part of the database). This presents a person licensing a database to another including terms in the licence agreement which purport to hinder access to and use of the database. It is essentially a non-derogation from grant provision. It is clear from this provision that a database may be made available in such way that a licensee may be restricted to part only of the database. The restrictions may be in terms of certain records or certain fields. For example, in a database of potential customers, a licenced user may be restricted to customers living in the South of England only or it may be that he user can retrieve names and addresses only and not data relating to individuals' financial standing. The right under section 50D cannot be prohibited or restricted and section 296B makes void any term or condition in an agreement in so far as it purports to prohibit or restrict those acts permitted under section 50D or any act necessary for the exercise of the rights granted by the agreement.

The Database Right

The Copyright, Designs and Patents Act 1988 was not mended to include the provisions relating to the database right. Instead it is provided for separately in Part III of the Copyright and Rights in Databases Regulations 1997.

The database right, described in the Directive as a right *sui generis*, was designed to protect the investment in obtaining, verifying or presenting the contents of a database.

It is of limited duration compared to copyright but the right is not restricted to non-copyright databases and many databases will be subject to both copyright and the database right. As with the copyright provisions, the database right is unaffected if the database contains works which are themselves subject to copyright. Take, for example, a database of original maps or charts which required the exercise of skill and judgment (assuming that this test is the same as 'author's intellectual creation') and which was also substantial investment, for example, in the presentation of its contents. The individual maps or charts will be works of copyright the database as whole will be a work of copyright and it will also be subject to the database right.

Definitions

The database right is a right given to the maker of a database prevent the unauthorised extraction or reutlisation of the contents of a database. To understand this basic right, it is important too look at the definitions in the Regulations which are set out below. However, it must be noted that the meaning of 'database' is the same as applies to databases subject to copyright. The definitions are contained in regulation 12 although the fine detail of some of them occur in other parts of the Regulations as indicated:

- 'database right' is defined in regulation 13(1) as a property right which subsists in a database if there has been a substantial investment in obtaining, verifying or presenting the contents of the database;
- 'investment' includes any investment, whether of financial, human or technical resources;
- 'substantial', in relation to any investment, extraction or reutilisation, means substantial in terms of quantity or quality or a combination of both;

- 'insubstantial' is relevant to infringement and, under regulation 16(2), the repeated and systematic extraction or reutilisation of insubstantial parts of the contents of a database may amount to the extraction or reutlisation of a substantial part of those contents;
- 'extraction', in relation to any contents of a database, means the permanent or temporary transfer of those contents to another medium by any means or in any form;
- reutlisation', in relation to any contents of a database, means making those contents available to the public by any means;
- 'maker' is defined in regulation 14(1) as the person who takes the initiative in obtaining, verifying or presenting the contents of a database and assumes the risk of investing in that obtaining, verification or presentation, such acts constituting the act of making the database. The basic rule is that the maker will be the first owner of the database right. Where a database is made by an employee in the course of his employment, the employer is regarded as the maker of the database and there is provision for Her Majesty to be regarded as the maker of a database where it is made by an officer or servant of the Crown in the course of his duties (Parliamentary database right is also provided for);
- 'jointly' in relation to the making of a database is defined in regulation 16(2) in terms of two or more persons who act in collaboration in taking the initiative and assuming the risk of investing; however, unlike the case in copyright law, there is no requirement that the contribution of each is not distinct.

- 'lawful user', in relation to a database, means any person who (whether under a licence to do any of the acts restricted by any database right in the database or otherwise) has a right to use the database.

A few points can be made about these definitions. First, the fact that the right is a property right (as is copyright, of course) should come to as no surprise. The meaning of 'substantial' is slightly different from that generally accepted (though not defined) for copyright purposes, because quality, quantity or both are factors, whereas for copyright purposes attention tends to focus on quality rather than quantity. However, that is not to say that the proportion of the work taken can never be a factor in determining infringement. A curious provision is that continuing to take or make available insubstantial parts may amount to a substantial taking or making available. This is to prevent any doubt as to whether such action would infringe the database right. There is some doubt under copyright law as to whether the repeated taking of insubstantial parts can infringe although it would seem sensible to view such taking as a connected series of takings and view them cumulatively, in the round.

The meanings of 'extraction' and 'investment' are quite wide. In particular, the latter is not restricted to financial investment and covers a situation where a person spends time and effort in making a database or simply where technical resources are tied up. This could be the situation where a central computer is dedicated to receiving information from remote users who submit information to the computer which is automatically collated and entered into a database. As quality of investment is a factor in the investment, it is possible that the skill of any person involved or the power or technical advancement of equipment used could be relevant in determining whether the right subsists.

The meaning of 'reutilisation' is directed to making the contents available to the public rather than simply making use of the contents. Thus, making use of the contents for one's own benefit without authorisation does not, *per se*, infringe the database right. However, it is likely that the person concerned will have previously infringed by extracting those contents and there may also be infringements of any copyright in the underlying works included in the database, where such copyright exists.

Lending a copy of a database (not for direct or indirect commercial advantage) by an establishment accessible to the public does not constitute extraction or reutlisation of the contents of a database but this exception does not extent to making available for on-the-spot reference use which could, therefore, fall within the meaning of extraction or reutlisation.

The doctrine of exhaustion of rights within the European Economic Area (EEA) applies to copies sold within the EEA by or with the consent of the owner of the database right to the extent that further sale of such copies does not constitute extraction or reutilisation of the contents of the database. Therefore, if a person lawfully buys a copy of a database, that person can resell that copy elsewhere in the EEA without infringing the database right. The fact that a database has been made available on-line for consultation by members of the public does not, however, exhaust the maker's right of reutilisation, It is only sale of copies that exhausts any right to control resale.

Qualification

For the database right to subsist, it must satisfy the qualification requirements. These are set out in regulation 18, and require that, at the 'material time', the maker (or at least one of the where there are joint makers) is:

- a national of an EEA state (or habitually resident in the state);
- a body incorporated in an EEA state, having its central administration or principal place of business in an EEA state or registered office in the EEA and the body's operations linked on an ongoing basis with the ceremony of an EEA state, or
- a partnership or other unincorporated body formed under the law of an EEA state, having at that time its central administration or principal place or business within the EEA.

The 'material time' is the time when the database is made or, if this extended over a period of time, a substantial part of that period. The qualification requirements do not apply in the case of Parliamentary database right although there is no express exception for Crown database right.

Duration

The Directive emphasised that the right is to be limited in time, subject to a new right arising if a database undergoes substantial change, and the term of protection afforded by the database right is stated in regulation 17 as 15 years from the end of the calendar year during which the making of the database is completed; although, if it is made available to the public before the end of that period, the right will continue to endure for 15 years from the end of the calendar year during which it was first made available. Of course, many databases are subject to continuing or periodic modification. Thus, a new period of protection arises if changes to the database are substantial and this includes any substantial change resulting from an accumulation of successive additions, deletions or alterations, provided the database would be considered to be a substantial new investment.

The definitions should again be reflected upon. It could be, for example, that a new database right arises simply because the maker has redesigned his software to improve the presentation of the contents of the database, or has put resources into checking the accuracy of the contents. For example, in the case of a database of customers, the owner has sent out a mailing asking for confirmation of the details of individuals and made corrections to the database as appropriate.

If the database in question was made on or before 1 January 1983 and the database right subsisted in the database immediately on 1 january 1988, the database right will last for 15 years beginning with 1 January 1998.

Infringement and Exceptions

Infringing acts are defined in regulation 16 in terms of the extraction or reutilisation of all or a substantial part of the contents of the database without the consent of the owner. Reflecting the special nature of databases and the damage that may be done to the owner's interests by a systematic course of unauthorised use of small parts of database, the repeated and systematic extraction or reutilisation of insubstantial parts of the contents of a database may amount to the extraction or reutilisation of a substantial part of those contents. In terms of 'insubstantial infringement'; the Directive stated that the repeated and systematic extraction or reutilisation must imply acts conflicting with a normal exploitation of the database or be unreasonably prejudicial to the legitimate interests of the maker of the database.

One way of looking at repeated insubstantial takings is to view them as a continuing act and as equivalent to a substantial taking by accumulating them. However, it is clear that what is intended is that an accumulation of insubstantial takings could infringe even if, when accumulated, they still do not amount to a substantial part of the database.

There are a number of exceptions to infringement. Regulation 19 contains a non-derogation from grant' provision which prevents the owner of the database right interfering with the subsequent use of insubstantial parts by a lawful user such as a person having access under a licence agreement. A lawful user of a database, which has been made available to the public, cannot be prevented from extracting or reutilising insubstantial parts of the database for any purpose. Any term in an agreement, under which the right to use a database or part of a database has been granted, which the right to use a database or part of a database has been granted, which attempts to prevent this is void. Regulation 20 contains a fair dealing exception to infringement. Where the database has been made available to the pubic in any manner, fair dealing with a substantial part of the contents does not infringe if:

- the part is extracted by a person who is otherwise a lawful user;
- it is extracted for the purposes of illustrations for teaching or research (but not for a commercial purpose), and
- the source is indicated.

Further exceptions are set out in Schedule 1 to the Regulations and relate to parliamentary and judicial proceedings, Royal Commissions and statutory inquiries, material open to public inspection or on official register, material communicated to the Crown in the course of public business, public records and acts done under statutory authority. These mirror the equivalent permitted acts for copyright. However, apart from these exceptions and those mentioned above, none of the other permitted acts that apply generally to literary works under copyright apply to the database right. For example, there is no provision for fair dealing for criticism or review or for reporting current events.

Where it is reasonable to assume that the database right has expired and the identity of the maker (or makers in the case of a database made jointly) cannot by reasonable enquiry be ascertained, the right will not be infringed by the extraction or reutilisation of a substantial part of the contents; regulation 21. It is important, therefore, for the owner of database to indicate the identity of the maker on copies of the database and the year during which it was first published. If the database is made available on-line, this information should appear on the title screen or other appropriate place. This is also worth doing so as to raise useful presumptions as discussed below.

It should be noticed that it is the identity of the maker which is important, not that of the owner, where the maker and owner are not the same person. This is similar to copyright where it is the identity of the author which is crucial. However, unlike copyright, the duration of the database right is not dependent on the life of the maker and is fixed by the act of making or first publication. Of course it may be dangerous to rely on this and other permitted acts which relate to the database right, as the database and/or its contents may be subject to copyright. Such copyright, where it subsists, to independent of and not prejudiced by the database right. Where Copyright subsists in the database or its contents, a person using a database must ensure that the agreement under which he is using it extends to the appropriate use of copyright materials. A person relying on the exceptions to infringement of the database right must also check to make sure that his intended use is also covered by the exceptions to copyright infringement. For example, if a person who has the right to use a database wants to extract any part for the purpose of illustration for teaching, he should confirm that he can rely on the equivalent permitted acts in relation to teaching which apply to copyright works if the part extracted is protected by copyright unless, of course, his right to use the database covers this.

Presumptions

There are some presumptions which apply to the database right and which may be helpful to the owner in an action for infringement. They are not dissimilar to the equivalent presumptions which apply in relation to copyright works. Under regulation 22, where a name purporting to be that of the maker of the database appears on copies of the database as published, it is presumed that person is the maker and the database was not made in circumstance where the employer would be the first owner and is not Crown or parliamentary databaser right. Where copies of a database as published beat a label or mark stating that a named person was the maker and that it was first published in a specified year; the label or mark shall admissible as evidence of those facts and presumed correct until the contrary be proved.

Where a database has been made jointly, these provisions apply in relation to each person alleged to be one of the makers. under copyright law, the usefulness of the equivalent presumptions was seen in the case of *Microsoft Corp* v *Electro-wide Ltd* [1997] FSR 580 where, in the absence of any evidence submitted by the defendant, the Microsoft Corporation did not have to prove that it owned the copyrights subsisting in software such as 'Windows 95.'

Other Provisions

The provisions which apply to dealing with rights in copyright works, the rights and remedies of the owner of copyright and of an exclusive licensee under the copyright are all applied without modification to the database right. Thus, assignment of the database right must be in writing and be signed by or on behalf of the assignor and exclusive licences are required to be in writing and be signed by or on behalf of the owner of the database right. This is helpful and where the database and/or its contents are also protected by copyright a simple form of works can be used. For example, an assignment may use the phrase 'I hereby assign the copyright and database right subsisting in [the database] and the copyright subsisting in its 'contents' or; more simply, 'I hereby assign all the rights subsisting in [the database] and its contents'.

Remedies are the same as for copyright and include damages, injunctions, accounts or otherwise as is available for infringement of any other property right, and additional damages are also possible in the case of flagrant infringement. Exclusive licences have rights concurrent to those of the owner and may bring an action themselves. As is usual, the owner would be expected to be joined in the action, for example, as co-plaintiff.

Schedule 2 to the Regulations contains provisions for licensing the database right and deals with licensing schemes, licensing bodies and referral of licensing schemes to the Copyright Tribunal. These provisions are equivalent to those in sections 116-129 and 144 of the Copyright, Designs and Patents Act 1988 which apply to copyright works. The jurisdiction of the Copyright Tribunal is enlarged accordingly to give it jurisdiction the database right.

Database Structure

As the non-literal elements of a computer program,including its structure, can be protected by copyright, it would seem sensible to assume that the structure of a database can also be protected by copyright.

However, in *Total Information Processing Systems Ltd* v *Daman Ltd* [1992] FSR 171, it was held that the field and record specifications as expressed in the data division of a COBOL program were not protected because, in this form, the information did not form a substantial part of the computer program as a whole. This part of the program defines the structure of the database in addition to setting out the variables and their nature and format. In the second edition of this book the author submitted that this approach was wring and that it would be better to consider the database structure as a form of expression in its own right and not as part of the computer program. This would accord with common sense because, in many cases, a great deal of work involving skill and judgment is expended in the design of database structure. Indeed, subsequently in *IBCOS Computers Ltd* v *Barclays Highland Mercantile Finance Ltd* [1994] FSR 275, Mr. Justice Jacob made a number of criticisms of the judgment in the *Total Information Processing Systems* case and he said that there may well be a considerable degree of skill in devising the data division of a program and so it would be considered to be a substantial part of a program as a whole.

In an earlier case, *Computer-Aided Systems (UK) Ltd* v *Bohvell* (unreported) 23 August 1989, Chancery Division, the mere fact that a new program had file compatibility with an earlier program written by the same people failed to impress the judge who considered the plaintiff's application for inspection of the defendant's program to be nothing more than a 'fishing expedition'. There was no evidence of copying and the two programs were written in different languages, the original being written in COBOL the latter one being written in a fourth-generation language called PROGRESS. The structure of the databases in terms of input and output formats must have been identical or similar but this did not seem to be sufficiently argued;

instead the plaintiff concentrated on an argument that the structure of the two programs must have been similar. Alternatively, the fact of file compatibility could have been the result of a 'filter', a program which converted the file structure from one format to another.

Although the Copyright and Rights in Databases Regulations 197 make no mention of the structure of a database, recital 15 to the European Directive on the legal protection of databases states that copyright protection should cover the structure of a database. The only major requirement for protection, apart from qualification, therefore, is that the database is an 'intellectual' creation'. If it is and someone copies he database structure is but not its contents without the permission of the owner this will infringe the copyright if the database structure represents a substantial part of the database. It should not be necessary to demonstrate that the database structure, as opposed to the database as a whole, is an intellectual creation. It would seem that if a database is subject to the database right only, its structure is not protected by that right. In order to further strengthen protection of databases, whether protected by copyright or the database right to both, the author or maker should retain copies of preparatory design materials such as diagrams, layouts and specifications. It is possible that anyone copying the structure of a database will indirectly infringe the copyright subsisting in such materials.

4 COMPUTER-GENERATED WORKS

The Copyright, Designs and Patents Act 1988 expressly recognises that works produced by or with the aid of a computer are worthy of copyright protection. Such works were protected before the 1988 Act but there were difficulties in determining the identity of the author of the work for copyright purposes. Grids of random numbers selected by computer for a newspaper competition called 'Millionaire of the Month' were held to be protected by copyright in *Express Newspapers plc* v *Liverpool Daily Post & Echo plc* [1985] 1 WLR 1089. Arguments that there was no human author and, consequently, the lists of numbers drawn by the computer were not protected by copyright were rejected by Whitford J who said that such a claim was as silly as saying that a pen could be the author of a literary work. The human expertise in computer-derived works could be found to reside in the programs which, in this case, produced the lists of random numbers.

In works produced by or with the aid of a computer, human skill can reside in the person who enters information into the computer to produce the output or in the programmer who writes the program used or a combination of them both. Section 178 of the Act defines a work as 'computer-generated' when it is generated by a computer in circumstances such that there is no human author of the work. Section 9(3) states that, in the case of a literary, dramatic, musical or artistic work which is computer-generated' the author is the person by whom the arrangements necessary for the creation of the work are undertaken. This will generally mean that the person who has control of the computer will be the author of any computer-generated work. These two definitions are tautologous when taken together: a computer-generated work is one created in circumstances such that there is no human author but if we attribute authorship to a human it cannot be computer-generated. The only way round this dilemma is to cannot be computer-generated. The only way round this dilemma is to determine authorship *after* the creation of the work but this seems illogical. Normally, creation and attribution of authorship are coincident in time.

The approach taken in the Act can lead to difficulties because in many cases of works produced *with the aid of a computer* it will not be possible to say with any certainty whether the work has a human author. At one end of the spectrum a work will be produced using a computer as a tool, just as a writer uses a pen or a typewriter, while, at the other end the computer will produce its works with little or no direct human effort. Neither of these situations should cause any great difficulty, but in between these two extremes lie a great many types of work which are the result of a modest amount of direct human input and classifying such works will not be easy. In order to consider this question further, works which involve computers in their production will be categorised as follows:

- works created using a computer,
- works created by a computer, and
- intermediate works.

In these cases 'computer' means a programmed computer.

Works Created Using a Computer

Examples of works which fall into this category are: documents produced using worked processing system CAD (computer-aided designs) such as plans for a house or a new car body panel; music written using a program designed to assist with the composition of the music (as opposed to a program designed to write music); and an accounts report created using a spreadsheet program. In all these cases, the person operating the system is using the computer to achieve the results that he wishes to obtain. The programmed computer is merely a tool that allows the operator to use his creativity and imagination to the fullest extent and efficiency. Such works are not computer-generated; the skill and expertise (or at least the greatest part of these) derives from the user of the system. Word-processed documents, drawings, music and reports produced using packages which facilitate the making of these works are protected the copyright as original literary, dramatic, musical or artistic works in their own right. Indeed, section 51 of the Act recognises that copyright can subsist in data stored in a computer representing a design as a form of design document.

The person using the computer to create the work provides the expertise necessary for the making of the work and is, for copyright purpose, the author of the work. That expertise may be applied directly or indirectly; for example, a person writing a report may draft it out on paper and then hand it to a word processor operator who enters it into the computer. In these circumstances, the author is not the operator but the person writing the report. It is similar to the process of amanuensis in which a person dictating a letter will be the author of that letter; the person who writes the dictation down is merely his agent.

The person who wrote the computer program used to assist in the creation of the types of works described above has a rights in the work because, although the programmer may control or influence the *format* of the finished work, he has no control or influence on the *content*. The fact that many works in this category may be produced directly using a computer before any other tangible form exists presents no serious problems because these works will exist, in terms of copyright protection, the instant they are recorded; that is, as soon as they are stored on a computer disk or printed out on paper.

Works Created by a Computer

These works, which may be literary, dramatic, musical or artistic, are those in which there is 'no human author' (section 178). This implies that the direct degree of human intervention in the making of the work is lacking or minimal. Examples include:

- the automatic generation of weather forecasts by a computer communication with satellites;
- the selection of lists of random numbers for a competition or for the Premium Bond draw;
- programs which produce artistic designs or music automatically, being based upon a set of rules or algorithms built into the program;
- a program designed to simulate some particular environment, such as climate, monetary systems battle scenarios, etc. and produce reports based on that simulation.

Many of the systems operate with no human effort or

skill apart from switching the equipment on and checking that there is sufficient paper in the computer printer or plotter and son on. The human operator has very little or so control over the *formal* or *content* of the output produced by the computer. The author of such a work is the person who makes the arrangements for the work to be created. Therefore, if a business organisation buys and installs computer equipment and software to produce such works, that business organisation will be regarded as the author and, as a result, the first owner of the copyright in the work. The Act contemplates non-human authors as, by section 154, an author can be a qualifying person if; *inter alia*, it is a body incorporated in the United Kingdom, such as a limited company. In the case of an unincorporated body, such as a partnership, the partners will be considered to be the joint authors of the work. If a company can be an author of a computer-generated work, there has to be a special rule for determining the duration of copyright in such works; the copyright expires at the end of the period of 50 years from the end of the calendar year in which the work was made (section 12(7).

Interestingly, and controversially, the Act appears to ignore the skill and expertise of the person or persons who wrote the computer program used to generate these works. It could be argued that the computer programmer whose skill lies behind the computer output should have some recognition of authorship. However, this could cause difficulties because a person obtaining a computer program would expect to own the copyright in anything produced using the program, and any provisions sharing the ownership of the copyright between the user and the programmer could result in an undesirable fetter on the subsequent use of information and reports generated by the computer. The owner of the copyright in the computer program, suddenly realising that he has rights with respect to the output generated from using the program, might attempt to interfere with the subsequent use of that output in the hope that he will be able to negotiate a fee for his permission.

A concept, as yet untested in the courts, is that there is no such thing as a computer-generated work; that is, a work without a human author. After all the argument that a list of numbers drawn at random by a programmed computer had no human author was rejected, as we have seen, in the *Express Newspapers* case. The approach adopted by a Copyright, Designs and Patents Act is a utilitarian one but it does not reflect the reality of the situation as it fails to recognise that all computer output is the result, albeit in many cases the indirect result, of human skill and effort. It would have been better if the programmer's skill was recognised making him the author or joint author of 'computer-generated' works. The practical difficulties resulting from this could be assuaged by raising a presumption that ownership of copyright would lie with the licensee, the ultimate user, of the computer program, subject to any agreement to the contrary.

Intermediate Works

These works lie in the area between computer-generated works and works made using the programmed computer as a tool. The *content* of the output produced is the result of the skill and effort of the person using the computer *and* the skill and effort of the person who wrote the computer program and/or the person who produced any database used. There are many examples of these intermediate works, such as a specialised accounting system for a particular type of business, builders' estimating systems or a music synthesiser designed to produce music from a basic framework of notes entered by the user and expert systems.

A great deal of specialised software falls into this category where the skill required to produce the finished results is contained partly within the program, the remainder being provided by the user of the computer system. In some systems, the skill may come from more than two sources. For examples, consider a computer system designed to used to estimate the cost of building work. The system itself will comprise a suite of computer programs, which include routines to provide analyses and breakdowns of the costs derived, and a database of standard prices, based on sets of sources and labour outputs. The person using the system to work out the cost of building brings a substantial degree of skill by deciding whether the standard prices are applicable and, if not, by building up, new prices and entering them into the database. As Fig. 4.1 shows, the resulting computer output has three sources of expertise; that of the programmer, of the persons responsible for developing the database of standard prices, and of the person using the system. Who is the author of the finished work? Because the person using the system beings an amount of skill to the task, it would not be unreasonable to suggest that he is the author. Indeed, the user has the most direct link with the finished product and has ultimate control but may, nevertheless, rely to a great extent on the programs and information contained in the database. It could be argued that the finished work is partly created by human author and partly computer-generated. Alternatively, all three persons - programmer, database developer and user - might be considered to be joint authors. In the absence of any clear guidance in the Act and until we have a judicial precedent which clarifies the meaning of 'computer-generated, it is important that contractual provisions are made to cover the ownership of rights in the output of such intermediate works. In some cases, because all the persons involved are employees of the company developing and using the software, there will be little difficulty, but if outsiders are involved at any stage, terms should be inserted in contractual agreements dealing with ownership and use of the computer output.

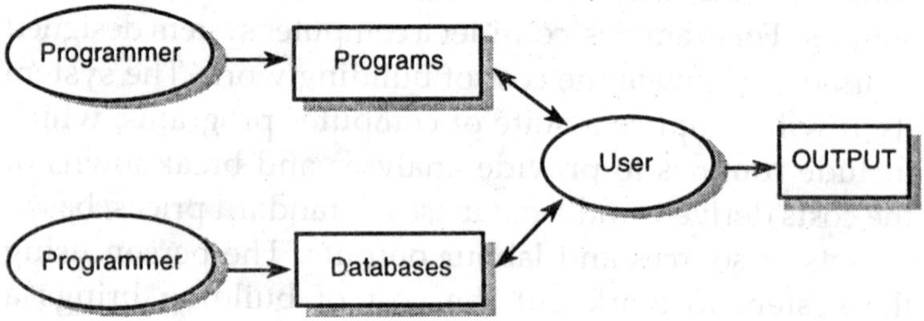

Fig. 4.1 Authorship of intermediate works

The same considerations apply to expert systems. These computer systems, which are intended to emulate the thought processes, analytical reasoning and advice of experts, contain a great deal of skill and expertise within the systems themselves. An expert system, in basic terms, contains three main elements: a knowledge base (rules and facts provided by experts), an inference engine (a computer program which manipulates the knowledge base and applies it to a particular problem) and a user interface to make the system 'user friendly' and to provide explanations of the reasoning adopted and advice given by the export system. When an expert system is used to produce some advice or a report, the expertise underlying the output comes from the following sources:

- the experts who provided the knowledge;
- the persons (sometimes called 'knowledge engineers') who refined the knowledge and formalised it so that it could be installed in the knowledge base;

- the person who wrote the inference engine and the user interface (or adapted existing ones); and
- the user of the system.

The user of the system provides expertise because he will have to understand and respond to the system, and he will have to interpret the questions asked by the system and know what the scope and limitations of the system are. At this stage, most if not all expert systems cannot be used by naive users; a reasonable general knowledge of the area of expertise covered by the system (its knowledge domain) is essential if the output produced is to be taken seriously, just as the scope, limitations, and difficulties presented by a new piece of legislation can only be predicted with any certainty by a lawyer and, even then, not always correctly.

What will the law make of the output of expert systems when it comes to deciding the authorship and ownership of the copyright in that output? To argue that it is computer generated and has no human author runs counter to common sense. To say that the user of this system is its sole author might be convenient but is unrealistic. To attribute authorship to the experts and knowledge engineers who developed the knowledge base is unsatisfactory because they cannot predict how the system will be used and what responses will be made by the user; they have no control over its use. In reality, all the persons listed above are the joint authors, in differing proportions, of the output resulting from the use of the system. It must be said, however, that, if the courts follow this interpretation, it will lead to all manner of complications regarding the commercial use of expert systems and other 'intermediate' systems. Although the court might be willing to imply terms - for example, that the licensee or 'purchaser' of such systems owns the copyright in any output - it is obviously more sensible to recognise the difficulties associated with this part of the Act and to make suitable contractual provision for ownership (as opposed to authorship) of computer output. Better still, the provisions relating to computer-generated works ought to be repealed.

5 COPYRIGHT AND ELECTRONIC PUBLISHING

All manner of works can be stored and made available electronically, Literature, music, works of art, audio-visual works, industrial designs can all be represented in digital form. Even three-dimensional works and moving images can be expressed digitally and, using appropriate software, displayed on screens, copied, manipulated or transmitted anywhere in the world 'at the touch of a button'.

The case with which all forms of creative expression can be exploited digitally has far-reaching consequences as regards the dissemination of information and has opened up the exciting prospect of a global information village. Al Gore's term 'The Information Super-Highway' is very apt to describe the technology, and the rate at which the largely unregulated Internet has grown and continues to grow is impressive. Another recent phenomenon is the growth of multimedia (CD-ROM) technology offering large storage of wide variety of works on a single disk. Typically, a CD-ROM may contain film, music, photographs, text and the spoken word, a collection of disparate works, each of which may be subject to copyright and may incorporate other rights such as rights in performances.

It is unsurprising that these new technologies pose considerable challenges to copyright law and the traditional role of copyright, which has only recently come to terms with the computer program and database. Already there are serious issues relating to balancing controls over the access and use of works and freedom of speech.

In the United States, a corporation which owns the copyright in certain works created by L Ron Hubbard, the founder of the Church of Scientology, used a former member who placed extracts of the works on the Internet for infringement of copyright and trade secret violations (BBC2, *The Net*, 15 May 1995.) It seems that the access provider was also threatened with legal action and that members of the Church sent cancel messages on the Internet to delete previously posted messages about the Church. The former member of the Church responsible for placing the works on the Internet, Dennis Erlich, said, 'We're using 18th and 17th century law to define what goes on in a 21 st and 22 nd century medium.' A a matter of note the defences of fair dealing and public interest were advisable to a defendant who had reproduced extracts of Mr Hubbard's writings in the United Kingdom in paper from (see *Hubbard* v *Vosper* [1972] 2 QB 84).

Before looking at the copyright implications of these new forms of information dissemination, it is worth looking at what is meant by electronic publishing.

What is Electronic Publishing?

The term 'electronic publishing' is lacking in precision and it is by no means clear what if encompasses. For example, it could include publication by one of the following methods:

- sale, rental or lending of a physical carrier containing a copy of the work or works in question - for example, CD-ROM, magnetic disk or magnetic tape;

- by means of communications networks - for example, the Internet or on-line facilities, or
- by means of a broadcast, whether or not encrypted or not in digital form - for example, Prestel and CEEFAX.

All these three forms of electronic publishing are capable of copyright subsistence. In all cases, the individual works so made available may be subject to copyright and, in some cases, there will be other copyrights, such as that in the broadcast or cable programme. Additionally, there may be a further copyright in the form of a compilation.

It should be noted that, for copyright purposes, the word 'electronic' has a particularly wide meaning, by section 178 of the Copyright, Designs and Patents Act1988, as being 'actuated by electric, magnetic, electro-magnetic, electro-chemical or electro-mechanical energy' and the term 'in electronic form' means in a form usable only by electronic means. However, even this width of definition may be incapable of keeping up with technological change. Would have above definitions be appropriate in relation to a liquid DNA computer described by Alexander (Alexander, G, 'DNA holds key to explosion in computer power', *The Sunday Times*, 30 April 1995, p 29)? Nevertheless, it is clear that the definitions of 'electronic' and 'in electronic form' apply to CD-ROM, laser disk and magnetic disk technology and this is important, as, under section 17(2), copying includes storage in any medium by electronic means. The Act has specific provisions for broadcasts and cable programmes and some forms of on-line publishing would be deemed to be cable programmer services. Information made available over the internet has been considered to be a cable programme or part of a cable programme.

This chapter concentrates on publication by means of multimedia and the internet. It also looks at the potential liability of Internet Service Providers for copyright infringement.

Multimedia

A CD-ROM typically may contain a whole range of works. For example, a multimedia product on the topic of romantic poems may include among other things:

- the text of poems to be displayed on screen;
- the sound of poems being recited;
- a commentary comprising an oral and/or textual description of material relating to the poets and their poems;
- film sequences showing the poets at work or meditating, for example, while walking a dog or smoking a pipe;
- photographs of the poets' birthplaces, homes, relatives and acquaintances, and
- introductory and background music.

A feature of multimedia is that the person using the product can move about it all will. The information is, therefore, structured and may have hypertext links. In terms of copyright subsistence, all the works above may be subject to copyright in addition to the whole as a compilation or database. The following example gives some idea of the complexity of rights in such a work.

MultiMega, a multimedia publisher, decides to produce a CD-ROM containing selected poems written by Andrew, Belinda and Clarence. Andrew is still alive, Belinda died some 20 years ago and Clarence has been dead for 80 years. Diana, a famous self-employed literary critic has been commissioned by MultiMega to select the poems to include in the CD-ROM and to write some material giving a critical appraisal of each poem. MultiMega's editing manager, Edward, selects some music written by Frances, who died 57 years ago, to use as background music. George, an actor, is commissioned to recite the poems in front of studio audience. A selection of modern photographs of the poets' homes and favourite haunts, taken by Harrier, is to be included in the work. There is also some old footage of Belinda being interviewed live on ICE television. MultiMega has created its own computer programs to access and display the works and has also created hypertext links.

Assuming that there has been no subsequent transfer of the various copyrights except on the death of a copyright owner, the following permissions will be required by MultiMega:

- a licence from Andrew and from Belinda's estate (as she is now deceased) allowing for the copying, performance and issue to the public of their poems;
- an assignment (or exclusive licence) from Diana in respect of the compilation copyright and the material she has written;
- an exclusive licence from George in respect of his live performance (this is protected as a right in a performance, a right analogous to copyright); and
- a licence from ICE in respect of the broadcast.

No permission is required in respect of Clarence's poems which are now out of copyright but care must be taken as far as Frances's music as concerned as the copyright in it might be revived as a result of the extension of the term of copyright to life plus 70 years (this will be so if her music is still protected in any member state of the European Community). As Edward presumably is an employee, none of his efforts will result in a copyright that belongs to him rather than MultiMega. Another problem for MultiMega is that some of the persons involved will have moral rights (in particular, Andrew, Diana and Harriet), and it must take account of moral rights, either by acknowledging the authors or seeking a waiver in respect of the right to be identified. It is clear that, in most cases, obtaining the necessary permissions for a work of multimedia will be difficult, drawn out and, probably, expensive!

The changes to copyright in relation to databases result in the ensuing multimedia product probably being considered to be a database rather than a compilation. The definition of a database is a collection of independent works, data or other materials which are arranged in a systematic or methodical way and are individually accessible by electronic or other means. This would certainly seem to be the case with MultiMega's CD-ROM. However, one proviso is that it may be that not all the works included are 'individually accessible'. For example, a particular piece of music may be played only when a specific film sequence is accessed and it may not be possible to access that music entirely on its own. This may seem overly pedantic but, if the CD-ROM does not qualify as a database, it almost certainly will as a compilation. As far as copyright is concerned, here is very little difference between copyright in a database and copyright in a compilation. But, databases must be personal intellectual creations to attract copyright whereas the requirement for originality for compilations is not further qualified. The other main difference is that fair dealing for the purposes of research or private study in respect of databases requires an indication of the source and does not extent to research for a commercial purpose. There is also a provision protecting the carrying out of any act necessary for access and use of the contents of a database by a person having a right to use it.

On balance, it seems most likely that CD-ROM products will be classified as databases, except CD-ROMS of music compilations which are excluded by the Directive on the legal protection of databases; these will be protected as compilations. If a CD-ROM like that made by MultiMega is a database, the next question is whether it is a copyright database or whether it is only subject to the database right. As seen in the preceding chapter, this is a question as to whether its making was the result of a personal intellectual creation and/or whether it required as substantial investment. In the above example, it is possible that both of these rights subsist.

A further issue is whether the hypertext links built into the software are protected by copyright. These may be considered to be a structural element of the database protected as a non-literal element. As a Directive on the legal protection of databases makes clean, the protection of copyright databases extends to their structure. It seems entirely reasonable to assume that a person copying the structure of hypertext links from one multimedia product to another, different, product may infringe the copyright in the first if those parts taken represent a substantial part of the first, providing it is a copyright database. Of course, it would be rare that much would be gained simply by copying the structure of hypertext works alone.

The Internet

Publishing works on the Internet looks very attractive at first sight. It is a really effective way of making a work available to a wide audience at minimal expense. Many academic writers have been quick to seize the opportunity to spread their work on a world-wide scale. A number of academic journals are now appearing on the Internet and while many authors may be happy to distribute their work in this way, without recompense, there are large numbers of authors who depend on the income they receive from publishing their work. There is a view, held by many, that the Internet is equivalent to the public domain and anything available there should be freely copied and used. This view is misguided.

Typically, individuals gain access to works on the Internet, which are stored on host computers, via an access provider (see Fig. 5.1).

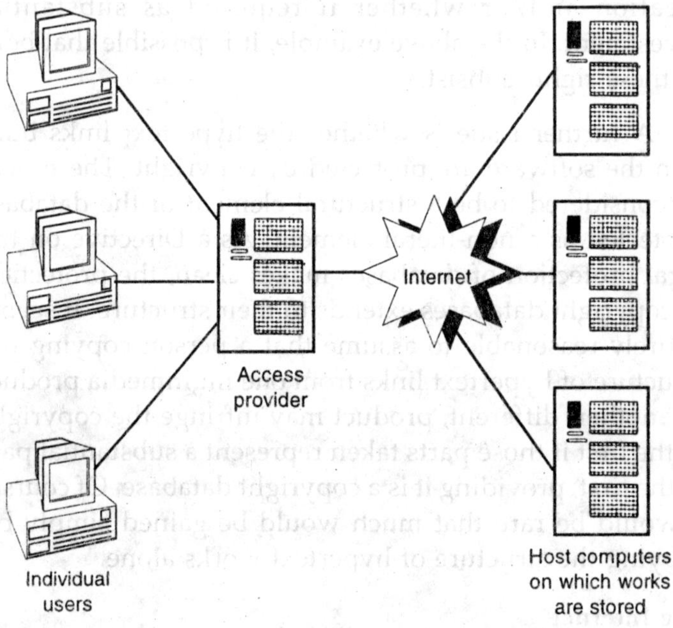

Fig 5.1 the Internet

The Internet itself is, basically, made up of public telecommunications systems which are used to carry information from host computers. The technology makes use of the most effective path through the system at the time of transmission, rerouting to avoid busy lines. No one is in overall control of the Internet.

Individual works available on the Internet will normally have their own copyright which may well be a foreign copyright. Contrary to the view that the Internet is equivalent to the public domain, this does not affect the fact of subsistence of copyright. A copyright owner may choose to make his work available freely but it will remain a work of copyright and will not affect the copyright position of other works. It is advisable for owners of copyright works to make it clear whether the work can be printed or downloaded or used in other ways. While it is almost impossible to police the use of works on the Internet the copyright position, including moral rights, should be spelt out.

There are proposals for harmonisation of certain aspects of copyright and related rights in the Information Society. This results from the Copyright and Performing Rights Treaties of the World Intellectual Property Organisation which will modify the Berne Copyright Convention. Apart from a communication right and controls over the circumvention of technological measures to prevent unauthorised copying (both of which already exist under United Kingdom copyright law), a particular feature is the protection of electronic frights management information'. This is information which identifies the work, the author, the owner of any right in the work, or information about terms and conditions of use. Remedies will be available also against any person who, without consent, disseminates any works in respect of which such information has been removed or altered with express knowledge of this. Compliance is likely to be required by 30 June 2000. The utility of protecting rights management information is obvious.

If information such as the name of the author or owner of the copyright in a work or any conditions as to its use is removed and a work is placed on a Website, anyone accessing it might think they can do with it as they wish. They may think that they can download it, make copies of it, modify it or distribute it freely. In view of this, and the forthcoming protection afforded to rights management information, it is doubly important for owners of copyright works to clearly mark them with the name of the author and owner, if different, the year or creation and any conditions as to its use. For example, if Fred Smith decides to make his new composition available on his Web site, he may decide to add the following information:

> Copyright F. Smith 1999. The right of F Smith to be identified as the author of this music is hereby asserted. This music may be listened to in private and a single copy may be downloaded for your personal and domestic use only. Any further use may infringe copyright and moral rights and may attract civil remedies and criminal penalties.

Under United Kingdom law, apart from any copyright in the individual works, databases of compilations of works, there may be separate copyrights as cable programmes included in a cable programme service. This is defined by section 7(1) of the Copyright. Designs and Patents Act 1988 as a service consisting wholly or mainly in sending visual images, sounds or other information by means of a telecommunications system otherwise than by wireless telegraphy, for reception.

(a) at two or more places (whether for simultaneous reception or at different times in response to request by different users), or

(b) It seems clear that information available via the Internet falls within (a) above. There are a number of exceptions (including systems which are

> predominantly interactive such as electronic mail). There are difficulties, however, with applying cable programme copyright to the Internet. This form of copyright was intended to be the equivalent to the broadcast copyright for providers of cable television. In this sense it works well but, by section 9(2)(c), the author of a cable programme is the person providing the cable programme service in which the programme is included. The question here is: who is the person providing the service? As no one person is in overall control this is not easily answered. The access provider who arranges connection to the Internet does not, in reality, provide the service in which the programmes (or works) are included. Rather, the service provider is a facilitator rather than a provider.

The first case on the copyright nature of the Internet was heard in Scotland. It involved Web pages of the *Shetland Times* on which extracts of news items appearing in printed editions of its newspapers were placed. It was hoped that advertises would want to advertise on the front page of the Web site. The defender, Dr Jonathan Wills had a Web site called 'The Shetland News' on which he had placed verbatim headlines from the *Shetland Times*. Anyone accessing these headlines could, by clicking the mouse button on them, gain access to the news items on the *Shetland Times* Web site, by-passing the front lines had been infringed. In *Shetland Times Ltd* v *Dr Jonathan Wills* [1997] FSR 604, in the Outer House of the Court of Session, Scotland, Lord Hamilton granted an interim interdict (interjunction). He said that it was arguable that the copyright in the headlines had been infringed by including them in a cable programme service. He also said it was at least arguable that operating a Web site was operating a cable programme service within section 7(1) of the Copyright, Designs and Patents Act 1988 (see above).

There is an exception in section 7(2)(a), where an essential feature of the service is that it is interactive. However, Lord Hamilton did not accept that this provision applied to save the defender as although persons accessing the Web site could send messages and communicate with the *Shetland Times* via the Internet, this was to an essential feature of the service. Alternatively that part of the service was severable, leaving the remainder of the service to be classed as a cable programme service. An appeal was lodged but the parties settled the dispute before the appeal got properly under way. That being so, it is not beyond doubt whether operating a Web site is within the meaning of operating a cable programme service, although that does seen to be the most appropriate form of copywright.

If operating a Web site is operating a cable programme service, this has important consequences. A cable programme is defined as 'any item included in a cable programme service by section 7(1) of the Copyright, Designs and Patents Act 1988. As a cable programme service consists wholly or mainly in sending visual images sounds or other information and infringement extends to including a cable programme in a cable programme service, this could mean even very small items, normally regarded as too small or trivial to attract copyright protection otherwise could be protected. In particular, an item of 'information' could be quite small. It should be sufficient to convey something (a dictionary definition of 'information' is 'something told, knowledge, items of knowledge') and it is likely that even a small newspaper headline could do this. Somewhat controversially, in the *Shetland Times* case, Lord Hamilton considered that the headlines were literary works in their own right. Normally these would be considered too small for copyright protection and, in the past, phrases such as 'Beauty is a social necessity, not a luxury' and 'The man who broke the bank at Monte Carlo' and words such as 'EXXON', 'Kojak' and 'Elvis' have been held not to be works of copyright. However, if a generous view is taken o 'information,' very trivial things could be protected by virtue of cable programme copyright. Apart from continuing doubts as to the copyright status of the Internet as a service (notwithstanding that individual works placed on Web pages will in most cases, have their own independent copyright) there are other serious problems for copyright in 'cyberspace' such as:

- powerful copyright owners may use 'bully-boy tactics,' obtaining or threatening injunctions against individuals and, more seriously, against access providers,
- it becomes impossible to control copying and unauthorised use of works (copies can be made on disk virtually instantaneously — much cheaper and quicker than photocopying) and
- the international dimension is a nightmare in terms of policing, jurisdiction and acting against infringers.

Until recently, there has been an emphasis on the medium on which a work is stored with too little appreciation of the nature of copyright. For example, a book comprises two separate and distinct property rights. The paper, ink and binding together make in item of tangible property as a 'good'. The work contained within the book and expressed therein is subject to a copyright which is a form of intangible property. There has been insufficient focus on the existence of the intangible right that is copyright and, with the advent of the Internet, freeing the copyright from its medium, like releasing the genie from the bottle, will have interesting and probably unexpected consequences.

Licensing

When it is required to commercially exploit works published electronically (whether by cable, broadcast or in multimedia products) it is usual for access to be provided by means of a licence agreement. A licence is necessary because accessing the works will involve an act restricted by copyright. For example, retrieving a document from a database of documents will require a copy to be made in the computer's memory and the copyright owner's permission to do this must be obtained. This is not so with traditional paper materials. Taking a book from a library shelf and reading it does not require any acts to be done which are restricted by copyright. Any use of a work involving computer technology will usually require copies to be made even if they are only transient. By section 17(6) of the Copyright, Designs and Patents Act 1988, it is an infringement of copyright to make a transient copy.

The use of licence agreements brings contract law into play in addition to copyright law. A licencee agreement will contain terms concerning the use of the work and may impose restrictions going beyond copyright. Typically, a licence may specify the acts that may be done in a negative way by stating what may not be done. For example, a licence for the use of a multimedia product such as a CD-ROM may state that the licensee shall not duplicate the CD-ROM or print out any of the works contained in it or download any of those works apart from viewing on a screen. If the product is available with an updating service there may be a term requiring that old copies are destroyed or returned to the licensor. The licence may also require that the licensee place notices near computer terminals warning of copyright infringement. Failure to abide by the terms of the licence will be a breach of contract and, in many cases, also an infringement of copyright.

There are important international differences in the protection of creative works. For example, the United Kingdom does not yet provide for an artist's resale right as applies in France. This can make the identification of rights and obtaining the permissions required very difficult, especially with a product such as multimedia. The person acquiring a multimedia product should satisfy himself that all the relevant permissions have been obtained and provided for in thee licence and should check that the licence agreement also contains an indemnity. If it turns out that a relevant permission has not been obtained, the licensor should indemnify the licensee against any claims arising and which are directed at the licensee. An example of the difficulty that might be experienced is whether a consent that had been obtained 40 years ago in respect of playing music from a vinyl sound recording in public would now extend to incorporating the music in a multimedia product. Peggy Lee obtained some $3.8 million in an award of damages resulting from an action against Walt Disney. She claimed that here original agreement with Walt Disney for her work on *Lady and the Tramp* did not extend to selling videos of the film. Video had not been invented at the time! (*The Times*, 7 October 1992, p.16.)

On-line databases are already well established and, usually, made available through a subscription in the form of a licence agreement. In addition to paying an annual fee, it is common for each search of the database to be charged individually. An interesting feature of an on-line database is that the provider can keep an exact record of the use of the database and can charge a sum reflecting the precise use that has been made of the database by the subscriber. The ability to monitor use in this way will have increasingly significant implications in the future.

An on-line database may comprise a number of

copyrights as is the case with CD-ROM products. Taking LEXIS as an example, a database containing the full text of legislation and cases, the legislation is, in the United Kingdom, a work of copyright which belongs to Her Majesty (Crown copyright). The cases contain court judgments each of which comprise catchwords, a headnote and the judgment itself. The copyright in the catch-wo~ds and headnote will belong in the first instance to the organisation employing the law reporter but the judgment will be Crown copyright on the basis that a judge is probably a servant of the Crown who writes the judgment in the course of his duties (section 163). The database maker will have a copyright in the whole database as a compilation and will have been permitted to enter the individual materials into the database under licence agreements. The licence under which the subscriber is permitted to use the database will restrict that use, particularly in terms of downloading and copying.

Other questions are raised in relation to databases. For example, is a particular database protected by copyright or by the database right or both? How is substantiality of determined in relation to a database? Is the copyright in a database refreshed from time to time as it evolves and undergoes changes? At what stage does an aggregation of incremental changes give rise to a fresh copyright or database right?

Collecting societies such as the Performing Right Society and the Copyright Licensing. Agency assist in the exploitation of copyright by increasing the accessibility of works and allowing a certain amount of copying while providing copyright owners with income. However, most collecting societies do not, at the moment in the United Kingdom, cover electronic publishing with their blanket licence schemes. The disparate nature of works available electronically makes the establishment of a workable and equitable set of rules governing the use of works very difficult.

Special Copyright Problems Posed by Electronic Publishing

Apart from the issues identified above, there are a number of specific problems that may result from the widespread use of electronic storage and publishing of works. These problems relate to digitisation, typographical arrangements, electronic publication of old works and the liability of 'facilitators', persons or organisations (such as libraries) which make electronically published works available to end users and especially, Internet Service Providers. These are considered below.

Digitisation

Some doubts have been expressed as to whether digitising (storing in digital form) is within the restricted act of copying for copyright purposes. In *Anacon Corp Ltd* v *Environmental Research Technology Ltd* [1994] FSR 659, the defendant had used the plaintiff's circuit diagram to create a printed circuit board. As an intermediate step, the defendant made a net list (a list of the electronic components with details of their interconnection) from the circuit diagram. Although a circuit diagram is, *prima facie,* an artistic work, the judge held that it was not an infringement of the copyright in the circuit diagram as an artistic work because the circuit board did not look like an artistic work. He said that it was the visual significance of an artistic work that mattered.

On this basis, making a digital copy of an artistic work will not infringe as the digital copy will not look like the original work or, for that matter, any artistic work. Previous case law under the Copyright Act 1956 supports this view but the Copyright, Designs and Patents Act 1988 contains a provision that clearly contradicts this approach. Section 17(2) states that copying a literary, dramatic, musical or artistic work 'includes storing the work in any medium by electronic means' - a phrase that was not mentioned by the judge, Mr Justice Jacob. Of course, the words of the statute, if they are clear and unambiguous, which they are, prevail. Therefore, that part of the judgment dealing with infringement of copyright in artistic works must be read with caption.

Jacob J. overcame this apparent (and mistaken) limitation by holding that the circuit diagram was also a literary work because it was intended to be read. A person making a circuit board would have to read the information contained in the diagram, which also included written information such as the rating of components. By doing so and creating a net list, the defendant had reproduced the literary work in material form.

The definitions of sound recordings, films, broadcasts and cable programmes are very wide and, for these works, converting or storing the work in digital form should present no particular problems. For example, by section 5(1) a 'film' means ' a recording on any medium from which a moving image may be any means be produced'. Of course reproducing a work from a digital recording will normally infringe copyright if done without the copyright owner's licence and this is so even if any intervening act does not infringe (see section 16(3)). For example, say that Mary in London buys an LS Lowry print. Mary converts this into digital form and then transmits it to Thomas in Cardiff who then reproduces the work on screen and prints it out on paper. Neither Mary not Thomas has the permission of LS Lowry's estate to do any act restricted by copyright. By section 17(2), by storing the work electronically, Mary has infringed copyright. Transmitting the work digitally does not infringe (assuming that act does not fall within the restricted acts of broadcasting, inclusion in a cable programme service or issuing to the public). However, storage in Thomas's computer probably infringes because, by section 17(6), copying includes making copies which are transient or are incidental to some other use of the work. Furthermore, by printing the work out on paper, Thomas has reproduced the Lowry print in a material form. The fact that in intervening act (transmission) did not infringe does not break the chain as far as Thomas is concerned. Mary will probably be liable also for the infringing acts of Thomas because infringement includes authorising another to do any of the acts restricted by copyright. This is shown diagrammatically in Fig. 5.2.

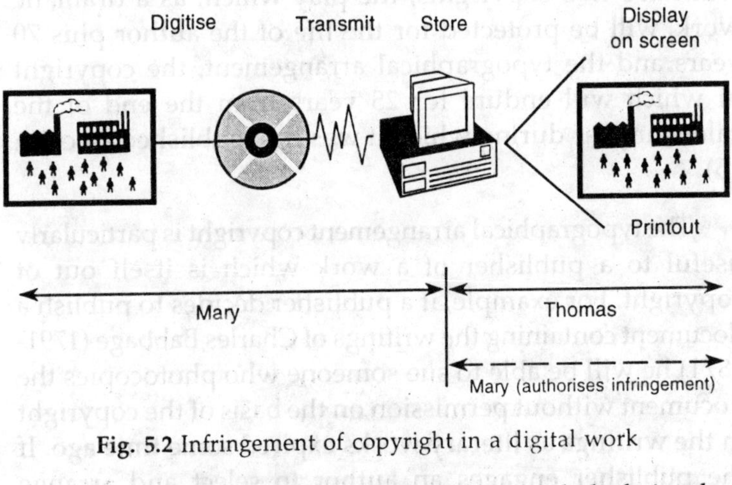

Fig. 5.2 Infringement of copyright in a digital work

It is arguable that because of the weak link in the above acts (transmission other than by way of a broadcast or cable programme service) there should be a strengthening of the Copyright, Designs and Patents Act 1988 in this respect. Through it should cause no particular difficulties within the United Kingdom, it could if a copy of the work is obtained already in digital form (e.g. CD-ROM) and it is then transmitted to another country. On the face of it, the person transmitting the work from the United Kingdom does not himself infringe copyright. Liability might still accrue, however, on the basis that he was authorised the infringement by facilitating it and this form of liability is considered later in this chapter.

Typographical Arrangements of Published Editions

Typographical arrangements of published editions are protected as a distinct form of copyright (section 1(1) of the Copyright, Designs and Patents Act 1988.) This copyright gives protection to publishers of literary, dramatic and musical works irrespective of the copyright subsisting in those works as such. Thus a new publication of a new play will have two copyrights; the play which, as a dramatic work, will be protected for the life of the author plus 70 years and the typographical arrangement, the copyright of which will endure for 25 years from the end of the calendar year during which it was first published (section 15).

The typographical arrangement copyright is particularly useful to a publisher of a work which is itself out of copyright. For example, if a publisher decides to publish a document containing the writings of Charles Babbage (1791-1871) he will be able to sue someone who photocopies the document without permission on the basis of the copyright in the writings as literary works expired some time ago. If the publisher engages an author to select and arrange Babbage's writings and to add a commentary there will arise additional new copyrights in the commentary, providing it is more than trivial and, potentially, in the work expended on the selection and arrangement resulting in a compilation copyright.

The purpose of copyright in typographical arrangements is to protect the publisher's work in selecting the typeface, margins, headings, spacing and other typographical details; in other works, the layout of the print on the page. This is all well and good in the context of print on paper but what is the position where the work in question is published electronically? To take an example say that Charles decides to store the entire known works of William Shakespeare (1564-1616) on computer disk. Copyright in Shakespeare's works expired some centuries ago and, as the entire known works are to be stored, it is unlikely that there is any copyright in the whole as a database because, on the basis of *G A Cramp & Sons Ltd* v *Frank Smythson Ltd* [1944] AC 329, there is no room for skill and judgment in selecting the materials to include. For the sake of this example, it is assumed that the individual works are not entered in any particular order or subject to a newly devised classification system.

For copyright to subsist in a typographical arrangement, the following requirements must be met:

- the arrangement must qualify for United Kingdom copyright (this will not usually be an issue),
- it must not simply bee a reproduction of the typographical arrangement of a previous edition, and
- It must be applied to a published edition of the whole or part of one or more literary, dramatic or musical works (section 8).

The last point is doubtful in terms of electronic publishing. The phrase 'published edition' is not defined in the Act other than as above although it is reasonable to suppose that the meaning of 'publication' will be relevant.

This is defined in section 175 as issuing copies to the public and include, in the case of literary, dramatic, musical or artistic work, making it available to the public by means of an electronic retrieval system. Thus, electronic publishing of the original works of copyright is specifically covered, but typographical arrangements are not mentioned. Even if it does extend to typographical arrangements are not mentioned. Even if it does extend to typographical arrangements, there may be further difficulty with the word 'edition'. This reflects traditional publishing but may be inappropriate in the context of, say, a database which is continually being updated. Certainly, when a database is first made available to the public that could be said to be its first edition. But when does a second or subsequent edition exist? Does the owner of the database have to change the font, point size, margins, etc. to obtain a new typographical arrangement copyright? Typographic arrangement's is not defined in the Act and this may allow the courts to take a flexible view and to confirm, if the need should arise that it applies to the layout of text or musical notation on a screen and/or the details of font, spacing, page and style setting, etc. embedded within the relevant computer file containing the work. That there are doubts about typographical arrangements of published editions in the context of electronic publishing is regrettable. Perhaps there should be a new electronic document format copyright which would extend not only to the choice of fonts, margins, page settings and such like but also to protect the work involved in creating hypertext links and other structural or indexing systems used in computer documents. Electronic publishers should not be disadvantaged compared to traditional paper publishers.

Returning to our example, if Charles sells CD-ROM disks containing the works of Shakespeare, even if his electronic arrangement is deemed to be a typographical arrangement of a published edition, this will not enable him to take legal action to prevent someone copying out the work sin a different form, for example, by handwriting. Converting the format by changing details such as font, point size, margins, etc. to produce a different format will not infringe copyright as the restricted act of making an adaptation does not apply to typographical arrangements of published editions. Thus Charles may have limited protection only and the situation should be the same if he makes the works available to the public on-line.

It has already been noted that a copyright might arise if Charles has to expend skill on judgment in selecting what to include and in arranging the individual works, perhaps using a classification system based on type of work; tragedy, love sonnet, etc. Certainly, if he adds commentary and criticism that itself should attract copyright. The position is less clear where Charles has carried out extensive research in an effort to get to the precise wording of Shakespeare's works as written, correcting errors in knows texts. Can there be a copyright in correcting mistakes in old works? It would seem reasonable to reward the skill, effort and judgment expended by Charles but it he succeeds in recreating the true text as written by Shakespeare that would produce the anomaly of resurrecting a long extinct copyright?

Clearly, there are problems with typographical arrangements in electronic publishing. Although it is entirely reasonable to accept that the provisions protecting typographical arrangements also ought to apply to the format of electronically published works it is far too easy to copy the work without the format. For example, a word processed document which has been carefully set out and formatted to look attractive on a computer screen or as printed and has numerous font changes, indents, headings, etc. can simply be converted to ASCII code to avoid infringing the copyright in the typographical arrangement. Some word processors have 'style sheets' which determine the format and layout of the document. Could these be deemed to be typographical arrangements? The difficulties are amplified where the copyright in the work itself has expired because of its age.

Legal Liability of Internet Service Providers

Internet Service Providers (ISPs) facilitate access to material on the Internet. Through their agreements with persons to whom they provide access, ISPs have some measure of control, for example, by requiring the client to adhere to copyright law and not to make infringing material available to others, whether on a Web page or by transmitting by e-mail. ISPs may even seek indemnities from their clients for copyright infringement attributable to their actions. Nevertheless, ISPs may be vulnerable for copyright infringement in a number of ways:

- by being secondary infringers,
- by authorising infringement, or
- by joint infringement.

These are considered below.

Secondary Infringement

Under section 24(2) of the Copyright, Designs and Patents Act 1988 it is an infringement of copyright to transmit a work, without the licence of the copyright owner, by a telecommunications system knowing or having reason to believe that infringing copies will be made by means of the reception of the transmission in the United Kingdom or elsewhere. Although it matters not where the reception takes place, the definition of 'infringing copy' provides territorial constraint as, in relation to infringing copies made outside the United Kingdom, the copy must either have been imported or is proposed to be imported into the

United Kingdom. Also, had it been made in the United Kingdom that would have been an infringement of the copyright in the work or a breach of exclusive licence agreement relating to the work.

A serious limitation is that the transmission must be otherwise than by broadcasting or inclusion in cable programme service. As discussed above, the *Shetland Times* case is authority for the view that operating a Web site is within the meaning of operating a cable programme service. If this is confirmed, then this form of infringement does not apply to those parts of the service deemed to be cable programme services. However, parts of the service intended to be interactive, such as a e-mail or bulletin boards, may still be caught by section 24(2) as these will fall within the express exception to cable programme services.

If a person who subscribes to an ISP gains access to an infringing work of copyright, that person will infringe copyright by making a copy, whether transient or otherwise. Innocent copying still infringes, although innocence may be a factor in whether damages are available. However, an ISP will infringe under section 24(2) only if he has reason to believe that infringing copies will be made by means of the reception of the transmission in the United Kingdom or elsewhere. This is an objective test. Would a reasonable person, with knowledge of the facts knows to the alleged infringer, have reason to believe infringing copies would be made?

Authorising Infringement

Section 16(2) of thee Copyright, Designs and Patents Act 1988 states that copyright in a work is infringed by a person who without the licence of the copyright owner does, *or authorises another to do,* any of the acts restricted by the copyright. If the act which infringes is done in the United Kingdom, it does not matter if the authorisation comes from elsewhere. In ABKCO *Music & Records Inc* v *Music Collection International Ltd* [1995] RPC 657 a Danish company granted a licence to an English company to make and issue to the public recordings of the plaintiff's sound recordings in the United Kingdom and Eire. It was held that it did not matter where the authorisation was given as ling as the restricted act was carried out within the jurisdiction of the United Kingdom courts. Thus, if an Australian ISP authorises someone in the United Kingdom to make infringing material available on the Internet, the ISP is caught by section 16(2) and is liable for the infringement together with the person responsible for making the material available.

It is important to understand what is meant by authorisation. It has been construed by the courts in a fairly wide sense and turning blind eye can amount to authorisation. Indifference or even failing to inform persons of the implications of copyright law may suffer. In *Moorehouse* v *University of New South Wales* [1976] RPC 151 a failure to inform users of a library with photocopying facilities as tocopyright law and to supervise the use of the copiers was held to be authorising infringement of copyright. In the United Kingdom, judges have equated with the grant or purported grant, which may express or implied, of the right to do the act complained of.

An ISP could be said to authorise infringement if it fails to inform its clients of copyright law and the need to avoid infringement of copyright. It is possible that an even stronger duty could be placed on an ISP, for example, a positive duty to check material made available through its service. This may require spot checks or sampling or material made available through its service by its clients.

Joint Inringement

It is possible that an ISP could be claimed to be a joint

infringer along with the client responsible for making infringing material availablc through its service. Joint infringement occurs where two or more persons act in concert pursuant to a common design to infringe. In terms of stereo equipment having dual cassette tape players, in *Amstrad Consumer Electronic plc* v *The British Phonograph Industry Ltd* [1986] FSR 159, it was held that supplying machines which would be likely to be used to unlawfully copy pre-recorded cassettes subject to copyright protection was not authorising infringement of copyright. The supplier had no control over the way the machines were used once sold.

In the case of ISPs, things are different. They do have some control. They can monitor and check what is being made available through their service. They can erase or block infringing material. The problem they have is that the sheer volume of material involved makes effective control and policing almost impossible. The best they can do is not warn their clients about the dangers of copyright infringement. But if they encourage, even implicitly, a disregard of copyright. A sensible approach for an ISP is to inform their clients and to carry out a reasonable level of policing and checks on what material is being made available and transmitted through their service, the only difficulty being that they may then be accused of invasion of privacy.

What has been said above in relation to ISPs also applies to others who facilitate access to material over the Internet. Thus, libraries with with on-line facilities of employers who allow or encourage employees to make use of the Internet should be careful as regards copyright infringement by their clients of employees. Education and vigilance seem to be the key words in respect of the Internet.

The Future

It is arguable that the mass storage of all manner of

works on electronic media will create insuperable problems for copyright law. Until recently copies of copyright works were only available as stored in or on some tangible item, for example, a book, disk, oil on canvas, magnetic tape and so on. Now, as we are entering an information 'Cyberspace', these tangible items are on longer necessary to the distribution or use of copyright works and there are unprecedented challenges ahead for copyright law. This gloomy view of copyright, however, takes no account of future development and refinement of the law. In the past, copyright law has proved itself to be capable of adapting to protect new forms of technological expression such as the photograph, sound recordings, broadcasts, cable programmes and computer programs. Technology is both a threat to copyright law and its potential saviour. For example, developments in cryptography, the increasing power of computers to monitor and record the use and copying of copyright works and to extract payment of electronic funds transfer and to precisely distribute that income among the plethora of right holders must not be undeprated. Authors and copyright owners will be reimbursed for the actual use made of their work. This could diminish the role of the traditional publisher. Authors of works of copyright instead may deal directly with the providers of electronic databases and Internet access providers. Agents may become more important, being persons who will negotiate the best deals for authors to enable the work to be made available by the most effective providers.

Collecting societies such as the Copyright Licensing Agency may have a role to play in the above developments. One danger of the technological control of works of copyright is that the permitted acts under copyright law may be reduced to vanishing point as access may be denied without the appropriate licence fee being paid. Because of this we can expect that compulsory licensing provisions will be extended more and more into the copyright field. The mechanism already exists in the United Kingdom Copyright, Designs and Patents Act 1988 for provision to be made for compulsory licensing in respect of rental of sound recordings, films and computer programs by section 66, and the Commission of the European Communities has not entirely ruled out the need for compulsory licensing in the copyright field. One thing that is certain is that copyright law is facing unprecedented challenges and it will be interesting to see how it develops. At the end of the day, however, given the power of technology to make works available anywhere at any time the main issues may be concerned more with policing copyright and bringing pressure to bear on countries with weak or unenforced copyright laws.

6 LAW OF CONFIDENCE

The law of confidence is concerned with the protection of secrets whether they be trade secrets, secrets of a personal nature or concerning the government of the country. The fundamental rationale underlying the law of confidence is that it can prevent a person divulging information which has been given to him in confidence, on an express or implicit understanding that the information should not be disclosed to others or otherwise used by the recipient of the information. Alternatively, if the information has already been disclosed or used in breach of confidence, damages may be awarded against the person divulging or using the information. The roots of the law of confidence lie in equity and it is almost entirely based on case law. It is given statutory recognition in the Copyright, Designs and Parents Act 1988, section 171, which states:

> ... nothing in this part [the part dealing with copyright] affects ... the operation of any rule of equity relating to breaches of trust or confidence...

Although of older pedigree, the modern law of confidence developed in the nineteenth century and then lay relatively dormant until the middle of the twentieth century. It soon became clear that breach of confidence was actionable *per se,* and did not require a contractual relationship between the parties. An important case, *Prince Albert* v *Strange* [1849] 1 Mac & G 25, helped to establish this area of law and concerned etchings made by Queen Victoria and her consort, Prince Albert. The Queen and Prince made etchings for their own amusement, intended only for their own private entertainment, although they sometimes had prints made to give to friends. Etchings were sent to a printer to make some impressions and someone surreptitiously made copies which he passed on to the defendant who intended to display them in an exhibition which the public could attend on payment of an admission charge. It was held that relief would be given against the defendant even though he was a third party. He had argued that the prints were not improperly taken but it was said that his possession must have originated in breach of trust, confidence or contract and, therefore, an injunction was granted preventing the exhibition.

The law of confidence can be a very useful adjunct to other intellectual property rights. Copyright protects the expression of an idea, but the law of confidence is wider and can protect the idea itself. In *Andersen Consulting* v *CHP Consulting Ltd* (unreported) 26 July 1991, Chancery Division, a case concerning a dispute about maintenance of computer software by third parties, it was said that confidence is frequently used in connection with copyright material as it is:

> ... of course notorious that copyright protects only the expression of ideas and does not protect the idea itself ...

The law of breach of confidence can supplement copyright and patent protection especially in the early stages when there is nothing tangible or substantial enough for copyright law or patent law to protect. Additionally, the law or confidence can be useful for certain types of secrets for which other rights are inappropriate such as the recipe for Coca-Cola or a secret research technique or industrial process.

Basic Requirements

A good working formula for the application of the law of confidence was laid down in *Coco* v *AN Clark (Engineers) Ltd* [1969] RPC 41, by Megarry J. (as he then was). This involved a moped engine designed by the plaintiff who entered into informal negotiations with the defendant; no contract was executed. Megarry J. held that the defendant owed the plaintiff an obligation of confidence (although) he doubted the confidential quality of the information) and said that, apart from contract, an action for breach of confidence will require three elements:

1. The information must have the necessary quality of confidence about it.
2. The information must have been imparted in circumstances importing an obligation of confidence.
3. There must be an unauthorised use of that information to the detriment of the party communicating it.

The third of these elements is self-evident, but the first two require further discussion.

Quality of Confidence

To be protected by the law of confidence, the information must have a quality of confidence about it. If the information is commonplace or is common knowledge to a group of persons (for example, it is well known to computer programmers) or to the public at large, it cannot be confidential, instead, it will be considered to be in the public domain. Often, it will be obvious whether the information is or is not confidential. The concept of confidentiality was considered in the case of *Thomas Marshall (Exports) Ltd* v *Guinle* [1976] FSR 345, in which the defendant, who was the managing director of the plaintiff company, resigned half way through his 10 year service contract to set up a rival business. The information involved sources of supply and the names of officials and other contacts in Europe and the Far East. Megarry VC found for the plaintiff and he said that four elements were necessary in testing for confidential quality.

1. Release of the information would injure the owner of the information or benefit others.
2. The owner must believe the information to be secret and not already in the public domain.
3. The owner's belief in 1 and 2 above must be reasonable.
4. The information must be judged in the light of usages and practices of the particular trade or industry concerned.

To come within the scope of the law of confidence, the information does not have to be particularly special and, as in the above case, ordinary and mundane information can be the proper subject matter of confidence as long as it is private to the person who has compiled the information, even though others could gather similar information if they took the trouble to do so. In this way, the law of confidence prevents others from gaining benefit from the work of the person who accumulated the information in the first place. As a result, a great deal of material related to the running of a business will fall within the ambit of the law of confidence. Examples of information relevant to computers which may be the subject matter of confidence include:

- ideas for a new or improved computer system, hardware and software, and research and development work generally;
- details of existing computer systems as would be known by computer analysts or programmers or even users of system (in terms of users, the system would have to be uncommon in some respect);
- lists of customers or sub-contractors and associated information - for example, what services they perform, what their credit rating is. Information stored in computer databases is often confidential;
- a company's strategy of future research and development, production and marketing.

Obligation of Confidence

An obligation of confidence will not be imposed on everyone. A person who is given confidential information and is unaware of its confidential nature (and has no reason to be aware) will be able to use the information freely. This is a major weakness of the law of confidence as it is largely ineffective against innocent third-party recipients of the information. For example, if A tells B something in confidence and B (without A's permission) passes the information on to C, who has not been told that it is confidential and the circumstances are such that an obligations of confidence cannot be imputed to C; then C will be able to use the information freely although B himself can be prevented from using the information or divulging it further. However, it may still be possible for A to obtain an injunction against C in respect of future disclosure or use by C if the information has not yet entered the public domain. C will not, of course, be liable for any acts that he may have carried out innocently before notification that b had divulged the information in breach of his obligation of confidence to A.

Obviously, and obligation of confidence can arise by express agreement; for example, where a freelance computer programmer is engaged to carry out some work under a contract which contains a term stating that the programmer will not use or divulge details of the client's business. An obligation of confidence may also be implied by the courts where there is a duty of good faith as in the relationship between a client and a solicitor, patent agent or bank manager. Another situation where the obligation will be imposed is where a person discusses his ideas with business organisations with a view to the commercial exploitation of those ideas; for example, if a computer analyst has an idea for a new computer system and discusses that idea with software houses interested in developing and marketing the system.

Employee

The employee-employer relationship is a special case may be governed by express terms, as incorporated in the contract of employment, or implied terms or both. Generally, the duty of confidence owed by ex-employees will by less than for current employees who should always act in their employer's best interest. A present employee must respect the confidentiality of his employer's information even to the extent that he should not pry into information he has been told not to look at. In *Denco Ltd* v *Joinson* [1991] IRLR 63, an employee who had a right of access to certain information in his employer's computer system used another employee's password to gain access to other parts of the computer system - something he has not entitled to do. It was held that the employer was entitled to dismiss the employee summarily for his unauthorised use of the password.

Ex-employee have to make a living and much of the ex-employee's skill will involve what he learnt while in his previous employment, thus providing the courts with a dilemma. In many cases, to complicate matters, there may be an overlap with copyright law. However, the courts have developed rules for resolving the conflict which strike a reasonable balance between the interests of employee and employer alike.

When there are no express terms, the employer will not be protected to any great extent. If the ex-employee remembers details of some of the previous employer's customers, there is nothing to stop him using this information. Of course, it would be different if he deliberately memorised the cutomers' names of made a copy of them. In the absence of an express term in the contract of employment dealing with confidentiality, it was said, in *Printers and Finishers Ltd* v *Holloway* [1965] RPC 239, that there would be nothing improper in the employee putting his memory of particular features of his previous employer's plant at the disposal of his new employer. Even if there is an express term the employer would have to show that the information was over and above the employee's normal skill in the job and amounted to a trade secret. The nature of a trade secret was considered in *Lansing Linde Ltd* v *Kerr* [1991] 1 WLR 251, in which it was recognised that it was not confined to secret formulae or processes but could, in appropriate cases, extend to names of customers and the goods which they buy.

In *Northern Office Microcomputer (Pty) Ltd* v *Rosenstein* [19821] FSR 124, a South African case, the problem of where to draw the line between the employer's and employee's interests was considered. In this case, a computer programmer developed a computer program which was similar to one he had written for his previous employer.

The case involved copyright matters in addition to the law of confidence and is notable in that the court recognised that computer programs were protected by South African copyright law as literary works. The trail judge agreed that the computer programs were protected by confidence but said that the protection should be of a limited nature. Although the defendant programmer would not be allowed simply to copy the programs in question, he would not be required to 'wipe clean the state of his memory' because to do so would unduly restrict his use of his own training, skill and experience. There would be nothing, in principle, to prevent an ex-employee computer programmer writing a similar program by the exercise of his own mental effort provided he did not simply plagiarise his previous employer's program. To some extent, an important factor is the computer program itself, whether it is a commonplace program, carrying out mundane operations, or whether it is designed to do something novel, that is, whether the purpose of the program can be said to be in the nature of a trade secret.

In many cases, the employer's trade secrets' may be no more than the result of the application by an employee of his own skill and judgment, but if the employee was engaged specifically to produce that information then it can still amount to a trade secret. If the material is commonplace, however, there would be nothing to stop an ex-employee deriving the same or similar material again as long as he did not simply copy his employer's material. In such circumstances, all that would be protected would be employer's 'lead time' the advantage of getting his product to the market place first.

An important case laying down principles which can be applied to the employer-employee relationship was *Faccenda Chicken Ltd* v *Fowler* [1986] 1 All ER 617. The employer's business was supplying fresh chickens and it was alleged that the employee had made wrongful use of sales information such as customers' names and addresses. The employer's action failed, but the following guidelines were laid down in the Court of Appeal.

1. If there is a a contract of employment, the employee's obligations were to be determined from the contract.
2. If there were no express terms, the employee's obligations would bee implied.
3. While still in employment, there was an implied term imposing a duty of good faith. This duty might vary according to the nature of the contract of employment but would be broken if the employee copied or deliberately memorised a list of customers.
4. The implied term imposing an obligation on the employee after the termination of his employment was more restricted. It might cover secret processes and trade secrets.
5. Whether information fell within this implied term to prevent its use or disclosure by an ex-employee depended on the circumstances, and attention should be given to the following.

- the nature of the employment;
- the nature of the information;
- whether the employer stressed the confidential nature of the material;
- whether the information could be easily isolated from other material the employee was free to use.

An ex-employee is thus allowed to make use of his own memory of the work he has carried out in his previous employment unless it involves genuine secrets or is covered by an express term in the contract of employment. Computer programmers and analysts will be allowed to make use of programming techniques and skills which they have learnt and which have become part of their own skill and experience, unless there is something very special about them or they have expressly agreed not to make further use of them. However, a very restrictive express term will be struck out by the courts as being in restraint of trade. The same fate will await any terms which restrict the ex-employee's future employment prospects to any great extent - for example, a term which states that a computer programmer cannot work for computer software companies in the United Kingdom for five years following the termination of his employment. Such restrictive terms will be upheld by the courts only if they are reasonable, such as when a computer programmer working for a bank agree s not to work for another similar bank within a five-mile radious for the first year following the termination of his employment. The purpose of a covenant in restraint of trade should be to protect the employer's legitimate interests rather than simply preventing competition. Essentially, to be enforceable, the term should be aimed at protecting the employer's genuine business interests rather than trying to prevent lawful competition.

It is not easy to lay down an all-purpose formula based on time and geographical area as each case will turn on its own facts. For example, in *Office Angels Ltd* v *Rainer-Thomas* [1991] IRLR 214, it was held that a covenant precluding an ex-employee from opening an employment agency anywhere in an area only within a 1000-metre radius of the previous employer's agency for a period of only six months was inappropriate and would do link to protect the employer's interests because clients usually placed orders over the telephone and the geographical location of the office was of no consequences to them. In that case, the Court of Appeal also confirmed that, where a covenant in restraint of trade was ambiguous, the narrower construction would be taken.

Computer Hackers

A computer hacker is a person who gains access to a computer system without permission. Computer hackers pose a serious threat to the security of computer systems and some of the activities in which they engage are potentially criminal in nature. However, computer hackers also might be liable under the law of confidence, depending on the circumstances. If a hacker gains access to confidential files stored on a computer, it is just possible that the law of confidence might be used to prevent the Backer from making use of the information assuming, of course, that the hacker can be identified. In many cases, information stored in computer systems is highly confidential. It might, for example, concern medical records, creditworthiness, employment or lifestyle details. But will an obligation of confidence attach to a computer hacker? The case of *Prince Albert* v *Strage,* discussed above, suggests that an action might lie in breach of confidence even if the information was obtained surreptitiously. The court in that case was quite happy to imply an obligation of confidence even though if was not possible to say how the confidential information (that is, the prints taken from the engravings) came into the defendant's hands. It could only be assumed that the prints had been obtained in a clandestine manner. In principle, this is very similar to the position of a computer hacker. A hacker must know that there is a strong possibility that the information he accesses will be confidential and, therefore, he will be fixed with an obligation of confidence. If the information turns out to have a quality of confidence, then their is no reason in principle why the hacker should not be sued for breach of confidence if he uses that information or discloses it to others.

If the information is accidentally overheard or intercepted in circumstances where the owner of the information utters it or transmits it by insecure means (for example, by telling it to someone in a crowded room or by transmittting the information by a public telecommunications system) an obligation of confidence might not be imposed on the person obtaining the information in this manner. In *Maline* v *Metropolitan Police Commissioner* [1979] Ch 344, information overheard during an authorised telephone tapping operation by the police was held not to have been disclosed in confidence. However, the law on the matter of unauthorised interception of information is not clear.

The Law Commission recommended codifying the law of confidence and its report, *Breach of Confidence* (Cmnd 8388, HMSO 1980), contains a draft breach of confidence Bill. Clause 5 of the Bill would impose an obligation of confidence on a person who improperly acquires information by using or interfering with any computer or data retrieval mechanism - a welcome clarification. However, there has been no resulting legislation along these lines and it is unlikely that such action will be taken in the foreseeable future.

Remedies for Breach of Confidence

The most important remedy for breach of confidence is an injunction preventing the use or disclosure of the information. If the information has been divulged to sufficient will not be of any help; it would be like locking the stable door after the horse has bolted. If this has happened and the information has been used to the detriment of the person to whom it 'belongs', however, damages will be available against the person responsible and a limited injunction may be granted against that person.

As an alternative to damages, an account of profits may be available and this may be more advantageous to the plaintiff, especially if the defendant has made substantial profit from his use of the information. Being an equitable remedy it is discretionary and the plaintiff must have 'clean hands' and have acted promptly in enforcing his rights. An example of the use of this remedy is the case of *Peter Pan Manufacturing Corp* v *Corsets Silhouette Ltd* [1963] RPC 45, which involved the use of confidential information, after the expiry of a licence agreement, in the manufacture of brassieres. The plaintiff asked for the whole of the profits on the brassieres but the defendant said that the account of profits should only be based on the profit resulting from the wrongful use of the confidential information; that is, the profit relating to the parts of the brassieres incorporating the confidential information. The difference between the two sums was substantial and the plaintiff was awarded the higher sum because the defendants would not have been able to make the brassieres at all without using the confidential information.

It can be seen that the law of confidence is very useful at an early stage when ideas are being formulated and discussed. Although the law of copyright gives some protection at this stage by protecting plans, specifications and notes, the protection does not extend to the ideas behind them. Confidence is particularly important during the development of inventions before they are granted patents because a patent will be refused if details of the invention have been made available to the public, as we shall see. In the computer industry, as with any other, ideas have to be discussed with various persons and organisations with a view to raising finance and granting licences to use or reproduce the resulting invention or copyright work. Many licences for the use of patented inventions include permission to use 'know-how', the confidential information needed to work the invention to best effect. Some licenses may be purely for know-how where there is no patent involved. In most circumstances, during negotiations, an obligation of confidence will be implied but it is sensible to stress confidentiality - for example, by stating that the information is confidential and not be disclosed to anyone else without permission.

7 PATENT LAW

A patent is a very desirable form of intellectual property because it gives to the owner a monopoly in his invention, enabling him to exploit the invention for a number of years to the exclusion of all others (subject to provisions designed to prevent abuse of the monopoly granted). Patent law has a long history and has developed as a means of protecting innovation which has a benefit to innovator and public alike. Inventors are encouraged to invent and investors are more likely to risk money in the development of new inventions if a monopoly right is available for inventions. Society reaps a benefit because the invention will eventually fall into the public domain and because, in the meantime, commercial enterprise is stimulated.

There are two types of patentable invention — a product invention and a process invention — and it has been said that an invention is a new way of making something old or an old way of making something new. A patentable invention could relate to a new piece of computer hardware such as a new interface device, a new type of output device such as a more efficient flat screen display or a new form of storage medium or it could be a new way of making integrated circuits or flat screens. There have been many patent applications for computer hardware and other electronic materials: for example, the invention of the printed circuit board, the transistor and the integrated circuit have all been patented. Sometimes, other forms of protection may be available such as design law or copyright. If the invention fails to meet the rigorous standards required for patentability, these nd other forms of protection may still be available. For example, a new layout of components on a printed circuit board may be protected by the design right even if there is no inventive step for patent purposes.

Fundamentally, the inventor (or more usually, the employer of the inventor) applies for a patent to the Patent Office in London, whether the inventor wants a United Kingdom patent or one which extends to other countries as well. If the application is successful, a patent will be granted for four years initially and may be renewed, annually, up to a maximum of 20 years from the date the application is first filed (the priority date). The renewal fees become progressively steeper throughout the life of the patent and most patents do not run the full 20 years. Obtaining a patent is a complex, expensive and lengthy process and the services of a patent agent are desirable because the drafting of the patent specification and claims is extremely important as regards the future scope of the patent. Until the Copyright, Designs and Patents Act 1988, only a registered patent agent on a solicitor could act for gain as an agent for persons seeking patents, but now anyone can do this as long as he does not describe himself as, or hold himself out to be, a 'patent agent' or 'patent attorney.' In view of the complicated nature of the process, however the person applying for a patent would be well advised to satisfy himself as to the ability of his agent. In some circumstances, it may be preferable simply to keep the idea secret and rely on the law of confidence; this costs nothing and there is no requirement that the invention must eventually fall into the public domain. Examples of the effectiveness of this approach are the recipes and processes used in many familiar drinks and foodstuffs such as Coca-Cola and Kentucky Fried Chicken. In many cases, however, the invention cannot be kept secret, especially if articles made to the invention are to be marketed commercially or if a large number of employees know of the invention, in which case a patent is the only realistic solution.

Procedure

The ponderous patent application process seems to be unsuited to a fastmoving technology as it can take several years from initial application before a patent is finally granted. The procedure for obtaining a patent in the United Kingdom is as follows.

1. The application is field together with a specification describing the invention, an abstract (the title for the invention and concise summary) and the claims (defining the scope of the monopoly claimed). Drawings will usually be included in the specification.
2. The Patent Office will carry out a search for patents and other documents which may be relevant to the invention. Typically, this will find previous patents in the same field which might have a bearing on the patentability of the invention. It is common for the application to be amended following the search.
3. Eighteen months following the first filing of the patent it is published. This is referred to as 'A' publication.
4. The Patent Office examiners then carry out an extensive examination of the patent application to check for conformity with the requirements of the Patents Act 1977. Again, some amendments

may be necessary at this stage, though it should be noted that the monopoly claimed cannot be widened.

5. Finally, the patent will be granted (all being well) and it will be published again - 'B' publication.

The procedure is shown in Fig. 7.1. It is greatly simplified and assumes no problems are encountered. Since 1995, the United Kingdom Patent Office has offered a speedier procedure whereby the applicant can request a combined search and examination and earlier publication. This procedure may be suitable for straightforward applications. It is unlikely to be appropriate for software patents.

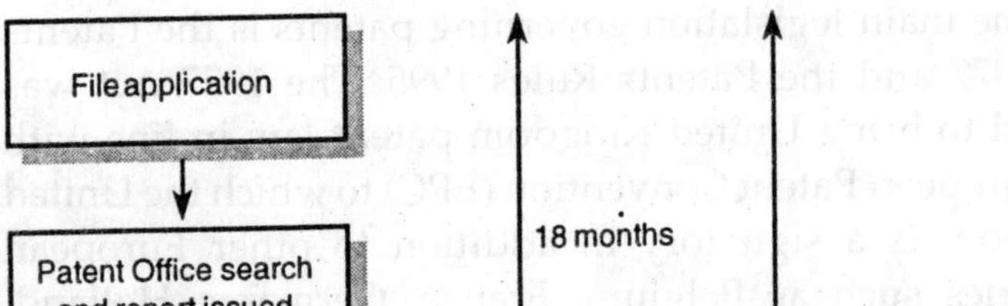

Fig. 7.1 Patent procedure (simplified)

The proprietor's monopoly dates back, effectively, to the date of 'A' publication. Although he cannot sue until the patent is granted, he will be entitled to damages in respect of any infringement carried out after publication.

The date when the patent application is first filed becomes its priority date. As a result of international countries within the next 12 months and the novelty of the invention will still be judged as at its priority date. Thus, the applicant has 12 months to decide in which other countries he wishes to obtain a patent. To international conventions - the European Patent Convention and the Patent Co-operation Treaty - facilitate for obtaining of patents in a number of other countries.

The main legislation governing patents is the Patents Act 1977 and the Patents Rules 1995. The 1977 Act was passed to bring United Kingdom patent law in line with the European Patent Convention (EPC) to which the United Kingdom is a signatory in addition to other European countries such as Belgium, France, Germany, Holland, Italy, Sweden and Spain. A number of non-EC countries also belong to the EPC, including Norway and Switzerland. The EPC is not a European Community institution although the European Patent Office (EPO) will administer the proposed Community Patent Convention, providing a Community wide patent system, when it comes into force. In addition to the Patents Act 1977, there are a number of rules and regulations dealing with details such as registration procedure, fees and the Patents Country Court in London. The Comptroller of Patents also has jurisdiction to hear certain patent disputes if the parties are willing and to hear other matters, such as determining who should be the true proprietor or whether an employee inventor should be awarded compensation for an invention belonging to his employer which is of outstanding benefit to the employer.

Not all inventions are capable of supporting a patent. The Patents Act 1977 lays down several requirements which must be satisfied before a patent can be granted and, furthermore, certain things are specifically excluded from patentability. The basic requirements for the grant of a patent will now be explained, followed by a consideration of the exclusions and their impact, especially with respect to computer software.

Basic Requirements

The basic requirements for the grant of a patent are stated in section 1(1) of the Patents Act 1977 as follows:

> A patent may be granted only for an invention in respect of which the following conditions are satisfied, that is to say:
>
> (a) the invention is new;
> (b) it involves an inventive step;
> (c) it is capable of industrial application;
> (d) the grant of a patent for it is not excluded by subsections (2) and (3) below....

The exclusions referred to in (d), which include computer programs, will be considered later but first the interpretation of the first three conditions will be examined.

New Invention

The word 'invention' is not defined in the Act but its meaning is really a matter of common sense and it can be used in a fairly wide sense. It is obvious that a patent should not be granted for anything which is not new, which is already in the public domain, otherwise the grant of the patent could make illegal and act which was previously legal. For example, if a company has been making integrated circuits by a special process for several years but has failed to apply for a patent, a second company, wishing to do the same type of work, will be refused a patent on the grounds that the invention is not new. The first company could set up such prior use as a defence against a patent infringement action under section 64. The prior use could invalidate for parent unless such use had not made the invention available to the public. This might be the case where the prior use was in secret until after the priority date of the patent. The prior use must have occurred before the priority date or serious and effective preparations must have been made in respect of such use before that date.

Section 2 of the Act expands on the meaning of 'new' and says that an invention is new if it does not form part of the 'state of the art'; this expression comprises all matter which has been made available to the public in the United Kingdom of elsewhere, by written or oral description, by use or in any other way. Matters contained in prior patent applications are also included. There is no need for the invention to have been made widely available to the public and, in *Windsurfing International Inc* v *Tabur Marine (GB) Ltd* [1985] RPC 59, it was held that 12-year-old boy, who had made his own sailboard which he used at Hayling Island on summer weekends, had made the invention available to the public with the effect that the patent later granted to the plaintiff for a sailboard was declared invalid after the defendant had challenged its validity on the grounds of lack of novelty and lack of inventive step.

The inventor must resist any temptation he might have to publish details of his invention before the first filing date (the priority date), otherwise he could inadvertently add his invention to the state of the art and anticipate his own invention. Similarly, the inventor must be careful when discussing his invention with potential manufacturers and the like and the law of confidence is very important at this stage. However, if details of the invention are disclosed by a person acting in breach of confidence or who has obtained details unlawfully, that disclosure will be disregarded in determining the state of the art if such breach occurs no earlier than six months preceding the filing of the patent.

As technology advances and the pool of knowledge in the public domain grows, it is increasingly difficult to devise something which is absolutely 'new'. Indeed, it is not an easy task to find out if the invention has been anticipated and is already part of the state of the art, given the massive world-wide volume of published work, and it is possible that a publication which anticipates the invention will not be discovered. If that material is subsequently found and shows that the invention was not new when the patent was applied for, the patent is in danger of being revoked. A number of patents may be on shaky ground as far as novelty is concerned if sufficient time and effort were expended on trying to trace anticipatory materials or prior use. A person who is being sued for infringing a patent will try to find such material.

Inventive Step

By section 3 of the Patents Act 1977 an invention involves an inventive step if it is not obvious to a person skilled in the art. This test, known as the 'notional skilled worker test', takes account of the complexity of technology, hence the reference to a skilled person rather than the ubiquitous 'reasonable man', so often used as a benchmark by judges. The reason is that a great many 'inventions' would not be obvious to a layman but would be to someone who knew something of the technology involved. It has been accepted that the 'skilled person' may be a team of highly qualified research workers such as team of analysts and computer programmers. When it comes to applying the test, the skilled person is not endowed with any inventive faculties himself, a somewhat artificial premise, but to hold otherwise would mean that virtually all inventions would be obvious and not patentable.

'Obvious' has no special meaning but is judged by looking at the invention as a whole and considering the entire state of the art. Whether the invention is obvious is a question of fact. In the *Windsurfing* case discussed earlier in connection with novelty, Lord Justice Oliver suggested the following four-stage test for determining whether an invention is obvious.

1. Identify the inventive concept embodied in the patent.
2. The court then assumes the mantle of the normally skilled but unimaginative person in the art at the priority date of the patent and imputes to him what was, at the date, common general knowledge in the art.
3. Identify what, if any differences exist between that knowledge and the patented invention.
4. Consider whether, without knowledge of the invention, those differences constitute steps which would have been obvious to the person skilled in the art or whether they require any degree of invention.

Commercial success is a factor which can be taken into account in determining obviousness though it is not conclusive. In *Technographic Printed Circuits Ltd* v *Mills & Rockley (Electronics) Ltd* [1969] RPC 395, a case involving a patent for a method of making printed circuits, Harman J. said:

> It was objected that in fact it was not until ten years after the invention was published that it was

> commercially adopted.. and it was argued from this that it was not a case of filing a long felt want. I do not accept this argument. In the years immediately following the war, manufacturers could sell all the machines they wanted using the old point-to-point wiring and had no need to trouble themselves with anything better.

Computer technology spreads into all kinds of other technologies and this may lead to patentable inventions even though the computer technology itself is not new, if the application of the technology is new. In principle there is nothing to prevent the application of well-known technology to a particular problem being the proper subject matter of a patent. This many not be obvious if there has been a major problem and a solution has evaded many attempts to reach it. Again, the commercial success of the invention is a useful guide. In *Parks-Cramer Co* v *G.W. Thornton & Sons Ltd.* [1966] RPS 407, the invention was a method of cleaning floors between rows of textile machines. There had been many unsuccessful attempts to find a satisfactory solution but none of them, unlike the present invention, actually worked. Essentially, all the invention consisted of was an overhead vacuum cleaner which moved back and forth between the textile machines and which had attached to it a long vertical tube, reaching almost to the floor. It was argued that this was obvious because every competent housewife knows that dust can be removed from a floor by the passage of a vacuum cleaner. This argument was rejected and the patent was held to be valid as the many unsuccessful attempts by inventors to find a solution coupled with the immediate commercial success of the present invention denied the possibility of a finding of obviousness.

The courts have to draw a line somewhere when it comes to obviousness although it is difficult to lay down hard and fast rules. It is clear, however, that there must be a sufficient inventive step and merely taking two older inventions and sticking them together will not necessarily be regarded as an inventive step.

Industrial Application

Another requirement for the grant of a patent is that the invention must have an industrial application but this is widely defined by section 4 of the Patents Act 1977 which states that the invention must be capable of being made or used in any kind of industry, including agriculture. However, a method of treatment of the human or animal body by surgery or therapy or a method of diagnosis practised on the human or animal body is not capable of industrial application although this does not prevent the patenting of drugs to be used in any such treatment or diagnosis.

The need for industrial application shows the practical nature of patent law, which require that the invention should be something which can be produced or that it relates to some sort of industrial process.

Examples of refusal on the grounds that the invention does not have an industrial application are rare, but one example is provided by *Hiller's Application* [1969] RPC 267. This case concerned an improved plan for underground service distribution schemes for housing estates; that is, the layout of the gas, sewerage and water pipes and electricity cables. It was held that this could not constitute a 'manner of manufacture' (the phrase used instead of 'industrial application' prior to the 1977 Act). Therefore, if someone develops a new form of layout for the components in a computer or a new configuration for printed circuit bards, these are unlikely to be granted patents. However, the layout of components and the configuration of a printed circuit board may be protected by copyright through any drawings which have been made indicating the layout or by the design right. Methods or principles of construction are excluded from the design right. A new form of layout cannot, without more, be said to be capable of industrial application.

Exclusions from Patentability

Several things are excluded from the scope of patent law. Section 1(2) of the Patents Act 1977 contains those which can generally be classified as coming within the scope of copyright law or the law of confidence and, in that context, computer programs are of particular interest. (Section 1(3) concerns things which might encourage offensive, immoral or antisocial behaviour or new varieties of animals or plants.) Section 1(2) of the Act states that the following are not inventions for the purposes of the Act:

> (a) a discovery, scientific theory or mathematical method;
>
> (b) a literary, dramatic, musical or artistic work or any other aesthetic creation whatsoever;
>
> (c) a scheme, rule or method for performing any mental act, playing a game or doing business, or a program for a computer;
>
> (d) the presentation of information;
>
> but the foregoing provisions shall prevent anything from being treated as an invention for the purposes of this Act only to the extent that a patent or application for a patent relates to that thing *as such* [emphasis added].

Note that the above exceptions only apply to the extent that a *patent relates to that thing as such.* This means that these particular things mentioned in the above list of exclusions can be protected by patent indirectly if they are part of a patent application which includes other elements which are patentable in their own right. For example, a computer program *as such* to control the temperature of a furnace cannot be patented (it will, of course, be protected by copyright). If an application is made to patent a computer-controlled furnace, however, it may well succeed and be granted a patent.

Computer Programs

The exclusion from patent of computer programs reflects international trends. Copyright is seen as the proper vehicle for the protection of computer programs although, when the current Patents Act was passed in 1977, it was far from clear whether copyright did protect computer programs. Even before the 1977 Act, computer programs were not generally patentable *per se*, but there have been cases, both in the United Kingdom and in the United States, where computer programs have been granted patents indirectly, usually as being part of a piece of machinery or an industrial process. For example, in *Diamond* v *Diehr* [1981] 209 USPQ 1, the United States Supreme Court confirmed that a computer-controlled process used in rubber curing was patentable.

In *Gever's Application* [1970] RPC 91, data processing apparatus was arranged to work in certain way associated with punched cards inserted into it. The purpose of the apparatus was to file world trade marks in such a way that they could be easily produced to check for similarity and prior registration. The patent application, which concerned a piece of machinery which functioned in a certain way because of the punched cards, was allowed to proceed. The cards were described by the judge as a 'manner of manufacture' because he thought that a punched card was analogous to a cam for controlling the cutting path of a lathe. This was distinguished from a card which merely had written or printed material on it, intended to convey information to the human eye or mind, and not meant to be ancillary to some machine by being specially shaped for that purpose. However, because of subsequent technological developments, integrated circuits, magnetic disks and tapes and optical character readers now are used to enter information into a computer or to store the programs which control the computer. The analogy with a mechanical process no longer true and it is unlikely that this case will be followed.

In another case, *Burrough's Corporation (Perking's) Application* [1974] RPC 147, computer programs controlled the transmission of data to terminals from a central computer (a communications system). The system, including the computer programs, was held to be the proper subject matter of a patent because the programs were embodied in physical form; they were 'hard-wired' - permanently embedded in the electronic circuits of the equipment. In many respects the significance of the physical form of a program, whether hard-wired on a silicon chip or stored on magnetic disks, is an irrelevance and should not affect patentability.

The distinction between modes of storage and their effect on patentability was considered more recently in *Gale's Application* [1991] RPC 305, concerning an application for a method of calculating square roots by program instructions contained in a ROM chip. The Comptroller of Patents, Designs and Trade Marks rejected the application but the applicant's appeal to the Patents Court was allowed by Aldous J who said that the claimed invention related to a product (the ROM chip) and was, therefore, patentable. He then said that the program would not have been patentable had it been stored on a floppy disk. This decision would have had the effect of making a software designer's choice of storage medium crucial to the question of patentability but it was, fortunately, quickly overruled in the Court of Appeal where Lord Justice Nicholls said:

> It would equally be nonsense of a floppy disc containing a computer program was not patentable that a ROM characterised only by the instruction in that program should be patentable.

The Court of Appeal's decision conforms with common sense and the simple expedient of hard-writing a computer program should not, *per se,* make the program patentable. Something else must be present such as a technical effect.

Technical Effect

Two alternative approach have been made to the question of the patent protection of inventions which include a computer program. The first is that the patent application should be considered without the contribution of the excepted thing. For example, if a machine includes a computer program it is then a question of whether the machine, without taking the computer program into account, adds anything to the state of the art. Does the machine, ignoring the computer program, meet the requirements for patentability? If the only novel and inventive step concerns the computer program itself, then the machine as a whole is not patentable. The case of *Re Merrill Lynch, Piece Fenner & Smith Incorporated's Application* [1988] RPC 1, illustrates this approach. The invention related to an improved data processing system for implementing an automatic trading market for securities. The system received and stored the best current bids, qualified customer buy and sell orders, executed orders as well as monitoring stock inventory and profit. The Principal Examiner of the Patent Office rejected the application for a patent and the appeal against his decision was dismissed. On appeal to the Patents Court, it was held that where an invention involves any of the excluded materials in section 1(2) the proper construction of the qualification in that subsection requires that the Patent Office inquires into whether the inventive step resides in the contribution of the excluded matter alone. If the inventive step comes only from the excluded material, then the invention is not patentable because of section 1(2). The judge, Falconer J. said that the novel and inventive effect reside outside the computer program even though it may be defined by program.

In a further appeal to the Court of Appeal (*Merrill Lynch's Application* [1989] RPC 561], the approach of Falconer J was qualified and that taken by the European Patent Office, as described below, was approved. However, the Court of Appeal still confirmed that the invention in *Merrill Lynch* was not patentable but on the grounds that was no technical effect, the operation being entirely software based.

In *Vicom Systems Incorporated's Patent Application* [1987] OJ EPO 14, a different approach to that of Falconer J. was taken. This case concerned an application to the European Patent Office (EPO) and the invention was a new digital image processing system, the process steps being expressed mathematically in the form of an algorithm. It was held that this claim was allowable. It was said that if a claim is directed to a technical process which is carried out under the control of a program (whether implemented in the hardware or the software), then the claim cannot be regarded as related to a computer program as such. It is an application of the program for determining the sequence of steps in the process and it is the process for which protection is sought. In the present case, the subject matter of the invention was the practical application of a computer program, the technical effect resulting from the operation of the programmed computer and not the computer program itself. The EPO's approach has been followed and approved subsequently by the English courts. In *Genentech Inc's Patent*[1989] RPC 147, it was held, *inter alia*, in the Court of Appeal that a patent which claimed the practical application of a discovery did not relate to the discovery as such and was not excluded by section 1(2) of the Patents Act 1977 even if the practical application might be obvious once the discovery had been made. *Gale's Application* [1991]RPC 305, discussed above, confirms this as the correct approach.

It would seem that the technical effect does not have to be external to the computer and, in principle, operating systems are patentable because they determine how a computer operates technically. Indeed, there are patents in the United Kingdom and the United States in respect of operating systems including the recently litigated data compression software. With applications programs it is more difficult to achieve a technical advance and, in *Wang Laboratories Inc's Application* [1991]RPC 463, an application for a patent for an expert system shell was rejected because there was no new technical effect. Aldous J. said that the computer (being a conventional machine) and the program combined do not produce a new computer. In *Hitachi Ltd's Application* [1991]RPC 415, an application in respect of a compiler program was rejected by the Patent Office as being no more than an application for a computer program as such.

While a patent will be refused for a computer program *simpliciter* (or any of the other exceptions in section 1(2) for that matter) it will be allowed if the purpose of the program is to bring about some technical effect and it is that effect which is the subject matter of the patent application. The subject matter should make a technical contribution to the state of the art.

Commercial Effect

The emphasis on technical effect applies to most countries, but in Australia following *IBM* v *Commissioner of Patents* (1992) AIPS 90-853, a case where a method of creating a visual representation of a curve by a series of calculations was allowed, it seems that an effect which is commercially useful may be patentable even though it is entirely software based. Some commentators argue that patents will be allowed eventually in Australia and, perhaps, in the United States for computer programs as such.

The European Patent Office remains steadfastly loyal to the technical effect approach and in *IMB/Card Reader* [1994]EPOR 89, the Technical Board of Appeal dismissed an appeal against a refusal to grant a patent in relation to an invention whereby an automatic card-reading machine could read any card. This would allow the use of any bank card with a machine such as an automated teller machine (ATM or cashpoint machine) to carry out a transaction. The Board of Appeal confirmed that the subject matter of a patent must have a technical character and be industrially applicable. It also went on to say that applying technical means to perform a business activity does not mean that the business activity has a technical character and is thus an invention. It should be noted that a method of doing business is also excluded according to section 1(2) of the Patents Act 1977.

It is submitted that the approach of the EPO is correct and accords with the basic historical nature of a patent. England's first patent legislation was the Statute of Monopolies 1623 which allowed patents for new manners of manufacture, a phrase which was used right up to the 1977 Act. Insisting on a new technical effect whether inside or outside the computer is entirely consistent with that phrase and its replacement 'industrial application'.

Mental Steps

The operation of a novel computer program may product a technical effect which is itself caught by the exceptions to patentability as in the *IBM/Card Reader* case above. Another exception is a scheme, rule or method of performing a mental act and it seems that simply programming a computer to carry out something that can be performed by the human intellect will not be patentable. For example, in *Re The Computer Generation of Chinese Characters* [1993] FSR 315, an application for a patent in respect of a method of storing, processing, displaying and printing Chinese characters was turned down in Germany. It was said that the subject matter neither solved a technical problem by a technical method nor did it make a technical contribution to the state of the art.

Similarly, in the United Kingdom, a patent was refused for a software means of identifying ships by comparing the silhouette of an unknown ship with a database of ship's silhouettes in *Raytheon Co's Application* [1993] RPC 427. The fact that the equivalent mental act in the human mind would not be deliberate conscious process did not bring the application out of the exception. Recognises of shapes by humans is almost instantaneous, whereas a computer program doing this would be based on algorithms that may operate quite differently, in logical terms, to the human brain. The deputy judge was not prepared to read the exception in a narrow sense. Thus, it appears that a computer program that simply does something that can be done by mental acts in the human brain will not be patentable even though the program may do it differently and in a totally new way. The same must apply to the other exceptions such as methods of doing business.

The mental steps doctrine has become even more ingrained in United Kingdom patent law. *Fujitsu Ltd's*

Application [1997] RPC 610 involved an application for a patent in relation to software which was developed to help chemists design new chemical compounds. A computer screen displayed the crystalline structure of two known chemicals and these images could be rotated and manipulated so as to align one face of one crystal to be aligned with the complementary face of the other crystal. This then formed the blue-print for a new hybrid 'designer' chemical.

It was held that the application was for a method of performing a mental act as such. In the Court of Appeal, Lord Justice Aldous rejected the submission that, as it was not possible to perform a mental act using a computer, a claim for a method of using a computer could not be a claim to a method of performing a mental act. He stressed that it was important to look at the substance of an application. Thus, a claim for a computer program operating in a particular way is no more than a claim to a computer program. Furthermore, a claim to a method of carrying out a calculation, which is a method of performing a mental act, can never become more patentable simply because the calculation is being performed by a computer rather than being done manually on a piece of paper.

It was also accepted by the Court of Appeal that the application was for a computer program as such and not patentable on this ground also. The invention used a conventional computer to do what was previously done using plastic models. The only advance was that of using a computer to enable the result to be portrayed more quickly. Mr Justice Aldous said that this was just the sort of advantage to be obtained by the application of a computer program. In other words, there was nothing special in it.

In the context of computers, the exception for methods of performing a mental act is potentially very wide. Many programs automate what used to be done by the human mind, even if a computer does it on the basis of a completely different algorithm. Although not really discussed, it was highly arguable that the application would also have failed for lack of novelty (the exercise was done before but by using physical models) or through lack of inventive step. It is fairly obvious that advantages can be achieved by automating existing processes. This is why most computer programs would fail to be patentable. However, there are some programs that make new and effective technical contributions and it is for these that the patent system is important. Incidentally, the Fujitsu patent appears to have been granted in Japan.

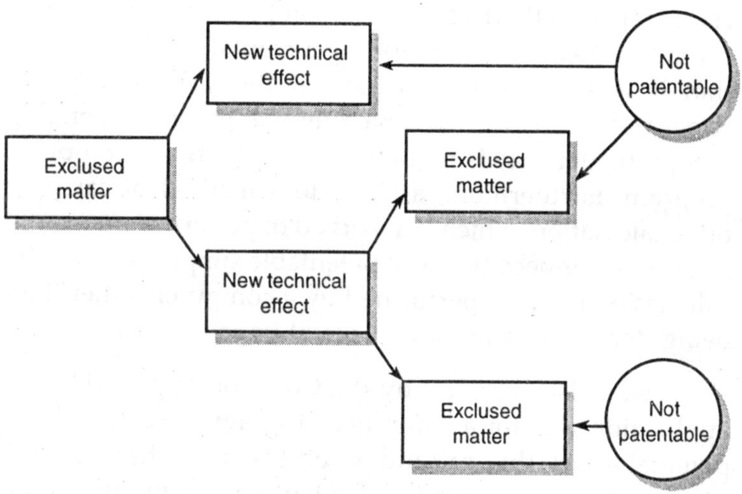

Fig 7.2 Patentability of excluded matter such as computer programs

To summarise, if a patent application includes excluded matter, such as a computer program, there must be an associated technical effect which does not result in something which is itself excluded (Fig. 7.2)

It has been argued that a special hybrid type of right should be introduced for computer programs-something between a patent and copyright. Such a right would give a monopoly in the program, thus protecting the underlying ideas more effectively than copyright, but the right would last for a shorter period than a patent, say five or seven years maximum. Given the developments both in the United Kingdom and elsewhere over the last few years, however, it is now unlikely that this course will be taken. The Copyright, Designs and Patents Act 1988 confirms this forcibly by its clear inclusion of computer programs in literary work category of works protected by copyright.

Infringement, Defences and Remedies

A patent is infringed if a person does one of certain things in relation to the invention in the United Kingdom without the permission of the proprietor (owner) of the patent. Section 60 of the Patents Act 1977 defines what does and what does not constitute infringements. The nature of the infringement depends on whether the invention is a product (for example, a new type of computer printer) or a process (for example, a new method of making integrated circuits). If the invention is a product, the patent is infringed by making, disposing of or offering to dispose of, using, importing or keeping the product. Similar provision apply to a process: for example, using the process infringes but, additionally, the patented process may be infringed by using or disposing of, etc. any product obtained directly from that process. Another difference between products and processes relates to the knowledge of the infringer. For a process, knowledge that a patent is being infringed is required. However, 'knowledge' is used in a special way and a person can still be deemed to have the requisite knowledge if it would be obvious to a reasonable man that a patent was being infringed. There is no requirement for knowledge as regards a product and, therefore, in the absence of a defence, liability for infringement is strict.

A patent is also infringed if a person supplies or offers to supply some other person with any of the means, relating to an essential element of the invention, for putting the invention into effect. Knowledge is required in that the person supplying knows, or it is obvious to a reasonable man, that those means are suitable for putting the invention into effect and that person so intends. This 'supplying the means' infringement is useful as it applies to persons who supply products in kit form. For example, if a person supplies a computer in kit form which, when assembled, infringes a patent, then the supplier of the computer kit infringes the patent even if the he is just a middleman as long as he has the requisite knowledge. This prevents a possible loophole in patent law such as where a person imports components made in a foreign country to be sold as as kit. The person assembling the kit computer will not be liable under patent law, however, if he assembles and uses the computer privately and for non-commercial purposes. To give a practical example of infringement, consider the following situation.

> An inventor A has invented a new type of computer 'chip' and a new process which will be used for making those chips. He has taken out patents for the process and for the chips. B finds out about the process and decides to build a similar process for making these computer chips. B asks C to supply equipment which is essential to the process. B then makes some computer chips and sells them to D, a trade supplier.
>
> The position is:
>
> B, if he knows, or it would be obvious to a reasonable man, that the process was patented, has infringed the patent for the process. Even if

B had no actual knowledge it would be most likely that he would be fixed with knowledge on the basis of the reasonable man test. (Patent specifications are available for public inspection - would a reasonable man check first?)

B has infringed the patent for the computer chips even if he did not know or could not be expected to know of the patent.

C and infringed the patent for the process if he knows, or it would be obvious to reasonable man, that the equipment he supplied was suitable for putting the process into effect and the equipment was intended to do so.

D infringes the patent for the computer chips, regardless of knowledge.

The fact that some infringements do not require any form of knowledge may seem unduly harsh, but knowledge is required for some of the remedies and the situation is not as inequitable as it might appear, bearing in mind the need to protect the patent.

There are certain defences or exceptions to infringement: for example, if the act is done privately and for non-commercial purposes or for experimental purposes (on the basis that the proprietor's interests are not harmed by such use). There are other, unusual defences, but these are outside the scope of this book. Of more importance is whether, if someone has 'copied' an invention but has introduced some minor changes, the patent has been infringed. What is the scope of the patent? To determine whether there has been an infringement, the specification and, in particular, the claims for the patent must be looked at and interpreted to find the limits of the patent. Although judges tend to interpret Acts of Parliament and legal documents literally (unless this leads to an absurd result), patent specifications are interpreted purposively; that is, in line with the presumed intention of the person who wrote it. In *Catnic Components Ltd* v *Hill & Smith Ltd* [1982] RPC 183, the plaintiff obtained a patent for a load bearing lintel, the main strength of which came from a vertical metal rear face. The specification and claims in the patent referred to the rear face as being vertical. Claim 1 described the rear face as '.... a second rigid support member extending vertically from or from near the rear edge of the first horizontal plate....' The defendant made a similar lintel but with a rear face inclined at 6 degree from the vertical. The House of Lords, by interpreting the word 'vertical' to mean, in effect, 'vertical or nearly vertical' held that the patent had been infringed. The important feature was the metal face, the purpose of which was to support the load. This approach is in line with both common sense and the European Patent Convention and prevents others from flouting patent law by making minor changes to details of an invention while retaining the underlying principles involved, and is justified on the basis that patent specifications and claims are directed to technical people, not lawyers. It also shows the different scope of patent law compared with copyright law, because patent law can protect purpose and principle whereas, generally, copyright law cannot. The so-called purpose and principle whereas, generally, copyright law cannot. The so-called 'Catnic Test' has recently survived an attack upon its validity and it has been confirmed by the Court of Appeal that it is still useful.

A patent, once granted, can be revoked if it is subsequently shown to fail to meet the requirements for patentability: for example, it was not novel at the priority date or does not involve an inventive step, or if it was not granted to the person entitled to it. The fact that a patent has been granted by the Patent Office is not conclusive proof that the invention has satisfied all the requirements and the discovery of a prior publication disclosing the invention can result in the patent being revoked. Often, a person sued for infringement of patent will attack the validity of the patent. As far as the alleged infringer is concerned, this can be a useful ploy as the proceedings will be drawn out and the proprietor of the patent will be put to extra expense in defending his patent. Although the validity of patents is frequently brought into issue by defendants, only a handful of patents are revoked each year.

The remedies available for infringement of a patent are injunctions, delivery up or destruction of infringing articles, damages or an account of profits and a declaration that the patent is valid and infringed by the defendant. Damages and accounts of profits are alternatives. If the defendant proves that he was not aware and had no reasonable grounds for supposing that the patent existed, then neither damages not accounts of profits are available. If a product carries the word 'patent' or 'patented' or similar, this does not automatically mean that the defendant knows of patent unless the number of the patent also appears on the product concerned. This enables anyone to look up and inspect the patent specification to determine its scope.

The proprietor of a patent must be careful how he warns alleged infringers. There is a remedy under section 70 in respect of groundless threats of infringement proceedings. A person aggrieved by the threat may bring an action, unless the person making the threat can show that the acts in respect of which the threats were made were or would constitute an infringement of the patent, and the patent is not shown to be invalid by the person bringing the action. The remedies available are a declaration that the threats are unjustified, an injunction against a continuance of the threats, and damages for any loss sustained by the person aggrieved who has brought the action. Groundless threats actions do not apply to all forms of infringement (making or importing a product or using a process) and simply notifying any person of the existence of the patent does not constitute a groundless threat.

An example where a groundless threats action might be appropriate is where it is alleged that a computer imported into the United Kingdom by Acme Importers Ltd and is alleged to infringe a United Kingdom patent belonging to Esoteric Computers plc. Thee computers are sold by Acme to Krafty Computer Sales Ltd, a retail outlet. Esoteric send a letter a Krafty threatening to sue Krafty unless it ceases selling the computers forthwith. Krafty will be 'a person aggrieved' and so many Acme, if Krafty stops buying computers from Acme. Either should be above to bring an action for groundless threats and will be entitled to remedies unless Esoteric can show that the sale of the computers infringes the patent and, if a challenge has been made on the validitty of the patent, or any relevant part of it, that it invalid.

Miscellaneous

Certain other provisions contained in the patents Act 1977 are worthy of brief mention. An invention may be potentially very beneficial but might also destroy or seriously undermine an existing business: for example, a car engine that does 200 miles to a gallon, or an everlasting light bulb. To prevent the proprietor sitting on his patent, deliberately failing to use it, section 48 of the Act allows any person to apply for a compulsory license under the patent, after the expiry of the three years from grant if, for example, the patent is not being worked or some abuse is being made of the patent monopoly such as if the product is not being made available at reasonable terms.

An employee who, in the course of his employment, has made an invention which belongs to his employer may be awarded compensation to be paid by the employer if the patent is of outstanding benefit to the employer (section 40). This provision is seldom used, perhaps because reasonable employers reward such employees sufficiently well so that they do not apply for compensation. However, it is clear that the benefit must be truly outstanding if the employee is to stand any chance of obtaining compensation. The author is not aware of any examples of compensation awarded under section 40.

Utility Model

There are plans for a new form of protection in the United Kingdom which is called the utility model and is like lesser version of a patent, sometimes referred to as a 'petty patent'. This new right will come about through moves to harmonise this form of protection throughout the EC; Proposal for a Directive for the protection of inventions by a utility model, COM (97) 691, OJ[1998]C36/13. At the present time, only three member states do not have any equivalent form of protection, these being the United Kingdom, Luxembourg and Sweden. In its original form, computer programs were excluded from protection by the utility model, but as a result of an amended proposal in June 1999, computer programs will be appropriate subject matter for protection, providing they are new, involve an inventive step and are suitable for industrial application. Protection will be for up 10 years and the harmonised utility model is intended to be implemented some time during 2001.

8 TRADE MARKS

Trade Marks

Marks have been used to identify the makers of goods for thousands of years. Individual marks become associated with a particular product and with the quality of that product. As regards the value of trade mark to a manufacturer, two factors are important: the buying public's familiarity with the mark and their experience of reasonable quality or value for money in the past associated with the mark. A trade mark which is used with a successful product is of tremendous value to the owner of the mark and he will want to prevent others from using the mark or a similar one to capture some of his trade. Trade marks law serves two main purpose: first it protects the good will and reputation which a trader has built up around the mark involved and, second, it prevents the public from being deceived as to the origin of goods or services. By doing so, it establishes a property right in the mark in question and requires that the mark be used (failure to use a mark may result in it being revoked).

A manufacture, trader or person who makes goods or provides a service may register a mark for one or more classes of goods or services. This will give the owner of the mark a monopoly in the use of that mark in the classes under which the mark has been registered. There are a total of 34 classes of marks for goods (for example, chemicals, electrical goods and scientific apparatus, vehicles, clothing, fancy goods and smokers' articles) and a further eight classes for services (for example, advertising and business, insurance and financial, communications and miscellaneous). Software trade marks may be registered in Class 9 which includes data processing equipment and computers. A person providing services by writing software would register a mark in Class 42 which includes computer programming.

If anyone else uses the mark, or one deceptively similar, in the course of trade without the owner's permission, that person can be sued for infringement of the trade mark. Depending on the circumstances, a criminal offence may also be committed. The remedies available to the owner of the trade mark are as usual: injunctions, damages or an account of profits as an alternative to damages plus removal of offending marks. The infringing articles may be ordered to be destroyed if the offending marks cannot be removed.

In the computer industry, the power of trade marks can readily be seen as, in a relatively short space of time, names such as Apple computer, IBM, WordPerfect, Lotus 1-2-3 and Microsoft became household names. Trade marks are especially important in a fast-moving industry and it is very comforting to buy goods with familiar names when so many products and businesses come and to in rapid succession, as happened with microcomputers in the early 1980s. A familiar name or mark is very influential as many who buy computer hardware and software will look for a product which is likely to be of reasonable quality and will be supported in years to come. There have been few examples of trade mark infringement in the world of computers and most counterfeiters have used different names or marks: for example, copies of the Apple computer imported into

Australia were called 'Wombats'. Other Apple lookalikes have been called 'Pineapples' and 'Microprofessors'. Perhaps this is a testimony to the effectiveness of trade mark law.

Until 1994 trade mark law was provided for by the Trade Marks Act 1938 which was widely recognised as being difficult and outdated. The new law is contained in the Trade Marks Act 1994 which is a result of a European Directive harmonising trade mark law (OJ [1989] L40/1), though some of the old case law is still relevant. The new Act is a welcome and much awaited improvement of trade mark law.

What is a Trade Mark?

By section 1 of the Trade Marks Act 1994, a trade mark is:

> ... Any sign capable of being represented grapohically which is capable of distinguishing goods or services of one undertaking form those of other undertakings.

It goes on to say that a trade mark may, in particular, consist of words (including personal names), designs, letters, numerals or the shape of goods or their packaging. This definition is much wider than that in the 1938 Act, under which an application to register the Coca-Cola bottle as a trade mark failed in *Re Coca-Cola Co's Application*[1986] 2 All ER 274. The new definition allows the registration, potentially, of music and even smells (represented by chemical formulae or a written description of the fragrance perhaps). There should be little difficulty for software companies to register marks embedded in software such as a moving image produced on a screen when a computer game is being loaded together with any associated distinctive musical motif.

Even the threshold for registration has been eased by the new law. Under the 1938 Act, there were two parts to the register of trade marks. Part A was for marks adapted to distinguish the goods of one trader from those of other traders while Part B was for marks which were capable of distinguishing, a lower standard which offered less protection. Now the lower requirement 'capable of distinguishing' applies to all marks and the nonsense of a two part register has been abolished. In *Davies* v *Sussex Rubber Co* (1927) 44 RPC 412, case involving 'Ustikon' for stick-on rubber soles for shoes, it was said that a mark was capable of distinguishing if it would become distinctive through use; in other words, if it was not incapable of becoming distinctively associated with the goods of the trade mark proprietor.

This approach was accepted as also being appropriate under the 1994 Act in *AD2000 Trade Mark*[1997] RPC 168. In that case an application to register AD2000 as a trade mark failed. A combination of two letters and four numbers could be capable of distinguishing if it was idiosyncratic. However, that was not the case here as AD2000 naturally referred to the year 2000 and was not idiosyncratic. Mr Geoffrey Hobbs QC, hearing the case, refused to be swayed by the fact the the word 'MILLENNIUM' had previously been accepted for registration as a trade mark.

Unregistrable Marks

The fundamental purpose of trade mark is to distinguish goods or services of one undertaking from those of other undertakings. In other words the mark must serve as an indicator of trade origin. If it does not do this, it is not registrable. For example, 'TARZAN', 'ELVIS' and 'ELVIS PRESLEY' were held to be unregistrable. By the time the applications were received, these names were so well known as 'household' words that they could not serve the function of indicating a connection in the course of trade between a trader and his goods. Although 'three-dimensional' signs are now potentially registrable, the same principle applies. In *Philips Electronics NV* v *Remington Consumer Products* [1998] RPC 283, a registration as a trade mark of a representation of a three-headed electric razor was declared invalid because it denoted function rather than trade origin.

Apart from the basic requirement that a trade mark must serve as a badge of origin, there are two types of grounds for refusal of registration - absolute grounds and relative grounds - the latter being so called because refusal depends on the mark's similarity with other marks. The absolute grounds for refusal, are, by section 3 of the Trade Marks Act 1994, where the mark is:

- not capable of graphical representation or not capable of distinguishing;
- devoid of any distinctive character;
- exclusively descriptive or laudatory (words of praise) - for example, 'Superb Computers';
- in *bona fide* use in the trade - for example, 'Software Bug';
- of a shape necessary to achieve a technical result which gives substantial value to the goods; or
- contrary to public policy, accepted principles of morality or deceptive - for example, where a dating agency that does not possess or use a computer wishes to register the mark 'ComputaDate'.

Also excluded are certain flags and emblems; not will a mark be registered if it was applied for in bad faith, such as where a tobacco company registered 'Nerit' to try to protect us 'Merit' mark. 'Merit' is a laudatory word and not registrable. The 'Nerit' mark was ordered to be removed from the register of trade marks.

The meaning of 'bad faith' under the 1994 Act is not entirely clear. In *Road Tech Computer Systems Ltd.* v *Unison Software (UK) Ltd.* [1996] FSR 805, the plaintiff traded in computer software for the transportation business and was the registered proprietor of the trade mark 'Roadrunner', which was registered in respect of 'computer software and programs; all included in Class 9 but not including any such goods relating to birds'. The reason for the latter exception was that an American bird, the paisano, is also known as a road-runner. The defendant claimed that the registration was not *bona fide* as the plaintiff had no intention of using the mark. The plaintiff argued that bad faith was more restrictive and required dishonesty. The judge pointed to the difficulty of determining the meaning of bad faith under the 1994 Act, which was not helped by looking at the Directive. Accordingly, he granted the defendant leave to defend the plaintiff's action for infringement as he considered that the plaintiff's argument was not sufficiently clear to allow it summary judgment against the defendant. He added that if the hearing had been a full trail, he would have considered referring this issue to the European Court of Justice for a preliminary ruling.

A mark will be refused on relative grounds if it is identical to an earlier mark or sufficiently similar as to be likely to cause confusion on the part of the public (section 5). This also applies where the earlier mark is used to different goods or services but has achieved such a reputation that the later use of a similar mark would take unfair advantage of it or would be detrimental to it. Thus, attempts by companies other than the Microsoft Corporation to register the word Mocrosoft for software, computer hardware or even bicycles will all fail. Indeed, use of the word in those circumstances without permission would undoubtedly infringe the Microsoft trade mark. Not only will similarity to earlier registered trade marks be grounds for refusal but similarity with works of copyright, designs or unregistered marks will also be likely to lead to a refusal to register the later mark.

Examples of marks turned down in the basis of a similarity with an earlier mark (under the 1938 Act) are:

- 'Huntsman' - earlier mark 'Sportsman' (both cherry brandy), and
- an application showing a picture of three pigs was refused because of a prior word mark 'Three Pigs Brand' (bacon).

In *Coca-Cola of Canada Ltd* v *Pepsi-Cola Co of Canada Ltd* (1942) 59 RPC 127, however, it was held that 'Pepsi-Cola' was not too close to 'Coca-Cola' because the suffix 'Cola' was a word that had become common and descriptive of a type of beverage - that is, a generic word.

Rights and Infringement

The registered proprietor of a trade mark has, by section 9 of the Trade Marks Act 1994, the exclusive right to use the mark in the United Kingdom. Use by another without the proprietor's consent will infringe if within section 10. This states that use of an identical mark for identical goods or services infringes *per se.* Otherwise use of identical or similar marks for similar or identical goods or services infringes only where there exists a likelihood of confusion. Well-known marks may be infringe if an identical or similar mark is used for different goods. However, in this case it still appears that confusion is required. Use must be in the course of trade and extends to signs under which gods are sold, business stationery and advertising.

In respect of whether goods or services are similar, Mr. Justice Jacob laid down some guidelines based on an old test under the 1938 Act which he said was still applicable under the 1994 Act. In *British Sugar plc* v *James Robertson & Sons Ltd* [1996] RPC 281, he said that respective uses and users, the physical nature of the goods or services, the respective trade channels, whether goods are sold alongside each other in supermarkets and the extent to which the goods compete are all useful factors to consider.

Practice as developed at the Trade Mark Registry may also be a factor. In *Avnet Inc* v *Isoact Ltd* [1998] FSR 16, the defendant used the word 'Avnet' for his Internet service for the aviation industry. This service also allowed subscribers to place advertisements on their own Web pages. The plaintiff had registered 'AVNET' for advertising and promotional services and complained of the defendant's use of the word. However, summary judgment was refused. An important factor was that, at the time, Registry practice was to classify the plaintiff's and defendant's activities in different classes of the trade marks register.

Comparative advertising occurs where a trader advertises his goods or services in comparison with those of another trader in a way which includes a reference to that other trader's registered trade mark. It used to infringe under the 1938 Act and may still do so under the 1994 Act. However, under section 10(6) of the 1994 Act comparative advertising will not infringe if it is in accordance with honest practices in industrial or commercial matters and the use without due cause does not takes unfair advantage of, and is not detrimental to, the distinctive character or repute of the trade mark.

Under the 1938 Act the case of *Compaq Computer Corp* v *Dell Computer Corp Ltd* [1992] FSR 93 gives an example of comparative advertising. Dell advertised its computers with a photograph showing its computer and a 'Compaq' computer with both makers names (including the word 'Compaq'; a registered trade mark) and the price of the machines. The plaintiff, Compaq, sued for trade mark infringement, passing off and trade libel. The court granted an interlocutory injunction to Compaq. It was at least highly arguable that Dell infringed the Compaq mark through its advertising. However, there was some doubt as to whether the Compaq mark should have been accepted for registration because of its phonetic similarity with 'Compact', an everyday word.

The 1994 Act marked a sea change in legal response to comparative advertising and it was not long before traders were exploring the boundaries of what was permissible. In *Barclays Bank for plc* v *RBS Advanta* [1996] RPC 307, the defendant advertised its new credit card by reference to the Barclaycard trade mark with a list of features comparing with both cards. Of course, the features selected were designed to show the defendant's card in the best light. The judge said that it was for the proprietor of the trade mark to show that the use was not in accordance with honest practices. Further, persons reading the advertisement would realise that the advertiser would be selective in choosing which features to compare and would also expect a certain amount of hyperbole. What an advertiser can get away with would depend to some extent on the nature of the goods of services concerned.

In *Vodafone Group plc* v *Orange Personal Communication Ltd* [1997] FSR 34, where the defendant advertised by stating that on average subscribers would save £20 per month by switching to its service, the judge accepted that the public would expect some elasticity of price and usage in relation to the quoted average saving. However, if the information is clearly untrue or misleading, comparative advertising is likely to infringe as in *Emaco & Aktiebolaget Electrolux* v *Dyson Appliances, The Times,* 8 February 1999.

Remedies for trade mark infringement are, by section 14, damages, injunctions, accounts or otherwise. There are also orders for delivery-up, erasure or destruction.

Exceptions to Infringement

There are a number of exceptions to trade mark infringement which may be set up as a defence. They include, by section 11:

- use by a person of his own name or address;
- use of indications of the kind, quality, intended purpose, value, geographical origin, the time of production of goods or rendering of services, or other characteristics of goods or services;
- use, where it is necessary, to indicate the intended purpose of a product or service, in particular, as accessories or spare parts (for this and the exceptions above to apply, the use must be in accordance with honest practices in industrial or commercial matters); or
- use of an earlier right (such as an unregistered mark protected by the law of passing off) in a particular locality.

The third exception (actually, its equivalent under section 4(3) of the Trade Marks Act 1938) was considered in *IBM Corp* v *Phoenix International (Computers) Ltd* [1994] RPC 251. Phoenix supplied computer equipment including 'reworked' memory cards which contained IBM components. Phoenix advertised these cards as 'IBM manufactured' and IBM sued for trade mark infringement and for passing off. Phoenix argued, as far as the trade mark infringement was concerned, that it had IBM's implied consent or that the use indicated that the boards were adapted from IBM components. The judge refused to strike out this defence. However, this does not mean that the defence would succeed at a full trial. The wording of section 11 in the 1994 Act is much simpler and, provided the use of the mark in such cases is necessary to indicate the intended purpose (for example, that the cards will work in IBM mainframe computers) and such use accords with honest practices, the defence ought to succeed. It is submitted that the use of the phrase 'manufactured from IBM components' would be more likely to be acceptable than simply 'IBM manufactured'.

As with patents (and designs) there is a remedy in respect of groundless threats of infringement proceedings. This was introduced into trade mark law by the 1994 Act. An example of a successful action was *Prince Plc* v *Prince Sports Group Inc* [1998] FSR 21 in which the defendant, a United States company with a United Kingdom registration in respect of the word 'Prince', threatened the plaintiff, which had registered 'prince.com' as its Internet name, with litigation if it did not transfer the domain name to the defendant. The court held that the threats were unjustified and granted in injunction against their continuance.

Licensing of Trade Marks

The 1938 Act and previous trade mark legislation were very concerned with protecting the public from deceptive practices and one consequence was that an owner of a mark could not register the mark if he intended to allow other persons to use it unless he maintained a link with the other persons' business operations. One way this was done was to register a user of the mark and maintain quality control over the goods to which it was applied. However, if the owner of the mark simply wished to grant licences to others allowing them to use the mark on their own goods in return for a royalty this would result in any application to register the mark being refused. This happened in *Holly Hobbie Trade Mark* [1984] FSR 199 where the applicant to register the mark (a drawing of a little girl in an old-fashioned dress) wished to grant licences to companies in the United Kingdom so that they could apply the drawing to their own products. The House of Lords remarked on how this ban on 'trafficking' in registered trade marks was out of tough with commercial reality. Thankfully, it has now been repealed by the 1994 Act.

The Trade Marks Act 1994 containes much improved provisions for the licensing and sub-licensing of trade marks and takes due account of the existence of character merchandising. Licences may be exclusive or non-exclusive and, in some circumstances, licenses can sue in their own right for infrigement of the trade mark.

For example, say a computer manufacturer, A, owns the trade mark 'Comquik' which is registered in relation to Class 9 (computers and data processing equipment) and Class 41 (education and training etc.) Another hardware company, B making accessories has devised an optical character reader. Company A grants company B an exclusive licence, in respect of the Class 9 mark, to apply the 'Comquik' mark to the OCR equipment it makes in return for a 5 per cent royalty on net sales. A number of organisations providing training in the use of computers, C, D and E, each have non-exclusive licences from Company A allowing them to provide computer training under the name 'Comquik' on the basis of the Class 41 mark. Each pays a small annual fee to Company A. All the organisations B,C, D and E may call upon A to sue in respect of any infringement of the marks and, unless the licence agreement states otherwise, sue in their own name if A refuses to take action or fails to do so within two months of the request. The licence agreements must be in writing, signed by the licensor, and the licences must be noted on the register of trade marks.

Registration of a Trade Mark

Initial registration of a trade mark is for ten years and the renewal period is also ten years (under the old law the periods were seven years and 14 years respectively). There is no upper limit to the duration of a trade mark, which can be renewed again and again providing it has not suffered a period of non-use of five or more years. Many of the trade marks first registered under the Trade Marks Registration Act 1875 (the first Act allowing registration of trade marks) are still registered and in use today, demonstrating the importance of trade marks, including Britain's No.1 trade mark. the BASS 'red triangle' mark.

The fee for registration, which can has recently been reduced, is £200 against one class of goods or services. For each additional class the fee is £50. The renewal fee is £200 plus £50 for each additional class.

The Trade Marks Act 1994 is important in that it paves the way for the European Community Trade Mark (CTM) and provides for the accession of the United Kingdom to the Protocol to the Madrid Agreement which allows for international registration of trade marks. The CTM has a unitary nature and applies throughout the European Community. It is already proving popular and should be a serious consideration for any software company hoping to trade in Europe.

Passing Off

In many ways, the law of passing off is a common law version of trade marks law although of older pedigree. Passing off protects business goodwill and safeguards the public from deception by giving a right of action against anyone who tries to pass off his goods or services as those of someone else. One trader might try to 'cash in' on the goodwill and reputation of another trader by dressing up his goods in such a way that they look like those of that other trader. There is a large overlap between trade marks and passing off and it is not unusual for a legal action to involve both passing off and trade marks. The law of passing off is particularly useful if there is no registered mark to be infringed; perhaps a trader or manufacturer has used a mark for several years without registering it as a trade mark. The mark may fail to qualify for registration or the act complained of might fall outside the scope of trade marks - for example, if it relates to the format of an advertising campaign.

The following example shows the application of passing off. A computer retailer has been operating for three years under the name of 'Computer Equipment Sales' and has a chain of stores in the South of England. The retailer has acquired a reputation for low prices and efficient service. Recently, another retailer has opened a store in the South of England and uses the name of 'Computer Equipment Sales and Service'. Neither name is registered as a trade mark; in fact the names would be refused registration because they are too descriptive of computer retailing generally and would make it difficult for other traders to describe their business activities. As there is a danger that people will be confused and might buy from the second retailer thinking that they are buying from the first, the first should be able to obtain an injunction preventing the second retailer from continuing to use the name he has chosen. If the first retailer has only been in business a short time before the second retailer opens his store then it is unlikely that anything can be done. This is because there has not been sufficient time to build up goodwill connected with the name and, hence, there is little danger that the public will be confused. Similarly, if the second trader's store was in North Wales, it would be unlikely that the first trader's business would be affected, unless his goodwill extends to that location, for example, because he advertises nationally.

Basic Requirements for a Passing-off Action

Before the plaintiff can suffer the type of damage caused by passing off, he must have a reputation associated with goodwill. He must be able to show that his name, mark, get-up or something else which is distinctive about his business will be associated with his goods by the public. If a trader has just started in business he will not succeed in a passing-off action but a newly registered trade mark has immediate protection. However, the necessary reputation could be obtained relatively quickly by an intensive advertising campaign on the national scale.

The ingredients necessary to a successful passing-off action were described in *Erven Warnink Besloten Vennootschap* v *Townend & Sons (Hill) Ltd* [1979] AC 734. The plaintiffs made a liqueur called advocaat which came to be well known. It was made from brandwijn, egg yolks and sugar. The defendants decided to enter this market and they made a drink called 'Keeling's Old English Advocaat' which was made from Cyprus sherry and dried egg powder, an inferior but cheaper drink. This captured a large part of the plaintiff's market in the United Kingdom. It was held that, because of the reputation the plaintiff's product had gained, it should be protected from deceptive use of its name by competitors even though the goodwill was shared by several traders. There was a misrepresentation made by the defendant calculated to injure the plaintiff's business or goodwill and an injunction was granted in favour of the plaintiffs. Lord Diplock laid down the essentials for a passing-off action as:

- a misrepresentation,
- made by a trader in the course of trade,

- to prospective customers of his or ultimate consumers of goods or services supplied by him,
- which is calculated to injure the business or goodwill of another trader, and
- which causes actual damage to a business or goodwill of the trader by whom the action is brought.

Lord Oliver, in *Reckitt & Colman Products Ltd* v *Borden Inc* [1990] 1 All ER 873 (which involved the Jif Lemon and a competing lemon-shaped container for lemon juice), usefully condensed the test for passing off into the presence of the plaintiff's goodwill, a misrepresentation as to the goods or services offered by the defendant and damage or likely damage to the plaintiff's goodwill.

Normally, one would expect damage in the form of lost sales as a result of the defendant's misrepresentation. However, it also extends to damage to the plaintiff's goodwill itself such as where its unique character is eroded. This happened in *Taittinger SA* v *Allbev Ltd* [1993] FSR 641, in which the defendant produced a sparkling non-alcoholic drink which he called 'Elderflower Champagne'. It was sold in green bottles which resembled champagne bottles for £3.50. It was held that this was passing off. Although it was unlikely that many would be deceived in fact, the use of the name champagne in this way would reduce its distinctiveness and, hence injure the champagne manufacturer's goodwill. Although this case has not been overturned, doubts have been expressed about it as it could be perceived to be an undesirable extension of passing off.

The Misrepresentation

The misrepresentation is not necessarily limited to an exact copy of the name or get-up. It may be sufficient if it unfairly imputes a quality into some product or service, such as where a new trader uses another, established, trader's name or mark. An important factor is whether the buying public will be deceived by this unauthorised use of another's name. In deciding this it is not necessary to consider whether members of the public who are knowledgeable about the product are deceived; it may be sufficient if members of the public who have very little knowledge of the product concerned are likely to be deceived (see *J Bollinger* v *Costa Bravo Wine Co Ltd (No.2)* [1961] 1 All ER 561, where an injunction was granted to prevent the use of the name'Spanish Champagne').

As mentioned earlier, a misrepresentation does not have to be confined to a name or mark. The tort of passing off is wide enough to encompass other descriptive material such as slogans nd visual images associated with an advertising campaign if this material has become part of the goodwill of the plaintiff's product. The test is whether the plaintiff has acquired an intangible property right for his product deriving from the distinctive nature of this material which is recognised by the market. In applying the test, the courts have to bear in mind the balance between the plaintiff's investment in the product and the protection of free competition.

In one respect, Lord Diplock's judgment is misleading. He spoke of the misrepresentation being calculated to injure. This suggests that passing off must be deliberate. However, this is not necessary and innocence is not an absolute defence although it may influence the remedies granted.

Common Fields of Activity

If the traders in a passing-off action operate in different fields of activity, it will usually be assumed that there is less danger of confusion and thus less danger of damage to the plaintiff. For example, in *Granada Group Ltd* v *Ford Motor Company Ltd* [1973] RPC 49, the Granada television group could not prevent the Ford Motor Company calling one of their cars a Ford Granada; the court held that there was no danger of confusion because of the different fields of activity- namely television and cars. However, in *Lego UK Ltd* v *Lego M Lemelstrich Ltd* [1983]FSR 155, the Lego company, which makes children's construction kits comprising coloured plastic bricks, was granted an injunction against the manufacturers of coloured plastic irrigation material preventing them using the name 'Lego' as part of the description of the material. The plaintiff was able to show that there was a real danger of confusion and damage to its goodwill.

The plaintiff in *Silicon Graphics Inc* v *Indigo Graphic Systems (UK) Ltd* [1994] FSR 403 supplied computer work-stations for computer-aided design under the 'lingo' mark and had 3 to 5 per cent of the top end of the pre-press market, that is the market for all stages in the printing process prior to actual printing. The defendant made printing equipment under the Indigo name and although the plaintiff did not make printers it sued for trade mark infringement and passing off and applied for an interlocutory injunction. As far as passing off was concerned the plaintiff based its claim on a natural future extension of its business into the manufacture of printers. The judge accepted that there was a triable issue on passing off but, on the balance of convenience, refused the injunction requested.

There is no copyright in a fictitious name and an action in passing off is unlikely to be of much help if the defendant uses that name in relation to different goods or services. The test, as always, is whether the public is likely to be deceived by the use of the name, and in applying this test it is important to consider the fields of activity involved: do the two parties operate in the same or different fields? In the past, judges have not assumed that the public has a detailed knowledge of character merchandising. An example is provided by the case of *Wombles Ltd* v *Wombles Skips Ltd* [1977]RPC 99. Wombles were fictitious animals from a TV series noted for their cleanliness, and for cleaning up litter and putting it to god use. The plaintiff company owed the copyright in the books and drawings of the Wombles, and their main business was granting licences so that manufacturers, in return for a fee, could use the Womble characters to promote their goods. They granted one such licence for waste-paper baskets. The defendant formed a company to lease builder's skips for rubbish. After considerable thought, and remembering the Wombles' clean habits, he decided to call his company Wombles Skips Ltd. In finding for the defendant, the court held that there was no common field of activity and, therefore, no danger of confusion. However, some judges do seem prepared to accept that the public are now more aware of character merchandising and there may be a change in this aspect of passing off before too long.

As technology moves on, sometimes two distinct fields of activity may converge. In *Nad Electronics Inc* v *Nad Computer Systems Ltd*[1997] FSR 380, the plaintiff sold high quality hi-fi systems and the defendant sold computers. Developments in computer technology have resulted in modern personal computers being equipped with compact disc drives capable of playing music CDs. As the fields of audio entertainment and computers are converging, the judge held that the defendant was liable in passing off. An important factor was that the parties' respective goods were similarly advertised and were sold alongside each other in retail outlets.

Internet Domain Names

Every Internet domain name must be different to every other one. However, computers can distinguish the smallest changes, so changing a hyphen to an underscore or a full stop will result in two potentially usable and distinct domain names: for example, smith-jones.com and smith jones.com. If such close names are registered by different persons, it is highly likely there will be confusion on the part of person accessing the relevant internet addresses. There is a distinct possibility of passing off where traders are using similar domain names.

Although a dispute resolution procedure is taking shape, in the past, names have been registered on a first-come, first-served basis without any consideration as to whether the applicant had the right to register the name. Individuals have registered names such as 'mcdonalds.com', 'mtv.com' and 'harrods.com'. Such registrations may have been made in order to sell the addresses to the relevant organisations but, in the United Kingdom, the law of passing off has proved valuable in respect of such practices.

In *Pitman Training Ltd* v *Nominet UK* [1997] FSR 797 two companies, now distinct but sharing a common origin, had similar names; Pitman Training Ltd and Pitman Publishing. The case concerned the right to the domain name 'pitman-co.uk'. Pitman Publishing, which was the second defendant, successfully applied to register that name but did not make use of it for a period of time. Due to an error, the name was re-allocated to Pitman Training Ltd. Pitman Publishing complained when it found out and the name was re-allocated to Pitman Publishing. Pitman Training Ltd commenced proceedings, wanting the name transferred back to it, claiming, *inter alia,* that its use by Pitman Publishing was passing off. However, this failed to impress the judge who thought it highly unlikely that the public would associate the domain name with Pitman Publishing as it had been trading under that name for nearly 150 years. An additional factor was that, when the Pitman companies were sold off in 1985, there was an express agreement that Pitman Training Ltd would not use the Word Pitman without the word 'Training'.

In another case, a company with no connection to Harrods (the famous store in Knightsbridge) registered 'harrods.com' as a domain name. Use of the name was suspended pending the outcome of the dispute resolution procedure provided by the registration body in the United States that but, in the meantime, Harrods launched an action in England for passing off and trade mark infringement: *Harrods Ltd* v *UK Network Services Ltd* [1997] EIPR D-106. Summary judgment was granted and the defendant was ordered to release the domain name to the plaintiff.

In a subsequent case, *Marks & Spencer plc* v *One in a Million Ltd* [1998] FSR 265, five actions were brought by well-known organisations, each of which had substantial goodwill, against the defendant which was a dealer in Internet domain names. It had registered names such as 'bt.org', 'sainsbury.com', 'marksandspencer.co.uk'. The defendant wrote to the organisations offering to sell the domain names. The judge considered that threats of passing off and trade mark infringement were made out and he granted injunctions ordering the defendant to transfer the domain names to the plaintiffs. Similar activities in relation to company names have been described by one judge as a 'scam'.

It is clear that the courts will not look sympathetically at persons who register famous names as domain names with the intention of selling them for large sums of money.

The law of passing off is appropriate, though at the time there may not have been any actual use of the name. The threat of passing off of the intended buyer does not accede is very real where someone registers a name in bad faith. However, real difficulties still may arise, for example, because of the international nature of the Internet. What if an American company, having a Web site in the United States but which can be accessed in the United Kingdom, has a very similar name for its Internet address to that of an English company having an established goodwill? Furthermore, what if a sole trader whose name happens to be John Sainsbury wishes to register john-sainsbury.com as his domain name?

The problems of Internet domain names are taken very seriously by organisations such as the Commission to the European Communities and the World Intellectual Property Organisations, which are looking at ways of regulating the allocation of domain names and resolving disputes.

Remedies for Passing Off

The available remedies are injunctions, including interlocutory injunctions, and damages. An account of profits may be available as an alternative to damages. The damages are assessed by considering the harm done to the plaintiff's goodwill and the lost sales of the plaintiff's product as a result of the passing off. The most desirable remedy is an injunction, preventing the other person or business from continuing to use the plaintiff's established name, get-up or style.

Trade Libel

As action related to passing off is trade label, sometimes referred to as malicious falsehood. This is the commercial equipment of defamation and an example is where a person publishes untrue information concerning the quality of a trader's goods. In terms of computer technology, trade libel would occur if someone falsely claimed that a particular software dealer was trading in pirated software or was in financial difficulties or that a software house's products were defective or would not operate on a particular make of computer. Of course, the information must be false and must be published or stated maliciously. This means made without good cause or excuse and could extend to a reckless statement. In *Compaq Computer Corp* v *Dell Computer Corp Ltd* [1992] FSR 93, discussed earlier in this chapter, it was held that there was an arguable case of trade libel because the computer systems compared were materially different and the representation as to price were misleading and not justified. However, the requirement to prove malice reduces the frequency with which trade libel actions are brought.

In *Joyce* v *Sengupta* [1993] 1 All ER 897, the Vice Chancellor said that essential ingredients for an action in trade libel were falsity and malice. Proof of financial loss was also required, subject to the realisation in section 3 of the Defamation Act 1952 (that is, where the offending words are calculated to cause pecuniary damage and are published in writing or other permanent form).

9 DESIGNS

Introduction and Background

Designs are relevant to computer hardware and semiconductor products. Computer equipment may be designed in such a way that it is aesthetically pleasing as well as functional or there may be something novel about the design which falls short of the scope of patents. Examples of these are an attractive outer case for a computer monitor, a useful case for computer disks with built-in carrying handle, a desk for a computer or a new shape for a portable computer. A considerable amount of effort may have been expended on the design of such items and their components so that they perform their intended function efficiently or are visually attractive. It is right that such effort should be rewarded and this is the purpose of design law which applies to new or original shapes or decorative features.

Unfortunately, this area of law is far from straightforward and the Copyright, Designs and Patents Acts 1988 has done little to simplify matters. To add to the confusion, there are now two forms of right relating to designs; one is subject to registration, the other not. Registered designs are provided for by the Registered Designs Act 1949, amended by the Copyright, Designs and Patents Act 1988. The design right was introduced by the 1988 Act. The history of designs and their relationship with copyright is an interesting study in its own right and in many cases an original design was capable of dual protection under the 1949 Act as a registered design and, through any drawings of the design, under the Copyright Act 1956 (as amended) as an artistic work. The duration of copyright protection was limited to 15 years if the design was registrable; that is, if new and had eye-appeal. However, many functional designs were protected through the artistic copyright subsisting in drawings of the design for the full term of life of author plus 50 years.

Drawings are prepared for most designs and drawings are protected by copyright as artistic works, irrespective of artistic quality. Before the 1988 Act, anyone copying a design would infringe the copyright in a drawing made for the design even though that person had never seen the drawing, because making a three-dimensional copy of a two-dimensional work infringed the copyright in the latter and vice versa. For example, in *Valeo Vision SA* v *Flexible Lamps Ltd* [1995]RPC 205, it was held that the defendant had infringed the copyright in the plaintiff's drawings by making the rear light clusters for lorries represented in the drawings. The only proviso to indirect copying of drawings was that a layman would be able to recognise the one from the other. For example, in *British Leyland Motor Corp Ltd* v *Armstrong Patents Co Ltd* [1986] 2 WLR 400, the defendant made replacement exhaust pipes for the plaintiff's cars by copying the shape and dimensions of the original pipes - a process known as 'reverse engineering'. The plaintiff claimed that the exhaust pipes made by the defendant infringed the copyright in the original drawings of the exhaust systems, although the defendant had not seen the drawings. This argument was accepted by the House of Lords but their lordships refused to allow the plaintiff to assert its rights under copyright law. They said that car owners have an inherent right to repair their cars in the most economical way possible and, for that purpose, are to have access to a free market in spare parts.

Before the 1988 Act, all a person had to do to gain copyright protection for a design was to make a drawing of the design in such a way that the design could be recognised from the drawing (as long as the design did not relate to a spare part). However, the overlap between designs and copyright has been eroded by section 51 of the Copyright, Designs and Patents Act 1988 which states that it is not an infringement of any copyright in a design document or model recording or embodying a design for anything other than an artistic work (or a typeface), to make a article to the design or to copy an article made to the design. In this context, 'design' has the same definition as it does for the purposes of the design right and a design document includes a drawing or other documents such as specifications, photographs and data stored in a computer. This means that industrial designs must fall either within the design right or be registered as a design to be protected unless they are copies or artistic works - for example, sculptures. It is no longer possible, in most cases, to rely on copyright in any drawings or computer data relating to the design. In the case or designs created before 1 August 1989, however, under the transitional provisions in the 1988 Act, a limited copyright protection existed until no later than 1 August 1999. The *Valeo Vision* case mentioned above is an example of the workings of these transitional provisions. It should be noted that the unregistered design right does not subsist in designs created before 1 August 1989.

Many of the intricacies of the law of designs have little relevance to computer technology and a complete discussion of the rights is outside the scope of this book. The following description of the two forms of right is thus necessarily brief and the emphasis is on computer equipment rather than attempting to give a detailed account of design law. Nevertheless, computer equipment manufacturers may find that design law gives valuable protection, either in its own right or as a supplement to other intellectual property rights.

Registered Designs

Section 1 of the Registered Designs Act 1949, as amended, defines registrable designs as being:

> ... features of shape, configuration or ornament applied to an article by any industrial process, being features which in the finished article appeal to and are judged by the eye.

The design must be one intended to be applied to an article. By section 44(1), 'article' means any article of manufacture and includes any part of an article if that part is made and sold separately. In *Ford Motor Co Ltd's Design Applications* [1995] RPC 167, the House of Lords held that the phrase should include the words 'to be' because it was the design that was protected rather than the article. The House suggested the phrase should read... if that part is to be made and sold separately. This requires that the article should have an independent life as an article of commerce and be not merely an adjunct to some larger article of which it is a part. Thus, spare parts which are simply replacements for worn or damaged components are not registrable.

Does this mean that the design of a new computer keyboard or a new computer mouse is not registrable? This is probably going too far as new shapes of such articles are likely to be made to enhance the overall eye-appeal rather than simply be acquired to replace existing components.

Registered design law is concerned primarily with aesthetic aspects and it is not sufficient that the article simply looks pretty or pleasing but the eye-appeal of the article should be such that persons acquiring or using the article do so because of the appearance of articles made to the design. By section 1(3), a design shall not be registered if the appearance of the article is not material; that is, if aesthetic considerations are not normally taken into account to a material extent by persons acquiring or using articles made to the design. In addition, to be registrable, the design must be new (section 1(2)). Examples are a new shape of coffee cup or a new transfer pattern applied to plates or attractive and novel computer furniture and, with such articles, the appearance is important to a person buying it. Even if a person is buying desks for computers or word processors for an office, the appearance of the furniture is a major factor influencing choice. Although, at first sight, an attractively designed computer is less likely to be registrable as a design because the person acquiring one will be primarily influenced by performance rather than appearance, it may still be registrable as the appearance of an item of hardware is not without aesthetic impact, as the current range of Apple computers demonstrate.

Certain things are excluded from registration, such as a method or principle of construction or features of shape or configuration dictated solely in the function the article has to perform, or which depend upon the appearance of another article of which the former article is intended to form an integral part. Methods or principles of construction are verging on patent law, while eye-appeal resulting from function, or from having to match another article, is excluded because it is an indirect effect and would severely restrict, spare part manufacturers. The proprietor (owner) of a design is the author, the person who created it, unless the author is acting in the course of employment or has been commissioned, for money or money's worth, to create the design. If the design has been generated by a computer in circumstances where there is no human author, the person making the arrangements necessary for its creation is treated as the proprietor of the design. The right lasts for five years initially from the date of registration but may be renewed in five-year stages up to a maximum of 25 years. Registration fees are relatively inexpensive.

There are some transitional arrangements to cope with designs which had been registered on or after 12 January 1988 but prior to the more rigorous standards now applicable (that is, prior to 1 August 1989) and which would fail to be registrable subsequently. Those design registrations are limited to a maximum of ten years. Examples are designs which depend upon the appearance of another article of which the article is intended by the author of the design to form an integral part. This exception was introduced by the 1988 Act and does not apply to pre-1 August 1989 designs. Other designs registered prior to 1 August 1989 are limited to 15 years maximum.

The proprietor of a design is given certain exclusive rights in relation to articles embodying the design (for example, making or importing such articles for trade or business purposes or selling or hiring them). A person infringes a registered design by doing any of these acts without the licence of the registered proprietor. Infringement is judged through the eyes of the interested person (typically a consumer), and an infringing design is one which, when applied to the type of article for which the design is registered, is not substantially different. There are other infringements such as making anything to enable articles to be made or doing anything in relation to a kit. Remedies available include injunctions, damages and orders for delivery up or destruction of infringing articles.

The Design Right

Like copyright, this right is automatic and does not depend on registration but, unlike registered designs, there is no requirement for the design to have eye-appeal, althogh if it does, it is not barred from protection by the design right. The result is that the design right will apply to both functional and aesthetic articles and, hence, there is an overalp with registered designs. The potentially longer duration of registered designs is the main reason why a design which lies in this overlap should be registered. Another reason is that a registered design gives a monopoly right while infringement of a design right depends on proof of copying. The design right does not apply to designs recorded (or having articles made in respect of them) prior to 1 August 1989.

A 'design' in the context of the design right is, by section 213 of the Copyright, Designs and Patens Act 1988:

> ... the design of any aspect of the shape of configuration (whether external or internal) of the whole or part of the article.

This definition is not too dissimilar to that relating to registered designs. The design right applies to all manner of industrial designs whether functional or not. A design must be original and section 213(4) states that a design is not original if it is commonplace in the design field in question at the time of its creation. It has been held, in *C & H Engineering* v *F Klucznik & Sons Ltd* [1992] FSR 421, that this requires a two-stage test. First, is the design original in a copyright sense; that is, did the design originate from the author? If the answer is 'yes' then it must be determined whether the design is commonplace (at the time of its creation). The design, therefore, must be the independent work of the designer which was not commonplace in the relevant field when created.

The test for originality was once more considered in *Ocular Sciences Ltd* v *Aspect Vision Care Ltd* [1997] RPC 289. Mr Justice Laddie pointed out that the word 'commonplace' is new to English law and could be traced back to the EC Directive on the legal protection of semiconductor topographies, discussed in the next chapter. He accepted as plausible a definition that any design which is 'trite, trivial, common-or garden, hackneyed or of the type which would excite no peculiar attention in those in the relevant art is likely to be commonplace'. Nevertheless; that did not mean that a design which is made up of such commonplace features must necessarily itself be commonplace. A new and exciting design could be produced from the most trite of ingredients providing the combination itself is no commonplace.

The *Ocular Sciences* case is also authority for the view that detail differences, which may be too small to be readily distinguished by the naked eye, could be protected by the design right. In that case, it was accepted that, in principle, the design right could apply to details of a range of soft contact lenses, although, in the event, Mr Justice Laddie decided that the designs, as a whole, were commonplace.

As with registered designs, there are exceptions to design right protection. The first exception, a method or principle of construction, is common to both rights. The second exception is subdivided into features of shape or configuration of an article which:

- enable the article to be connected to, or placed in, around or against, another article so that either article may perform its function (the 'must-fit' exception); or
- are dependent upon the appearance of another article of which the article is intended by the

designer to form an integral part (the 'must-match exception).

These exceptions are significant for manufacturers and suppliers of spare parts. The former part of the exception applies to 'functional' spare parts which have to be a particular shape to fit another article. An exhaust pipe for a car will fall into this exception. Any piece of computer equipment which has to be fitted to some other equipment, such as a replacement 'card' (printed circuit board containing integrated circuits) which has to be a certain shape, or have a certain type of connector, in order to fit into a computer, will also fall into the first part of the exception. This exception is directed at rationalising the *British Leyland* case eventually may need replacement or additional parts should be able to obtain those parts in a free market at reasonable cost. It a design right monopoly were to be granted to spare parts, manufacturers of cars, washing machines, computers, etc. would be able to control the supply the price of spare parts and might be tempted to charge exorbitant prices for them.

The second part of the exception (which is, in effect, identical to the equivalent exception for registered designs) would apply to spare parts such as replacement body panels for cars where the design is dictated by the appearances of the car, but it is unlikely that many computer spare parts will fall into this category.

It could apply in respect of replacement parts for items of computer equipment such as a replacement paper feed tray or some other part, having visual significance intended to replace some worn out or damaged part. A further exception to design right protection is surface decoration, being more appropriately protected by registration as a design.

The surface decoration exception was considered in *Mark Wilkson Furniture Ltd* v *Woodcraft Designs (Radcliffe) Ltd* [1998] FSR 63, a case concerning fitted kitchen furniture. It was said, in that context, that the exclusion was not restricted to features lying on he surface which were essentially two-dimensional such as a painted finish but could extend to other features such as small grooves. However, other features might not be excepted where, for example, they themselves were subject to surface decoration. A cornice or recessed door panels might be subject to the right.

With registered designs the person creating the design is known as the author but, and for no explicable reason, the person creating the design is known as the author but, and for no explicable reason, the person creating a design which is subject to a design right is known is its designer. The owner of a design right is the designer unless he creates the design in the course of his employment or has been commissioned to create it. A computer-generated design belongs to the person making the arrangements necessary for the creation of the design. Design right lasts for 15 years from the end of the calendar year in which it was first recorded in a design document (which includes storage in a computer) or an article was made to the design, unless articles have been made available for sale or hire within the first five years, in which case the right lasts only a further ten years.

The result of the provisions relating to duration is that the owner of the right can only have a maximum of ten years to exploit the design commercially. This period will be reduced if the owner fails to market articles made to the design within the first five years. Effectively, and in a commercial sense, the right lasts for ten years with the owner being given a five-year breathing space within which to bring articles made to the design to the market place. The right is further diluted because licences are available as of right during the last five years. This means that anyone can exploit the design during its last five years subject to the payment of a royalty to the design right owner. Failing agreement of the terms of the license, the Comptroller-General of Patents, Designs and Trade Marks will settle the terms.

Infringement occurs when a person makes articles to the design or makes a design document recording the design for the purpose of enabling such articles to be made. This covers identical articles and articles made to substantially the same design. There are also secondary infringements where a person 'deals' with infringing articles, for example, by importing, selling or hiring. Remedies for infringement are as for copyright but there are no criminal penalties for dealing with infringing articles, In *C & H Engineering* v *F Klucznik & Sons Ltd* [1992] FSR 421, the defendant claimed his design right in a pig fender, a three-sided box structure, had been infringed. The 'original' part of the design was a round bar welded around the top. Aldous J. said the question of infringement involved an objective test through the eyes of a person to whom the design is directed. There was no infringement here because the plaintiff's and defendant's articles were not exactly or substantially the same. Although a design can relate to a part of an article, it seems that the whole article must be looked at when deciding infringement.

Apart from the appearance of computer hardware, the design right is important for the computer industry because a variant of it is used to protect the layout of circuitry within semiconductor products, particularly silicon chips.

European Community Developments

There are proposals for harmonising design rights

throughout the European Community and for Community-wide design rights. A proposal for a harmonising Directive has been published (OJ [1993] C345/14]. This proposes a two-tier system of rights - one based on registration, the other coming into existence automatically, not unlike the present mechanisms for design protection in the United Kingdom. The registered design will last for up to 25 years though there will be no requirement for eye- appeal. The integrated informal right will endure for three years only but will, in other respects, apply to designs that are registrable.

A one-year period of grace is proposed so that the owner of the design can test the market by selling articles made to the design without compromising the novelty of the design. The informal design right will afford protection during this period and will also be useful for designs with a short commercial life, in fields where fashions change regularly.

A Directive on harmonising registered design systems was adopted by the European Parliament and the Council on 13 October 1998 (OJ [1998] L289/28. This affects only the registered design system. There are some similarities to the present United Kingdom registered design law system but the Directive does not have any specific requirement for eye-appeal apart from being focused on the appearance of the whole or part of a product.

The design must be new and have an individual character and component parts are registrable only if they remain visible in normal use and it is those visible features which are new and have an individual character. A design is not new if it has been made available to the public before the date of the filling (or priority date) of the application. As with the proposed Community design there is a 12-

month period of grace, something new to United Kingdom intellectual property law.

The right will last for five years initially and be renewable in five-year periods up to a maximum of 25 years. It has come into effect by 28 October 2001.

10 SEMICONDUCTOR PRODUCTS

Integrated circuits, commonly known as 'silicon chips' or, simply 'chips' are of tremendous importance to the computer industry and to other areas of industry and commerce which rely heavily on information technology. Without the miniaturisation that they bring, the powerful personal computer of today would have remained an impossibility. Integrated circuits are made from layers of materials by a process which includes etching using various 'masks'(templates) which are made photographically. Alternatively, electron beam machines are used. The simplest integrated circuit consists of three layers, one of which is made of semiconductor material. A semiconducting material, in terms of its ability to conduct electricity, is one which lies between a conductor such as copper and an insulator such as rubber. Examples of semiconducting materials include silicon, germanium, selenium and gallium arsenide. A wafer of semiconductor material is coated with a layer of silicon oxide (an insulator) and the electronic components (for example, transistors) are made by chemically doping the semiconductor material with impurities through holes etched through the oxide. Finally, an aluminium coating is applied which is partly evaporated using a mask, leaving behind the interconnections between components formed in the semiconductor layer.

The patterns formed by the processes of etching and/or evaporation of the conductor make the electrical circuitry of the integrated circuit. These patterns represent the circuit design. The processes involved in the making of integrated circuits fall within the province of patent law and the first patents for integrated circuits were filed in the late 1950s, the most important one being developed by Noyce of the Fairchild Semiconductor Corporation in 1959. Licences were readily available and in 1961 the first chips were available commercially. Now that tthe early patents have expired and much of the know-how lies in the public domain, it is essential that the considerable effort that goes into the design and development of new integrated circuits is protected. New types of integrated circuits are unlikely to be patentable for lack of novelty because many are simply more efficient or miniatured forms of well-known electronic circuits or because, even if new, they do not involve an inventive step, being obvious to persons skilled in the art.

Semiconductor Design Right

One view was that integrated circuits were protected by copyright through drawings or photographs as most of the masks used in the manufacturing process were produced photographically and would be protected as photographs. This was uncertain, however, because of the requirements in the Copyright Act 1956 for a non-expert to recognise the circuit as being a three dimensional reproduction of the drawings or photographs. As a result of a European Community Directive (Legal Protection of Topographies of Semiconductor Products (87/54/EEC, OJ [1987] L24/36)), the Semiconductor Products (Protection of Topography) Regulations 1987 were laid before Parliament and came into force on 7 November 1987. These regulations gave a right (called a topography right) in the layout of an integrated circuit. With the advent of the Copyright, Designs and Patents Act 1988, however, it was decided to replace these regulations with an amended version of the new design right by the Design Right (Semiconductor Regulations) 1989, which came into force on 1 August 1989. The new right, referred to hereinafter as the 'semiconductor design right', draws heavily from Part III of the Copyright, Designs and Patents Act 1988 which deals with the unregistered design right but with some differences as far as semiconductor topographies are concerned. The manner in which this has been done is most inept and we now have the situation where some sections of the 1988 Act are different depending on whether they are being applied to semiconductors or other designs. References below to the 1988 Act are to the Copyright, Designs and Patents Act 1988 as it applies to the semiconductor design right.

The 1989 regulations are similar to the 1987 regulations in several respects; for example, it is the topography of a semiconductor which is protected, being, by regulation 2, a design which is either:

(a) the pattern fixed, or intended to be fixed, in or upon
   (i) a layer of a semiconductor product, or
   (ii) a layer of material in the course of and for the purpose of the manufacture of semiconductor product, or

(b) the arrangement of the patterns fixed, or intended to be fixed, in or upon the layers of a semiconductor product in relation to one another.

A semiconductor product is defined as:

> ... an article the purpose, or one of the purposes, of which is the performance of an electronic function and which consists of two or more layers, at least one of which is composed of

> semiconducting material and in or upon one or more of which is fixed a pattern appertaining to that or another function.

These definitions are not very helpful being somewhat tautologous but despite that is fairly plain that all original integrated circuits will be covered by the regulations. If the description of integrated circuits given earlier is now considered, it can be seen that the requirements are met: there are two or more layers (usually three), one layer is made of a semiconducting material and a pattern is fixed upon it for the purpose of performing an electronic function. Normally, the ingenuity which requires protection is in the circuitry represented by the patterns formed by the conducting materials, but the regulations are wider in the sense that they will apply in situations where the ingenuity lies not so much in the horizontal patterns themselves but in the vertical arrangements of layers.

Incidentally, the printed circuit boards commonly found inside most electronic equipment, ranging from transistor radios to computers, are not protected by these regulations because, although composed of layers (usually two), neither layer is made from semiconductor material. The board is made of insulating material and a conductor which is etched away leaving the circuitry to which electronic components are later attached by solder. Generally, however, printed circuit boards will be protected, through their preparatory drawings, by copyright as artistic works and, as they are intended to be read by the person making the printed circuit board, as literary works. Alternatively, they could be considered to be protected by the design right as a configuration when all the components are mounted onto the board. A single electronic component such as a silicon diode or a transistor is not protected because it possesses no topography within the meaning of the regulations. A novel electronic device or component might be patentable in its own right if the other requirements for a patent are satisfied, as may be a new process for manufacturing integrated circuits and other electronic devices.

Subsistence and Ownership

To be protected, the semiconductor topography must be original and it is not original if it is commonplace in the design field in question at the time of its creation (section 213 of the 1988 of Act). 'Original' is liberally integrated in copyright law, but the requirement that the topography is not commonplace is likely to lead to a much narrower interpretation (see the discussion of *C & H Engineering* v *F Klucznik & Sons Ltd* in Chapter 11). The two-stage test of originality and not being commonplace derives directly from the European Directive on the legal protection of topographies of semiconductor products, Article 2(2), which states:

> The topographicality of a semiconductor topography shall be protected in so far as it satisfies the conditions that it is the result of its creator's own intellectual effort and is not commonplace in the semiconductor industry.

Note the preferred European definition of originality being the creator's own intellectual effort, a similar test to that used in respect of copyright databases and, although not expressly stated in the Copyright, Designs and Patents Act 1988, computer programs. It is arguable that the United Kingdom model of protection for semiconductor topographies is unsatisfactory as the first part of the test remains that of originality not intellectual effort. The traditional United Kingdom approach to originality has been fairly generous.

Article 2(2) goes on to confirm that where a topography comprises, commonplace elements, it may still be protected if, taken as whole, the conditions of originality and not being commonplace are satisfied. The modified version of the design right which applies to semiconductor topographies, like the Directive, does not attempt to define 'commonplace'. In *Ocular Sciences Ltd* v *Aspect Vision Care Ltd* [1997] RPC 289, Mr Justice Laddie accepted counsel's submission that it would be likely to cover designs which were 'trite, trivial, common-or-garden, hackneyed or of a type which would excite no peculiar attention in those in the relevant art'. Although this seems to be a good working definition, equally applicable to semiconductor topographies and other designs protected by the design right, it must be noted that this part of Laddie J's judgment can only be regarded as a helpful guideline as he had already decided that the defendant had not copied the plaintiff's designs.

Apart from being required to be original (and not commonplace), the design has to qualify for protection. These requirements differ somewhat from those that apply to copyright. Qualification is based on the citizenship or domicile of the creator of the topography (or his employer or commissioner) or the person by whom and country in which semiconductors containing the topography are first marketed.

The qualification requirements are similar to those that apply in respect of the design right but there are a number of differences. In particular, the rule that a commissioned design qualifies by virtue of the commissioner (if he is a qualifying person) is subject to any agreement in writing to the contrary. This proviso is missing from the basic design right model. The same applies to designs created in the course of employment. There is also a change with respect to semiconductor designs which qualify by virtue of the first marketing, in that the person must be exclusively authorised to put the semiconductor products on the market in every member state of the EU, whereas for other designs the exclusively relates to the United Kingdom only. There are a number of other differences concerning territorial scope for qualification purposes. Protection is also afforded to semiconductor topography designs to persons from the Isle of Man, the Channel Islands and any colony and to firms or companies formed under the law of Gibraltar and to firms or companies having a substantial business activity in a number of other countries including Iceland, Japan, Liechtenstein, Norway, Switzerland and the United States of America.

One reason the 1989 regulations were passed was to satisfy the United States as to the protection offered in the United Kingdom, otherwise there might have been some doubt as to whether topographies derived from the United Kingdom would have been afforded protection in the United States.

Ownership of the semiconductor design right is dealt with by amending section 215 of the 1988 Act. The first owner of the right is the designer unless the design is created in pursuance of a commission or in the course of employment in which cases the commissioner or the employer respectively is the first owner of the right, subject to any written agreement to the contrary. If the right arises by reference to the first marketing of the article, such as where a semiconductor topography is designed by a Brazilian in Brazil but is marketed in the United Kingdom by an importer who is exclusively authorised to put articles made to the design on the market in every member state of the EC, then the importer will be deemed to own the semiconductor design right. By section 214 of the 1988 Act, the designer is the person who creates the design and in the case of a computer-generated design, the designer is the person by whom the arrangements necessary for the creation of the design are undertaken. The recognition of computer-generated topographies was added by the 1989 regulations.

Duration

The duration of the semiconductor design right depends on if and when the topography is commercially exploited. Normally, by section 216 of the 1988 Act, the right endures for ten years from the end of the year in which it was first commercially exploited (anywhere in the world). If the right is not commercially exploited within 15 years of the creation of the topography, however; the right expires 15 years from the time the topography was first recorded in a design document or the time when an article was first made to the design, whichever is the earlier. These rules mean that it might benefit the owner of a topography right for him to sit on that right until such a time as it can be exploited to its full potential as long as this is done a reasonable period before the 15 years have expired. Given the speed of development in the industry, however, this is unlikely to be a great advantage as there is a danger that the product will be obsolete before it has been exploited. As with the unregistered design right as it applies to other articles, the semiconductor design right is automatic and does not require registration. Bearing this on mind (and the same applies to the unregistered design right generally and to copyright works) it is worthwhile keeping good records of the development of the topography so that the date it was created can be proved in a court of law. This is to prevent a copier claiming that he was the first to develop the topography in question. By regulation 9 of the 1989 regulations, licences of right are not available in relation to semiconductors as they are with other designs (such licences are normally available in the last five years of a design right).

Right and Infrigement

The semiconductor design right is, by section 226(1) of the 1988 Act as substituted for semiconductor topographies, the exclusive right to reproduce the design by making a design document (which includes data stored in a computer) recording the design for the purpose of enabling such articles to be made. A person doing either of the above infringes the right whether he does it in relation to the whole or a substantial part of the topography. There are important exceptions to infringement connected with research, non-commercial or educational purposes. The regulations have one very unusual effect in that it is permissible to make a reproduction of a topography for the purpose of analysing or evaluating that topography or the concepts, processes, systems or techniques embodied in it by section 226(1A) of the 1988 Act as substituted. Furthermore, by regulation 8(4), it is not an infringement of the semiconductor design right to create another original topography as a result of such analysis or evaluation or to reproduce that other topography. Therefore, a form of reverse engineering' is positively encouraged allowing the knowledge gained from an inspection of an existing topography to be used in the design of a new topography. In practice, a limiting factor will be the requirement for the new topography to be original and not commonplace. On reflection, this exception is probably justified on the grounds that to provide otherwise might inhibit innovation in this very fast-moving field where the existing technology is being built upon all the time while property rights still subsist in that existing technology. However, this runs counter to basic principles of intellectual property rights; such an activity with respect to a copyright work would probably infringe copyright because any derivative work would contain a copy of a substantial part of the first work. It will really depend on how the word 'substantial' is interpreted in terms of the semiconductor design right. For the reverse engineering provisions to have any real effect, the word 'substantial' would have to be interpreted in quantitative sense which would run counter to copyright law.

If an infringement of a topography right also infringes copyright, the semiconductor design right is suppressed leaving remedies to be pursued under copyright law only, by section 236 of the 1988 Act. This is the same as with other designs. Regard must be had to section 51 of the Copyright, Designs and Patents Act 1988, however, which removes from the scope of copyright infringement the making of articles to designs recorded in design documents (or embodied in models) unless the design is for an artistic work. It is highly unlikely that semiconductor designs will be considered to be artistic works. Design documents include drawings, photographs and computer data and the effect of section 51 is to remove copyright protection from semiconductor topographies leaving: the modified right with its limited duration as the only form of legal protection, apart from the law of confidence which will protect until, at least, the semiconductor products are made available to the public. Compliance with the European Directive, following pressure from the United States, has had the opposite effect to that intended: it has significantly reduced protection in the United Kingdom from what was potentially available under copyright law.

Remedies for Infringement

Remedies for infringement are as for the design right generally and are injunctions, damages and accounts of profits 'or otherwise' (section 229 of the 1988 Act). Additional damages are also provided for as they are for copyright infringement and the unregistered design right generally. Orders for delivery up and destruction are also available. In the case of innocent infringement (if the defendant did not know and had no reason to believe that the semiconductor design right subsisted in the article) damages are not available although other remedies may be, such as an account of profits.

Secondary infringement — for example, where a person imports or deals with infringing copies of semiconductors - does not apply if they have already been marketed in the United Kingdom or any member state of the European Community by or with the licence of the owner of the right or other person entitled to do so.

11 CYBERPSYCHOLOGY AND CYBORGS

The impact and extension of computer technology continues unabated as schools and businesses are encouraged to get on-line and join the microserf bandwagon. At stake is the ability to access, and make available, information: 'Information has become our clothing, our food, our air and free access to it has become a basic human right' (Pesce, 1992). But as the computer revolution increases its influence and hold on everyday life social and cultural patterns swirl into place which connect with a variety of discourses that inhabit the pullulating technological matrix. Such technologies map the virtual territories that are being opened up and colonised. This mapping also throws into question the relationship that humans have with technology and therefore also remaps the lived world. For example: Weather satellites alter perceptions of weather systems, as land masses and hot and cold fronts offer visible plans far broader than the depiction of merely local effects. Such changes are not possible unless articulated through a technological paradigm (see Berland, 1996; Zizek, 1997).

A variety of approaches has been employed to examine the discourses of new technology and, as such, interest in its effects and consequences are not restricted to a single discipline. Links are forged between cultural theory and technoscience that map the extent of the technological matrix and its political effects. *Cyberpsychology* is one of the approaches. It rests uncomfortably, we hope, on a boundary. This allows it to engage with debates and wider issues within the matrix while acknowledging the long association that psychology, and particularly cognitive psychology, has with new technologies. In doing, so, cyberpsychology, highlights 'some of the relationships between psychological knowledge and social control' (Gordo-Lopez, 1995: 7).

Cyberpsychology looks to the emerging psycho-social spaces and virtual communities of the technological matrix as sites of possibility that aid the development of strategies and political critiques. It is therefore subversive and enabling, indicating points and means of resistance. The cyborg is a central image and concept within cyberpsychology. It is the site, the 'body' that can be made legible and can be thought of as the starting point for explorations of the relationships between humans and technology.

Interest in cyborgs has been fuelled by speculative science fiction narratives that offer the opportunity to return to the present: 'New forms of experience and social relationships are created as science fiction, and these new forms offer distinctive vantage points, different arrays of subject positions from which to view the present' (Parker, 1997: 190). Another related vantage point from which to view the present is the corpus of superhero narratives. The superhero genre often partakes of science fiction discourse but, for the most part, the stories are set in the present. In this instance superhero narratives offer an instructive means of comparison with cyborg imagery.

The American comic book has two main tributary sources. First, the popularity of dime novels in the first half of the twentieth century and, second, collections of comic strips used in marketing campaigns in the mid-1930s. The first issue of *Action Comics* (a DC Comics title) in June 1938 featured a brightly coloured figure in dramatic pose on its front cover. The character was Superman, and his popularity was to forge the success of the superhero genre. Many imitators soon followed in his speeding wake. One of these, a year later, was Batman. They are probably the best known comic characters, having had continuous success in comics and other media.

The focus in this chapter is on the construction of superhero and cyborg identity. We display similarities between superheroes and cyborgs as they appear in popular cultural representations, and demonstrate that the cyborg and superhero resist the consequences of boundary transgression and that the political affinities, so often desired of cyborgs, are open to naturalisation, for example around the thematic of masculinity. However, when the emphasis is moved away from the analysis if identity to that of reporting *events* then the superhero and the cyborg can be reconfigured politically to enable various forms of domination and transgression to be examined from a number of alternative vantage points. In this way it is possible to develop strategies that examine and map the resistances and changes within emerging psycho-social spaces and develop and cyborg language that maps and inscribes more than just individual bodies.

What is a Cyborg?

Theory and descriptions pertaining to cyborgs resonate uncomfortably with the salient features of many comic book heroes. The cyborg offers a critical approach to superheroes, but this is reciprocated as superheroes offer a critical approach to cyborgs. Before comparing cyborgs with superheroes it is necessary to outline some of their chief characteristics.

The term 'cyborg' (coined by Clynes and Kline, 1960) is a contraction of 'cybernetic organism' and a result of research into cybernetic systems. These are 'complex, feedback-controlled systems, responsive to the flows of matter and energy that pass or "dissipate" through them' (Marsden, 1996:7) Research into such systems was important during and after the war for military and space research.

Haraway's (1985) germinal essay, ' A cyborg manifesto: science, technology and socialist- feminism in the late twentieth century' has, as Marsden (1996: 6) indicates, 'attained cult status in many branches of contemporary theory', and is important for its explicitly political description and definition of cyborg imagery.

A cyborg at its simplest is the conjunction of humans and technology. More frequently it refers to the extension or enhancement of the body through its fusion with technology. Cyborgs are therefore *hybrids* of human and machine, or machines and organisms. Cyborgs are not static or held to one form. Different types of prosthesis lead to a variety of cyborg types that relate to the environment through a technological paradigm which re-articulates notions of identity and subjectivity. This is one of the starting points for Haraway's exploration of cyborg affectivity. Cyborgs are more than the technological enhancement of human ability, but the site where the relationship between nature and culture are reworked.

Haraway's cyborg is a complex hybrid. It integrates more than a technological paradigm connecting with a variety of competing discourses in order to reinvigorate feminist-socialist politics - hence the subtitle of the paper. The cyborg is the central figure in an attempt to write an ironic myth which also functions as a 'rhetorical strategy and political method', one Haraway ' would like to see more honoured within socialist-feminism' (1991:149). It is a boundary creaturc resident in the hinterland between fact and fiction, and it partakes in science fiction discourse and lived experience. Haraway argues for the cyborg as a 'fiction mapping our social and bodily reality and as an imaginative resource suggesting some very fruitful couplings' (ibid: 150). The cyborg therefore appears to function as a descriptive mechanism that aids critiques and suggests possibilities, but it is a great deal more than just 'an imaginative resource'. The cyborg is our ontology; it gives us our politics' (ibid.). There is, as Marsden reminds us, something 'unashamedly utopian' about Haraway's cyborg vision (Marsden, 1996:6). It does not revel in the dystopian visions of cyberpunk but prefers to consider the possibilities inherent to affinity and hybridity. An important aspect of Haraway's cyborg vision is the rejection of 'Western' origin stories.

The cyborg appears, and is politicised, at the points where boundaries are transgressed. Such transgressions are also acts of creation that occur outside Oedipal narratives: 'In a sense, the cyborg has no origin story in the Western sense' (Haraway, 1991: 150). Cyborgs are illegitimate, unimpressed by notions of organic wholeness and are 'oppositional, utopian, and completely without innocence' (ibid: 151). They are, of course, the progeny of military research, of patriarchal capitalism and state socialism. This is not a handicap as there is no need to remain faithful to their fathers, who are 'inessential' (ibid.)

The cyborg myth written by Haraway, then, is a fiction, a seductive non-Oedipal narrative that functions are utopian cyberpunk and political manifesto. The cyborg characteristics she describes desired characteristics. She is, in effect, defining a cyborg identity that has nothing to do with any actual lived empirical subjectivity, that refuses hierarchies and dualisms and posits a postgender world in which 'we are all chimeras, theorised and fabricated hybrids of machine and organism' (ibid.: 150). It is in the sidestepping of the Western origin story that the cyborg has its roots. I will now look at two characters whose origin stories are clearly based within Oedipal narratives in order to problematise some cyborg characteristics.

Superheroes and Origin Stories

One of the defining characteristics of superheroes is the *origin story*. Such stories provide explanations of the characters' powers, why they assumed hero identities and the nature of their campaigns. As such, they supply the characters with personal histories and psychological motivation and so render them meaningful. Origin stories, therefore, can be understood as myths of origin that are invoked to offer convincing accounts of superhero subjectivity. Probably the best known examples of superhero origin stories are those of Batman and Superman. The origin stories have been extensively used in the comic books to update the characters for new audiences (most notably in the 1986 revamp of *Superman: The Man of Steel*), to help the transition to other media, to transfer the characters to other times and settings (for example in the *Elseworld* series) and to explain the characters' actions in the face of adversity and possible (but never final) defeat. The origin stories are simple and easily precised. For Batman it is thus:

> As Bruce [Wayne] and his parents walked home from a movie, a nameless thug attacked them. Attempting to steal the mother's necklace, the hoodlum shot and killed both mother and father when the latter attempted to resist. A traumatised Bruce swore to take vengeance through a war on crimilals... Seeking both disguise and

> psychological advantage he decided that 'I shall become a bat'. (Urichio and Pearson 1991: 194).

And for Superman:

> A brilliant scientist fails to persuade the ruling council of his planet's imminent demise. To save his son he places him in a rocket ship and blasts him toward a distant planet. The child is found by a Kansas farmer and his wife, who raise him as their own. As he grows he develops amazing abilities. He realises that he must put these powers to the benefit of mankind and so takes the role of Superman to be able to act anonymously and protect his identity. (Heggs, 1996:3)

These two stories have underpinned the enduring nature of the characters. Over the period during which the characters have been fighting to preserve the public peace they have not aged. The origin story confers authenticity on the various versions of the characters and all take place in the present. The origin story therefore functions as a fountain of youth and bestows a form of textual immoratality. There is obviously a history to the various versions of the characters, but each incarnation contains its own present and refers to its own past and future. There is therefore a spatial relationship between version that resignifies the present of the narrative around common themes. For Walter Benjamin (1992:91) 'storytelling is the art of repeating stories, and this art is lost when the stories are no longer retained'. The Superman and Batman origin stories have been endlessly repeated and in the process altered to fit the needs of the plotlines.

This is what Barthes (1977), referring to the 'myth', called the 'privation of history'. Each innovation of an origin story is drained of meaning and resignified. As the process is repeated 'history' evaporates' leaving only a 'beautiful object'. Myths are, therefore, constructed, they 'cannot possibly evolve from the "nature" of things' (1977: 110). As the public becomes aware of these mythic stories, and as these stories are retold and elaborated upon, they are also *depoliticised*. In other words the constant repetition make politically constructed relationships appear to be natural. So, we might now even take it for granted that a young Bruce Wayne should grow up to take on the guise of a Batman, and that an alien baby should land in Kansas and eventually become Superman. Narrative coherence is therefore structured by the use of origin stories. By placing them into wider contexts the characters can be read alongside contemporary concerns and anxieties that are reflected and resisted within the texts. It is therefore possible to see how the narratives operate as a screen for the projection of fantasies and desires. These fantasies and desires are also found within other genres and disciplines, in this instance, cyborgs.

A closer look at one version of both origin stories will aid the critique and comparison with cyborgs. The example I have chosen is *World's Finest* (Gibbons and Rude, 1992). The story focuses on two orphanages in Gotham and Metropolis and the interest shown in them by Lex Luthor and the Joker, the best known adversaries of Batman and Superman. As the plot unfolds it becomes evident that Luthor intends to expand his business concerns in Gotham, while the Joker seizes the opportunity to holiday in Metropolis. Neither Superman nor Batman can cope with the series of disturbances caused by the visiting foe. An agreement is reached whereby the heroes swap cities in order to maintain the peace and thwart the plans of their antagonists. The origin stories are invoked early in the story, following an introduction to both cities and the problems faced therein.

There is a juxtaposition of the panels in the comic which visually demonstrates that the form of the stories are structurally equivalent, and also that the characters are opposites, positioned at either extreme of a superhero spectrum: 'Their primal, complementary qualities have given rise to the entire field [of comics] and, arguably, they define its parameters' (Gibbons, 1992: in introduction). The origin stories, as they are represented in this instance, show how the tragic loss of (biological) parents haunts the characters. An EEG-like framing of the panels indicates tthe increasing excitement and agitation connected with the recollection of the origin stories. These stories are shown to haunt the characters. The first frames of the origin story show concerned and caring parents, and the actions taken to protect the children. The first two panels of the second page show the moments in which the course of the characters' lives are irrevocably changed. The following panels contain the consequences of the freeze-framed irreversible moments. A small child is held in the arms of a woman while a man behind her fights to put out a fire; a young boy is led away by a policeman while another searches for a pen and readies his notebook. In the background of each panel is what has been lost by the characters, their biological parents. In the foreground there are indications of their future roles. Such dreams are disturbing, threatening, they awaken the characters, who react in different ways.

The origin, stories, as outlined and described, are indicative of exactly the kind of 'Western' origin stories maligned by Haraway. A fall from grace, 'from originary fullness is illustrated to which the heroes yearn to return. Clark Kent and Bruce Wayne have been wrenched- more than separate - from the comfortable state of fullness. But where the cyborg 'skips the step of original unity, of identification with nature in the Western sense' (Haraway,

1991: 151), the superhero places a firm foot on the ladder's first rung. They are beholden to the Oedipal narrative, and donning a tight-fitting costume acts as a cover that allows Batman and Superman to operate at a distance from societal regulation. The origin stories of Batman and Superman are precisely that, they refer to the subjective origins of the heroes, not of the mild-mannered reporter or of the playboy millionaire. The origin stories may be thought of as *primal scene fantasies* (Laplanche and Pontalis, 1973). Such scenes are concerned with the origins of the subject (in this instance, of the superheroic individual) and refer to a past event that can be returned to and retroactivity resignified in order to make sense of the subject's current situation. They are fantasies, and need not necessarily have occurred to be psychically effective. Each case is rooted in the Oedipal narrative.

In Freudian theory it is through the internalisation of the Oedipal narrative that society is supported. The desire to kill the father leads to feelings of guilt, the inevitable effect of the oedipus complex and development of superegoic structures. The constant return to the origin story is indicative of a compulsion to repeat 'and the regression it implies leads to the annihilation of the subject' (Penley, 1986: 81). Becoming Batman or Superman might, therefore, be seen as the visible symptom of guilt. The superhero identity therefore serves to protect, not the society in which it appears, but the individual against threats to a past fantasy state found in the 'family'.

Superman and Batman may, then, be thought of as boundary creatures but not as boundary transgressors. To transgress the boundary between human and non-human would require Superman and Batman to retire from their day jobs. Their opponents do not have this reservation, particularly those of the Batman. The Joker, for instance, rarely tries to hide the stigmata of his appearance. Batman and Superman serve the societies in which they act by protecting it, by combating threats to the status quo and this is supported by their close associations with institutional signs of public morality, Gotham City Police and *The Daily Planet*. To act within the boundary is to mark its limits and signal and resistance to its transgression. The origin stories depict a rupture in the natural order of things, based in a family structure, that opens a subjective space in which the superhero identity can eventually be placed.

There is, then, a double bind that holds the hero identity in place. On the one hand, Clark Kent and Bruce Wayne need to transcend their physical limitations and to be freed to signify different relations on the margins of the societal order, in order to be able to protect the populace from danger. On the other hand, their rootedness in Oedipal narratives armours them with a rampant individuality that prevents them from transgressing the boundaries produced by societal norms. This rootedness pulls them back and prevents them from exploring the consequences of their actions or their need to continue acting. The actions of Batman and Superman armour the subjectivity of Bruce Wayne and Clark Kent. Guilt is transformed into trauma and the repetition of the origin story neutralizes the possibility for collective action. The prospect of a utopian ending is negated before it can arise. The child-like innocence of the characters requires them to adopt a superheroic guise. They are monstrous inflated humanist characters unable to acknowledge their own culpability and to face their own fears and desires. They act to support the status quo, but in doing so also highlight, for critical readers, forms of domination.

Superman and Batman offer images of a masculine ideal. Strong, self-sufficient bodies acting independently in the world. The characters fit comfortably into the mould of the American monomyth (Lang and Trimble, 1988) where individual solutions are preferred over societal problems. However, the individual solutions in offer are symptomatic of the pathology of Batman and Superman and their desire to reinstate an impossible originary fullness.

Cyborgs and Superheroes, or Some Problems with Cyborg Identity

Cyborgs are everywhere, populating cyberpunk and science fiction texts, as well as within the lived experience of the social body. And as the number of breaches between the human and the non-human increases so does the importance of the cyborg as an imaginative resource. 'This figure of the cyborg helps us bring together myths and tools, representations and embodied realities, as a way of understanding postmodernity'(Gray *et al.*, 1995:2). This cyborg has the marks of its hybridity written upon its body and it is rendered intelligible, or at lest identifiable, by such inscriptions. Yet, as the figure of the cyborg accumulates more and more prostheses and as the number of possible combinations and configurations proliferates, and connects with a wider variety of discourses and technologies, so too does the image of the cyborg become increasingly complicated and disputed.

Haraway highlighted the border transgression that marked the point of emergence for the cyborg. However, the image placed at the centre of her blasphemy is felt undescribed while its properties are defined and described. The cyborg occupies a cypher-like space of possibility. Its qualities and characteristics are outlined but not inscribed in physical bodies. The body of the cyborg is, therefore, also a constructed concept, with theory functioning as a technological implant that provides it with a political and descriptive valency. I shall argue that a focus on cyborg identity, characterised by forms of cybernetic implant, is open to naturalisation and reclamation, particularly when the the focus is placed on the individual body.

Clearly, many of the descriptions of cyborg identity have been inspired by popular culture representations. Such images of the cyborg, as seen in film and comics and novels, obviously are related to the theorised cyborg that inhabits some strands of academic discourse. They are, however, different in a number of ways. Rather then opening up utopian and political opportunities, characters such as the *Terminator* (dir. Cameron, 1984) and *RoboCop* (dir. Verhoeven, 1987) violently resist any such possibility. An outline of comic book counterparts will aid a critique of the construction of the film cyborg.

Within the panelled world of comic books there are increasing numbers of cyborgs that 'reveal much about how these characters are perceived. [They] represent the most prevalent medium in which many children and adults are forming their impressions of cyborgian culture' (Oehlert, 1995:219). Comic books have long had a tradition of cyborg-like characters ranging from the Nazi-bashing adventures of *Captain America* during the Second World War to the industrialist Tony Stark acting as *Iron Man* (whose suit also helped him to live with his heart condition). However, with the dawning of a more distinct cyborg age the cyborg figure has become more clearly articulated within comic book narratives. Oehlert distinguishes between three main categories which refer to different levels of integration and of an increasing complexity. The first is called *simple controller* (simple implants or removable suits). Such systems augment natural abilities and 'would seem to be the equivalent of mental Waldos [prosthetically operated machines]' (ibid.: 224). The next category is that of the *bio-tech integrator*. These are non-removable systems of greater complexity.

Characters have greater control over intimate and alterable implants. Whereas characters in the first category cannot reconfigure the functioning of their cyborg implants, characters in this category are able to do so. The final category is that of *genetic cyborgs*. This is where there is purposeful alteration of genetic code that leads to enhancement of abilities. Characters, such as Superman, do not fall into this category as no deliberate alteration has taken place.

This categorisation, while it identifies three different possible varieties of cyborg prosthesis, does not consider the manner of the boundary transgression between the human and non-human and fails to examine the extent of the political ramifications of such hybrid identities. These are all high-tech cyborgs. Oehlert's categorisation is based on research on cyborg soldiers, it appears that they do remain faithful to their fathers in a way that is not desired by Haraway: 'The issue of humanity with comic book cyborgs then is not if the machine will take over the human side of the equation but what will the human half choose to do with his new abilities' (Oehlert, 1995: 227). Such cyborg characters have a tendency to violence, to dealing with problems in a personal and graphic style that highlights an ambiguity of the comic book cyborg. The clear cut moral divide between heroes and villains is blurred and is 'indicative of our unease with these creations' (ibid.: 226).

An example of this follows from the exaggerated reports of Superman's death in 1993 in *The Return of Superman*. Four retenders to his crown appeared in Metropolis. The different versions of Superman and the public's doubtful response to their presence over Metropolis seems to indicate a general feeling of insecurity, one that is connected to the truth of the Superman identity. The first is a clone of the original Superman, the second an old kryptonian weapon in the shape of Superman, the third a man in a suit (not unlike the Iron Man) and the last a cyborg Superman. While all of these characters fit into the categories used by Oelhert, only the cyborg Superman - who here does have his own origin story - is truly dangerous with his face permanently cut away in a style reminiscent of scenes from *The Terminator* and the ability to alter parts of his body at will and combine with different machines. This 'Superman' intends to destroy Metropolis, to ruin the reputation of the 'Man of Tomorrow'. It would appear that in the Superman narratives fully integrated polymorphing cyborgs are a threat (especially as they also have at their command great war machines capable of destroying cities at a stroke). The resurrected Superman, acting in concert with the remaining superman, defeats the cyborg and in so doing asserts the legitimacy of the Superman role. With the defeat of the cyborg Superman by the hand of the one true Superman affairs in Metropolis settle down to 'normal' once more.

The Return of Superman story are can be read alongside fears and anxieties connected to the dissipation of concrete subjects. A discourse on identity is played out through the narratives whereby 'true' identities are being sought as guarantors of the truth of the subject. The confirmation of Superman's return by Lois Lane reinstates the figure of Superman as a master signifier that guarantees a concrete subject against boundary transgressions and the disintegration of the subject. The only person upset by the return of Superman is Lex Luthor, as Superman is a threat to his plans to dominate Metropolis through his company LexCorp. Corporations and multinationals are the great evils of the cyborg comic book world, a concern shared with film cyborgs (see Oelhert, 1995:228.) The influence and power of the nation state is perceived as waning in comparison to the hegemony of corporate strategy who are the producers and controllers of cyborg technology, in film and comics at least (see Gray *et al.,* 1995). In the *Terminator* and *RoboCop* films the central characters struggle against the control exerted over them by the corporations Omni Consumer Product and Cyberdine Systems. There is a sense in which RoboCop and, to a lesser extent, Terminator rebel against the systems which produced, maintain and manipulate them. The only form of response, however, is one of extreme violence. The use of violence would then appear to be a defining trait for comic book and film cyborgs.

Making a stand against the impersonal corporation is, again, an attempt to assert a concrete identity and re-find a sense of wholeness. The armoured bodies of RoboCop and Terminator transgress the boundary between the human and the non-human and between the machine and organism but they are seemingly unaware and resistant to their cyborg nature. They seek identity rather than affinities, and the site where nature and culture should be reworked becomes a point of resistance. These characters are reminiscent of the *Freikorps* members described by Klaus Theweleit (1989) where bodies were armoured in leather 'to assert their solidity against the threat of fluid women' (Claudia Springer, quoted in Bukatman, 1993:306). Now the bodies of cyborgs are armoured 'against a new age (political and technological)' (Bukatman, 1993: 306). Springer suggests that it is that passivity of the interaction with computers that cyborgs resist. The feminisation of the technology, concealed and fluid systems, is a threat forms of masculinity. Thus, through the battle with the morphing T-100 in *Terminator 2: Judgment Day* (dir: Cameron, 1991) film 'the mechanical Terminator expunges the nightmare of masculine and industrial obsolescence' (Bukatman, 1993).

Film cyborgs integrate with technology precisely in

order to inoculate themselves against the threat to fragment identity. They can therefore resist thc consequences of full integration with the machine and preserve a sense of self. Such hybrid identities are, then, immune to the spread of the matrix. The example from the *The Return of Superman* highlights how superheroes can function as a defense against the threat of the dangerous cyborg; they protect the 'body' from invasion. Film cyborgs, on the other hand, stand in a similar position on the boundary but are immunised against the spread of implantation. In both cases, the threat may still be thought of as emanating from an unseen female body.

Here the cyborg is similar to the superhero, at least in its popular culture versions. Figures like *Terminator* and *RoboCop* are particularly conservative and violent, attempting to gain and regain a sense of identity and wholeness. However, in the next section I shall took at how the superhero might be reconfigured in a progressive manner.

Reconfiguring Superheroes

To longevity and remarkable ability of Batman and Superman to remain popular and adapt to changing audiences and social situations while desperately trying to stay the same is an outcome of the effective use of the origin stories. Such adaptation and constant renewal is a form of reconfiguration. The characters are merely reflections of their former selves. however, as the storyline have become more complex with more fixed elements accruing to the narratives the characters have become increasingly conservative. For example, Siegel and Shuster's original 1930s Superman frequently confronted social issues in a way that is now unthinkable. As the 'champion of the oppressed' Superman made munitions manufacturers and mine owners face the consequences of their business actions. A process of naturalisation has taken place that has rounded the politically and socially sensitive corners from the characters, but while the construction of identify within the Superman and Batman narratives is deeply conservative and and reliant on an origin story in the 'Western' sense, there is still a sense in which such characters may be reactivated politically against the grain.

In 1986, for example, DC Comics published *Batman: The Dark Knight Returns*. This was a radical reworking of the Batman mythos written and pencilled by Frank Miller. The story starts when Bruce Wayne narrowly survives the explosion of the car he is racing and has pushed past the limits of its capabilities. The explosion is reported in a news report which also includes items on the current heat and crime waves and also the anniversary of the 'last recorded sighting of the Batman' (Miller, 1986: 3). From this news item we learn that Bruce Wayne has returned from the Batman role, that debate continues as to the morality of Batman's actions and that many people 'consider him a myth' (Miller, 1986: 3). Obviously, Batman does not remain retired. As events unfold we are shown Bruce Wayne struggling to repress the beast inside: 'You are nothing - a hollow shell, a rusty trap that cannot hold me' (ibid.: 17). Shortly after, Batman is seen once again in the streets of Gotham dealing with a gang of teenagers called the Mutants, coping with the reappearance of Two-Face and the Joker and, finally facing down Superman following the detonation of a nuclear bomb.

The 'cyberpunk rebirth' (Rushkoff, 1994: 233) of an aged Batman placed the geriatric hero into a media-saturated city where his actions are reported, interpreted and debated. However other than being much older, Miller's version of the Batman is little different from earlier (and later) versions of the character. He still triumphs in the face of adversity and the origin story remains a core motivating force for the character. What is markedly different in *The Dark Knight Returns* is the narrative setting. 'He is the same batman who fought criminals in earlier, simpler decades, who now, as an older man, is utterly unequipped for the challenges of Cyberia' (Rushkoff, 1994:233). There are evident difficulties in overcoming the compulsion to repeat and the need of Bruce Wayne to act as the Batman. As Bukatman (1993: 307) puts it 'Miller has become the poet laureate of last-gasp cyborgism.. his characters are always "returning" to their killing ways despite their perceived obsolescence.' Such a statement alludes to the cyborgian nature of this version of Batman and also implies that similar characters may be seen as anachronistic, displaced from a society they no longer understand the dealing with problems using the only method they know, violence. However, it is necessary for characters like Superman and Batman to obscure their age-old origins in order to retain an audience. But if the characters remain 'essentially' the same then how ought the use of the origin story be understood, especially for progressive political purposes? The invocation of origin stories function not to update the character but to realign the character to the needs of an updated narrative. A shift in emphasis away from the construction of identity to one that considers the actions and interactions of characters can enable the site of the superhero body' to be reconfigured politically. Explicit emphasis on events enables political critiques that would be overlooked if their focus is only on a fixed Batman 'identity'.

Reconfiguring Cyborgs

The reconfiguration of cyborgs is more problematic than that of superheroes. These are a number of reasons for this that arise as a result of the cyborg being the 'always already' theorised body. This is to say that the figure of the cyborg draws together a hybrid body of theory that is politicised as it is enunciated. For example,

Haraway's descriptive definition of cyborg characteristics reworks the hybridised body in a politically progressive direction and in doing so refuses less politically astutue cyborg bodies political valency. However, the blasphemous image of the cyborg that Haraway promotes remains a hybrid of fact that fiction, of myth and lived experience. The cyborg figures I have examined clearly reside in the popular imagination. While such figures are cyborgian there is often a resistance, an armouring of the body against change. RoboCop and Terminator do not gain their ontology from their hybrid body forms. Rather they carry their prosthesis as stigmata, as signs of their suffering at the hands of the corporation. The armoured body marks its limits precisely and stalwartly defends it against all comers.

The cyborg in film shed light on the fears and anxieties that surround the penetration, of the body through new technologies. These particularly masculine fantasies are little different from the constructed superhero figures of comic books and film. Oehlert's categorisation of cyborg types in comics ignored the similarities shared with other superhero types. In fact, the current plethora of cyborgs in comics might be best seen in line with the superhero genre's unerring ability to update narratives. In other words, the fascination with cyborgs reflects current preoccupations and fears in the same way that mutant and alien hero characters did in previous stages of the genesis of the superhero genre. As such, the characters might be best seen as part of a continuum that plots the changing visage of 'the hero of a thousand faces'. The cyborg hero-type in film and comics therefore resists the temptations of cultural change and collective action so that 'it is not society that is to guide and save the creative hero, but precisely the reverse' (Campbell, 1993:391).

The focus here has been on the construction of identity of the superhero and and so of the cyborg within popular-cultural texts. This focus has stressed the difficulty in side-stepping the initial identification with nature in the 'Western' sense and he difficulty in overcoming essentialist accounts of subjectivity. However, as I argued in the previous section, a shift in emphasis can rework the politically conservative figure against the grain. By placing the accent upon actions and events the emphasis is displaced onto the connections forged by cyborgs and so highlights forms of domination that would otherwise remain invisible.

The image of the cyborg described by Haraway functions as a tool or more accurately as a theoretical prosthesis, as a nexus for accounts of changing notions of subjectivity and identity within postmodernity. However, it appears that there is a resistance to changing accounts of the construction of identity. What Haraway, and other 'cyborgologists', successfully highlight are the boundary breakdowns between human and machine and human and animal (see Pfeil, 1990:93). When the accent is moved from the construction of identity to that of cyborg events then the monstrous cyborg unites enable 'the politicla struggle [to be seen] form both perspectives at once because each reveals dominations and possibilities unimaginable from the other vantager point' (Haraway, 1991:154). The cyborg, as I have described it, suffers from single vision and only looks from one perspective. But it does allow others to gaze upon it and view political struggles from other perspectives.

My concern with Haraway's cyborg as a myth of political identity is that it too is naturalised and that, maybe, seeing from the point of view of the cyborg, is to suffer from the illusion of single vision. The cyborg figure is open to reclamation in a number of directions and this might also be to naturalise its political potency. A focus on identity is seductive and alluring. To become a cyborg is an exciting, consciously chosen, origin. But to look to cyborg events is to confront oppositions and be made to question the functioning of discourse as it appears in various situations.

Reconfiguring Cyberpsychology

The use of cyborg imagery within cyberpsychology provides a potent myth which enables alternative perspectives to be highlighted. As is stressed, however, this can lead to a set of oppositions being maintained between critical perspectives and the institutions such perspectives hope to disrupt. It allows affinities and different vantage points to be explored which may be overlooked when the emphasis is simply placed on the construction of identity.

REFERENCES

Aronowitz, S., Martinsons, B. and Menser, M. (eds) (1996) *Techo Science and Cyber Culture* London: Routledge.

Barhes. R. ([1957][1977] *Mythologies:* London: Johnathan Cape.

Benjamin, W. ([1970][1992] *Illuminations.* London: Fontana Press.

Berland. J. (1996) 'Mapping space: imaging technologies and the planetary body', in Aronowitz, S., Martinsons, B. and Menser, M. (eds). *Techno Science and Cyber Culture.* London: Routledge.

Bukatman, S. (1993) *Terminal Identity: The Virtual Subject in Postmodern Science Fiction.* Durham: Duke University Press.

Byrne. J, and Giorodano, D. (1993) *Superman: The Man of Steel.* New York: DC Comics Inc.

Campbell, J. ([1949]1993) *The Hero of a Thousand Faces.* London: Fontana Press.

Clynes, M. and Kline, N.S. (1960) 'Cyborgs and space', *Astronautics,* Sept., 26-7, 74-6.

Fuchs, C.J (1995) 'Death is irrevelant: Cyborgs, reproduction and the future of male hysteria', in Gray, C.H., Figueroa-Sarriera, H.J. an Mentor. S. (eds), *The Cyborg Handbook.* London: Routledge.

Gibbons, D. (1992) 'Introduction,' in Gibbons, D. and Rude, S. (eds) *World's Finest.* New York : DC Comics Inc.

Gibbons, D. and Rude, S. (1992) *World's Finest*. New York: DC Comics Inc.

Gordo-Lopez, A. (1995)'Cyberpsychology: an introduction'. in Burman, E., Gordo-Lopez, A.J. Macualey, R. and Parker, I. (eds) *Cyberpsychology: Conference, Interventions and Reflections* Manchester, Discourse Unit.

Gray, C.H., Figueroa-Sarriera, H.J. and Mentor, S. (eds) (19950 *The Cyborg Handbook*. London: Routledge.

Haraway, D. 91985) ' A manifesto for cyborgs: science, technology and specialist-feminism in the late twentieth century', reproduced in Haraway, D. (1991).

Haraway, D, (1991) *Siminans Cyborgs and Women: The Reinvention of Nature*. London: Free Association Press.

Haraway, D. (1995) 'Cyborgs and symbionts: living together in the new world order', in Gray, C.H., Figueroa-Sarriera, H.J. and Mentor, S. (eds)*The Cyborg Handbook*. London: Routledge.

Heggs, D. (1996) 'Origin stories: psychology and popular culture. Unpublished Presentation at the University of Valencia, Valencia.

Jurgens, D., Kesel, K., Simonson, L. *et al.* (1993) *The Return of Superman*. New York: DC Comics.

Lang and Trimble (1988) Whatever happened to the man of tomorrow? An examination of the American monomyth and the comic book superhero' *The Journal of Popular Culture*, 22(30: 157-73.

Laplanche J. and Pontalis, J. B. (1973). *The Language of Psychoanalysis*, London: Karnac.

Marsden. J. (1996) 'Virtual sexes and feminist futures: the philosophy of "cyberfeminism", *Radical Philosophy*, 78: 6-16.

Miller. F. (1986) *Batman: The Dark Knight Returns*. New York: DC Comics Inc.

Oehlert, O. (1995) 'From Captain America to Wolverine: cyborgs in comic books, alternative images of cybernetic heroes and villains' in Gray, C.H. Figueroa-Sarriera, H.J. and Mentor, S. (eds) *The Cyborg Handbook*. London: Routledge.

Parker, I. (1997) *Psychoanalytic Culture: Psychoanalytic Discourse in Western* Society. London: Sage.

Penley C. (1986) 'Time travel, primal scene and the critical dystopia", *Camera Obscura*, 15: 66-85.

Pesce, M.D. (1992) 'Final amputation: pathogenic ontology in cyberspace', gopher:/ alisha w.ucsb.edu:70/00/.speed/.s1.1/.articles/.pesce.txt

Pfeil, F.(1990) 'These disintegrations I'm looking forward to:science fiction from new wave to nes age', in Pfeil, F (ed.) *Another Tale to Tell: Politics and Narrative in Postmodern Culture.* London: Verso.

Raymond. E.S. (compiler) (1996) *The New Hacker's Dictionary.* Cambridge, MA: MIT Press.

Reynolds. R. (1992) *Superheroes.* London: Batsford.

Rushkoff, D. (1994) *Cyberia: Life in the Trenches of Cyberspace.* London: Flamingo.

Theweleit, K. ([1977]1989) *Male Fantasies,* Volume 2. Cambridge: Polity Press.

Uricchio, W. and Pearson. E. (1991) 'I' m not fooled by that cheap disguise,' in Pearson, E. and Uricchio, W. (eds) *The Many Lives of the Batman: Critical Approaches to a Superhero and His Media:* London: BFI Publishing.

Zizek, S. (1997) *The Plague of Fantasies.* London: Verso.

12 AGAINST SOCIAL CONSTRUCTIONIST CYBORGIAN TERRITORIALISATIONS

What do we know about cyborgs? We know that 'cyborg' is a neologism formed by the fusion of terms 'cybernetics' and 'organism', coined by Clynes and Kline (1969). We know that cyborg is a metaphor (Haraway, 1991; Piscitelli, 1995; Wolmark, 1995), that it speaks of what we are becoming; it speaks of the transgression of boundaries and of a way of breaking through old limits; between the modern oppositions '1/other'; 'mind/body', 'culture/ nature', 'man/woman', 'civilised/primitive', 'reality/ appearance', 'whole/part', and so on. We also know that the cyborg can develop into a discipline of knowledge, such as cyberanthroplogy (Escobar, 1996).

But what do we *not* know about cyborgs? Although the cyborg brings transgression and is a notion which speaks of hybridisation and crossbreeding rather than purity, we have hardly started to follow through the implications of this, we do not thoroughly hybridise, we are not transgressors of old academic disciplines or hegemonic conceptual positions. Instead, it seems we are moving in the opposite direction. We do this, for example, precisely when we create specific disciplines, as is the case of 'cyborg anthropology' or when we try to describe its imaginary quality and the means it uses to produce knowledge. It seems we that we seek the *isolation* of cyborgs as if they were discrete things rather than studying their insertion in our everyday experience. In this sense, we have hardly done anything more than affirm that with this notion the categories of modernity break down. The main exception to this is the work of subversion epitomised by Donna Haraway (1991) within a feminist frame of reference. She has shown how must North American feminists assume profound dualisms between mind-body and animal-machine in social practices. For this reason, they have developed analytical tools that are no more than the mere reflection of the object of their critique.

The purpose of this chapter is twofold. First, I shall try to subvert he commonly used notion of cyborg. To this end, I will pose three questions:

1. What is cyborg? Here I will argue that it is not a metaphor but a *becoming.*
2. Do cyborgs have a history? Here I will argue that they are ahistorical and more than being simply processes, they are *events.*
3. What are the consequences of cyborgs? Here I will recover Haraway's portrayal of cyborgs as our ontology and will try to develop it in order to extract from it as many consequences as possible.

I will defend the idea that cyborgs are 'folds upon folds' as opposed to the forms of 'folding' and 'unfolding' involved in classicism and modernity respectively. Second, I will use this re-encounter with the idea of the cyborg to propitiate a re-encounter with social constructionism. The encounter with this perspective seeks to alter, at least to criticise, and even perhaps to contaminate it. We will then be in a better position to develop a definition of the term 'cyberpsychology' and to comment on the possibilities this opens up.

Cyborgs Revisited

The cyborg is often treated as a metaphor, but it also operate as a form of transgression. The problem with treating it merely as a metaphor is that the notion of metaphor itself belongs to the realm of analogy, and to representationist thinking. Representation entails the subordination of something original which does not reveal itself as such, and which only does so through an image.

As long as the cyborg is treated as a metaphor, then, it seems that it would be well nigh impossible to ask what it represents, what underlying object and relations give it meaning, how the foundation for such a metaphor was laid, and what synthesizes its presence. Thus, within the realm of analogy, the cyborg appears to us like the figure represented by he hybridisation between humans and animals, or animal-humans and machines, or a network of organic, inorganic entities and interests, or things and beings in general. As long as the cyborg remains within representationist thinking, then, it will be subject to *limits*. It will always depend on the original object from which it takes its meaning. For Bergson (1957), the transgression offered by metaphor, in this case the cyborg, operates on the underlying idea that concepts are formed to exactly resemble solid bodies. Constant, stable and consistent, with distinct and distinguishable borders. Indeed, this is what our concepts are like in Western culture, and this is what our conceptualisation of the individual, artefact, attitude, gender, and so on is like in contemporary psychology. But the cyborg is a figure, a concept which *defies* these distinct and uniform borders. It introduces an oscillation between frontiers, shaking around he edges, borders with mobility and flexibility. The effect of the cyborg as metaphor is to force us to picture concepts with images other than that of solid bodies.

The controlled transgression which metaphor normally produces has other implications for cyborgs. It means that they lose their potential for subversion as, in the end, they are homogenised and turned into a unique, identifiable species. The metaphor converts cyborgs into go-between beings and thins, leading to the appearance of another seemingly solid entity, the cyborg. The cyborg is placed in an intermediary position as a third element, fenced in by the previous two, continually dependent on them and at a point held on the same plane as the others. And so, despite transgression this idea that concepts are like solids, the cyborg ends up being turned into a simple meeting point between beings and things. From his it follows that the representation of the cyborg is possible, albeit as a transgressive blend, but it is still a representation nevertheless. This is good certainly, but not good enough.

Let us try to think of cyborgs in another way. Let us try to tear hem from the ambit of he metaphor and, therefore, from the terrain of representation. In his way we can make them more subversive and corrosive, and avoid the ultimate homogenisation that converts them and reifies them into a species apart, as another species for the inventory of knowledge. We can do his by going further along the path which Bergson's reasoning opened up.

The metaphor of the cyborg can be employed as part of a kind of critique which affords the possibility of intermediary concepts which oscillate, fluctuate between other limits, which are further apart but present nonetheless. Michel Serres (1980), following Bergson, calls this situation or possibility of intermediary or oscillating concepts the logic of what is liquid or fluid. Fluids oscillate, change, vary, but always within certain boundaries, wide but unsurmountable, so the ultimate transgression of these limits is never reached. To think that a cyborg is a metaphor can help us to think of it as being fluid, like a liquid element.

Is it possible to cross these last frontiers? It is possible if we continue with Serres' proposal. Let us abandon this object model of liquids and think of fire, specifically of a flame. The topology of a flame is extremely paradoxical. The edges of the flame vary at such a speed for us that it is impossible to say either if they are actually present or where they are. All of a sudden, the flame disappears, it moves somewhere else, or it represents itself right here and it is no longer the same flame. It continues and discontinues. It is more than unstable and less than stable. It is not a flow, as it lacks any constant to give it order. It is random fluctuation, always the same flame but bearing no relation to what it was a moment ago. It dances unpredictably. It has no constant edges, frontiers or margins. The flame enables us to get away from representationist thinking.

But if 'cyborg' has broken beyond the limits of metaphor, what is it now? What shall we call it? How do we understand it? We could say it is a flame, that it is like a flame. But this alone is just an image without concept; we need a concept which might take root in this image and escape from that of sold and fluid.

The logic of the flame is taken up in the notion of 'becoming' put forward by Deleuze (1977, 1990, 1993) and Deleuze and Guattari (1977, 1980). What is becoming, or a becoming for these authors? Becoming is not evolution, it does not operate by filiation, likeness, relationship or inheritance. It engenders mutual transformation between heterogeneous entities, establishing meetings and relations between them. Becoming does not imitate, but establishes relations between multiplicities.

So what does becoming cyborg or a becoming cyborg involve? It means that, in the first place, cyborgs are not intersections, midpoints or meetings between beings and thing,s subjects or object. They are not even fluid concepts among solid concepts. Becoming cyborg is movement without pause, without brakes, with a random speed which traps beings, things, subjects and objects. It is sudden event. It is a movement which never ceases, with different speeds and different intensities. As becoming, cyborgs are not identical to each neither are they self-identical, there are no two cyborgs the same, they vary in size and appearance. They are in networks which continually joint up and then disappear. There is no space or empty moment in which they can be considered a simple mixture of flesh and metal, of life and artificial organ. The cyborg is a logic in its own right, a movement of endless incorporation.

Haraway (1991: 254) claims that we are cyborgs. I think it is more a question of claiming that we *become* cyborgs. The difference in approach is important. It would seem from Haraway's text that each one of us is a distinct identificable cyborg in time and space, we are always becoming different cyborgs. We become mixtures at the intersection of animal and machine, perhaps but also with specific various interest and ideologies. These mixtures are not constant but change repeatedly. It is an agonising process, without origins or teleologies.

We become cyborgs then, and becoming cyborg includes the possibility of participating on different planes simultaneously. The cyborg is a to-and-fro between things and beings, languages and meanings. There is a multitude of superimposed planes, a gyration in endless movement, and the logic of this action is a *becoming cyborg*.

Cyborgs are Ahistorical

A corollary of the argument so far is that cyborgs do not have a history. Does a flame have a history? A flame lights up and goes out, nothing more. In the flame, there is no history, only change. The flame is lacking in a point or moment which contains anything permanent or which sets a standard for writing its history. The flame either exists or it does not, simply that.

There are sometimes attempts made to make a history of the notion of cyborg. In these cases, we come across three different situations. In the first, we find a work of the etymological type which runs around, of course, in 1960 with the article by Clynes and Kline in which the neologism 'cyborg' is coined. In the second, an effort is made to give depth to this neologism, and cyborgs or records of them in literature and mythology are sought and found. Frankenstein or the Greek god Hephaestus are well- tried examples in such cases. as a third strategy, we find a blend of etymological work and literary criticism.

There are two conditions for the realisation of history. It requires an object perfectly identifiable in space, univocal, and homogeneous in its components. It also needs to inscribe in this object a single temporality which begins to unfold from the present moment. But what happens when we have an object with limits unidentifiable in space? What happens when our object has a present in which it is formed and deformed from a heterogeneous multiplicity of entities? What happens when an analyst freezes a becoming cyborg in an attempt to understand it, only to find that it possesses a multitude of temporalities?

The cyborg *surpasses the historical*. This is not because

cyborgs are outside or on the edge of time, but because they condense a multitude of temporalities. They condense all possible times; unforseeable, accelerated, determined, related, dead, forgotten, continued, and so on. Also such condensation is continuous, random; it varies, and depends on each new relation which is established or dies. To picture this, let us imagine a network of associations continually growing and diminishing, encompassing new elements and eliminating them, moving, and shrinking. This situation does not allow us to describe either lineal genesis or continuous evolution. Rather than history or histories, we should be in the business of cartography and topology if we really want to get closer to cyborgs. If cyborgs are a collage of alien parts, it is then absurd to think about an origin in their identity. So how may we write the history of something containing a multitude of alien, unrelated temporalities?

It is not enough to say that cyborgs are a process because to know the process is to describe it in its temporal trajectory, to risk attributing that sedimented temporal process with an essence of some kind. Cyborgs are without essence. They are completely different one from another and have heterogeneity built into them. So, more than a process, cyborgs are an event. They refer to the singularity of their appearance or disappearance, singular emergencies; they do not represent the successive figures of a same meaning or use; they do not obey any pre-established logic or unwavering teleology. In a way, cyborgs are just a , perpetual present, without a past that might be distinguished, without a future to dream of. Events are always different; difference is what is gathered up in events. They contain a law of absolute singularity, the knowledge of which is all we can aspire to, without any possibility of generalisation. The cyborg is more a question of description of context than a history of succession.

Archaeology: The Cyborg Form

If, as Haraway (1991) claims, cyborgs are our ontology, we do need to know what form they take and how they came about. To this end, we shall turn to the archaeological approaches developed by Foucault (1966) in *The Order of Things*. Archaeology aims to establish that basic unit which at a given moment lays down the conditions which organise the order of things, the relation between beings and things, the possibilities of knowledge, of what can and cannot be said. Archaeology seeks to establish conditions of possibility in the same terrain of knowledge:

> One thing in any case is certain: man is neither the oldest nor the most constant problem that has been posed for human knowledge. In fact, among all the mutations that have affected knowledge of things and heir order... only one alone, that which began a century and a half ago and is now perhaps drawing to a close has made it possible for the figure of man to appear.. man is an invention of recent date. And one perhaps nearing its end. If those arrangements were to disappear as hey appeared, if some event of which we can at the moment do no more than sense the possibility - without knowing either what its form will be or what it promises - were to cause them to crumble, as the ground of Classical thought did, at the end of the eighteenth century, then one can certainly wager that man would be erased, like a face drawn in sand at the edge of the sea. (Foucault, 1966: 386-387).

The 'man' to which Foucault refers here, or the man-form speaking in the terrain of knowledge, has not always existed. We maintain that term 'man' here quite deliberately, for this category is something that the cyborg will disrupt later. Let us see how, from the archaeology of man as a figure of knowledge and all that it implies, we may gain access to the cyborg as an ontological figure.

As Serres (1980) and Deleuze (1986) maintain, classical thought is notable for its passion and the central role it gives to the idea of the infinite. The most significant texts of the seventeenth century make reference to orders of infinitude: the infinite in size, the infinite for its own sake, the infinite within limits. Classical thought forever pursues and is lost in the infinite. Forever committed to this pursuit, it ends up without a centre or territory, it strives to establish a finite place among all these infinites so as to set about putting them in order. With this infinite, the individual in their everyday existence is limited, and cannot account for these infinite powers which transcend and surpass it. The encounter, the resulting compound of infinitude gives rise to the god-from (Deleuze, 1986). The sciences which emerge in this age are general disciplines because everything that is general indicates an order of infinitude, it approaches the infinite. Thus, for instance, there is no biology but natural history, no political economy but analysis of wealth, and instead of philology or linguistics, general grammar. To refer to the operations of this knowledge and in harmony with the task of representation, Foucault (1966) uses the word 'unfolding". Classical thought explains reality by unfolding it, unfolding is the operation which leads to the infinite. Unfolding is the operator of classical knowledge, it is the movement which carries the finite towards the infinite, and man towards God.

Modernity presents a mutation in classical knowledge and the order of things. The god-form is substituted by the man-form. The individual, finite, measurable, comes into contact or relation with an exterior which is no longer infinite, but finite too. That which is exterior to man is an finite as he is. What has happened in this exterior? What is that made it change? For Foucault, the answer can be given in archaeological terms. At the end of the eighteenth and into the nineteenth century, historicism enters into things, isolating hem and defining them in line with its own coherence. It imposes on them a new form of order, the form of order implicit in the logic of time; that is, finitude. In their mere becoming, things find heir principle of intelligibility. The individual's contact will not now be made with God, but with semi-transcendental categories such as life, work and language (Foucault, 1966). This is a triple root of finitude which will originate biology, political economy and language. This substitution of the original infinitude for finitude will be called he Kantian revolution. Instead of generalisation in knowledge, there is comparison. For Foucault, knowledge folds over onto finitude which is the finitude of man himself. The world folds over onto the man-form. This form becomes the epicentre and the reference point of all knowledge. Biology, political economy and language will search for their foundation in this figure.'It is rigorously contemporary of man, as an epistemic bond, the paradox which governs all modern philosophy: to look for foundation in a finite being' (Wahl, 1975:73).

Has this man-form now died, been erased, an Foucault claims? And if this is the case, what new form has emerged? Can we continue the archaeological explanations which Foucault brought to an end with the man-form to make explicit how this new form emerges? The dispositions of knowledge of things and their order which gave birth to the man-form or man, of our sciences, have *disappeared*. In their place a new figure is emerging, a substitute which is the *cyborg-form*. The characterisation of such a new ontology, however, has not been explored, and we believe that this is fundamental with regard to understanding the possibilities for thinking of and conceiving the reality offered by this figure.

The relation between the individual in their everyday existence and heir exterior has changed. The cyborg-form has emerged from the relation of individual with an exterior which is unlimited-finite. This form is neither god nor man. Nor is it the mere transgression of limits. It is the ability or possibility to act, to exist and to be on different planes simultaneously. It is the capacity to be defined in different ways through multiple positions, chains of genetic codes folded over on top of one another, the potential relations of silicon, information stored in cybernetic machines the contours of the sentence and the dispersion of words in postmodern literature. Human subjects and conceptual or material objects among those living can now no longer be conceived in singularities isolated from the dynamic, correlative, multipartite systems, within which they appear. The fold upon fold expresses something of the way the cyborg-form is more than a figure and a network, but is a logic of continual incorporations of things, beings and structures, in totalities which emerge, develop, and repeatedly fold over on themselves to the point of saturation and redundancy.

Let us now revisit social constructionism in order to contaminate its basic boundary markers, to infect its clean, clear limits.

Social Constructionism Revisited

Authors such a Michael (1996) have started to demand of social constructionism that it incorporate role of the non-social and the non-human in it. According to Michael, the reasons which impel us not to exclude the non-human and the non-social from our descriptions and explanations are aesthetic, historical, and political. Social constructionism has shown itself to be highly sensitive to the linguistic resources which operate in the production of meaning from what surrounds us. These, in their turn, are systematically located in spaces as diffuse and abstract as those ambits, called 'culture' 'ideology', or 'language', spaces which are populated by ideas and thoughts, and empty of walls, doors, dogs, computers, fish. The effect of all this is to make the social omnipresent.

Michael's claim seems to me to be sound. However, in its form, it fails to convince me. Simply incorporating the non-social and the non-human in our explanations has two effects. The first is to leave intact the dichotomy between the social and the non-social. The second is a corollary of the first. We leave the notion of the social present in social constructionism intact. This is still a relationship, now between humans and non-humans, but a relationship all the same, and a process.

Why should we question that the social be a process? Is it not the case that when social constructionism conceived of the social as process, it broke away from thinking which understood the social to be fact, objective, external to the individual and beyond time and the historical? When Gergen (1994: 49) writes that 'the terms and forms by which we achieve understanding of the world and ourselves are social artifacts, products of historically and culturally situated interchanges among people', is he not subverting traditional social psychology? He is, but he is also still trapping the social in time, in the hegemony or tyranny of the temporal.

There are two elements to the confinement of the social—of 'territorialisation' in Deleuzian Terminology, or 'stratification' in that of Foucault - in time. On the one hand, social reality is historical, subjected to the vicissitudes of, and keeping step with the historical, and nowadays it seems unquestionable that:

> Society constitutes a human production which is modified through time.... social phenomena,

> social practices, social structures have memory, and 'what they are' at a given moment is inextricable from the history of their production... to say that social reality is intrinsically historical is to say that it results to a great extent from the cultural peculiarities of the traditions, the way of life that a society has gradually built up throughout its development (Ibanez, 1994:229)

By the same token, the social is a process. As I said earlier, the procedural is inextricably linked to time. This is the case to such an extent that one of the meanings of the word process is that of the passage of time. Process is the action of continuing a series of things which have no end.

This means that the true mechanism of intelligibility of the objects of social constructionism is time, or history. The social as process is conceived of as a set of phases or moments which unfold in time. For instance, racism is that set of actions which, unfolded, lead to discrimination. However, it is time which allows us to gather and agglutinate them in a meaningful unit. Time gives a logic to, or unites along a line, the dispersion marked out by these practices of violence. Furthermore, however, racism is limited as a phenomenon which appears in a particular culture and in a specific historical period. Here we have the double encapsulation of the social by time: it labels a process and thereby employs the trope of homogeneity. This double confinement of the social has an important effect. It makes 'the social' seem like the designation of something coherent, univocal, homogeneous and identical in its appearance and recognition. The social as a process is a species, recognisable in its manifestations, identifiable.

Knorr-Centina (1995:75) seems to be pointing to something similar to this:

> Sociology considers many of its categories as 'primitives' - as categories constitutive of daily life and applicable to any arrangement of human subjects. Categories such as actor, action, interaction, social, social structure and organisation, are such primitives. Can we watch human beings 'do' things with each other and yet not call this behavior interaction? Is it conceivable that a group of people who live together in a village is not a social group? Is not anything people do as long as they do it within collective arrangements by definition social?

Let us make this author's questions our own, and add one more to the list: Is possible to break, alter or contaminate this notion of the social? Can we escape from it? Let us do a simple exercise: try to think of the social from the cyborg angle.

Let us think of two people - for example; a scientist in a subatomic-particle laboratory and her husband at the supermarket. Here we have two individuals in very specific and different circumstances. If I were a social constructionist, I would accept that identity is no more than the theory we use to understand ourselves, or which others use and which is subject to contextual, variations. To say something about our scientist in her laboratory, I had only to observe how she relates to her colleagues, how she speaks, what she speaks about, how she defines herself, how she is defined, what she writes. In her husband's case, things are not so simple. The supermarket seems a tricky context to talk about social identity, but I would, nevertheless, end up resorting to standards, norms, lessons, the sort of relationship he has with the cashier and the other customers, and I could also say something about how his identity is constituted in the supermarket.

The point I wish to arrive at with this, perhaps excessively caricatural, example is to show that he social is the result of an exercise in abstraction in which I set off a process of vacuum production. In it, I take the actors out of their most immediate material context and transport them to a plane in which only hey, their relaionships with other humans and pre-defined elements such as language, norms, and so on exist. I do not suppose that the shopping trolley, the Geiger counter, or the microscope can tell me anything about their identities. In the final analysis, the word context boils down to certain questions: When is she in the laboratory? When is he at the supermarket? Who do they see, who do they talk to? Why do they talk about that in a supermarket? How do they write? How do they talk?

Do we wish to think of the social in another way? Can we say of these individuals that they are cyborgs? Not a *priori.* It does not seem appropriate. However, if a cyborg is not just a metaphor, we may answer affirmatively. They *become cyborgs.* She becomes cyborg in her laboratory. He becomes cyborg at the supermarket. Why? In the laboratory, she establishes relationships with non-human entities (the microscope, the electron-accelerator, Einstein as myth, radioactivity, and so on) which have no place in the usual explanations of the social sciences. Moreover, these relationships have standards of meaning, possess symbolism and are not merely automatic actions. Thus, she can treat the Geigercounter as an actor in a social network whereas she can relate to her assistant as if they were not human.

All the myriad relationships with their meaning and symbolism support, give foundation to, and guide her actions and behaviour in this context. In the laboratory, she forms part of a network through which things and beings are organised and related. The operations carried out in this network are continually crossing the limits which classical and the natural. For this reason, I claim that she becomes cyborg. In order to understand her, to get closer to her in this context, I cannot make the *a prior* abstraction of only considering relevant in it the relationships that she makes with human beings, that she has a set standard which guides them, and that the non-human are only things for her. A similar thing would happen with her husband at the supermarket.

Each becoming cyborg is an event and not a process. To approach these becomings, it is not enough for us to relate their history. It is not enough for us to make a narration, with a beginning, middle and end. We would be better off making a map, charting the set of relationships of which she is a part, and observing the variations in this map. Does all this mean that there is a need to give up the notion of the social? Not necessarily. We can consider that the social is not a presupposition but an effect, a product which may emerge or not. When it appears, it is thanks to the becoming cyborg which incorporates it as just another element. The social may appear in distinct forms, particular ways of materialising and particular ways of being given meaning. These are going to depend on a framework, on a map which distributes relationships and actions. This distribution respects none of the limits that the social sciences have assumed until now as *a prioris* of their thinking.

If there are no hidden planes organising daily life in the laboratory, but only a becoming cyborg, and that in this becoming our scientist and the things and beings which interact with her acquire their identity, then we are dealing with ontological reorganisations - with a framework of ontological activity. And ontology or ontological activiy is politics.

Becoming Cyborg is a Becoming Political

Gergen (1994) claims that social constructionism is

marked by a refusal tc speak of things ontological, but this proves to be an untenable position. When Ibanez (1994) sets an agenda for he new critical social psychology, he includes a section dedicated to the ontological presuppositions of this tendency. He has seen that when it is stated that social reality is historical, that it has a historical nature, a movement into the ontological terrain is made. Surely this statement is about the historical becoming of social practices a theorisation about the logic of things, about their being and, then, about ontology?

What has to be highlighted, however briefly, is that it is not a matter of discovering, foundational discourses, but of elaborating them, even knowing them to be untrue. It is a question of the use value that these discourses have. Given that a plane called 'out there' as opposed to another called 'in here' does not exist, but that these and their differentiation are constructed and that this elaboration has consequences, we may try to exploit this construction's possibilities.

On this point I follow Lopez Petit (1994) in maintaining that ontology is not an ideological and obfuscatory instrument. Ontology is a space of confrontation, a political space. Examples to support this statement are to be found in the work of Deleuze or Negri, where ontology is more of a toolbox for experimentation than an attempted explanation of reality, of things just the way they are. Ontology affords us new ways of thinking of what surrounds us, of organising, of understanding.

As Haraway (1991: 254) states, 'The cyborg is our ontology, it gives us our politics. Cyborgs allow us to redefine and continually alter the limits of our world, of our everyday existence. Ontology is no longer the space of the thinking of 'being' which philosophy used to manage; now it belongs o the everyday becoming of cyborgs.

As opposed to ontological silence, it is necessary to call for an excess of ontological discourse. I claimed earlier that cyborgs are a 'fold on a fold', this form or idea enables us to approach this excess, this piling up and accumulation of differences and entities set against each other which are integrated in one unit. Becoming cyborg continually removes order in so far as it transgresses all limits or unceasingly reconstitutes them. Order in its own dynamics is unrelentingly removed in this becoming. We need a different logic to that of frontiers to try to approach an everyday existence populated by becoming cyborg. This search is in itself a political action. The becoming cyborg is a 'fold upon fold'. It forces us, therefore, to confront the multiple and the varied, the fragmentary and the unfinished, the nomadic and the hybrid.

The Forms of Cyberpsychology

In conclusion, we would like to explain how we imagine the forms of cyberpsychology. Above all, believe that it cannot be a doctrine, a school or a method. We imagine cyberpsychology as a project that is always open, without doctrinal or methodological limits. We imagine it as a critical analytic tool, as a way of reading that which currently surround us. This manner of reading has an express political commitment.

We imagine a cyberpsychology that does not substitute ontology with a refusal to speak but which searches for the polyphony of creations, of ontological inventions. If cyberpsychology is a critical tool, we imagine it incorporating within its reflection what has always been the great otherness of social thought, technology, to be more precise, that which is not human; the events that populate our days spread out in networks, in chains made up of human and non-human assemblies. Nature and society, or society and technology are not concepts that operate as a starting point in order to explain or day to day, on the contrary, they are points of arrival. Purification exercises where human action is separated from that which is not human and where the mechanisms of intelligibility are separated from these actions. Cyberpsychology would not recognise artificial limits between the subjective world of politics-culture-morality and the objective world of science-technology-nature. We live in a present with a different logic to the one expressed by this dichotomy, we could call it the logic of assembly. Neither human subjects, nor conceptual or material objects can be considered in heir singularity or isolation from the networks and dynamic systems within which they appear. All things and all individuals arise, develop and disappear by joining together or by being incorporated in other structures that arise, develop and disintegrate.

Finally, we imagine cyberpsychology as vagrant knowledge which, at the same time, is not lacking in objects. We imagine it as an analysis of a changing, heteromorphological present, populated with a multitude of sensitive data that do not cease to be produced, fractual, unassimilable. We do not imagine it as a renunciation of the study of that which surrounds us, as an abandonment to the mere flow of data and experience. We imagine cyberpsychology made by a fragile, uncertain being, shifting in like manner to the terrain upon which it moves. Approximate and momentary, without firmly capturing its object, without drawning it in final explanations. In particular, We imagine a knowledge made up of 'mini-concepts', previously made up of ancient words with new meanings, ancient words in original combinations. We imagine a knowledge of dispersed remnants, more or less achieved, provisional.

REFERENCES

Bergson, H. ([1957]1977) *Memoria y vida. Madrid: Alianza Editorial.*

Clynes, M. and Kline, N.S. (1960) *Cyorgs and space.* Astronautics, Sept., 26-7, 74-5.

Deleuze, G. ([1977]1980) *Diologos con Claire Parnet.* Valencia.: Pre-Textos.

Deleuxe, G. ([1986]1987) *Foucault.* Barcelona: Edictions 62.

Deleuze, G. ([1990]1995) *Conversactions.* Valencia: Pre-Textos.

Deleuze, G. ([1993]1996) *Critica y Clinica.* Barecelona: Anagrama.

Deleuze, G. and Guattari, F.([1972]1977) *El AntiEdipo.* Barceloana: Paidos.

Deleuze, G. and Guattari, F, ([1980]1988) *Mil Mesetas.* Valencia: Pre-Textos.

Escobar, A. (1996) 'Welcom to Cyberia: notes on the anthropology of cyberculture', in Sardar, Z. and Ravetz. J.R. (eds.) *Cyberfutures: Culture and Patterns on the Information Highway.* London: Pluto Press.

Foucault, M. ([1961]1991)*Historia de la locura.* Madrid: Fondo de Cultura Economic.

Foucault. M. ([1963]1989) *El Nacimiento de la Clinica.* Madrid: Siglo XXI de Espanda editores.

Foucault, M. ([1966]1970) *The Order of Things.* London: Tavistock.

Gergen, K.J. (1994) *Realities and Relationships.* Cambridge: Harvard University Press.

Haraway, D. ([1991]1995) *Ciencia, Cyborgs y Mujeres.* Madrid: Catedra.

Ibanez, T. (1994) *Psicolgia Social Consructionsita.* Guadalajara: Universidad de Guadalajara.

Knort-Cetina. K. (1995) *Epistermic Cultures.* Chicago. Chicago Universiy Press.

Lepex Petit, S (1994) *Entire of Sery el Poder.* Madrid. Siglo XXI de Espana Editores.

Michael, M. (1996) *Constructing Identities.* London: Sage.

Piscitelli, A. (1995) *Ciberculturas.* Barcelona: Paidos.

Serres. M. ([1980]1991)*El paso del Noroeste:* Madrid: Debate.

Wahl. F. (1975) *Qu'est-ce que le Structuralisme?* Paris: Seuil.

Wolmark. J. (1995) 'Cyborg bodies and problems of representation', in Burman E.A., Gordo-Lopez, Macauley, J.R. and Parker, I. (eds) *Cyberpsychology: Conference, Interventions and Reflections.* Manchester, Discourse Unit.

13 THE CYBER AND THE SUBJECTIVE

It has been often mentioned that technologies shape our images of ourselves, but little has been made of how our selves shape technology. Once science overcame superstition, the explanatory narratives humans used to make sense of life processes mirrored the scientific narratives explaining nature. Holy fires and vital life forces gave way in the Enlightenment to complex narratives concerning mechanics, physics and biology. Industry operated on the basis of hydraulics, and science estimated that the human body operated as a machine, that various connections of pipes, tubes motors, governors, made life possible. genetics forms the foundation for the life sciences at present, and our computer technologies/ binary codes mimic DNA.

What has happened to our human narratives, though? Do they, too, mimic the digitised, fragmented bits to which we have become accustomed the digitised, fragmented bits to which we have become accustomed by science? Postmodern discourse as a form of human and social narrative would seem to suggest that in fact we have adopted a kind of narrative would seem to suggest that in fact we have adopted a kind of digital, or at least digitised, viewpoint. Postmodernism has much to offer as we try to determine who we are in the late twentieth century, approaching a new millennium. But as Postmodern philosophers would probably readily admit, it is but one of many explanatory schemes. Perhaps that will be the legacy of digitisation: as the bit has standardised the format by which the media of communication operate, it has also levelled the value of the content mediated. At least it has inscribed valuation within the subjective, for if, as Nicholas Negroponte (1995) and other 'digerati' are wont to point out, 'bits are bits,' then it is only what individuals do with bits that matters. If we understand humans in a fashion similar to the way we understand digital being, might we not also level the value of our selves, or at least imagine into being a hypersubjective realm in which mediation of the self through communication is the *sine qua non* of networked technologies?

As other chapters in this volume remind us, our most recent technologies are indeed particularly ones of the self. They conflate the narratives we construct about who we are with ones we construct about who we are in relation to technology, rather than in relation to one another. One might even say that these are not only technologies of the self, but selfish technologies. The affective dimension of network technologies is difficult to assay, but is of great importance. The contributors to this volume have done a masterful job of mapping out that terrain, altering us to the tasks that lay ahead as we come grips with new subjectives.

A note about the subjective; I am an interloper into the discussion of cyberpsychology. My training is in the study of communication and in cultural and critical studies. Any scholars in the social sciences and humanities, however, ignoring the consequences of network technologies for their work, do so at their peril. The issue is not merely whether the Internet, for instance, can disseminate information more rapidly, whether on-line journals are a suitable arena for publication, or whether educational technology will displace traditional teaching methods. An overarching issue is the manner in which these technologies implicate the objects and subjects of scholarship, along with scholars themselves, in new webs of significance and meaning that impart new frameworks to our experiences and encounters. In addition to encapsulating us in any variety of Foucauldian panopticons, like some global Hawthorne effect, network technologies affect or thinking and behaviour as much because of the attention we pay the technology (and ourselves embedded in it) as because of anything else.

Additionally, we must attend to the very definitions of selfhood as these technologies engage us more than imaginatively in realms other than the ones we physically occupy. Marshall McLuhan's (1964) characterisation of the media of communication as 'extensions of man' was meant to make sense in the realm of the senses. The Internet however, is in these terms extrasensory. It less extends our senses and more extends our selves. The discussion in these pages of cyborgs and bodies is relevant and important. We must continue that discussion and consider the nature of software agents and bots to best understand the social system being envisioned and engaged in these networks. In addition to asking who we are when we are online, and who we are when we are off-line, what heuristic power may derive from asking who we are when we are, simply, not present? Does telepresence fundamentally alter not only the nature of both presence and selfhood but also the nature of absence?

The critical nature of these chapters is of great importance, too. We must more critical discourse about cyberculture to the forefront or our debates about network technologies. And when we doe so we must keep at bay nostalgia, not for the past, but for the future. Behind much of what has been written about cyberculture lies a series of 'if onlys' that at best make its authors seem presumptuous, and at worst reveal an uncritical perspective. One is reminded of a type of Country and Western song with the refrain, 'We could have had it all'. Predictions of the future are as much about the past as they are about our imagination, and David Abrahamson (cited in Carey), ' the only thing certain about the future is that we know nothing about it'.

What is needed, I believe, is an interpretive turn to our discussions of cyberculture. Let us asks of ourselves. for whom are our words meant? For the psycho-technological complex in its entirely? For the individuals engaged in it in innumerable ways? For ourselves, the disciplines of which we are a part and/or for (not necessarily) because of) the experiences we have had of technology? As we write, debate, speak about these matters, do we repress what we explain? Do we explain it away? Do we explain it into being? In what ways do we make meanings even as we understand those extant? Vannevar Bush's (1945) fortunate phrase in the title of one of his essays, 'As We May Think', inspired not only the artefact we term the Internet, and its hypertextual character, but the meaningful and deep structures of thought with which it is overlaid. The network of networks mimics human thought, but at a level beyond the individual it mimics culture itself. Post-structuralists should recognise the Internet's character as an articulative process and not only a technology. In Lewis Mumford's (1934) terms, it is the *technics* of the Internet that are of greatest importance. The Internet more than any other modern technology embeds technics in reference to social relations. Consequently, our inquiries and interventions into cyberculture are, as Stuart Hall (personal communication) said in relation to cultural studies, deadly serious intellectual work. And cyberculture appears to be a particularly resonant site for such work. Will the work we do also have serious material, cultural effects on cyberculture in turn? The Internet particularly has roots in academia, and we should be attentive to that rootedness as we examine both its past and its future.

In regard to articulation, the Internet's meaning, as meanings within and among culture(s) generally, is not simply in its structures, nor is it in its users, although at any one given time it is located specifically there. Rather, its meaning is in the connecting between and among nodes, accreting and dispersing, (virtually) ahistorically, or so the technology makes it seem to us. The Internet, and thus cyberculture (although I do not equate those but only refer to them in the same sentence to note their for-better-or-worse constant conflation and necessary interdependence) are technology-as-process rather then technology-as-produce.

Within a technology-as-process where and how does none locate the self? Judging from the chapters in this book (although this is the least of its contributions), the relationships between society and self are in flux, and self (itself) is in flux. Self has always been multiple, as most recently and popularly noted by Verve singer Richard Ashcroft declaring 'I'm a million different people from one day to the next,' although he goes on to note that he 'can't change the mould' he's in. A pertinent question, then: who has made the mould? Is it indeed a human construction at all, or a technological one, or a combination of those? In what ways is cyberculture a mould, a cyberstructure, as a technology-as-process, perhaps one akin to a coral reef that grows, is eaten away, regrows? An example: Most of us have a variety of voices we use on the telephone. One voice is for friends, another for family, still another for telemarketers, and so on. Those are typically voices we do not use in person, or at least we are not conscious of using them. Did the telephone split our selves via our voice? Was the potential for such a split there already? Does networked communication fragment us similarly, along lines of identity forged by email address, IP mode, Internet tool, or something else altogether?

Answers to these questions have typically engaged issues of culture, technology and communication, and in turn those issues fall upward to analyses of the human relation to space and time. The chapters in this book do as well, to an extent. But they also focus on subjectivity in a way that must force us to a more substantive discourse of what space and time mean in relation to communication. Marshall McLuhan (1964). Harold Innis (1972) and James Carey (1980) have greatly added to our understanding of space and time in relation to communication. This volume's contributors in in their own way further that work and allow us to bring subjectivity into these discourse. We have this far had a tendency to apply subjectivity only at those times when we need to explain how and why digital media, quintessentially linear, bounded, discrete forms, seem anything but linear, bounded and discrete. How has it come to be that these technological forms seem analogue, continuous and relative? Is it their speed? Is it that time is not linear, not flowing, but discrete, and that our perceptual processing provides sufficient closure, as it does when we hear a CD, or use a telephone, for example, and hear sounds made up of millions of discrete bits that form analogue sound?

I ask these questions because they have been much on my mind lately, as I have tried to make sense of the transition from one type of society to another, from one forged by the Industrial Revolution to one inscribed by bits and lasers. It took decades to make sense of the transition from an agrarian to an industrial society, and it will likely take decades to make sense of the one from an industrial society to a networked one. The upheavals the first transition brought to the surface were vast, and in many cases dangerous. Whether the ones we are now experiencing are, or will be, dangerous, we cannot yet know. That they are vast, however, is certain, We are beginning, however, to chase down that vastness, perhaps like William, Cowper's philologists 'who chase/A panting syllable through time and space/Start it at home, and hunt it in the dark' (1968:691). Illumination follows.

ARE MEDIA CYBORGS?

Virginia Nightingale

In the following comment on the changing (and anti-communicative) character of global culture, the late Michel de Certeau suggested that the shift flows of 'people, things and ideas' as the organising mode of culture is changing the structure and balance of our social and cultural worlds:

> Communication is the central myth of our societies split between the development of circulation and atomisation. On the one hand, emphasis is placed on everything that circulates (people, things, and ideas), on travels, on modes of transport, and on schools and the media, these two great interchanges of ideas and images. On the other hand our social organisation endlessly scatters and fragments groups, individuals, and traditions; it collapses the inner logic that used to structure former ways of thinking, a use of relations, a language of everyday life, and the memory that used to inhabit gestures and speech. As the information that is distributed throughout social space increases, the relation among the

> practitioners of this space tend to decrease. Communication thus becomes the paradox and the system of the juncture of what informs and what relays: distribution of communication increases, but its reality diminishes. At the core of these tensions is located the place and that which pertains to locality. (Certeau 1997: 91)

Certeau envisaged a relation between flow and culture such that as flow processes accelerate, the infrastructure of the old culture atomises into smaller and smaller units. Its logic collapses, and so do its traditions and social relations. The survival advantage, whether material, social, cultural, shifts to the capacity for flexibility with which cultural units can assemble, disassemble and reassemble again, no matter whether the assembling is assisted by post-Fordist commodity production or human reproductive technologies.

Certeau anticipated that the stress and tension which results from the pace of flows and from the fragmentation of social relations under such pressure places greater emphasis than ever before on 'locality' as the sites where flow 'fall-out', both good and bad, is likely to become evident and where strategies and tactics of resistance will occur. If I can be forgiven an analogy, this is a *Feng Shui* culture, where *chi* energy threatens to overwhelm locality unless controlled or deflected by tactics such as reflections, sound, barriers, screens, mazes and traps, It leads to the development of strategies for capturing the power of the *chi* in order to access its energy for human ends and its seems to me that work produced for this volume, *Cyberpsychology,* starts this process as he beginning of a strategic engagement with the most powerful flow humanity has yet encountered-cyberspace.

Clearly, there are likely to be both benefits and potential psychological harms in social, technological and specifically cybercultural changes of his order, and it is to the mapping of such impacts that his anthology speaks. *Cyberpsychology* presents theorisation and analysis of the psychological fall-our from the cultural shift to 'flow' (or 'circulation') as the increasingly dominating organising principle of our culture. Where traditional psychology was predicated on assumptions of the body as the origin of the drive and on the self as the author of a life, *Cyberpsychology* contemplates the possibility of extra-corporeal origins and non-Oedipal psycho-geneses. It explores, as Gordo-Lopez and Parker point out in he introduction to Part One, the nature of'cyberpsychological modes of corporeality and subjectivity' and the possibilities of submission and repression, resistance and subversion in the cyber-environment.

Anthropomorphism and Totemism as Cyborg Models

Nevertheless, my first reaction to *Cyberpsychology* is to wonder at the extensive anthropomorphism that permeates the discussion of cyborgs and patterns the developing agenda that will eventually be identified as 'cyberpsychology'. Somewhat strangely to me the regular punctuation of the readings with Haraway's judgement - 'we are cyborgs' - serves, in the 'cyberpsychology' context, to reinforce the imagining of cyborg agency as an elaboration of human agency, and of cyborg testifies as hybratical human testifies. Haraway, I cannot accept that this is an adequate apprehension of her position. Haraway seems to me to be affirming the present proliferation and hybridisation of cyborgs as a continuation of our phylogenetic dependence on technological and social intelligence - intelligences that Mithen claims have evolved with humans from pre-human times (Mithen 1996). In fact the discourse on the cyborg seems to place too much emphasis on only one of the two extremely early modes of thought (anthropomorphism and totemism) which have assisted human cultures in the prediction of the archetypal flow - nature.

Mithen usefully reminds us that anthropomorphism and totemism mirror each other as ways of conceiving nature and as precursors to controlling it. But in my reading of *Cyberpsychology* there is very little elaboration of the totemic cyborg and rather too much elaboration of the anthropomorphic cyborg.

The anthropormophisation of the cyborg worries me because it obstructs my contemplation of an alternative, totemic vision of the cyborg. My cyborg 'vision' is informed, I shamelessly admit, by my interest in readership, audience and fan cultures, and from this perspective I see no *a priori* requirement that a cyborg must possess physical form or bodily parts in the way that both humans and the anthropomorphised cyborg do. This issue became most strongly focused for me when reading Sey's thoughtful and erudite comments on the delusions of ageing hackers that humanity is about to be replaced by a cyborg superrace. Sey claims instead that 'the body provides the limit not only to experience, but to knowledge and power also'. I completely agree because I imagine the possibility that some extremely interesting cyborgs are dependent on transitory appropriations of human bodies and other physical and psychological properties of humans for their existence. They are humanoid rather than human-like. These electronic chimeras borrow human qualities by enticing humans into their flowing. They cathect human bodies to provide them with energy; they amass human bodies to command power. Without human service these cyborgs cease to exist; they evaporate almost without trace. Henri Lefebvre (1991; 116-7) defined flows as the energies which surround living organisms- capable of both threatening and supporting life. Media flows begin by supporting life. They facilitate in various ways our primordial fascinations with both sociality and technology. But with human power and psychology behind them, media flows are also capable of threatening life in a variety of ways, which is why a cyberpsychology capable of understanding them is so important.

My 'cyborgs' contrast most dramatically with Heggs' superheroes and cyborgs. Heggs imagines as augmented equivalence between human and cyborgian agency . He suggests that at the very least the two agentic psychogeneses are comparable and therein instructive of each other. he presents a very interesting argument that the non-Oedipal psychogenesis of the cyborg threatens the world with a cyborgian predetermination to act as programmed, to act totally egocentrically, since the cyborg is perversely narcissistic and lacks the capacity to take another's perspective. The cybernetic organism as human person 'gone wrong' simply shines more brightly and blinks alternately as human/non-human consciousness and human/non-human body. The figure of this non-human cyberorganism is valuable, as Heggs indicates, for allowing humans to imagine another perspective (and its alterity). The imagining of accidental hybridisation is the raw material of science fiction horror (see Heggs' account of *The Fly*), but here Heggs considers the accidental cooptation of insect agency and biological imperatives, while I remain haunted by images of spectral vectors and electronic Sirens.

My question, 'Are media cyborgs?", was prompted by a statement from Sey's essay and an example he used to explain it. Sey makes the following point. With the vast proliferation of technological systems beyond the initially crucial confines of the industrial relation between body and machine, we can discern that the ostensible disappearance of technology from the body, which might seem to mark a move into postmodernity, in fact emerges as the disappearance of the body into technology. Technological systems, that is, have extended to form the context of our experience of time and space, duration and extension.

This statement for me an even more radical understanding of 'audience' than that I proposed in my book, *Studying Audiences* (Nightingale, 1996). In particular it concretised a vision of media as cyborgs, and I immediately began to imagine example on example of places where people disappear 'into' media - video game play; TV viewing; net surfing; radio listening. This is the chilling reality explored in Alexander Besher's 'novel of virtual reality' *RIM* (Bescher, 1994) where children are lost in virtual reality, their bodies suspended, comatose in the real world until rescued by an unlikely veteran of virtual environments. With other media, such 'disappearances' are characteristically temporary and, usually but not always, voluntary excursions into an alternative experience of extension and duration from that of everyday life - but they have in various pre-electronic forms (from rock at to reading) always been a characteristic of human culture.

But then a few paragraphs down, I noticed that Sey expressed he view that it is 'sport' that has changed as a result of technology that allows 'the sedentary and distanced viewer to become either a wishful voyeur or a postmodern technographic scientist "manque". The example disconcerted me because in this case I strongly believe that neither sport nor the viewer has changed fundamentally. The viewers' expectations of what they consider they should be able to see and of how they should be able to see it *have* changed. Viewers expect the deployment and exploitation of technology, but that exploitation is not changing sport. It is changing the meaning of participation and engagement in sport on the one hand, and the expectations of the quality of the information brought to the contemplation of such participation and engagement on the other. In some cases sub-varieties of the particular sport may be developed to meet the requirements of media broadcasting (as in the development of one-day-cricket) but fundamentally 'sport' has not changed.

Sport is; as Sey understands, a very interesting example. Sporting events ar major socio-cultural fixtures. They pre-date the electronic media and are one of the contexts where contemporary totemism continues to be practised. Football teams in my home town, Sydney, are called Tigers, Bulldogs, Sharks, Sea Eagles, Eels - the list goes on. Broadcasting has added to the sporting event its parallel broadcast form and inadvertently created a level of competition between attendance at the broadcast form and the live form. The intensity of the competition is attested by the introduction of regulations and agreements about broadcasting rights which limit the synchronic presentation of sports broadcasts with the live event. Much more could be said about this, especially if social problems linked to off-course betting for horseracing and box-office takings for cricket and football games were more fully analysed.

The new twist in sports broadcasting is that it is now possible for the sporting field and its advertising to be altered for the broadcast image - advertisements for cigarette companies using billboards and hoardings on the field may become advertisements for entirely different products in the broadcast event. A potentially boring broadcast of a less than world-class local event can now be enhanced by the interweaving of other cultural forms (perhaps animation or comedy). Imagine for example the case of a home goal in a soccer match - suddenly it is possible to play mini-cartoons in the outfield which joke at the player's expense or which rehearse thc win presaged by such a mistake for either or each team. If viewers pay per view and select their team broadcast, even more intense programming is possible, with in-jokes and all pretence of impartiality by the commentators dispatched. Of one thing there can be no doubt, the direction this change takes will be to increase the intensity of the viewing experience for both live and broadcast events, to lure more people into the flow because without people there would be no broadcast. And yet the live event and the broadcast event remain necessary to each other. The broadcast event annexes not only the players, referees and linesmen, it also annexes he crowd - its look, its voice, its mood, its energy and vital essence, not to mention its buying power and its non-verbal commentary on the game. The broadcast event annexes these characteristics of humans and replays them as television entertainment, in the context of televisual flow, where the bodily amassing of a second (viewer) crowd completes the cyberphenomenon.

The cyborg hybrid lurking here is a variety of broadcast television entertainment. It is TV sports broadcasting. To be more precise, the cyborg is the phenomenon produced by the combined interaction of the technology, the viewers and the owners, financiers, broadcasters, producers, ratings agencies, technicians and all participants in television - that is by human labour and human technologies. The agency of this television cyborg is undirectional - towards self-maintenance and self-enhancement. It is based on the model of totemism, and it works with a logic of flow, feigns political and cultural weakness in order to encourage the largest possible number of people to lend it their bodies or the longest possible period of time. But one of its most interesting characteristics, and he reason why I raise it in the context of a discussion of cyberpsychology, is its capacity to develop a psychology of engagement that is parasitic of human psychology.

Media Psychologies

Each medium of communication is dependent on human bodies, some media (usually commercial media) develop their own psychological pitch or seduction - and yet we have been very slow to look closely at the psychologies of electronic media (radio and television) when compared with the volumes written on the psychologies of print, film and the photographic image.'Selling' psychologies have dominated these mass broadcasting terrains and this probably explains the lack of interest they hold for most academic researchers who prefer the more complex media psychology challenges of the novel or the film. The virulence of radio psychology was brought home to me recently when collaborating on a conference paper with my colleague, Jackle Cook (Nightingale and Cook, 1997). Cook's research on talk-back radio had revealed the capacity of the highest rating talk-back radio hosts to 'sex' the space of radio talk by deploying a hypermasculinity augmented by the production codes of radio. She demonstrates that the host cultivates seduction and 'dirty talk' from women callers, but challenges or 'calls out' male callers, 'beating them up' with bad language and unfair abuse to parade his dominant position. The talk-back host does not hesitate to mercilessly exercise his control of the studio and the production crew to censor callers. He uses gift giving (of sponsor-donated gifts) to repay favours or to hide his guilty conscience. His 'bad behaviour' attracts callers like bees to a honey pot!

Such behaviour is not confined to radio. A very similar spatial sexing is described in *Wired!* as the style of the late Tom Mandel, moderator of several, and contributor to most, *Well* conferences over a period of ten years (*Wired!* May 1997). Mandel's sexualisation and monstering of explorers in the cyberspaces created by *The Well* had an effect similar to that of the radio host - kept people involved as participants and as voyeurs, and demonstrated a commercial potential for the Web as an entertainment medium.

So are media psychologies part of cyberpsychology? The suductive hypermasculine environment of radio developed not only to hook listeners but also to sell the capitalist 'gift' of commodities. Cook's research examines how a production team and fan club coordinate the listening and buying activity that maintains the programme, and a technology of control operates to maintain the radio space as an a active one. Psychological strategies and techniques which exploit the frustrated sociality of frequently aged and isolated people are deployed to this end. Similarly the broadcast sports event, another environment promoting the advantages and power of the male, extols the virtues of male competitive strategies and muscular development. It parades the sociality of the crowd and in doing so hints at the managerial expertise of male power.

Certeau considered flows to be contemporary and culturally destructive phenomena. Henri Lefebvre considered 'space' - whether physical or mental, concrete or abstract - and the production of 'space' to be the key cultural product, and he defined 'flows' as the energies which surround living organisms- capable of both threatening and supporting life. He considered flows to be the 'spatio-temporal rhythms of nature as transposed by a social practice' (Lefebvre, 1991: 117): composed of 'raw materials and energy' (ibid.: 85). For lefebvre, flows could be contrasted with 'those realities which some geographers call 'networks' and which are subordinated to the frameworks of politics' (ibid.: 116). Media are obviously flows, and flows which are capable of supporting life. In fact they mostly facilitate life by offering opportunities for sociality in the spaces they colonise from absolute space;

> Absolute space cannot be understood in terms of a collection of sites and signs; to view it thus is to misapprehend it in the most fundamental way. Rather, it is indeed a space, at once and indistinguishably mental and social, which comprehends the entire existence of the group... and it must be so understood. In a space of this kind there is no 'environment', not properly speaking, any 'site' distinct from the overall texture. (Lefebvre, 1995:240)

Lefebvre (1995: 234ff.) explains the concept, absolute, space, by pointing to the relationship between town and countryside, a populated space of use patterning, irreducible to the blank abstraction of corporate representations. His description is usefully extended to the pioneering of cyberspace as a new media space and to the pioneering of cyberspace as a new media space and to the current attempts to transform it into a selling space. A gendered characterisation of the processes of engagement between town (website) and countryside (cyberspace), produces a symbiosis, following Lefebvre, which results in an initially unsexed space of power and sacredness. In the context of websites nd experiences of surfing the Internet, this engagement ostensibly remains 'outside' physicality, in a realm of disembodiment where there is no 'environment', only a 'texture' fabricated from the very interaction of websites with cyberspace. This 'dislocated' relation however, by its very claim to extra-terrestrial or terra nullius mythical states, becomes primordial and primogenitive. Both maternal and paternal, absolute (cyber)space becomes the antithesis of both, and in this absoluteness, invokes the sacred. The sense of the sacred is evident in the names chosen and in the fates befalling the more notorious Internet communities - for example 'The Well' and 'Heaven's Gate' - examples of the political and the religious identifications and intrigues which characterise Internet communities, and of the beginning of a totemism based on life source analogies of the ineffable. The sterility and emptiness of the unformed website is characteristic of the evacuated yet sublime character of cyberspace, and perhaps explains the determination with which the Heaven's Gate cult quit this earth-bound life and decided to seek permanent dissolution of their psyches in the mythical homeland behind the Hale-Bopp comet.

Reflection: Exhibitionism and Harassment

I once re-read the current week's crop of Internet stories. The focus was on net exhibitionism - Lorraine Chew replaced, or joined, Jennifer Ringley in living her life for her Web camera and the entertainment of the thousands who visit her website each day; Ty Taylor and Michelle Parma finally conceded that their loss of virginity is totally unrelated to their plans to have sex on the Internet; and the mother who gave birth to her fourth child on the Internet was arrested for writing false cheques (Sevrens, 1998). Such life transition phenomena, rites of passage - birth, defloration, initiation - remind me of the totemic identifications such transitions often accompany. Their expensiveness for the participants is obvious in the arrest for, fraud, unsolicited surveillance and other forms of harassment that stalk the unwary at every turn in this cyberfrontier.

Web panics about Internet rape and the unregulated preying of pornography and pederasty groups on unsuspecting young Web users are quickly outpaced by new panics about e-commerce and credit and fraud. In this discourse the press replays a popular litany of media anxieties, sometimes in and sometimes out of sync with the complex philosophical, psychoanalytic and socio-cultural reflection of the chapters in *Cyberpsychology*. *Cyberpsychology*, by contrast, focuses on the 'conditions' of cyberpsychology and at times seems troubled more by the ontological status of cyberpsychology itself than interested in its phenomenology and scientific development. Is it succumbing to or recoiling from the insistent, creeping and perverse narcissism of the cyberworld?

REFERENCES

Bescher, A (1994) *RIM : A Novel of Virtual Reality:* New York: HarpeCollins. Certeau, M.de (1997) *The Capture of Speech and Other Political Writings* (Conley T., trans.). Minneapolis and London: University of Minnesota Press.

Bush V. (1945) 'As we may think', *Atlantic Monthly,* 162(7): 33-40.

Carey, J.W. (1988) 'The Internet and the end of the national communication system: Uncertain predictions of an uncertain future', *Journalism and Mass Communications Quarterly,* 75(1) 28-34.

Carey, J.W. (1989) *Communication as Culture,* Boston: Unwin-Hyman.

Cowper, W. (1968[1785]) *Verse and Letters.* Cambridge, MA: Harvard University Press.

Haraway, D. (1991) 'A cyborg manifesto', in *Simians, Cyborgs, and Women* New York: Routledge.

Innis, H.A. (1964) *The Bias of Communication.* Toronto: University of Toronto Press.

Innis, H.A. (1972) *Empire and Communications.* Toronto: University of Toronto Press.

Lefebvre, H. (1991) *The Production of Space,* trans. (Nicholson-Smith, D., trans.). London and Cambridge, MA: Blackwell.

McLuhan, M.(1964)*Understanding Media: The Extensions of Man.* New York: McGraw-Hill.

Mithen, S. (1996) *The Prehistory of the Mind. A Search for the Origins of Art, Religion and Science.* London: Orion Books/Phoenix.

Mumford, L. (1934) *Technics and Civilisation.* New York: Harcourt Brace.

Negroponte, N. (1995) *Being Digital.* New York: Knopf.

Nightingale, V. and Cook, J. (1997) 'Hard buys and soft sells. Unpublished paper presented to IAMCR Mexico Conference July.

Nightingale. V.(1996) *Studying Audiences: The Shock of the Real.* London. Routledge.

Sevrens, J. (1998) 'Lust for fame', *The Weedend Australian,* August 29-30.

Wired! (1997) 'Pushi Kiss your browser goodbye the radical future beyond the Web'. Editorial (March 12-23).

14 COMPUTER CONTRACTS

Contracts for the acquisition and use of computer hardware and software are dealt with in this chapter. Many such contracts are not sale contracts as such but are license agreements; this is particularly so with respect to computer software where the owner of the rights subsisting in the software grants licences to customers, giving them permission to use the software in return for a licence fee. For these agreements, the existence and scope of intellectual property rights is of fundamental importance.The acts restricted by copyright may form a substantial part of the licence's subject matter. Contracts for the acquisition of hardware and software are subject to may of the legal constraints on contracts such as the Unfair Contract Terms Act 1977 and those provided for by copyright law.

Liability issues related to defective hardware and software are discussed next and in should be noted that, in some cases, liability is not dependent upon the existence of a contractual relationship and, where appropriate, liability for negligence and product liability is discussed. An employer's liability in relation to RSI (repetitive strain injury) caused by long periods of work at a keyboard is also discussed. In subsequent chapters, particular types of computer contracts are described: contracts for the writing of computer software, 'off-the -shelf' software licences, agreements between software authors and publishers, and hardware contracts. There is a separate chapter looking at the implications of electronic contracting, and area which is growing in importance at an exponential rate. The summary chapter includes a checklist of terms normally to be found in contracts concerning computer hardware and software.

INTRODUCTION TO COMPUTER CONTRACTS

Contracts for the acquisition of computer equipment and software present special problems, many of which flow from the unique nature of computer technology. For example, we cannot see or touch a computer program running in a computer; all we can do is experience its effects through a peripheral device such as a screen or a printer. It may be possible to read a listing of a computer program and perhaps make some sense of it but, certainly to many of us who have to use computer programs, they take on a quasi-mystical nature as they are, after all, intangible. It is the difficulty in coming to terms with the nature, effects and implications of computer equipment and software that is a direct cause of many of the contractual and other problems associated with computers.

The case of *Brownton Ltd* v *Edward Moore Inbucon Ltd* [1985] 3 All ER 499 provides an example of the financial implications of misunderstandings between the parties to a contract involving computer systems. A firm of commodity brokers sought advice from a computer consultant on the installation of a computer system. The consultant recommended a particular system which was installed in 1978. Unfortunately, the system never worked properly, was quite inadequate for the broker's needs and was eventually scrapped. The consultant had charged over £ 66,000 for his work and the computer system had cost in the region of £75,000. The broker claimed damages, for breach of contract, of over £ 250,000 based on the wasted expense and the difference in price between the system obtained and a new system that would be capable of doing the work. Later, the broker submitted better particulars and claimed that an alternative computer system capable of carrying out the work would cost in excess of £1.1 million. Eventually, a settlement of around £ 300,000 was reached.

In another case, a lack of understanding of the ORACLE fourth-generation computer language on the part of the client and software developer during the feasibility study for and initial development stages of complex accounting software led to the inevitable result. The software was delivered late and, because it contained a large number of errors, it was unusable. The client was awarded £662 962 in damages (see *The Salvage Association* v *GAP Financial Services Ltd* [1995] FSR 654). The software developed was unable to avail itself of a clause on the contract limiting stability for defects to £25,000.

A hypothetical example can further illustrate the difficulties. A company wants to install a computer system on one of its departments which has previously had to use slow, laborious (but reliable) manual methods. The initial decision to do this is probably based on some vague notion that a computer system will increase efficiency, or perhaps because all its competitors have installed computer systems. The company already may have a mainframe computer and the IT manager might suggest that some potentially suitable software packages be evaluated and that obtaining a ready-made package should be considerably less expensive than writing one from scratch. The first problem is to decide how the available packages should be evaluated and by whom. The people in the company who will use the proposed system ought to be involved in the selection process, but such people are unlikely to have much knowledge of computers and computer software although they may be familiar with word processing and spreadsheet systems running on their desktop computers.

The IT manager and other computer professionals, either within the company or brought in from outside as consultants, will have an important contribution to make to the decision. Although they will have an intimate knowledge of computers, they will probably not have a deep knowledge of the particular application of the proposed software. Their priorities will differ. The computer people will want to know how the software will fit in with their portfolio of software, whether it will require additional computer equipment, how well it will be maintained, now portable it is and so on. There may follow a lack of communication and understanding between the computer professionals, the legal advisers, the ultimate users and the supplier of the software resulting in the purchase of a system which is cumbersome, does not provide all the information the users now realise they would have liked and which runs far too slowly to be of any practical use. The software company which supplied the package is not unsympathetic but claims that it was just not given clear and sufficient guidance as to what was expected of the software. The software company may even suggest that the problems will be overcome if new and more powerful equipment is obtained. An allegation that the problem lies with the client's own computer installation might be difficult to refute. It is at this stage that the contract is carefully examined, perhaps for the first time, and the company obtaining the software realises, too late, that as far as it is concerned, the contract is little more than worthless and does not provide adequately for the situation. The client might refuse to make the final payments and the ensuing legal struggle is both predictable and inevitable. IT personnel and independent computer consultants must educate department heads and legal advisers as to the implications and dangers involved in acquiring computer equipment and software. Departmental heads and legal advisers, for their part, must be prepared to ask questions of their computer advisers and, even more importantly, so listen to the answers.

The point of the above story is to demonstrate the importance of the parties to a computer contract knowing precisely what is to be expected in terms of performance and the standards required. The role that the equipment or software is intended to build must be clearly identified and quantified, a comprehensive and precise specification must be drawn up. The lack of, or defects in, specification is probably at the heart of most disputes resulting from the aquisition of computer equipment and software.

The importance of choosing the most appropriate hardware and software should not be underestimated and, as a corollary, a contract which provides a reasonable and fair machinery for indentifying responsibilities and resolving disputes needs to be negotiated. A mistake in the choice of equipment or software coupled with a poor contract can be disastrous for a purchasing company. The problems are not all one-sided, however, as it may be that a supplier of equipment or software has to fall back on contractual remedies. If the acquiring company refuses to provide, or is incapable of providing, clear instructions, if it refuses to accept and/or pay for the equipment or software, if it tampers with the programs, misuses them and allows employees to copy them freely, the supplier will need to take action. The company making the acquisition will need to decide: how the contract can protect it if the equipment or software fails to perform as it should; how it should be maintained and how its staff should be trained; and what to do if the software or hardware infringes a third party's copyright or patent. Other decisions will concern the selection of the software developer or hardware supplier, the form of contract and whether a feasibility study or prototyping work is to be undertaken.

One thing is clear, whatever form of contract is used, and that is that great care must be taken in drafting the contract. Judges interpret contracts strictly and will use certain principles of construction when it comes to resolving inconsistencies and ambiguities. If a contract is silent on a particular matter, judges may if necessary imply terms to give the contract business efficacy on the basis of the presumed intention of the parties. As judge will not, however, write the contract for the parties. There must be, at least, something resembling a concrete agreement between the parties. It is certainly very unwise to use a form of contract designed for one jurisdiction in another, even though both have similar legal systems. In *Adersen Consulting v CHP Consulting Ltd* (unreported) 26 July 1991, ex-employees of the plaintiff set up in business on their own account, providing maintenance for the plaintiff's computer programs. The plaintiff argued that a term in their licence agreements prevented maintenance by third parties. Mr Justice Harman refused to grant an injunction in favour of the plaintiff and strongly criticised the use of an American contract which he described as having odd and inept phrasing. The contract should have been drafted to take account of United Kingdom law; it was simply not good enough to make a few modifications to an American form of contract.

The nature of the contract, contractual and tortious liabilities and the use of exclusion clauses will be considered. Individual terms which may be found in various types of computer contracts will then be discussed in subsequent chapters with a view to avoiding the disasters that await the unwary. Balanced, fair and thorough negotiation is the key to a smooth running contract and all the relevant contractual terms and mechanisms should be considered and agreed before the parties become committed to the contract. The final chapter in this part of the book contains a summary and checklist of terms commonly found in computer contracts.

FUNDAMENTALS OF COMPUTER CONTRACTS

Terms of the Contract

It is important to know precisely what the terms of a contract are. Of course, in many situations where the whole contract is in writing, this should be an easy matter. Providing one is skilled in 'legalese', the technical legal jargon is still commonly found in legal documents. But even here, things are not necessarily that straightforward and the law may insert additional terms into the contract or strike out some of the terms apparently agreed upon by the parties to the contract. This is notwithstanding the English tradition of freedom of contract - to the effect that their contract. Another problem may be where the contract is not in writing or is only partly in writing. An example of the latter is where a signed note or memorandum indicates that a contract exists but clearly does not contain all the terms on the face of it. For example, the note may state that Ace Software Ltd agrees to write process control software for Boris Boring and Drilling Co Ltd for the sum of £45,000. On its own such a note would be unenforceable because it lacks certainty. Apart from other missing information, there is no specification or other description of what is required of the software not any time for delivery. In relation to oral contracts and contracts partly in writing, it will be a matter of submitting evidence of the other terms to give the contract sufficient certainty. To over come some of these difficulties, the law may imply terms into the contract.

The first is to look at what has been expressly agreed by the parties. The *express terms,* whether oral or in writing, may be the only terms of the contract, although this would be rare. In many cases, the law will imply terms into the contract, particularly as a result of statute. These *implied terms,* such as those implied into certain contracts by the Sale of Goods Act 1979 or the Supply of Goods or Services Act 1982 are particularly important and are discussed later in this and subsequent chapters. Sometimes, the courts may imply terms into a contract. However, this will only be done in limited circumstances as indicated by Lord Pearson in *Trollope & Colls Ltd* v *North West Metropolitan Regional Hospital Board* [1973] 1 WLR 602 where he said (at 609):

> An unexpressed term can be implied if and only if the court finds that the parties must have intended that the term form part of their contract; it is not enough for the court to find that such a term would have been adopted by the parties as reasonable men if it had been suggested to them: it must have been a term that went without saying, a term necessary to give business efficacy to the contract, a term which although tacit, formed part of the contract which the parties made for themselves.

In other words the term must be such as is necessary to make the contract effective and must be a term which the parties would clearly have agreed must be included had it been mentioned to them at the time. It is not enough for the term to be one which would be reasonable to include. The above sentiment was agreed with in the Court of Appeal by Sir Iain Glidewell in *St Allians City & District Council* v *International Computers Ltd* [1997] FSR 251 where he held that, in a contract for wiring computer software without involving the transfer of property in tangible terms such as magnetic disks, the court could imply a term to the effect that the software was reasonably fit for its purpose. This important case of liability for defective software and the scope of exclusion clauses is discussed in more depth in the following chapter.

As well as implying terms into a contract, the law may impact upon the express terms. It may make a term, agreed by the parties, void and unenforceable. Normally, this will be the result of a statutory provision. For example a term in a software licence which prohibits or restricts the making of a necessary back-up copy or a computer program by a person having the right to use it under an agreement is declared void and unenforceable by section 296A(1) of the Copyright, Designs and Patents Act 1988. The Unfair Contract Terms Act 1977 is important in controlling the use of terms which try to exclude or limit liability for negligence and breach of contract among other things. Another way the courts will control contract terms is by using the common laws: for example, by declining to enforce a term which is in restraint of trade such as where a computer programmer's contract of employment prevents him working for a competitor of his employer for a period of five years without any geographical limitation. A common ploy in some contracts is where the party in the stronger bargaining position inserts some draconian terms and, knowing that the courts interfere with them, seeks to save as many of them as he can. A 'saving', sometimes referred to as a 'blue pencil' clause, may be worked as follows:

> In the event that any provision of this agreement is unenforceable but would be enforceable if

> part of the wording of the provision were to be deleted, it shall apply with the minimum of such deletions being made as required to make the provision enforceable.

Such terms are unlikely to be met with judicial favour Judges will not write the contract for the parties and draconian terms may be consigned to the court's waste bin rather than the judge striking out the offending parts. The general rule, however is that if a term is severable, that is, the contract can stand without it, the term will be deleted, leaving the rest of the contract in force. If the term in question is of fundamental importance to the contract, then the entire contract will be in jeopardy. Of course, the ploy of having draconian terms which may be unenforceable is that they may be accepted at face value by the other party and not tested in the courts. Nevertheless, great care must be taken not to attempt to take away certain statutory rights as to do so may result in criminal prosecution.

Nature of the Contract

It is not always easy to separate hardware and software and this fact has been demonstrated on several occasions in the courts. For example, in *Dyason* v *Autodesk Inc* (1990) 96 ALR 57, there was much confusion as to whether a 'dongle'; a device required to be inserted into a computer before a program would operate, contained a computer program and in *Gale's Application* [1991] RPC 305, the trial judge (erroneously) drew a distinction between a program on disk and one hard-wired into a ROM chip. Such confusion is largely a result of the difficulty many lawyers have when dealing with a highly technical field such a computer science but it does not stop there. Even if the technological aspects are fully understood, the application of the law to them may still peoples.

Although there is some common ground and some similarity in other provisions, contracts for hardware and software are governed by different legal rules. Computer hardware, if it is sold, will be subject to the Sale of Goods Act 1979 whereas an agreement to write software ('bespoke' software) will be within the scope of the Supply of Goods and Services Act 1982. There are other differences, for example, as regards the statutory is not always easy to apply in practice because hardware equipment often incorporate software and the contractual position of 'off-the-shelf' software is far from clear. Nevertheless, the classification in terms of the legal nature of the transaction is important and he author's suggested approach is to look at the predominant purpose of the transaction. In other words, did the person acquiring the subject matter thank that he was obtaining hardware or software?

Consider a person purchasing a new motor car. This is a 'good' and the transaction is clearly subject to the Sale of Good Act 1979, section 2(1), which states:

> ... a contract of sale of goods is a contract by which the seller transfers or agrees to transfer the property in goods to the buyer for a money consideration called the price.

The whole purpose of the transaction is to transfer ownership in the car. Suppose the car is faulty, however, and that fault is traced to computer program installed in the electronic ignition system. The purchaser would still expect. rightly, to the able to obtain a remedy from the seller under the Sale of Goods Acts seen though he has not obtained ownership of the copyright subsisting in the computer program. After all, the buyer wanted to acquire a car not a computer program. Therefore, a contract to purchase a computer is a sale of goods contract notwithstanding the inclusion of computer software embodied within the computer. If other software is provided (often referred to as 'bundled') that will usually be subject to a separate, collateral licence agreement.

Contracts for the acquisition of software alone cannot be sale of goods contracts, the title to the software is not normally transferred nor is a computer program or database a good. The only proviso is that, as far as manuals, disks and packaging are concerned, we might have a collateral sale of goods contract. However, the predominant nature of the contract is the provision of a service, the function of the software being the service in question. This is so even if the copyright ownership is transferred, that is, if the agreement is an assignment and no simply a licence.

The nature of software contracts has long puzzled judges and legal writers. Certainly, in the case of software which is specifically written for a client, it must be a service contract as opposed to a sale of goods contract. Although some writers have focused on the fact that tangible items such as magnetic disks may be provided, suggesting a sale of goods contract, where software is delivered on-line or by loading it onto the client's computer, the nature of the arrangement becomes clearer. The delivery of tangible items in addition to the software has only served to cloud the reality of the transaction.

A case which involved a book gave an indication of the approach preferred by the author of this book. In *Ashley* v *Sutton London Borough Council* (unreported) 8 December 1994, the appellant, Ashley, brought an appeal against his conviction for an offence under section 14 of the Trade Descriptions Act 1968. The charge was that he had made a statement which he knew to be false as to the nature of services he provided in the course of a trade or business.

Ashley had supplied books by mail order which described a winning strategy to be used with fixed odds gambling and he guaranteed to refund the purchase price if customers were not satisfied. If was argued on his behalf that he had supplied books, not services, and, consequently, could not be guilty under section 14 which only concerns services not goods. The Divisional Court of the Queen's Bench Division held that, although goods were supplied (that is, the books), the essential nature of the contract was the provision of a service- the service of providing information. The book was merely the medium through which the information was imparted and the contract was, therefore, predominantly a contract for services and the appeal against conviction was dismissed. The same can be said in terms of software even more forcefully. It is a copy of the programs and/on data that the customer wants. As in the *Ashley* case, the high price of the information relative to the tangible items delivered confirms this. The fact that software can be transmitted without the need for a tangible carrier reinforces the view that software contracts are service contracts. At best, any tangible items delivered with the software give rise to a collateral sale of goods contract in respect of those items only. To return to the analogy with a book, sale of goods law will give a remedy if the book is physically defectives for example, if it falls apart or has pages missing. It will not give a remedy simply because the plot it nor very good or if there are grammatical errors. Such defects relate to the information not the good itself.

Two software cases have reinforced the deceptive simplicity of that approach. In *St Albans City & District Council* v *International Computers Ltd* [1997] FSR 251, Sir Iain Glidewell said that a computer program is clearly not within the meaning of 'good' for the purposes of the Sale of Goods Act 1979 nor the Supply of Goods and Services Act 1982. However, at first instance, Mr Justice Scott-Baker accepted that software was goods within the Sale of Goods Act 1979 (although he did not have to decide the point) because '... it is difficult to see what it can be other than something to which no statutory rules apply....' Not a very convincing argument!

As the often been the case, it was a Scots judge who most ably defined the nature of a software contract in the context of licence for-off-the shelf software. In *Beta Computers (Europe) Ltd* v *Abode Systems (Europe) Ltd* [1996] FSR 367, Lord Penrose in the Outer House of the Court of Session in Ediburgh had to determine the nature of an agreement to acquire of-the- shelf software. He decided hat the supply of such software for a price is a *sui generis* (unique) contract rather than a sale of goods contract or a hybrid contract. He considered the Copyright, Designs and Patents Act 1988 and concluded that the supply of the medium on which the program is stored must be accompanied by an appropriate licence conferred directly or by implication from the acquisition of the software. An essential feature of the arrangement was that the supplier undertook to make available to the purchaser both the medium and the right of access and use of the software.

There are some differences between English and Scots contract law and, under the latter, it is possible to grant third parties rights under a contract. Nevertheless, the judgment is an excellent analysis of the nature of a software contract and an important feature of the case was that the predominant purpose of the contract - that is, to acquire the right to use of the software - would be subjugated if it were classed as a sale of goods contract.

Software Acquisition

The most common method of acquiring computer software is by way of a licence which is granted by the copyright owner to the person or company acquiring a copy of the software, giving permission to use the software in return for the licence fee - the 'price'. The licence may be for a fixed, perhaps renewable, period of time or there may no mention of duration, in which case it can be assumed that the licence will last as long as the software is subject to copyright protection. The copyright owner will prefer to grant a licence because he will want to retain the copyright in the software and be free to grant licence to others. The licence may be exclusive, however, which means that the copyright owner cannot grant licenses to other in respect of that software. More usually, the licence will be non-exclusive so that the copyright owner will be free to grant licences to anyone else he wishes to. An exclusive licence will be appropriate between an independent software writer and a software publisher who undertakes to market the programs on behalf of the writer. Sometimes, ownership will be transferred and his form of transaction is called an assignment of copyright.

The special nature of computer software and the fact that a copy of software is usually acquired by means of licence have several legal implications. To begin with, the Sale of Goods Act 1979 does not apply to computer software as such. This Act is very important in the commercial world; in addition to being a very comprehensive regulator of contracts of sale it implies importance terms into contracts such as requirements that the goods must match their description, be of satisfactory quality and that the seller has the right to sell the goods. However, 'goods' are defined by section 61(1) of the Act as including.

> ... all personal chattels other than things in action and money.

It seems unlikely, even if the copyright is transferred with the computer programs, that an intangible computer program resident on a magnetic disk or in a computer chip is a personal chattel (as opposed to the disk or chip), because copyright is a 'thing in action' like company shares or a money order, to be contrasted with the more tangible 'things in possession' such as motor cars or computers. Copyright is thus excluded from the definition of goods. In any case, a licence cannot be a sale of goods contract as there is no transfer of property. The result of all this is that the terms contained in the Sale of Goods Act which are implied into a contract for the sale of goods will not apply to a computer software contract at least as far as the software is concerned. Any tangible items such as magnetic disks transferred with the software may be subject to a collateral contract (a subsidiary or parallel contract). This may seem unfortunate as these implied terms are a very useful weapon for the buyer and, in the case of consumer sale,s the implied terms cannot be excluded or modified at all. In non consumer sales the implied terms can only be so excluded or modified if the terms purporting to do this are reasonable in accordance with it. Unfair Contract Terms Act 1977, sections 5 to 7. Service contracts are also subject to implied terms, however.

Supply of Goods and Services Act 1982

The Supply of Goods and Services Act 1982 implies terms who contracts under which are property (ownership) in goods passes, and also into contracts for the hire of goods and contracts for services. Some of the terms implied are similar to those implied by the Sale of Goods Act. Examples of contracts governed by the Supply of Goods and Services Act are hybrid contracts: that is those which involve part services and part goods such as a contract for the the painting of a portrait. In this particular instance the service is the actual Act of painting; the goods are the canvas, frame and paint. The Act also governs a contract purely for services, such as the contract for a haircut. Has the Supply of Goods and Services Act any relevance for computer software contracts? As far as 'goods' are concerned, the situation is the same as with a sale of goods contract because the definition of goods excludes things in action of which copyright is an example. The 1982 Act will be particularly relevant, however,if an independent computer firm or a programmer is engaged to write a computer program as this should come within the meaning of 'service'. The draftsmen of he Supply of Goods and Services Act elected not to attempt to define 'service' probably in deference to the very wide variety of services offered both to consumers and to businesses. There is good reason to believe, therefore, that a contract for writing a computer program will fall within that part of the Act dealing with the supply of services - sections 12 to 16. The fact that goods such as manuals and floppy disks may also be transferred does not prevent the contract from being a contract for the supply of services (section 12(3)).

Expert systems and other types of software, including databases, which provide information or advice could, arguably, be construed as supplying a service and thus fall within the ambit of the Supply of Goods and Services Act 1982. If this view is taken by the courts, bearing in mind that 'service' is not defined in the Act, it will result in the appropriate terms from the Act being implied into a contract for the supply of such computer software systems. The dealer who supplies in expert system may be deemed to be supplying a service (that is, providing the advice available from the system) even though others, such as the experts who provided the knowledge used in the system and the makers of the system, are responsible (in a non-legal sense) for how system Act 1982 states that a 'contract for the supply of a service means':

> ... a contract under which a person (the supplier) agrees to carry out a service.

It may sometimes be difficult to determine the identity of the supplier where computer software is obtained off the-shelf. For example, if an expert system is obtained from a dealer is he the supplier or is it the company which made the expert system? In other words, who is the contracting party? Two possibilities exist: either the contract is between the person acquiring a copy of the system (the 'acquirer') and the dealer or it is between the acquirer and the software company, in which case the dealer acts as the company's agent. The answer to this is of crucial importance because of the doctrine of privity of contract: only the parties to a contract can sue on it. If the expert system turns out to be defective the acquirer will need to know who is liable. Apart from contract law there may be liability in negligence which does not depend on a contractual relationship and may even extend to others involved in the development of the system such as the experts who provided the knowledge contained in the system.

If a dealer has been asked to supply a suitable expert system it is possible that by doing so, he carried out a service. By supplying expert systems, the dealer has enabled the advice-giving service to be performed and in some respects it is similar to the position where a supplier sub-contracts all or part of the work. The customer relies on the dealer to provide a suitable and effective system and, consequently, there is duty on the dealer to select and recommend an adequate system (see *Stewart* v *Reavell's Garage* [1952] 2 QB 545). Therefore, dealers marketing expert systems should satisfy themselves as to the veracity and reliability of these systems and their suitability for particular customers. Dealers may also wish to consider including appropriate and reasonable exemption clauses in their supply contracts with respect to advice-giving computer systems.

The dealer as agent for the software company is a more likely interpretation if the acquirer specifies the system the wants. Of course, the fact that there will, invariably, be a licence agreement with the software company reinforces the view that the dealer acts as an agent to bring about the contract between the software company and the acquirer. The legal position is far fro clear, however, and there is a lack of authority on this point. The situation is much simpler where software is written for and at the request of a client. This is a straightforward service contract between the client and the software developer and is covered by the Supply of Goods and Services Act 1982. This has been confirmed in *The Salvage Association* v *CAP Financial Services Ltd* [1995] FSR 654 in which the Official Referee in the High Court confirmed that a contract to develop new accounting software for a client was a service contract. He went on to imply into that contract section 13 of the Supply of Goods and Services Act 1982.

Section 13 implies a term that the supplier, if acting in the course of business, will carry out the service with reasonable care and skill. This restates the previous position at common lay, that person, who holds himself out as being prepared to carry out a service is expected to exercise a level of skill that could be expected of a reasonably competent member of the relevant trade or profession. Therefore, if a firm engaged to write a computer program fails to measure up to the standards that would normally be expected from able computer programmers and the program turns out to be sub-standard hen, *prima facie,* the firm will be liable in contract. It does not matter that the firm's employees tried their best; the question is: does the program meet this objective standard?

In the *Salvage Association* case it was held that there was a breach of section 13 and also a breach of an express term in the contract that the software developer would assign suitably qualified staff to perform the work. The staff originally assigned to write the software were insufficiently experienced in the use of ORACLE, the language in which the software was to be written.

Another term implied by the Supply of Goods and Services Act 1982 concerns the time for performance. Again, this only applies to suppliers acting in the course of business, although a similar term might be impled at common law. Section 14 states that, in the absence of an agreed time for performance or an agreed formula to determine the time for performance, the supplier will carry out the service in a reasonable time. The Act also says that what is reasonable is a question of fact that is, it depends on the facts of the case. The case of *Charnock* v *Liverpool Corporation* [1968] 1 WLR 1498 gives an example of an unreasonable time. The defendant garage was liable in damages because it took eight weeks to taken about five weeks. A contract for the writing of computer programs should have detailed provisions about completion times and all section 14 does is to provide a net to catch those instances where there has been an oversight. What is a reasonable time will depend on the nature of the programs and their complexity, taking into account the time required for testing and acceptance.

Section 15 of the Act states that, unless the contract fixes the payment or a method of calculating payment, the supplier will be paid a reasonable amount. Usually, the contract will mention the fee, but this provision might be useful if the supplier takes on additional work at the request of the other party and no mention is made at the time of agreement of the charge for this extra work. It means that the supplier cannot, much as he might like to, charge an unreasonably high price. Comparative fees and prices for writing similar software would provide a good indicator of what is reasonable.

Hardware Acquisition

As far as computer equipment (hardware) is concerned, this may be purchased outright or hire. If purchased then the Sale of Goods Act 1979 will apply and terms as to quality, complying with description, satisfactory quality, etc, will be implied into the contract, subject to any valid exemption clauses. There have been some important changes to this Act. The Sale and Supply of Goods Act 1994 replaces the old section 14(2) of the Sale of Goods Act 1979 (which required that goods were of merchantable quality) with a new requirement that goods must be of satisfactory quality. This is started by section 14(2A) to apply if the goods meet the standard that reasonable person would regard as satisfactory. Account is to be taken of the description of the goods, the price (if relevant) and all other relevant circumstances. In a welcome tightening of the implied term, section 14(2B) defines the aspects of quality to be taken into account, being:

(a) fitness for all the purposes for which goods of the kind in question are commonly supplied (this is simply a restatement of the previous law);
(b) appearance and finish;
(c) freedom from minor defects;
(d) safety; and
(e) durability.

This implied term is a condition in England, Wales and Northern Ireland and applies where goods are sold in the course of business. In Scotland, it is simply a term, the remedies depending on whether the breach is a material one. For a breach of condition (or a material breach in Scotland), the buyer may reject the goods without prejudice to any claim for damages.

The old requirements that goods must be of merchantable quality caused injustice in a number of cases. It did not appears that the goods had to be durable and he presence of minor defects did not necessarily render goods unmechantable. For example, in *Millars of Falkirk Ltd* v *Turpie*, 1987 SLT 66, it was held that an oil leak from the power-steering unit of a new car did not make the car unmechantable and, in *Bernstein* v *Pamson Motors* [1987] 2 All ER 220, and engine seizure in a three-week old car that had only covered 140 miles did not render the car unmerchantable. Only occasionally did the courts seem to take a sympathetic view of the buyer's position: for example, in *Rogers* v *Parish (Scarborough) Ltd* [1987] QB 933 the Court of Appeal recognised that the buyer of a luxury car such as a Range Rover had a right to expect a vehicle that did not continually break down and suffer from rust.

In the context of computers, the courts also took a fairly narrow view of unmerchantability and in the *Micron Computer Systems Ltd* v *Wang (UK) Ltd* (unreported) 9 May 1990, the High Court considered that the failure of a computer's hard disk was perfectly normal teething problem and did not give the buyer the right to reject the computer. Of course, the buyer may still have claim to damages in respect of such a defect. Now, because of the test of satisfactory quality, it is more likely that the buyer of a computer with a faulty hard disk would be able to reject the computer and insist on a refund of the purchase price. The same should apply if the computer has an intermitent but troublesome fault.

If the supplier goes beyond the mere supply of the equipment and carriers out some work such as assembling and installing the equipment, the Supply of Goods and Services Act 1982 will apply, discussed above. If the contract is for the hire of the equipment, then the Supply of Goods and Services Act will apply, whether or not installation or other services are also provided by the supplier. An agreement which is described as a lease or rental is essentially a contract of hire, and is a hire agreement is one under which the possession of the goods passes to the other party but the property in the goods (the ownership) remains with the supplier. 'Hire' does not include hire-purchase agreements, which are covered by the Supply of Goods (Implied Terms) Act 1973 - this Act implies similar terms into the contract as under the Sale of Goods Act 1979. The relevant provisions in the Supply of Goods and Services Act 1982 regarding hire agreements include implied terms about the right of the supplier to transfer possession of the goods, that the goods must correspond with ther description and impled terms about quality and fitness for purpose (sections 7 to 10). These terms are equivalent to those in the Sale of Goods Act.

Breach of Contract

If a party to a contract is in breach of one or more of its terms, the remedy depends on the status of the particular term or terms which have been broken. The aggrieved party may want to repudicate the contract treat the contract as discharged by reason of the other party's breach and recover any money he has paid out as well as any other expenses. In the *Salvage Association* case it was held that the client was entitled to repudiate the contract when it became clear that the software developer would fail to meet the extended deadline for delivery of the software. The delivery of the software. The client was entitled to £662 926 in damages being made up of:

- £ 291 388 paid under the contract;
- £ 231 866 wasted expenditure; and
- £ 139 672 wasted management time.

Alternatively the injured party might prefer to hold the other party to the contract but would like some compensation for the breach and if the breach concerns a minor term this is usually the better solution. However, the injured party does not always have a free choice as the law lays down rules determining and limiting the scope of remedies.

Traditionally there are tow types of terms in contracts: 'conditions' and 'warranties'. The distinction is important because breach of condition gives the other party the right to repudiate the contract and claim damages. For example, consider a contract to deliver a computer by '1 June at the latest'. If the machine has not been delivered by that date, the buyer can treat the failure to deliver as a breach of a condition and he can cancel the contract as time for delivery is usually construed as being a condition (see *Hartley* v *Hyams* [1920] 3 KB 475). Furthermore, the buyer can claim damages that would be equivalent to the difference in cost of buying another similar computer elsewhere and any other expenses and losses he has been put to as a direct consequence of the breach, with the proviso that he mitigates this losses - that is, he keeps them to a minimum. The buyer may have wanted the computer to expand his business and he will be able to claim the resulting loss in profits, provided the seller know or should have known of this - that is, it was in the reasonable contemplation of the parties.

On the other hand, a breach of warranty allows the aggrieved party to claim damages only. The contract is still in force and must be completed by both parties. They must both perform the remainder of their agreed duties under the contract. For example, if a suppler has agreed to deliver a computer system and the contract states that the terminals are to but a deep yellow colour but, instead, he delivers a computer with lemon coloured terminals, this will amount to a breach of warranty unless there is some special reason why the deep yellow color was specified. The buyer will be entitled to damages only and he will still have to pay the purchase price of the computer, although he may be able to set off a sum representing the damages. Damages are assessed on the basis of the damage naturally arising from the breach and in the contemplation of the parties. In the example given, the damages would be little more than nominal.

In *Koufos* v *Czarnikow Ltd* [1969] 1 AC 350, a ship was chartered by sugar merchants to transport a cargo of sugar. The shipowners knew that there was a sugar market at the port of destination but did not know that the merchants wanted to sell the sugar immediately on its arrival. The ship deviated from the agreed voyage and arrived about ten days late; in the meantime the price of sugar had fallen and the merchants lost over £4000. It was held that this loss should be recoverable from the shipowners because they should reasonably have contemplated that the delay would have resulted in a loss. The shipowners knew there was a commodity market at the destination and that prices would be liable to fluctuate, so that any delay could lead to a diminution of the value of the cargo. Unfortunately, this does not appear to work the other way - the shipowners would not be entitled to any share in a windfall profit if the market value of the cargo increased dramatically and was sold for much more than it would have done had it arrived on time.

How does the basic principle that damages are based on the losses that were within the contemplation of the parties when the contract was made work in the context of computers? Suppose that you run a computer bureau and carry out ordinary data processing work. You decide to expand the business and buy a more powerful computer to be delivered by a certain date. You tell the supplier that you need the computer to carry out some additional data processing but neglect to inform him that you are negotiating a very lucrative top secret government contract on the basis of having the new computer. If the computer is delivered late, then you would be entitled to damages based on the loss in profits in the normal of business but you would not be entitled to anything should you lose the government contract. This is simply because the supplier did not know, and could not reasonably be expected to know, of this potential contract. A buyer should therefore consider informing a supplier of all the uses to which the equipment or programs will be put, especially if they are unusual.

The distinction between conditions and warrants is not always clear. Sometimes a contractual term lies in a grey area between the two. If the term is broken, then it will be classified in the light of the facts surrounding the breach and it will depend on the facts as to whether the breach goes to the root of the contract. If it does, then the term will be effectively promoted to the rank of condition with all that entails; otherwise it will be classed as a warranty. These intermediate terms are called innominate terms and their nature is determined retrospectively, after a breach. The case which paved the way for this approach was *Hong Kong Fir Shipping Co Ltd* v *Kawasaki Kisen Kaisha*[1962] QB 26, in which it was held that a term implied in a hire contract for a ship that it must be seaworthy was such an innominate term. The nature of the breach determined the nature of the contractual term. For example, if the ship had a 5 degree list and was badly leaking it would be totally unseaworthy and this would be a breach of condition enabling the hirer to repudiate the contract. However, if the breach concerned some trifling defect, perhaps a mere technicality, which could be put right very quickly and easily, the term would be classed as a warranty. For example, if a word processing program is acquired which is claimed by the supplier to be a 'professional package' and it does not have a built-in-thesaurus, this might be considered to be a breach of warranty. It cannot be truly said that the breach goes to the root of the contract if the program has all the other usual features normally found in powerful word processing systems. However, if the package does not include features such as right-justification, a spelling checker and cut-and-past facilities this would be more serious and could make the system virtually useless in a business environment. Such a breach would go to the root of the contract and would be a breach of a condition, giving the person acquiring the program the right to cancel the contract and recover the cost of the system plus any direct losses.

This way of looking at terms and not deciding their status until there has been a breach is very useful as it gives a welcome degree of flexibility to contracts, although it could be criticised for introducing, uncertainty. There may be some terms, however, which are obviously conditions: for example, if the contract is for the delivery of a particular make of computer; and the seller attempts to deliver a different make altogether, this would clearly be a breach of condition.

What sort of terms in computer contracts could be described as innominate terms? Suppose that a contract is made for the provision of a network to link individual computers together, aterm in contract stating that the network will support at least 16 personal computers. If there is a small degradation of performance when 15 or more machines are in use but otherwise the network is fine, this might be regarded as a breach of warranty. On the other hand, if it turns out that the network fails when more than seven machines are in use, the term would be regarded as a condition. Sometimes a term can start as a condition, become a warranty and then revert to a condition. In *Rickards* v *Oppenheim* [1950] 1 KB 616, the defendant wanted a body built on his Rolls-Royce chassis and he agreed that the plaintiffs (from whom he had purchased the chassis) could use a sub-contractor to do this specialised work, which should have been completed in March 1948. The work was not complete by that time and, although time for delivery is usually a condition, the defendant did not cancel the contract as he was entitled to do, but continued to press for delivery, thereby waiving his right to cancel. In the end the defendant gave an ultimatum. He said that the car must be ready by 25 July 1948 and that he would refuse to take delivery after that date. The car was not ready by that date, so he defendant bought another car elsewhere and claimed back the price he had paid for the chassis. It was held that when time for delivery is of the essence of a contract for the sale of goods (that is, a condition) and, after the stipulated time was elapsed, the buyer waives his right to cancel by pressing for delivery, converting the term into a warranty, he may later give notice setting a reasonable deadline, once again making the time for delivery a condition of the contract.

It is not unusual for new software to be delivered late. In this case, the client must be careful when granting extensions of time and should bear in mind that he will hope to avoid fudging the issue of the date at which he can repudiate the contract on the grounds of the software developer's late delivery. It is essential that any extensions be agreed in writing with the new date being firmly stated as a condition. If this is not doe, the client must allow a reasonable time when delivering an ultimatum to the software developer. It is not satisfactory to allow work to drag on for months and then to suddenly state that the contract will be repudiated if the software is not completed by the end of this work'.

It is common to find provisions for late delivery and late payment included in contracts. The contract might state that the supplier will pay £150 per week if he delivers late, or that the buyer will pay interest at 0.75 per cent above the current base bank rate, should be late in making payment. Predetermined damages, known as liquidated damages, are frequently found in contracts. 'Liquidated' simply means that the damages or the method of calculating them are fixed and agreed. Liquidated damages are to be distinguished from a penalty. Liquidated damages are a genuine pre-estimate of the loss resulting from the breach, whereas a penalty, which might be out of all proportion to the loss sufferered, will not be enforced by the courts. The stipulation of liquidated damages for breach of a particular term contradicts the possibility of that term being a condition. Terms backed by liquidated damages will usually not be regarded as conditions, therefore, unless the scale of the breach is considerable.

In practice, many terms will be innominate terms, in which case it will only be possible to determine whether breach of the term allows a party to repudiate the contract in the light of the actual facts of the breach. This accords with Scots practice where the question is whether the breach is a material one. Provisions concerning the performance of a computer system, how fast the programs work in practice and the degree of compatibility with other equipment are likely to be innominate terms. Terms which will probably be classes as conditions from the beginning deal with aspects such as the time for delivery and the description of the actual computer concerned. Time for payment is usually treated as being a warranty unless the contract states otherwise or the circumstances suggest a different interpretation (see, for example, section 10(1) of the Sale of Goods Act 1979).

By its very nature, when delivered, bespoke software often contains errors and it may be some time before they can all be traced and corrected. It is a brave software producer who claims that his software is error-free. The contractual positon was considered in *Saphena Computing* v *Allied Collection Agencies* [1995] FSR 616. A contract for wiring a number of programs was terminated while there were still errors in the programs. The Court of Appeal accepted that software was not a commodity that was handed over once and for all and that it would usually require testing and further modification. It would not, therefore, be a breach of contract to deliver software that might, initially, have a defect in it. Usually, the supplier would have a right and a duty to correct the errors within a reasonable time. In this particular case the client, who had a copy of the source code, could carry out error correction himself but, because he had brought the contract to an end, the supplier would cease to be liable for the remaining errors.

Misrepresentation

If you are negotiating with a salesman with a view to acquiring computer software, he may make statements regarding the software and its performance. It is not unknown for a salesman to describe the product in glowing terms and you would expect him to highlight the best features. Sometimes, he can go too far; he may be anxious to make a sale and many make statements which are simply untrue in an effort to try to induce you to buy the product. Some statements are so wild that no one is expected to take them seriously; these are sometimes referred to as salesman's 'puff'. Examples abound from the second-hand motor trade: for example, an ageing car may be described as being 'immaculate'. Such statements are not to be taken seriously and the courts would not support a case brought on them. Less extravagant statements, however, if untrue, may give rise to remedies. The standing of the statements needs initially to be determined and it may be elevated to the rank of contractual term if the courts consider on the facts that this was the intention of the parties. If this happens then normal contractual remedies are available to the aggrieved party if the statement turns out to be untrue.

If the statement does not become incorporated into the contract, it is said to be a representation - something said in the course of the negotiations leading up to the contract itself. If may well induce the other party to conclude the contract, in which case a remedy may be available on the basis of misrepresentation if the statement turns out to be untrue. Obviously, if the party, to whom the representation is made, knows that the statement is untrue he will not have any remedy. He has entered into the contract with his eyes open to the true facts; the statement itself will not have influenced him.

There are three forms of misrepresentation: fraudulent, negligent and innocent. If the representation has been made fraudulently (or recklessly, not caring whether or not it is true), then at common law the remedy of rescission is available (setting the contract aside as if it had never been made at all), together with a right to recover any money laid out. Fraud may be difficult to prove; the person making the statement may simply say that he honestly believed, at the time he made it, that it was true. The Misrepresentation Act 1967, as amended by the Unfair Contract Terms Act 1977, made the situation more satisfactory. Rescission is the standard remedy for misrepresentation but this may cause hardship; therefore, in the case of negligent or innocent misrepresentation, a court may award damages in lieu of rescission by section

2 of the Misrepresentation Act. This is important because rescission is an equitable remedy and as such will not be ordered by the courts if the aggrieved party has acted promptly. Formerly, if the aggrieved party had already accepted the goods, the very fact of acceptance would mean that rescission would not be available. Imagine that a company buys a computer. It is important that his computer is directly compatible with its existing equipment and the supplier confirms in good faith, before the contract is made, that the computer is compatiable although the contract itself is silent on the matter. Some weeks after accepting delivery and paying for the computer, it is found that, although the computer works well in every other respect, it is not compatible with the company's other machines and cannot reasonably be made so. Before the 1967 Act, the company acquiring the computer would have no remedy for this innocent misrepresentation, unless it was deemed to be a contractual term, as it would be too late to have the contract set aside. Now the courts would be likely to award damages instead, which might be considerable in our example. The better approach would have been for the company to insist that an express term was inserted into the contract to the effect that the computer to be acquired must be compatible with the existing equipment.

Summary

In this chapter the basic implications of computer contracts have been discussed. Apart from the difficulties arising from classifying software contracts the law is relatively well settled. One remaining difficulty is to apply that law to computer technology. For example, how do we set the standards for reasonable care and skill and quality in relation to computer hardware and software? Fortunately, to date, judges have themselves reasonably well equipped to do this though some doubts remain.

Of greater uncertainty is the potential for liability for defective software and this is something which is examined in the following chapter together with a consideration of the effectiveness of exemption clauses, limiting or excluding liability for defective software or, indeed, for breach of contract. Case law has amply demonstrated the care that must be taken in this respect when drafting computer contracts.

15 LIABILITY FOR DEFECTIVE HARDWARE OR SOFTWARE

There have been a number of occasions when defects in software have had very serious implications. The term 'safety-critical' is applied to software (and hardware which is used in situations involving risk to life and limb. For example, in 1992 it was discovered that around 1000 patients at a North Staffordshire hospital had received incorrect dosages of radiation therapy beacuse of an alleged fault in a computer program. Later that same year the London Ambulance's new computer system failed dramatically throwing the ambulance services to chaos and, possibly, resulting in a number of deaths caused by the consequential delays in getting ambulances to their call-out destinations.

Defects in computer equipment and software can cause all manner of damage. The failure of flight control systems, nuclear power station systems and defence systems could result in major loss of life. The same could be true of software used to design buildings and vehicles. Defects in other systems might result in financial loss only such as where a expert system is used to provide financial advice. The fact that organisations developing or supplying software or manufacturing and distributing hardware could be liable for the consequences of failure requires them to consider means of reducing or limiting liability and, while practical measures such as quality control and testing are of vital importance, regard must be had to the legal position regarding defects.

The 'Millennium Bug' has focused minds recently as regards the potential for disaster caused by 'computer error'. That particular problem is caused by the old (and now clearly perceived to be foolish) convention of only using two digits to store the year of a date. Thus, the date 4 August 1999 would be stored in a form equivalent to 04/08/99. Where a calculation is performed which involves dates, such as in determining the duration of some computer controlled process or operation, it is obvious that things cna quickly go wrong on or after 1 January 2000. The convention of using two digits for the year was a result of a desire to save what was then very expensive computer storage. Additionally, most programmers working in the 1960s and 1970s thought the programs they were working on would become redundant long before the Millennium. In those days, in terms of the pace of development of computer technology, the terms of the century seemed an awful long way off.

If a person suffers loss or damage as a result of defective hardare or software, one or more of the following areas of law might provide a remedy;

- contract;
- law of negligence;
- negligent misstatement; or
- product liability.

The basic principles of contractual liability have already been discussed in previous chapters and often can provide the simplest route to a satisfactory remedy. However, because of the doctrine of privity of contract, only the parties to a contract can sue upon it. If the aggrieved person is not in a contractual relationship with the person responsible for the loss or damage, other areas of law must be looked to for a remedy.

Once the risks and liabilities have been identified, the contract should provide a suitable mechanism for apportioning liability between the parties. Insurance can then be obtained to cover the potential losses resulting from defects and from issues relating to the performance of the contract. This is important as recent case law has amply demonstrated that reliance on contract terms, limiting lioability to a relatively small sum, is misplaced.

In this chapter, forms of liability for defects, other than contractual, are examined. The focus is upon the alw of negligence, negligent misstatement and product liability. These areas are of particular concern because they impose liability in respect of loss or damage sustained by third parties. Finally, the legal control of exemption clauses and notices, which attempt to exclude or limit liability, is considered.

Negligence

Negligence is part of an area of law known as tort. Basically, a tort is a civil wrong, independent of contract. It imposes legal liabilities on a person who has acted carelessly or unreasonably omits to do something. Under certain circumstances a person will be liable to another for failing to exercise a required duty of care. In the case of consumer goods, such as a table lamp or television set, if the negligence of the manufacturer causes them to be defective, then the person injured as a result will be entitled to damages. A claim in negligence does not depend on the presence of a contract, so if the person injured is someone other than the buyer, that person can still sue. The buyer also should be able to sue, but on the basis of breach of contract if the item is defective and fails to comply with implied terms such as that concerning satisfactory quality. To be able ot sue in negligence, three essentil ingredients must be present:

- a duty of care owed to the injured party;
- a breach of that duty of care; and
- consequential loss- that is, loss which is a direct and natural result of the breach of duty of care.

The landmark case on negligence is *Donoghue* v *Stevenson* [1932] AC 562, in which the plaintiff had been bought a bottle of ginger beer by a friend in a cafe. The bottle was made of opaque glass and so the contents could not be seen. the cafe owner poured part of the contents into a glass which the plaintiff drank. The plaintiff's friend then poured out the rest of the contents and the decomposed remains of a snail came out of the bottle. The plaintiff sufered shock and severe gastroenteritis as a result of the revolting sight and the fact that she had already swallowed some of the ginger beer. The plaintiff could not sue in contract because she was not a party ot the contract—it had been her friend who had bought the drink. Nevertheless, the House of Lords held that a manufacturer who sold food or medicine or the like in containers of a nature that the distributor or ultimate purchasers or consumers could not discover the defect by inspection is under a legal duty to the ultimate purchaser or consumer to take reasonable care that the article is free from any defect likely ot cause injury to health. This duty of care is owed to any person who might be contemplated to be injured by the act or ommission of the manufacturer (the 'neighbour' or proximity test). Negligence cna be thought of as as early form of product liability and has developed over the years to its present wide scope, although this is tempered to some extent by the growth of insurance. It is also limited, to some extent, by policy considerations. This is particularly to where the loss is purely economic or the claim is in respect of nervous shock.

What is the significance of the tort of negligence as far as computers and software are concerned? Although it is unlikely that decomposing snails will be found within the workings of computers, it is possible to come across computer 'bugs' and there may still be some futher nasty surprises. At first sight it may seem unlikely that computers and computer software could kill or cause serious injury; however, negtligent liabiluty does not top at personal injury biut extends to damage to property. Computer equipment runs on electricity so there is always the danger of electrical shock and, if this results from negligence, there is a strong possibility of an action in negligence. But what if a large passenger aircraft has to be fulelled ready foro flight? A computer program is used to calculate the amount of fuel required This is based on information such as the number of passengers, the wright of baggage, the flight distance and prevailing winds, etc. Then, because of a hitherto undiscovered bug in the computer program, less fuel is loaded than required, with the result that the aircraft runs out of feul over the mid-Arlantic. It is possible that the company writing the computer program was negligent in its testing of the program. The total size of the claims resulting from such an incident might well be enormous, even though the copy of the computer program may have cost only a few hundred pounds.

Other nightmoare scenarious include where an air traffic control system contains a software error which incorrectly records the location of an aircraft or where a railway signalling system contains a fault or where guidance software directs a missile with a warhead to the wrong location. Of course, although most software errors do not have catastrophic effects, they can have very costly consquences if they are not spotted. A simple error in software to assist self-employed persons calculate their tax liability for the purposes of self-assessment of tax resulted in may people underestimating their tax liability bringing the possibility of fines from the Inland Revenue (*The Times*, 13 August 1997, p 5). The error was a mistake where pounds and pence were confused. In this case, most of the persons affected would have constractual remedies had they fined on the basis of the licence agreement with the software developer (subject to any valid exclusion or limitation clauses).

The fact that an action in negligence lies without the need for a contract is important both for computer program writers and manufacturers of computer equipment. If a program is lecenses by a publisher, the program author could be liable in negligence even though he is not a party to the licence agreement. In the case of computer hardware, a person suffering loss or injury as a result of the negligence of the manufacturer will have a calim in negligence against the manufacturer regardless of the fact that the equipment was bought from a dealer.

There are limitations, however, to the scope of the law of negligence and, as mentioned above, certain ingredients must be present. A person writing a computer program, or a company manufacturing computer equipment will not necessarily be potentially liable to the world at large in negligence; they will be liable, however, to those whom they could contemplate being adversely affected by any negligent act or omission by them. A further limiting factor is that the plaintiff bears the burden of proof; he has to show that the defendant was negligent and this is not always easy to do. There may be an exception if the event causing the injury or damage could only be reasonably explained by assuming there had been negligence. This is knows to lawyers as *res ipsa loquitor*, that is, 'the thing speaks for itself'. If you are hit on the head by a pot of paint while walking under a ladder you would not be asked to show the precise act of negligene that caused the paint to fall; it goes wihtout saying that someone had been negligent. This is the exception, however, and normally the plaiintiff must prove the negligent act or omission.

Even if negligence is proved, the amount of damages awarded may be reduced if the plaintiff has contributed in a causal sense to the negligence. If a computer has been badly make and is an electrical hazard them if the person who has been electrocuted had tampered with the machine, the damages awarded may be reduced in proportion to the extent of his contribution to the accident. Fortunately, death or personal injury resulting from the use of a computer has been a rare occurrence, but other forms of loss or damage might be more common; for example, in a business contex where a computer may be used ot assist with decision-making, there is a s trong probability that a financial loss will be blamed on the computer. However, an action based solely on economic loss is unlikely to succeed under the normal law of negligence due to policy considerations. It may be possible in such a case to base an action on negligent misstatement instead, as described later.

Negligence and RSI

Typists, word processor operators and data entry operators spend long periods of time at a keyboard. By doing so they may risk acquiring some form of cramp or painful condition in their writs and fingers which is often described as repetitive injury or RSI. That is not, however, a medical term of precision, but for some time the Department of Health has recognised a condition knows simply as PDA4 which is on a list of precribed diseases for the purposes of industrial injury benefit. It is defined as cramp of the hand or forearm due to repetitive movements, such as writer's cramp. The types of occupations where it is possible are those which involve prolonged periods of handwriting, tying or other repetitive movements of the fingers, hand or arm.

The most important case to date on RSI (or PDA4) in the context of a word processor operator was *Pickford* v *Imperial Chemical Industries Ltd* (unreported) 25 June 1998. The plaintiff worked for the defendant for a number of years as a secretary and spent around 50 per cent of her time using a word processor. She claimed that, at times, that went up to 75 per cent. Eventualy, she complained of pain both hands and, after consulting a number of doctors and specialists, she commenced proceddings against her employer alleging negligence. She claimed that it was reasonably foreseeable that operating the word processor for long periods without breaks or rest periods would cause the condition and that the employer was negligent in failing to warn her of it and the ned to take rest breaks. At the trial, the judge found that the plaintiff failed to establish the case against her employer but the Court of Appeal overturned that decision by a 2:1 majority. The employer appealed to the House of Lords which allowed the appeall by a 4:1 majority.

The majority in the House of Lords considered that the Court of Appeal was wrong to overturn the decision of the trial judge. All the relevant issues related to findings of fact and an appeal court will interfere with such a finding only in exceptional circumstances as it is the trial judge who has the benefit of seeing and hearing the witnesses including, in this case, a number of exper and lay witnesses. Lord Hope of Craighead made a number of observations as follows.

- PDA4 has two possible causes: one is organic and the other is that its basis is psychogenic (that is 'it is all in the mind'), the product of conversion hysteria whereby the mind uses the body to escape from an objectionable workiong situation,
- medical opinion is divided as to the cause,
- the trial judge rightly decided that the plaintiff failed to prove that the cause was organic and the defendant did not have to prove that the cause was psychogenic (the burdent of proof lay on the plaintiff),
- the judge was right to hold that PDA4 resulting from typing work was not reasonably foreseeable, in the light of the state of knowledge at the time of plaiontiff developed the conditioon (that is, in 1988-89).
- the nature of the work meant that the plaintiff had ample non-typing work to intersperse with her word processing and, consequently, there was no duty on the employer to prescribe rest periods,
- there was no duty on the employer to warn of the dangers of PDA4-this was particularly so as issuing such a warning might bring about the condition given that one possible cause was psychogenic.

Although the plaintiff failed in her claim, that does not mean to say that word processor operators and others who, as part of their work, spend long periods at a keyboard would also fail. In the present case, the plaintiff failed to prove causation - that is, that her injury was caused by the negligence of the employer. Indeed, the dissenting judge, Lord Steyn, said that among the 'tangled words and imperfect scientific insights' the central proved facts establisehd that the plaintiff's work caused her disability and this could, had the employer exercised reasonable care, have avoided the occurrence of the disability.

One point of make is that it appears that an action might lie only if the court accepts that the cause is an organic one. if the court finds that it is a result of mind (psychogenic), any claim is bound to fail. That is somewhat controversial as to the sufferer the pain and discomort will probably feel just as real and it might have been brought on by having to work at a keyboard at high speed for intolerable periods. In terms of causation, the injury will be the result of the work.

The case raises the question of what advice an employer should give to an employee about the dangers of working at a keyboard for long periods of time without breaks. To warn specifically of PDA4 might induce it in persons of a nervous disposition. The best approach, as was suggested in the above case, is to tell employees simply to go and see a doctor if unusual pain or discomfort is experienced. To warn word processor operators and the like that if they developed pain they would never work agian was, in the words of one expert witness, 'disgraceful'. The defendant had an excellent record with respect to health and safety and gave advice to persons using computers with respect to eye-strain and ensured that work stations were suitably designed and sited.

Computers have been claimed to be harmful to the bealth of the operator because of radioactive emissions, although at the present time there does not appear to be any conclusive proof that a real danger to health exists. If a definite association were to be found, however, between the occurrence of skin cancers or miscarriages and the continued use of computer monitors, then computr manufactuers and importers who continued to make or sell equipment giving off such dangerous emissions would be liable. There may also be implications under the Health and Safety at Work etc. Act 1974 if an employer persists in requiring his staff to use such machines. The producer would have to consider fittiong some device such as an ionisation screen to absorb the rays and, in the absence of a technolgical way of overcoming the problem, might be forced to withdraw the product until such time as a solution could be found. As regards computer display screens, there is specific legislation dealing with their use and safty and extending to the ergonomic features of the computer equipment and the desk at which the computer operator sits (Health and Safety (Display Screen Equipment) Regulations 1992.) These regulations came into force on 1 January 1993. Nowadays, most screen displays are designed to minimise radioactive emissions. Nevertheless, a good employer should ensure that the equipment and the manner in which it is used is not such as to give operators eye-strain or other injuries.

Negligent Misstatement

It is the terms of expert systems or other items of computer software designed to provide advice that the potential for liability for negligence takes on special signficance. If the system is used to derive advice for a professional to use in the execution of his duties, the ultimate recipient of the advice may find that he has a right of action against the professional or the system develpoer (or even the independent experts and knowledge engineers engaged by the system develper). The leading case on tortious liability for negligent advice, referred to as negligent misstatement, is *Hedley Byrne & Co Ltd* v *Heller & Partners Ltd*[1964] AC 465. In that case, the House of Lords concluded that a bank giving information is to the liquidity of one of its own customers to another bank so that the latter could show the information to one of its customers could be liable to that customer, even though the first bank did not know the identity of the second bank's customer - the ultimate recipient of the information. The fact was that the bank giving the reference must have appreciated that the information would be shown to a customer of the other bank and this was sufficient to satisfy the 'neighbour test'. Therefore, the required relationship exists where one person holds himself out as an expert and gives advice which is intended to be taken seriously and acted upon even though no contractual relationship exists.

This could have the effect of making the persons and organisations responsible for the creation of expert systems liable to the ultimate consumers of the advice generated. The experts who provided the rules and facts used by the system, the knowledge engineers who formalised the knowledge, the programmers and analysts responsible for desiging the inferencing and interface programs could find themselves liable if the advice generated by use of the system is incorrect. There are, howoever, two factors which might negate or reduce liability. The first is whether a duty of care will be imposed and the second is the status of any disclaimer. Although the people involved in the development of the system are directly responsible for the performance and accuracy of the system, they have little control over the way the system will be used or interpreted. Unlike a simple bank reference where the significance and use of the information provided is fairly obvious, the advice obtained from an expert system depends on the interation between the system and its user. As expert systems ar desgned for use by persons who have some general understanding of the knowledge domain, it is reasonable to assume that the user will take at least some of the responsibility for the output obtained. However, a professional such as a general medical practioner who has to seek the advice of a specialist consultant will find it difficult to verify and validate the advice of the spcialist and this is true also of expert systems which contain knowledge beyond that of the user of the system. Lack of control over the use to which the information will be put does not in itself negate liability. The central issue is whether a duty of care will be imposed by law. In *Caparo Industries plc* v *Dickman* [1990] 2 AC 605, it was held that there are three criteria for imposing a duty of care:

- foreseeability of damage;
- proximity of relationship; and
- the reasonableness or otherwise of imposing a duty of care.

In that case, a company bought additional shares in another company following receipt of audited accounts prepared by the defendant. The House of Lords said that liability for statements, put into general circulation in such circumstances that they might foresseably be relied on by strangers, would only be imposed when the maker of the statement knew it would be communicated to the person relying on it either as an individual or member of a calss and that it would be likely ot be relied on for a known purpose. In the present case it was held that in auditor owed no duty of care to the general public nor to individual shareholders who relied on the accounts to buy shares because of a lack of proximity. To hold otherwise would give rise to unlimited liability on the part of the auditor. However, in allowing a claim by the intended beneficiaries of a will which should, but for the negligence of the solicitor acting for the person making the will (the testator), have been prepared before the testator died, the House of Lords, *While* v *Jones* [1995] 2 AC 207, raised the spectre of widening the scope of persons to whom a duty of care was owed. Two of the five Law Lords dissented on the basis that this could lead ot the recognition of an extensive new area of potential liability.

Advice produced using expert systems or other decision-support systems is nearer to the *Hedley Byrne* facts than those of *Caparo* v *Dickman* in which the primary purpose of the information was to comply with a statutory requirement, that is, having the company's accounts audited. Advice flowing from expert systems is intended ot be taken seriously and acted upon. If the system is designed to produce advice as to trading in stocks and shares that is precisely the use ot which it will be put. Therefore, the law or negligent misstatement ought ot apply to such systems.

On the other hand factual software such as a database of vehicle performances lies nearer to the *Caparo* v *Dickman* case. The maker of the database has no clear idea as to the particular uses to which the data will be used, unless it has been sold for a specific purpose. Thus, the maker of the database should not be liable to a third party in respect of a mistake contained within it. He may be contractually liable, however, to the purchaser of a copy of the database. Of course, many computer systems lie between these two extremes.

In the *Hedley Byrne* case, the bank providing the advice was able to escape liability because it had printed a clear disclaimer on the information excluding legal responsibility for the advice. Since the *Hedley Byrne* case, the Unfair Contract Terms Act 1977 was enacted to control, *inter alia,* exclusion or limitation of liability for negligence, whether under contract or tort. As far as business liability for death or personal injury is concerned, it cannot be excluded or limited by a notice or term in a contract. In other cases, the notice or term must satisfy the requirement of reasonableness. Futhermore, the use of a disclaimer will be effective only if it is clear and unambiguous and drawn to the attention of the person relying on the advice. Figure 15.1 shows the potential liability (tortious and contractual) with respect to incorrect advice derived from a defective expert system. It assumes that the experts and knowledge engineers are consultants to the software company and not its employees (this will be common arrangement in practice).

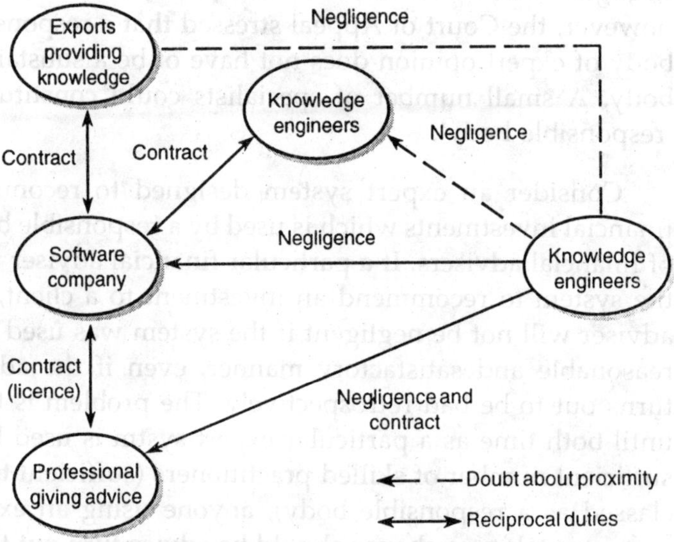

Fig 15.1 Liability for defective advice from an expert system

Note: For a duty to arise in negligence, owed to the client by anyone other than the person giving advice. It would have to be shown that the client relied on that person's statement rather than on the statement of the person giving advice.

The person using an export system to advise a client will be potentially liable under the laws of contract and negligence. Liability will not be avoided simply because the system has a fault and the same principles apply here as in the case of conventional computer software. It might be important to consider whether it would be reasonable for the person using the system for the purpose of advising others to rely on the system's output. In relation to the exercise of a profession such as medicine, the fact that a person has acted in accordance with practice which is recognised as proper by a responsible body of persons skiled in that profession means that there has been no negligence. In *De Freitas* v *O'Brien* [1995] 6 Med LR 108, however, the Court of Appeal stressed that a responsible body of expert opinion does not have ot be a substantial body. A small number of specialists could constitute a 'responsible body'.

Consider an expert system designed to recommed financial investments which is used by a responsible body of financial advisers. If a particular financial adviser uses the system to recommend an investment to a client, the adviser will not be negligent if the system was used in a reasonable and satisfactory manner, even if the advice turns out to be bad retrospectively. The problem is that, until both time as a particular expert systm is used by a sufficient number of skilled practitioners (sufficient to be classed as a responsible body), anyone using an expert system is taking a chance should be advice turn out to be wrong, although it must be stressed that the fact that advice is wrong does not inevitably and conclusively mean that there has been negligence, in *Whitehouse* v *Jordan* [1981] 1 All ER 267, the House of Lords confirmed that an error of judgment does not automatically indicate negligence; it depends whether the error would have been made by a reasonably competent professional mn professing to have the standard and type of skill that the defendant held himself out to have. If the person using the expert system does not have the degree of skill and knowledge contained in the system he should make this clear to the client and obtain his agreement prior to using the system. The advantage of negligent misstatement over normal negligence claims is that it can be used where the loss has been economic only, although it is not restricted to this.

Liability for Indirect Statements

Where the original maker of the statement does not directly communicate it to the person relying on it, it appears that for a duty of care to arise, the latter must realise who is the source of the statement. In *Abbott* v *Strong* (unreported) *The Times*, 9, July 1998, a firm of accountants made statements as to a profits forecast, which were included in a circular sent to shareholders inviting them to subscribe for new shares in a rights issue. It was held that the accountants were not potentially liable for any misstatement to shareholders who subscribed as they had not relied on the accounts' statement. Where a person makes a statement to anohter person who uses it to advise another but that other does not know of the first person's participation in the advice, then the recipient cannot be said to have relied on the first person. Thus, where a person uses computer software in order to advise a client who believes that the advice comes from the person using the software alone, then any person who has been involved in the development of the software cannot be liable to the client in tort. Of course, this will be different if the client knows that the advice derived from using the software emanates from a person or persons involved in the development of the software, such as in the case of an expert system which contains rules and advice set forware by a particular person.

This approach is based on the concept of reliance. The person originally giving the advivce cannot be liable if the ultimate recipient is knows not to have relied on that person but on advice given by another (even if originally given by that person) and can be contrasted with *Hedley*

Byrne where it was clear that the recipient of the advice did indeed rely upon the first bank. The recipient's bank was merely the messenger. Thus, if a patient, Tom Cobb, consults a general practitioner, Dr Akkerman, in respect of an illness and the doctor uses diagnostic software which includes diagnostic rules and suggested teatment devised by a specialist, Mr Rudge, he will not have a claim against Mr Rudge as he does not rely on him. It is Dr Akerman on whom Tom Cobb relies. It would be different if Dr Akerman first told Tom Cobb that he was goint to use a computer system which contained advice from Mr Rudge, a specialist in the field.

The need for reliance does not necessarily require that the recipient of the statement knows the precise identity of the person from whom the advice originated providing that he knew it came from some other person. Reliance as an essential ingredient in an action for negligent misstatement was confirmed by the House of Lords in *Willimas* v *Natural Health Foods Ltd* [1998] 2 All ER 577. In that case it was held that a director of a franchisor company (the franchise was in respect of health food shops) was not liable to the franchises for loss resulting from negligent advice *given by the franchisor company* as there was no evidnce that the franchisees believed that the direction was undertaking a personal responsibility to them. In the example given in Figure 15.1, if liability for negligent misstatement is to be imposed on anyone other than the professional giving the advice directly to the cleint, it would be necessary to show that the client relied on any statement made by that person.

Negligent Provision of a Service and Concurrent Liability

At first, it was thought that *Hedley Byrne* was limited to negligent statements but it is now apparent that it also applies to the negligent provison of a service. In *Henderson* v *Merrett Syndicates Ltd* [1995] 2 AC 145, discussed later, Lord Goff said that there was no reason why a person should not be liable under the *Hedley Byrne* principle for economic loss which flows from the negligent performance of a service, and this sentiment was approved in *Williams* v *Natural Health Food Ltd* [1998] 2 All ER 577. The provision of the service must be coupled with a concomitant reliance and will often be set in the context of a contract. This brings into question whether there can be concurrent liability under contract and tort where, for example, a service is provided under a contract.

At one time it was thought that where there was a contract between the parties, that contract would provide the sole basis for the injured party seeking a remedy. At least liability in negligence could not be imposed if it contradicted the express terms of a contract. However, the position was clarified in *Henderson* v *Merrett Syndicates Ltd* [1995] 2AC 145, where the main issue was whether the defendants (managers of syndicates at Lloyd's) could be liable concurrently in contract and tort to Lloyd's underwriters for the negligent management of syndicates to which the underwriters belonged.

The House of Lords held that such concurrent liability can exist unless the contract itself precludes it. This means that in many cases, the injured party may choose whether to sue on the contract or in tort. Althogh in may cases the outcome will be the same in practical terms, in some the contractual and tortius duties may be different and the limitation periods may be different. The limitation period is the time within which an action must be commenced, otherwise, it will be time-barred. For contract it is six years from the breach (Limitation Act 1980, section 5), while for negligence (and negligent misstatement) generally it is six years from the date of damage occurred (Limiation Act

1980, section 2); although for personal injury cases, the period is three years.

As an example of the above principles, consider a situation whereby Conway Computer Systems Ltd has agreed to maintain for one year the computer system of Willett & Co Ltd, a company with a parcel delivery operation. The contract states that Conway will remedy any defects within 24 hours of being informed by Willett and there is a clause in the contract providing for the payment of £500 per day in liquidated damages by Conway for every 24-hour period in excess of the first such period during which the computer system remains out of action because of a defect. One day, Willett informed Conway of a fault on its computer system. Due to the negligence of its programmers, Conway took 72 hours to remedy the defect. Under the contract Conway is liable to pay £1000 to Willett. However, under the circumstances, Willett's operations were badly disrupted and its total loss ws in the order of £15 000. It was reasonably foreseeable that Willett would be so affected by its computer system being inoperable for such a period of time. That being so, the damages arising out of negligence ought to be in the order of £15 000, whereas, under contract, they are only £1000. Although, theoretically, there are concurrent liabilities in contract and tort, it would be highly unlikely that a court would allow Willett to pursue a remedy in tort as the contract has an express limitation on the measure of damages for failure to repair the defect in time. If the limiting clause did not exist, however, it would seem that Willett could be free to chose which route to pursue. This might be advantageous, particularly if the duty of care under the contract is of a lesser standard than that under the tort of negligence.

Product Liability

Related to negligence are the product liability provisions

contained in the Consumer Protection Act 1987. Under the Act an ultimate consumer can claim against the producer of a defective product regardless of the lack of a contractual relationship between the consumer and the producer and without having to show the basic requirements for an action in negligence. Part 1 of the Act deals with product liability and stems from the Council of European Communities Directive on product liability (Directive on the approximation of the law, regulations and adminstrative provisions of member states concerning liability for defective products 85/374/EEC, OJ[1985] L210/29. A 'product' is defined by the Consumer Protection Act as being any goods including electricity and includes a product comprised in another product whether a component part or a raw material. A computer would therefore come within the meaning of product but computer software, *per se,* will be outside the scope of this part of the Act.

Although product liability does not appear to apply to software it will apply to a defective product which incorporates software such as a computer-controlled microwave oven. There would seem to be no reason why liability on the basis of product liability should be avoided even if the defect which causes the damage lies within the software. A defect in software controlling a microwave oven or any other product will result in the microwave oven itself being defective.

The producer of a defective product is liable for damage wholly or partly from that defect. Distributors and retailers selling 'own brand' goods can be liable if they can be said to be holding themselves out to be the producer. If a person imports a product, in the course of business, into a country belonging to the European Community from outside the Community in order to supply the product to another, then that importer will be regarded as the producer for the purposes of determining liability by section 2 of the Act.

This might have implications for the many companies which import computers made outside the European Community, especially importers who affix their own name to the equipment. If one of these machines is defective and someone is injured as a result, then the importer/distributor will be liable under the Act, apart from any remedies available against him under contract. The Consumer Protection Act also makes a supplier liable if he fails to identify the producer wihin a reasonable time; having been asked to do so by the claimant.

A defect is defined by reference to the expectation of safety in the product and this relates to property damage as well as death and personal injury. A computer with an exposed unearthed metal chassis would fall short of the expectation of safety.

State of the Art Defence

An important defence is the 'state of the art' defence contained in section 4(1) of the Consumer Protection Act 1987. This provides that it is defence in any civil proceedings to show that 'the state of scientific and technical knowledge at the relevant time was not such that a producer of products of the same description as the product in question might be expected to have discovered the defect if had existed in his products while they were under his control'. This defence would apply, for example, where a product failed suddenly as a result of a form of material fatigue higherto not widely known amongst producers of such products. The defence as set out in the Act has been criticised as introducing a subjective element is it is a question of whether the producer might be expected to discover the fault, not whethera reasonable producer would be expected to discover the defect. The Directive seems to imply a more objective test as it requires the state of scientific and technical knowledge to be such as to enable the existence of the defect to be discovered. However, in *Commission of the European Communities* v *United Kingdom*, *The Times*, 23 June 1997, the European Court of Justice concluded that the Act validly implemented that part of the Directive and rejected the Commission's argument that the United Kingdom had widened the defence so that the strict liability imposed by the Directive had been turned into mere liability for negligence. As Part I of the Consumer Protection Act 1987 is stated to be intended to comply with the Directive and shall be construed accordingly, it would appear that the courts in the United Kingdom are likely to ointerpret the 'state of the art' defence on an objective basis.

A possible application of the defence is in the aeronautical industry, for example, where software companies develop sophisticated software for 'fly-by-wire' aeroplanes. Imagine there are two such companies: one is a very large company, Goliath plc, with enormous resources at its disposal whereas the other company, David Software Ltd, is much smaller, being a new entrant into this field, and having proportionally less resources. As a result of considerable research and testing, Golioath is aware of an inherent danger in such software in that it takes a short period of time for the pilot to override the computer software. Consquently, Goliath has incorporated an emergency override commands in its software. David Software is not aware of this problem because it has not been published by Goliath and David Software has not carried out sufficent research to detect the problem. If the test in section 4 of the Consumer Protection Act 1987 is subjective, David Software might be able to avail itself of the defence but is less likely to if, as it appears it should be, the test is objective.

The defence is most-likely to be relevant in leading-edge technology where new types of products are being developed. This is particularly so where computer technology is being used in process control, traffic control, guidance systems and the like. Consider, for example, the implications of a car with a computer software designed to apply the brakes in an emergency, say if the traffic in front comes to an abrupt standstill. One day a cat runs across the road in front of the car. The software interprets the image of the cat as a stationary object immediately ahead and brings the car to an emergency stop. A lorry following the car runs into the back of it injuirng the occupants. Who is liable? The company making the braking system could be potentially liable subject to the state of the art defence (a product includes a product omprised in another product as a component part). The lorry direver, and his employer, may also be liable in negligence.

Extent of Liability

Under section 5 of the 1987 Act, the liability covered by Part 1 of the Act extends to:

(a) death or personal injury;

(b) damage to or destruction of any item of property (including land) other than the defective product itself (there is a lower thereshold of £275 before a claim can be made) provided that the property:

  (i) is the type normally intended for private use and consumption, and

  (ii) it is used mainly for the private use or consumption of the person claiming.

Therefore, in dealings between businesses, the product liability part of the Act will only apply to defective products causing death or personal injury. As far as property damage is concerned, the provisions are really aimed at the consumer market, so, if you buy a computer as a Christmas present for your uncle and because of a fault it catches fire and causes £1500 of damage to his house, your uncle will have a cliam under the 1987 Act against the manufacturer of computer for the damage to the house and furniture. Personally, you may have a separate claim aginst the retail outlet because the computer was not of satisfactory-quality under the Sale of Goods Act 1979.

Criminal Liability for Defective Products

Part 1 of the Consumer Protection Act 1987 imposes civil liability on producers. However, if a person is killed as a result of a defective product and the defect is attributable to the negligence of any person, that person could be exposed to a prosecution for manslaugher. This could evren expose a company ot prosecution if the negligence of a senior offier of the company is the root cause of the negligence and this is imputed to the company on the basis that the acts of its senior officers are the acts of the company.

Apart from liability for manslaugher resulting from defects in safety critical systems, there are numerous statuts which impose criminal liability and which may be triggered by a computer defect. Examples include the Health and Safety at Wrok etc. Act 1974, the Food Safety Act 1990 and the Environmental Protection Act 1990. An offence might be committed under the Food Safety Act where a computer is used to calculate cooking times and underestimates safe times because of a defect. A polution control system run by a computer may result in an offence under the Environmental Protection Act 1990 if toxic substances are released into a stream without treatment because of a software error. The areas where civil and criminal liability may result from the use of defective computer technology are immense and, with the growth or safety legislation and environmental protection law, these areas are increasing rapidly.

The General Product Safety Regulations 1994 impose criminal liability on producers and distributors in respect of products that are not safe. A 'product' means by product intended for consumers or likely to be used by consumers, whether new, used for reconditioned. A 'safe product' is one which, under normal or reasonably foreseeable conditions of use, including duration, does not present any risk or only the minimum risks compatible with the product's use considered as acceptable and consistent with a high level of protection for the safety and health of persons. Account is to be taken of the products, characteristics, presentation (including information given) and categories of consumers at serious risk (for example, children). There is a defence of due diligence.

These regulations are highly relevant in terms of second-hand computer equipment and any electrical equipment sold to children. In terms of software the same difficulty will apply as identified above - that is, that it is unlikely that software will be deemed to be a product although it is possible that the disks and other tangible items supplied with the software may be so classed.

Exemption Clauses

An exemption clause is one which excludes or restricts the liability of a party who is in breach of contract. Exemption clauses can be sub-divided into exclusion clauses and limitation clauses. An exclusion clause gives the party relying on it total exemption for the breach whereas a limitation clause limits liability to specified amount. An example of an exclusion clause is where a supplier totally excludes his liability under the contract for late delivery if this is caused by circumstances beyond his control such as industrial action. An example of a limitation clause is where a supplier of computer software limits his liability for faulty software to the licence fee he has received for that software.

When people draft contracts they are usually keen to limit or exclude their liabilities and yet wish to ensure that the other party is absolutely bound to perform his part of the contract. Such one-sided contracts were fairly common in the past (they are by no means extinct now), particularly in circumstances where there was an inequality of bargaining power. An ordinary individual buying a product from a supplier who had a monopoly in the product had little choice but to accept the terms imposed in him or manage without it. A golden principle in contract was 'freedom of contract' meaning that the parties should be free to agree whatever terms they wished. This doctrine was acceptable where two powerful companies were negotiating a contract in a ffree market, but contractually weaker persons suffered. Over the years, however, Parliament and the courts have intervened to mitigate the harshness of the situation and certain terms are now implied into sale of goods and similar contracts, while exclusion clauses have been disapproved of by the courts, especially if such clauses are demonstrably unfair.

The courts developed technques to limit the effects of exclusion clauses, including the interpretation of an ambiguous clause to the disadvantage of the party seeking to rely on it. For example, in *Andrews Brothers (Bournemouth) Ltd* v *Singer & Co Ltd* [1934] 1 KB 17, the plaintiff ordered a new Singer car from the defendants. When the car was delivered it was found to have done some 550 miles. The defendants sought to rely on an exclusion clause which stated that liability for terms implied by statute was excluded; one of these terms was that goods must comply with their description. The contract, however, repreatedly described the car as a 'new Singer car'. I was held that, because the car was referred to in the contract as a new car, this was an express term and since the exclusion clause sought to exclude liability for implied terms only, the defedants were liable. The exclusion clause was of no effect for this breach of an express term. The plaintiff was awarded £50 in damages.

Exemption clauses are also controlled by statute. The Unfair Contract Terms Act 1977 limits the extent to which liability can be excluded or limited for breach of contract, or for negligence, or under the terms implied by the Sale of Goods Act 1979 and other legislation containing similar provisions, such as the Supply of Goods and Services Act 1982. Sections 2 to 4 of the Unfair Contract Terms Act apply to contractual terms or notices which attempt to exclude or restrict liability for negligence terms or contract.

A person may seek to exclude or limit his liability for negligence by means of a notice or a term in a contract. Whether the liability arises in tort or contract, the legal controls are the same and mainly result from section 2 of the Unfair Contract Terms Act 1977. This applies to business liability for negligence whether a breach of a contractual obligations to exercise reasonable care and skill in the performance of a contract or a breach of an equivalent common law duty. Section 2 of the Act probibits the exclusion of limitation of laibility for death or personal injury resulting from negligence, while liability for other loss or damage may only be excluded for restricted in so far as the term or notice satisfies the requirement of reasonableness. Section 11 of the Act provides that a term in a contract is reasonable if it is fair and reasonable to have been included in a contract having regard to the circumstances which were, or ought reasonably to have been, known to or in the contemplation of the parties when the contract was made. In relation to a notice, the test is whether it is fair and reasonable to allow reliance on it having regard to the circumstances. By section 11(4), where the term or notice seeks ot limit liability to a specified sum of money, regard must be had to the resources available to the person who would have to meet the liability and how far it was open to that person to take out insurance cover. The burden of proof is on the person claiming that the term or notice is reasonable.

In terms of defective hardware, the basic provisions of the Unfair Contract Terms Act work reasonably predictably but it is in respect of software that doubts were expressed as to the reach of the Act, and this has been the source of some speculation. This is because Schedule 1, paragraph 1 to the Act states that:

> Section 2 to 4 of this Act do not extend to- ...
>
> (c) any contract so far as it relates to the creation or transfer of a right or interest in any patent, trade mark, copyright, registered design, technical or commercial or other intellectual property...

One view was that the important provisions in section 2 (liability for negligence), section 3 (contractual liability for breach or in relation to performance) and section 4 (unreasonable indemnity clauses) were inapplicable to software contracts because the essence of most software contracts is the granting of a licence to use the software - the creation of a right under copyright law. A number of software companies considered that they could largely ignore the effects of the Unfair Contract Terms Act 1977 and exclude or strictly limit their liability for defects. The courts have taken a more restrictive approach, however, to the scope of paragraph 1 of Schedule 1.

In *The Salvage Association* v *Cap Financial Services Ltd* [1995] FSR 654, the plaintiff invited tenders for the computerisation of its accounts system. The defendant submitted a successful bid for a feasibility study (strategy study and defintion age) and was awarded the contract in the sum of £30,000. Following this, a second contract was awarded to the defendant to develop and implement the software specified in the feasibility study. The date for completion of the second contract was 18 July 1988 and the contract price was £291 654. The system was to be implemented using ORACLE, a fourth-generation language operating as a relational database management system. In July 1988, the software was declared to be ready for user-training but almost immediately it became apparent that it was unusable and contained a large number of errors that would require substantial work to correct. Many of the errors could be attributed to the fact that the defendant's projet team was not sufficiently experienced in the use of ORACLE. Nevertheless, the plaintiff persevered and allowed additional time for the defendant to complete the work satisfactorily. Several new dates for delivery were agreed but, eventually, it became clear to the plaintiff that the work was likely never to be completed satisfactorily and, on 13 July 1989, the plaintif terminated the contract because of the serious braches of contract on the part of the defendant.

The plaintiff claimed that it was entitled to reject the system and terminate the second contract and claimed damages of £855 550 (being the sum of £291 388 already paid under both contracts and £564162 for wasted expenditure resulting from the defendant's breaches of contract). The defendant sought to rely on limitation clauses in the standard form contract which formed the basis of the first contract and, in relation to the second contract, terms which purported to exclude liability except as provided for by the contract and, in any case, to limit liability under that contract to £25,000. The limit in the first contract was £250,000 in respect of physical damage and £25,000 for other loss or damage (except for liability for death or physiucal injury where there was no limit).

Both contracts contained terms to the effect that the defendant would assign appropriately qualified staff to perform the work and the judge in the High Court held that there was a breach of these terms. Furthermore, the judge implied a term under section 13 of the Supply of Goods and Services Act 1982 to the effect that the defendant would exercise reasonable care and skill and held that the defendant was also in breach of this term.The time for completion of the second contract was extended on a number of occasions but the judge held that time was of the essence and the extensions agreed by the plaintiff did not alter that simple fact. The plaintiff's patience had been stretched to the limit and it was entitled to repudiate the contract at the time it did.

If sections 2 and 3 of the Unfair Contract Terms Act 1977 applied to the limitation clauses, they would be upheld only in as much as they met the requirements of reasonableness - otherwise the defendant would probably be able to rely on them. The judge decided that paragraph 1 in Schedule 1 only concerned those provisoins in a contract that dealt with the creation or transfer of right or interest in the relevant intellectual property and did not extend to all the other terms of a service contract simply because the service will result in a 'product' that is subject to intellectual property rights. Thus, terms concerned with aspects of the contract other than those relationg to sections 2 to 4 of the Unfair Contract Terms Act 1977. In other words, paragraph 1(c) does not creat a blanket exceptions for software contracts.

As mentioned above, the reasonableness test is expressed in section 11 of the Act. Schedule 2 provides guidelines for the application of the reasonableness test and, though not expressed as being applicable to sections 2 and 3 of the Act, the judge accepted the suggestion of Potter J in *Flamar Interocean Ltd* v *Denmac Ltd (The Flamar*

Pride) [1990] 1 Lloyd's Rep 434 that it would be sensible to take the guidelines into account in such cases. He referred also to the judgment of Lord Griffiths in *Smith* v *Eric S Bush* [1990] 1 AC 831 where his lordship identified four matters that should always be considered:

- the realtive bargaining power of the parties;
- whether it was reasonably practicable to obtain advice from an laterantive source;
- the difficulty and dangerouness of task to be undertaken - that is, the risk; and
- the practical consequences of the court's decision, the ability of the parties to bear the losses involved and the availability of insurance.

In the present case, the parties were of equal bargaining power but it would have bene almost impossible for the plaintiff to insure to cover the liability excluded by the defedant. The insurance factor was crucial to this case as the defendant itself had recognised the inadequacy of the £25 000 figure in its standard form contracts and it had been raised to £1 million at around the time of the first contract. Unfortunately for the defendant, it had not been able to explain convincingly why the higher figure had not ben used in its contrats with the plaintiff. The judge, therefore, held that the terms limiting liability to £25 000 were unreasonable and awarded a total of £662 926 in damages comprising £291 388 (already paid by the plaintiff), £231 866 for items of wasted expenditure (computer time, wster computer stationery; payments to consultants and for testing) and £139 672 for wasted management time.

In another important case, *St Albans City & District Council* v *International Computers Ltd* [1995] FSR 686, the judge had to consider the effectiveness of clauses limiting liability in the context of a software 'bug' which caused financial loss to the client. It concerned software used to administer the community charge (poll tax) and has far-reaching implications for software developers, who should look carefully at their standard term contracts and level of insurance cover.

The plaintiff, a local authority, was responsible for setting the level of and collecting the community charge and invited tenders for the supply of suitable hardware and software to keep a register of charge payers and to carry out additional functions such as raising the necessary bills. The contract was award to the defendant in 1988. Perhaps exacerbated and compounded by unbelievably tight deadlines, an error in the software resulted in the population being over-estimated by some 2966 persons and the community charge was set at too low a level as a consequence. This had a knock-on effect in terms of money flows to and from central government and the total fionancial loss to the plaintiff was £314 846. The contract was made on the defendant's standard written terms.

Mr. Justice Scott Baker accepted that the defendant was under an obligation to provide software that maintain a reliable database of names entered on to the community charge register, accurately count those names and accurately retrieve and display the population count. Furthermore, the software had to be reasonably fit for its purpose of maintaining and retrieving a reliable register. There was a plain breach of contract because of the erroneous figures produced by the software. Additionally, an assurance made by the defendant's project manager that the figures could be relied upon was a breach of the project manager's contract of service which was part of the overall agreement. This was a negligent misrepresentation and the project manager's obligations were not, as required, exercised with due diligence. A term in the contract that errors had to be notified to the defendant within three months was of no effect because the plaintiff was unaware of the error and had no way of discovering it.

The judge, in awarding the plaintiff the full amount claimed, said that the plaintiff was not at fault in failing to discover the error not in failing to take different action when it became apparent that there was a problem with the software. He was of the opinion that the defendant had failed to establish that the limitation clauses in the main agreement and the service agreement incorporated in it were reasonable in the circumstances. By section 3 of the Unfair Contract Terms Act 1977, where one party deals as consumer or on the other's written standard terms of business, the other cannot, by reference to any contract term, exclude or restrict any liability for his own breach of contract except in so far as the term satisfies the requirement of reasonableness. The plaintiff was not dealing as consumer but the judge held that the contract was based on the written standard terms of the defendant even though there had been some negotiation between the parties. He said that it was not necessary for all the terms to have bene fixed in advance by the supplier for the contract to be deemed to be on the basis of written standard terms. Some terms, such as those dealing with quality or price, would often be the result of negotiation but that did not necessarily take the contract out of the reach of section 3. In any case, the judge held that either section 5 or 7 of the unfair Contract Terms Act 1977 also applied.

Sections 6 and 7 deal with implied terms in contracts of sale or hire purchase of goods and other contracts under which the title to goods pass and also require that the reasonableness test be satisfied in relation in terms excluding or restricting liability. Scott Baker J followed the approach of Judge Thayne Forbes in *The Salvage Association* v *CAP*

Financial Services Ltd and considered that it would be better for the loss to fall on a large international computer company (which was well able to insure itself against such claims) rather than falling on a local authority. Other factors of particular note were the resources of the defendant and its total insurance cover which was claimed to amount to £50 million. The judge decided that the plaintiff was in a slightly weaker bargaining position than the defendant and, although the plaintiff knew of the term (indeed it had complained about its presence in the contract), had received no inducement, and was unable to enter into a similar contract with another without such a term, the defendant had failed to discharge its burden of establishing that the term was fair and reasonable in the circumstances.

The Court of Appeal confirmed that the limitation clause was unenforceable in *St Albans City & District Council* v *International Computers Ltd* [1997] FSR 251. However, the defendant's appeal was allowed in part in that the award of damages was reduced to £685 000. The plaintiff's claim in relation to payments by chargepayers was held not to be recoverable as they were under an obligation to pay (otherwise they would get a bonus) and the plaintiff could simply increase the charge the following year to recoup that loss. This was notwithstanding the fact that some persons would have left the district and some would have moved into the district in the meantime. However, the Court of Appeal confirmed that the plaintiff could recover for the increased precept payments made to the County Council which it was unable to recover.

The *St Albans* case is very instructive and shows the difficulty that a software company may have in convincing a judge that any term excluding or limiting liability for defective software is reasonable. Here, the defendant's term was deemed to be unreasonable even though the plaintiff was aware of the term, other software companies had comparable terms and the software was in use while still under development. However, the judge's view that the plaintiff was in a weaker bargaining position can be criticised. It was a local authority responsible for a population in excess of 100 000 persons, employing professional staff and making use of a respected firm of management consultants to advise on the tender process. The plaintiff would certainly be in a stronger bargaining position than most small and medium-sized commercial enterprises dealing with a major computer company. Nevertheless, there are important lessons for computer software companies contained within the judgment.

Before the Unfair Contract Terms Act 1977 came into force, the courts developed, somewhat erratically, the doctrine of 'fundamental breach' as way of curbing the worst excesses of exclusion clauses. *Pinnock Bros*v *Lewis & Peat Ltd* [1923] 1 KB 690 concerned a contact for the purchase of copra cake. When delivered, it was discovered to be poisonous because it had been contaminated with castor coil. It was held that it was not copra cake at all but a substance quite different to that contracted for and, because of this the sellers could not rely on an exclusion clause purporting to exempt them from liability. Later, it was said that where there had been a fundamental breach of contract - that is, of one party fails to carry out his part of the bargain at all or attempts to render a performance totally different from that contemplated - then the party in breach could not rely on an exclusion clause (see *Karsales (Harrow) Ltd* v *Wallis* [1956]2 All ER 61). However, the courts later look a more *lassez-faire* attitude to exclusion clause and fundamental breach on the basis that the parties should be free to agree that there should be no liability under the contract even for a fundamental breach, if that was their desire; see *Photo Production Ltd* v *Securicor Transport*

Ltd [1980] AC 827. This case concerned the law before the implementation of the Unfair Contract Terms Act 1977, but the impact of this Act on exclusion clauses was in the minds of their lordships.

Nevertheless, the doctrine of fundamental breach may still have some utility when it comes to controlling exclusion clauses an contracts which do not come within the scope of the Unfair Contract Terms Act - for example, where the breach concerns the grant of the licence itself such as where the licensor turns out not to be entitled to grant the licence or in the context of liability arising outside the course of business. Of course, where a purported licence for the use of software fails because the licensor does not have the right to grant the licence (for example, if he does not own the copyright and does not have the right to grant the licence (for example, if he does not own the copyright and does not have the copyright owner's permission to grant licences) then it could be said that the contract will be void on the basis of a total failure of consideration.

Section 8 of the unfair Contract Terms Act provides that a clause in a contract which purports to exclude or restrict liability for misrepresentation will only be effective if it satisfies the requirement of reasonableness. If a computer salesman claims that the computer he is selling will run a particular software package and this claim turns out to be untrue, it will be for the company selling the computer to show that any exemption clause it hopes to rely on passes the test of reasonableness. The test is laid out in section 11 of the Unfair Contract Terms Act 1977 which requires that the term be:

> ... fair and reasonable ... having regard to the circumstances which were, or ought reasonably to have been, known to or in the contemplation of the parties when the contract was made...

This is nebulous requirement which also applies to some of the other provisions in the Act. It gives the courts scope to be flexible and to take the facts of a particular case into account. Some indication of the court's approach was given by the decision in Garage *Mitchell (Chesterball) Ltd* v *Finney Lock Seeds Ltd* [1983] 2 All FR 737. The plaintiff bought cabbage seed from the defendant for £192. The seed was defective and the resulting crop was little better than useless. The loss to the plaintiff, a farmer, was in the order of £61000. When sued, the defendant claimed to be liable only for the cost of the seed because of a clause in their contract to that effect. Lord Denning (it was his last case) said that the term was not fair and reasonable in the circumstances, although he did say that this was a borderline case. The following were important factors:

- Farmers had no way of knowing or discovering that the seed was defective.
- The defendant seed merchant could have insured against the risk of defective seed but it was unlikely that an individual farmer could so insure.
- The defendants had not relied on the clause but had reached a negotiated settlement in similar prior cases.
- It was likely that was seed merchant or their Dutch supplies had been negligent.

In a subsequent appeal to the House of Lords, the Court of Appeal's decision was affirmed. It should be noted that, by section 7 of the Unfair Contract Terms Act 1977, liability for defective products under Part I of the Consumer Protection Act 1987 cannot be excluded or limited by any contact term.

Individual consumers making contracts for non-business purposes are given greater protection in relation to standard form contracts as from 1 July 1995, by the Unfair Terms in Consumer Contracts Regulations 1994. This controls terms which are unfair and, being contrary to the requirement of good faith, cause a significant imbalance in the parties' rights and obligations under the contract to the detriment of the consumer. The nature of the goods or services must be taken into account in assessing the unfair nature of the term in question. Schedule 2 to the Regulation gives a list of things to be taken into account when assessing fairness; the strength of bargaining position, whether the consumer receive an inducement to agree to the term, whether the goods or services were sold or supplied to the special order of the consumer and whether the seller or supplier has acted fairly and equitably.

Schedule 3 contains a list of terms that are likely to be regarded as unfair. Some of these would not be effective in any case under English law, an example being a term which allows the unilateral alteration of a term in the contract by the seller or supplier. The provision do not apply to terms which have been individually negotiated or , if written in plain intelligible language, which define the main subject matter of the contract or are concerned with the adequacy of the price or remuneration. The seller or supplier has the burden of proof in showing that a term was individually negotiated. Where there is any doubt as to the meaning of a term, the meaning most favourable to the consumer will be taken. If a contract contains an unfair term, it will not be binding on the consumer but the contract will continue in existence if it is capable of so doing without the unfair term.

16 CONTRACT LAW FOR WRITING SOFTWARE

If an organisation wishes to obtain some new computer software, there may be several options open to it. Appropriate software may be available as an 'off-the-shelf' package of the organisation may employ its own computer staff who can develop the software. In other circumstances, it may be advantageous to have the software written or adapted by a software development company — a firm specialising in particular types of computer software. The following example is typical of instances when software will be developed under a contractual agreement.

A company owns a mainframe computer and network of personal computers or terminals. It requires software to automate its accounting and invoicing systems. After reviewing software available off-the-shelf, the company comes to the conclusion that none is ideally suited to its methods of operation and it is neither appropriate nor satisfactory for it to change its methods to suit the available software. Although the company employs a number of analysts and programmers, it decides against asking them to write the software as they are not sufficiently experienced in the development software that is likely to be used as a platform to deliver the applications software. The company selects an experienced software company to carry out a comprehensive feasibility study which includes development and strategy studies. The software company produces a detailed plan and specification for the worm, and is awarded the contract to carry out the work following the submission of bids by it and a number of other experienced software companies. We will not turn to the terms and provisions commonly found in a contract for wiring computer software. The company commissioning the development of the software will be referred to as the 'client' and the company wiring the software will be called the 'software development company'.

Definitions

The very first clause in the contract is likely to deal with a description of the parties to the contract and appropriate definitions relating to the software and the equipment on which the software will be installed. Apart from being a word-saving provison in that the client's full business name can be abbreviated throughout to CLIENT or CUSTOMER, the definitions clause can usefully describe terms such as software and this assist with the interpretation and construction of the agreement. Consequently, any expressions defined here should be precisely and comprehensively as they will be the key to understanding the remainder of the contract and the scope of the parties' obligations and liabilities under it.

Licence Agreement

What will the software development company deliver to the client in return for the payment? On the face of it a set of programs, data files and associated documentation is what will be provided, but will the software development company really hand over ownership of the programs and other software?. This will be unlikely and an important term usually states that the software is being licensed; the contract is, first and foremost, a licence agreement. A licence is a permission to do something; in terms of computer software, a licence is a permission to use the software and, without this permission, using the software would be an infringement of the copyright subsisting in it. This is because loading programs and data into a computer's memory is making a copy and copyright can be infringed even if the copy is transient by section 17(6) of the Copyright, Designs and Patents Act 1988.

The software development company will undoubtedly want to retain the ownership of the intellectual property rights in the programs and the documentation, for its business is licensing software and it will want to grant licences in respect of the software, or variants of it or modules contained within it, to others. If it is especially important for the company acquiring the software that it is not make available to others, it should insist on an exclusive licence, which is likely to be much more expensive. Alternatively, ownership of the copyright subsisting in the software could be transferred to the client under an assignment of copyright. In practical terms, there is little difference between an exclusive licence and an assignment of copyright. Where an exclusive licence or assignment of copyright is granted, however, the software development company would be wise to reserve the right to reuse modules in other software or even in the wiring of new software to perform similar functions. The drafting of an appropriate and workable clause to allow for this will require a great deal of care and the implications must be thoroughly considered. On the one hand the client may not want its competitor obtaining similar software from the software development company while, on the other hand, the latter will not want to unduly constrain its future software development activities.

Important points to check in the licence agreement will include the duration of the licence and its scope (sometimes the licence will be silent on the matter of duration). Because a licence is a permission to do something which would otherwise be unlawful, it does not give any proprietary interest in the software. The implications of this are twofold.

1 The licence should be for a fixed duration or their should be some provisions for termination of the licence. If the licence appears, on the face of it, to be perpetual, this contradicts the nature of a licence and it might even be implied that the agreement is not a licence but an assignment of the copyright and other rights in the software, especially, if the rights granted appear to be exclusive. It is more likely, however, in the absence of any express reference to duration, that the licence will endure as long as the copyright subsists in the software. The wording of the agreement as a whole should give a clue as to which interpretation is correct.

2 The licence agreement should state whether the software can subsequently be transferred to a third party. In the absence of any provision covering this aspect, it would appear that the benefit of the licence is transferable, depending on the circumstances.

The scope of the licence is very important. Is it permissible to run the software on several computers or just one particular computer? If the acquiring company is part of a group of companies, can be programs be used throughout the group or just within the one company? In the licence a single-user licence (if so, can it be used on any computer by the user)? Is it a site licence, a company licence or group licence? Can the software be transferred to another company? Is transfer subject to approval? All these questions should be considered and discussed with the software development company in the light of the contract and the intended uses to which the software is to be put. The possibility of expanding computing facilities and usage in the future must not be overlooked. In this respect, the client should carry out regular audits to make sure that its licensed software is not being used in excess of the licence agreements and to identify whether existing licences are adequate.

Assignment of Agreement

It is common for contracts to contain a term dealing with the assignment of the benefit of the contract. That is, the transfer of the might to use the software. For example, in an agreement for the writing of new software by a software development company for a client, there may be a term stating that neither party shall assign the agreement. Sometimes, assignment is permitted providing the other party consents. Note that in the context, we are talking about the assignment of the benefit of a contract rather than the assignment of the ownership of copyright. Terms dealing with assignment are particularly relevant where the performance of the contract will be carried out over a period of time, such as a building contract or a contract for writing new software.

Both parties to a contract enjoy benefits and suffer burdens emanating from the contract. For example a client for whom software is to be written under a contract may have the benefits and burdens listed in Table 16.1.

Unless prohibited, a party to a contract may assign (that is, transfer) the benefit of the contract but not the burden. The original parties remain liable for their obligations under the contract. In *Linden Gardens Trust Ltd* v *Lenesta Sludge Disposals Ltd* [1993] 3 WLR 408, a building contract contained a term which stated 'The employer [the client] shall not without the written consent of the contractor assign this contract'. There was a purported assignment of the contract but the House of Lords held that this was void. There was some criticism of the drafting of the above term. Lord Browne-Wilkinson said:

TABLE 16.1

Benefits and burdens in software contract

	Benefits		*Burdens*
1	The services of the software development company in writing the software	1	The obligation to pay the software development company
2	A copyright licence allowing use of the software	2	Providing facilities and information to the software development company
3	The grant of ownership of the property in disks, manuals, etc.	3	Accepting the software after attending testing.
4	The services of the software development company in maintaining the software and correcting errors		

On any basis, clause 17 is unhappily drafted in that it refers to an assignment of 'the contract'. It is trite law that it is, in any event, impossible to assign 'the contract' as a whole, i.e. including both burden and benefit. The burden of a contract can never be assigned without the consent of the other party to the contract in which event such consent will give rise to a novation.

(A novation is where a new contract is substituted for an old one.) Lord Browne-Wilkinsons also said, later:

> ...lawyers frequently use those words ['assign this contract'] inaccurately to describe an assignment of the benefit of a contract since

> every lawyer knows that the burden of a contract can never be assigned.

The House of Lords confirmed that a party to a contract might have good commercial reasons for refusing to grant consent to an assignment. For example, if a software company is providing continuing maintenance of software it might not want to maintain it if the software is transferred by the client to a third party. As the burden cannot be assigned the original party remains liable to fulfill his obligations under the contract. For example, if a client transfers the benefit of a software licence to a third party, that original client remains liable for any outstanding payment. Where there is an assignment, the original party, the assignor, might want to consider an indemnity clause to protect himself against any legal action brought by the other party in respect of his obligations under the contract.

It is common for a licence agreement (and the same applies to other forms of agreement such as a maintenance agreement) to state that the benefit of the agreement shall not be assigned without the prior written permission of the other party.

In *Circuit Systems Ltd & Basten* v *Zuken-Redac (UK)Ltd* (1995) Const LJ 201, the defendant rented computer equipment to the first plaintiff (Circuit Systems) and also entered into a maintenance agreement with it. Both agreements prohibited assignment though, in the case of the maintenance agreement, assignment with written consent was possible. The same day that the first plaintiff issued a writ against the defendant alleging, *inter alia*, breach of contract and economic duress, the first plaintiff went into liquidation. The second plaintiff, Basten (who owned at lest 98 per cent of the shares in Circuit Systems) took an assignment of Circuit Systems' rights of action for

£1 and was granted legal aid to pursue the claim. It was held that the assignments were not valid. However, in *Orion Finance Ltd* v *Crown Financial Management Ltd* (unreported) 30 March 1994, the assignment was subject to consent but the party whose consent was required, Crown, knew that the assignment had been made without consent but failed to draw the other party's attention to this Companies Act 1985. Crown was estopped from relying on the lack of consent. Crown's lack of activity was in effect a representation that it accepted the assignment as valid.

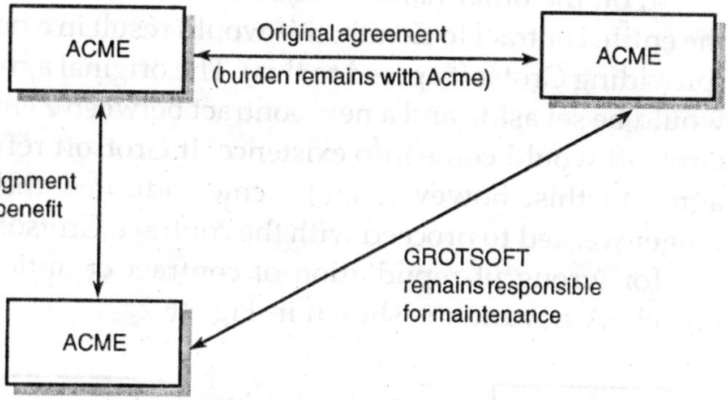

Fig. 16.1. Assignment of benefit of agreements.

Under what circumstances might an assignment of the benefit of contract be appropriate? Consider a client, Acme Manufacturing Ltd, which is member of a group of companies and which makes an agreement with Grotsoft Ltd, a software development company for the development, installation and maintenance of stock control software. After a while, because of changes in Acme's manufacturing methods, the software is no longer useful but another company in the group, Zenith Fabrications Ltd, would like to use the software. After seeking Grotsoft's permission as required in the contract, Acme assigns the benefit of the agreement to Zenith and Grotsoft will continue to maintain the software at Zenith's offices for the remainder of the maintenance period. Assuming that Grotsoft will be entitled to a final payment at the end of the maintenance period, this will be payable by Acme which remains responsible for this. In the separate agreement between Acme and Zenith in which the benefit of the agreement with Grotsoft is transferred to Zenith, there is provision for Zenith to refund Acme after it has made the final payment. Figure 16.1 shows the effect of the assignment to zenith.

If, on the other hand, Acme had wished to hand over the entire contract to Zenith, this would result in a novation (providing Grotsoft agreed to this). The original agreement would be set aside and a new contract between Zenith and Grotsoft would come into existence. If Grotsoft refused to agree to this, however, and Acme indicated that it no longer wanted to proceed with the contract, Grotsoft could sue for wrongful repudiation of contract or anticipatory breach. A novation is shown in Fig. 16.2.

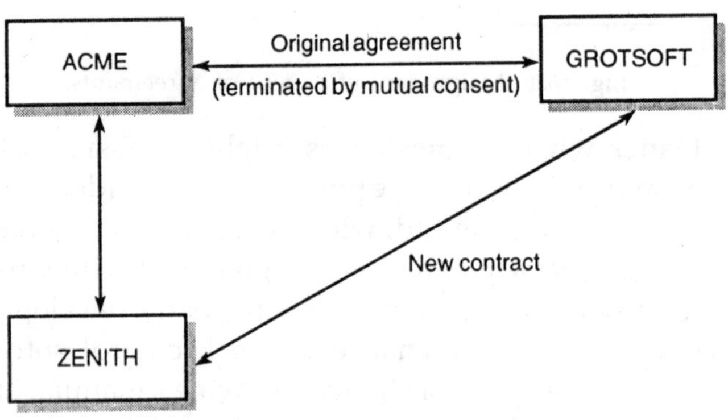

Fig. 16.2. Novation.

The Contract Price

As the agreement will be almost certainly in the nature of a licence, the sum payable should be termed a licence fee. This fee is often described as the price, however and often it will include other things such as training and tangible items such as disks and documentations. The word 'price' will be used, therefore, bearing in mind that this will include a once and for all licence fee which will usually make up the largest portion of the overall price. In some cases, the agreement will not be a licence, but instead, will provide for the assignment of the copyright subsisting in the completed software to the client. Nevertheless, similar considerations will apply as regards he price and many other aspects of the contract.

Wherever possible, the question of price should be tied down precisely. If it comprises licence fee; maintenance fee, price for any hardware supplied, etc. there should be a breakdown of the constituent costs. Apart from anything else, this could be a important for tax reasons. In addition, the contract should provide some machinery for calculating the cost of any extra work or services provided other than those which the software development company has agreed to provides its consideration for the contact. There may be unanticipated problems with the computer equipment, for example, or the client may change his mind half-way through the work and require modifications to be made to the specification. Therefore, the contract should include a list of hourly rates for programmers, analysts and others.

If a lump-sum price is agreed, it should be clear from one contract exactly what this includes: whether maintenance and training ar included, whether the price includes the documentation and, if so, how many copies. What about the cost of the media much as magnetic disks and tapes? If the payment is to be made in instalments, when are they due? If they become due following the performance of certain stages of the work, can these stages be clearly identified? For example, the contract might provide for payment of two-thirds of the total price when certain specified programs are operational and draft documentation has been provided. If the client is late in paying, does the contract include provision for charging interest? What if the client shows no intention of paying? It is in the interests of both parties that there should be no ambiguity as far as time for payment is concerned.

It may be that the software development company feels unable to quote a firm price form the start. Perhaps the client's computer equipment is unusual or unfamiliar in some respect. A software development company may refuse point blank to the tied down to a fixed price, particularly if the work involves modifying existing software to run on unusual equipment. If the software development company refuses to quote a fixed price the reason should be ascertained. Is it because the software development company is tackling something beyond its capabilities or are there more acceptable reasons? Is it genuinely difficult even for an experienced company to forecast the amount of work and the timescale because of the complexity of the work? One way round this problem is to ask the software development company or, preferably, a competent and independent consultant, to carry out a feasibility study. This will enable the viability of the project to be determined before the parties ar committed, and the actual amount of work involved and the price can be more accurately predicted. If carried through to the writing of a detailed specification, it can form the basis for inviting tenders or quotations from a number of software development companies to carry out the work. The cost of the feasibility study, however, can be a considerable addition to the overall cost of implementing the software though it may prove money well spent in the long run.

If the work involved in writing the software is

substantial, the possibility of obtaining quotations by competitive tender should be considered but, if this course is chosen, specialist advice should be sought as to the specification and other aspects of the tender documentation. The company inviting tenders is taking upon itself the responsibility for the feasibility of the project and the quality of the documentation provided to the tenders. If the specification is inadequate, any software development company awarded the contract will be able to point to this in its defence should the programs fail to be satisfactory, or use the deficiencies as a basis for claiming additional payment. Therefore, this approach can only be recommended for companies who have access to the necessary professional expertise. A major problem with comparing quotations and tenders is that it is unlikely that all those submitting will have put their bids together on the same basis. The chances are that some or all will have modified the specification in some way or another in spite of a request not to diverge from the specification. Some of those quoting may be unable to obtain a particular piece of equipment or software tool and will offer an alternative or they may offer an alternative simply because it is cheaper and they hope this will make their quotation appear more attractive. Although it could be argued that initiative should be rewarded, in fairness to the others quoting, all should be asked to reconsider their quotes in the light of the alternative should it appear to be worthwhile considering.

Specification

Whether the company acquiring the software, an independent consultant or the software development company writes the specification, there are several important points to be made in respect of it. The specification is the main provision in the contract which concerns the performance and capabilities of the software. It should be a detailed description of what the software is, what it will do and how quickly it will do it. The specification may well be contained in a separate document or be an appendix to the contract, but it must be noted that it is of crucial importance being the yardstick by which the software will be measured in the case of a dispute about the character and performance of the software.

Ideally, the specification will be clear, comprehensive and exactly mirror the client's requirements. Alas, this is not always the case and one of the most common problems is that the client moves the goalposts part way through the work, typically asking for changes to be made to the specification. The client may decide that he requires different or additional reports to be generated, links to other software not envisaged at the outset or the inclusion of additional routines, none of which are mentioned in the specification. Alternatively, some parts of the specification may have to be compromised became of operational and other difficulties not envisaged at the time the specification was written and agreed on by the parties to the contract. For example, the client may want to take advantage of a newly available upgrade to his operating system software which will require changes to the application software being written under the agreement. While changes made to the specification during the performance of the contract may result in the completed software being of a higher standard, more powerful or of increased functionality, the contractual implications of such changes must be catered for in the original agreement.

While the law will imply terms, based on reasonableness, dealing with additional payment and extensions to the time for completion, for example, under the Supply of Goods and Services Act 1982, it is better to build mechanisms into the contract for this purpose. A schedule of rates is a useful addition to a contract to be used or the determination of the additional price to be paid for extra work not included in the original contract because of changes to the specification made part-way through the work. Another term dealing with extensions to the time for completion would also be useful, as discussed later. If the changes are required because of unforeseen problems, then it would be useful to provide a term allowing additional payment it, and only if, a reasonably competent software company would not have anticipated the problem. The use of an independent professional contract supervisor, as advocated implications of changes to the specification.

It is useful to include a mechanism for variation orders in the agreement. A basic method is for any variation to the specification or work required to be set out in writing and signed by both parties before the changes are implemented or incorporated in the work programme. The additional cost (or reduction to the overall price) should be agreed by the parties as should the impact on the overall time for completion. It is far better to have agreement before any additional work is done or any other changes made to the planned programme of work implemented and for the consequences of any changes to be thoroughly considered and agreed. Trying to agree additional costs and extensions to the time for completion after the event can often result in acrimonious disputes although it has to be admitted that time pressures sometimes force retrospective action on the parties. At least a schedule of rates provides a safety curtain and a wise software development company will ensure that all the additional or modified work is carefully noted in terms of resources and duration.

If the changes made to the specification are considerable, the contracting parties ought to contemplate whether it would be better to terminate the existing contract and substitute it with another after negotiating a new contract and any settlement under the old contract. This is an example of novation. If the changes made are substantial this is probably the best route. Of course, the costs, and liabilities under the original contract which had already been incurred must be dealt with by mutual agreement (otherwise there could be an action for breach of contract). An experienced software development company should not get into a situation such that the the original contract has to be substituted by a new one. Where the work to be carried out is particularly difficult or covers new ground, it may be better to make an agreement to build a prototype system first backed by a broad specification, with a view to a subsequent contract to build the finished system backed by a much more detailed and explicit specification, written with the benefit of the experience gained in building the prototype.

The specification will have to address all the technical issues associated with the performance of the software. In particular, the three most important items which the specification should discuss are:

* a detailed description of the tasks the software will perform;
* the equipment on which the software will run and other software with which it will interface; and
* how quickly the software will carry out the operations involved, bearing in mind any networking and concurrent use requirements.

The client may have little knowledge of the mysteries of computer science and will hope to receive some guidance on these matters from the experts writing the programs. Here, as elsewhere, however, the client should contemplate seeking independent advice unless he has his own computer professionals to consult. There ware real dangers at this stage of over-optimism by both parties, plain misunderstanding or just a difference in emphasis of priorities. A great number of retrospectively ill-founded assumptions can be made about performance; computer programmers and analysts cannot be expected to know all the intricacies of the client's business, the nature of which may call for very fast information processing.

If the client does rely on the software development company to supply a system that will do a particular job, he can expect that it will bring a certain degree of expertise to bear upon the work and will perform its part of the contract in a workmanlike manner, using reasonable care and skill. Companies in the business of writing computer systems are implicitly holding themselves out to possess a minimum level of skill and experience when it comes to writing their particular type of system, and the courts have long been prepared to imply an appropriate duty in contracts for supplying services, such as in the case of hairdressers, garages and the like. A contract to write or modify computer software is analogous to such contracts; indeed it is a service contract. In *Stewart* v *Reavell's Garage* [1952] 2 QB 545, a customer relied on a garage to reline the brakes on his 1929 Bentley. The garage obtained a quotation from a sub-contractors; the quotation was recommended to the customer who agreed to it. The work by the sub contractor was carried out in a way unsuitable for Bentley cars and because of this the customer crashed the car, causing £362 worth of damage. It was held that, because the customer had relied on the garage to repair the brakes in a suitable an defficient manner and because the garage owed a duty to provide good workmanship and materials of good quality so that the braking system would be reasonably fit for its purpose, the garage was liable for the faulty work, even though the work itself was carried out by a sub-contractor. The garage had a duty to select and recommend a suitable sub-contractor. The implications of this are very appropriate in the field of software development, given that it is very common for sub-contractors and freelance programmers to be used by the main contractor.

An equivalent duty of care and skill is now implied into service contracts, where the supplier of the service is acting in the course of business, by section 13 of the Supply of Goods and Services Act 1982. The courts are willing to imply these terms into contracts for writing software and, indeed, into contracts for feasibility studies for software. Liability for loss resulting from failure to exercise reasonable care and skill can be excluded or limited subject the provisions in the Unfair Contract Terms Act 1977. However, the inclusion of such an exemption clause would be unlikely to add to the client's confidence in the software development company and, in any case, the courts have shown a vigorous reluctance to enforce such terms. The fact that the burden of proof in respect of the reasonableness of an exclusion clause lies with the party seeking to rely on it is another point to bear in mind. Generally, it will be better (and safer) business practice for the software development company to provide a reasonable level of insurance cover against its own negligence and to use that as a basis of any limitation of liability clause. It should be noted that, by section 2(1) of the Unfair Contract Terms Act 1977, business liability for death or personal injury cannot be excluded or restricted at all.

In terms of computers, if you have a particular computer and approach a company to write software for that computer, the company has a duty to bring a reasonable amount of skill to the task and to supply software that will be fit for its purpose. If your computer is particularly demanding about the nature of the software it will run, or it has a strange or outdated operating system, then you can expect the software development company to use its skill in taking such matters into account.If it sub-lets part of the work, it is under a duty also to select a sub-contractor capable of carrying out the work in a like manner. The software development company cannot avoid liability for defective software merely because it has asked you to agree to the particular sub-contractor recommended by it. An example of a sub-contract is where a software development company, contracted to write an accounts package, uses another specialist firm or, perhaps, freelance programmers to carry out part of the work. The software development company ownes a duty to the client to choose the specialist firm and freelance programmers carefully.

Other matters to which the specification should address itself include details of any data files and information to be entered to be used by the programs and how they will be entered. Will entry be by keyboard, optical character reader, from magnetic disk or through a modem? Will the entry be of an interactive nature and can be programs operate quickly enough? What results and reports are expected from the system and is there any likelihood of further being required once the programs have become established in use? What files, temporary and permanent, will be created? Is access to be controlled by passwords and, if so, is a hierarchical system of passwords required? With that other software must the new software interact or be interoperable?

The feature of computer systems which lies at the root of many disputes is the speed of operation. Computers wok at fantastic speeds, measured in microseconds, but they have a great disadvantage in that the vast majority are designed to process information in serial fashion, a piece at a time. The human brain, because of its massive parallel processing capabilities, can easily outperform a computer and, when given real work to do, computers are anything but fast. Therefore,it is essential that the specification contains information about the speed of the programs in use- for example, response times at the keyboard (two seconds can seem an eternity), the time taken to sort items into ascending or descending order, the time taken to compile and print reports. These timings should indicate the effect of multiple concurrent use of the same files and the fact that the equipment might be carrying out other demanding work at the same time. The specification should also describe the portability of the software — that is, can it be run on other equipment with little effort or will a major 'refit' be needed? The client should ask questions about the effect of a future change of or a modification to his computer equipment or operating software. Another problem might concern the compatibility of the software with other systems run by the client; can data be easily transferred from the new system to the client's existing computer systems and vice versa?

Time for Completion

A contract for wiring computer programs and preparing associated documentation is fundamentally different in character from a contract for the sale of goods but is, however, analogous to a building contract. The performance of the contract is not a single event but rather extends over a period of time. This fact alone brings some doubt to any assumption that time is of the essence of the contract. We have already seen that, although time for payment is not usually a condition in a commercial sale of goods contract, time for delivery is. If we enter into a contract with a builder for the construction of a house, however, we would not expect that we could repudiate the contract if the house was completed a day late and the position is similar with contracts for writing computer software. A delay of a few days might give rise to a claim for damages but would be unlikely to give the client the right to cancel the contract altogether, although if competition is very late the client may be entitled to cancel.

Writing computer software carries with it a degree of unpredictability and the client should be aware of this, especially if he is planning his business operations around a particular completion date. Unexpected problems frequently arise which can add considerably to the overall time for performance, just as construction projects are often delayed because of unanticipated problems with the sub-soil which has to support a new building, requiring extensive changes to be made to the design of the foundations. In *The Salvage Association* v *CAP Financial Services Ltd* [1995] FSR 654, however, the judge held that time is of the essence in a contract for wiring software, though, in that case, the delay was inordinately long. It is submitted that, if the delivery of the software is late by only a few days, this would not amount to a breach of condition (or a material breach in Scotland) giving the client the option of cancelling the contract. An exception would be where the delivery date was particularly important such as where the software was to be written for some special event such as the launch of a new product at an internatioal exhibition.

In case the software is completed late, it would be sensible to have some contractual provisions to cover this situation rather than arguing about the damages. The usual method of dealing with late completion is to include a term which gives the client a right to liquidated damages. These damages may be quantified as a certain sum of money for every week completion is late - for example,

£200 per week. The sum must be a genuine pre-estimate of the financial losses which the client will suffer as a result of the delay and it must not be in the nature of a penalty. The courts will not enforce a 'penalty clause'. An example of acceptable damages would be an estimate of the loss of profits arising from the late completion. Sometimes, it may be in the client's interests to offer a bonus for early completion.

It is not always easy to determine when completion has taken place. The software might have been installed on the client's computer and be working in a fashion, but it requires some further work to be carried out. Alternatively, the programs may be finished but the documentation is only available in draft form. It is clear that problems might arise in determining when completion takes place and it is advisable to define completion in the contract. Does it include testing and documentation? What, if anything, does the client have to do to signify his acceptance of the software? What is the effect of completion on payment? Do all outstanding moneys become due? The concept of substantial completion could be used whereby upon substantial completion a large percentage of the agreed price becomes due with the moiety retained by the client until the remaining work has been completed. Of course, substantial completion must be defined if this approach is used.

If completion is late, this will not necessarily be the fault of the software development company. The completion of the work could be late as a result of the inaction of the client in providing information necessary the continuation of the work or the client might fail to provide on time the facilities required by the software development company. The contract should clearly state what information and facilities the client must provide and when he must provide them. The contract should also contain machinery dealing with extensions to the time for completion as a result of the client's default in his duties under the contract and compensation for the additional expenses incurred. Ideally, the contract should include rates or formulae to help determine such additional costs.

Maintenance of and Enhancements to the Software

No matter how much skill and care have been put into the writing of the software or how much testing has been carried out, the odds are overwhelmingly in favour of it containing errors, or, colloquially, 'bugs'. Some of these bugs might not appear for a considerable period of time and they may be discoverable only under a very rare combination of factors. If a bug does appear this will normally be a breach of warranty and the client can expect that the software development company will correct the error. Naturally, the latter will wish to limit responsibility to correct such errors to a specified period of time. It is therefore important that the contract takes account of the maintenance of the software. A compromise might have to be struck: perhaps the software development company will be happy to rectify errors in the programs and manuals free of charge for a period of time and thereafter they will be prepared to offer this service for a fee. The Court of Appeal in *Saphena Computing* v *Allied Collection Agencies* [1995] FSR 616 has recognised that even when software is delivered there will still be some work to be done. The software sill almost certainly contain errors and the software development company will normally be expected to test the software to locate errors and make the necessary modifications. This duty will endure for a period of time though it is difficult to predict how long.

A software development company will usually offer an ancillary contract for maintenance for which the client will have to pay it. It would be reckless to eschew a maintenance agreement and the cost of it should be allowed for in the overall budget for the work. A maintenance agreement may also provide for enhancements and updates to be made available to the client, which can be very useful because software is continually being developed having new features added to it. There is likely to be a long term relationship between the client and the software development company if the software is complex or likely to require ongoing development and enhancement.

Section 50C of the Copyright, Designs and Patents Act 1988 (inserted by the Copyright (Computer Programs) Regulations 1992) allows the lawful user to copy or adapt a computer program for error correction purposes. Terms in a licence agreement prohibiting this are not automatically void under copyright law though they may be subject to other legal controls such as the principle of non-derogation from grant or competition law. Without a copy of the source code (and preparatory materials), however, maintenance of a computer program is, to all intents and purposes, a practical impossibility.

In many cases, the software development company will be unwilling to allow third parties, or even the client himself, to modify the software. The person carrying out the work might do so badly an the software could acquire a bad reputation as a result and this would reflect on the software development company. If the client considers it vary important to be allowed to modify the software himself or use the services of a third party providing software maintenance, this should be discussed before the contract is made and a suitable term incorporated. It is highly desirable that the client receives a copy of the source code to facilitate the making of modifications should this be permitted and the contract must clearly provide for this.

The contract should also cover questions of copyright ownership on the modifications, the assignment of modifications and whether the software development company has any other rights in respect of them.

Escrow

It is worthwhile considering what happens if the software development company goes out of business. Will the client be able to maintain and modify the software or find another company to do this for him? If the software development company has only supplied the object code this will be very difficult, if not impossible. A receiver or a company taking over the software development company's business may obtain the source coded and expect to be paid by the client for a copy. If the software development company is taken over, the new parent company might refuse to support the software yet not be willing to make the source code available. Many licence agreements include an escrow clause which is invaluable in such situations - that is, where the client is not given a copy of the source code.

Sources code escrow describes a situation where the software development company deposits, with an independent person, a source code copy of the programs together with copies of all the documentation and preparatory materials essential to the continuing maintenance of the software - in short, all the materials that will enable the client or a third party to take over the maintenance and further development of the software. The independent person (the 'stakeholder') holding these materials is instructed not to divulge them to anyone and to keep them generally secure. If a specified event occurs, such as the software development company going out of business or being unable to continue to support the software, then the stakeholder will release all the materials to the client who will then have all the information he needs to arrange for the software to be supported. Escrow works on the form of a guarantee or as insurance should something unfortunate happen to the software development company. The stakeholder must obviously be someone who can be absolutely trusted in the performance of his duties under the escrow arrangement and the details of the agreement need to be carefully thought out. It should include terms dealing with the following matters:

* definitions of the source code and other materials subject to the escrow;
* confidentiality of the source code imposed on the escrow organisation and the client should the source code be released under the agreement;
* delivery of updates to the escrow organisation;
* payment details and provisions in respect of late payment;
* a detailed description of the eventualities which will bring about the client's right to obtain the source code;
* an indemnity that the software development company owns the rights in the source code or otherwise has the right to deposit the source code and eventually, if the right to obtain the source code comes to fruition, that the client will be able to use the source code without hindrance ('quiet enjoyment');
* a system of formal notices requiring the software development company to carry out maintenance by a given deadline subject to the release of the source code;
* termination of the agreement, for example, because of the failure of the client to pay an outstanding fee after receipt of a written demand; and

* the liability of the escrow organisation for loss of or damage to the source code and other materials.

An organisation which provides an escrow service is the National Computing Centre at Oxford House, Oxford Road, Manchester MI 7ED.

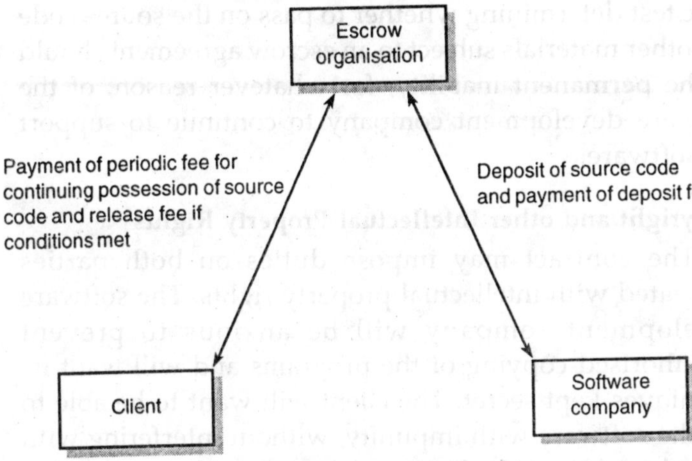

Fig. 16.3. Escrow arrangement

The typical mechanism is that an agreement is signed by the client, the software development company and the organisation offering the escrow service. This is a strange tripartite arrangement as shown in Fig. 16.3. A basic rule of English contract law is that there can only be two parties to a contract. An escrow agreement can thus be seen as two separate contracts; one between the software development company and the escrow organisation, the other between the escrow organisation and the client. The way the service will be paid for reinforces this analysis. Usually, the software development company will pay a fee upon depositing the materials with the escrow organisation and the client will then pay the periodic fees to the escrow organisation and, if it becomes necessary, a release fee.

The implications of mergers and takeovers will need to be carefully dealt with the new company might want to carry on business as usual, keeping the source code from the client, for reasons connected with confidentiality. The basic test determining whether to pass on the source code and other materials subject to an escrow agreement should be the permanent inability, for whatever reason, of the software development company to continue to support the software.

Copyright and other Intellectual Property Rights

The contract may impose duties on both parties associated with intellectual property rights. The software development company will be anxious to prevent unauthorised copying of the programs and will want its techniques kept secret. The client will want to be able to use the software with impunity, without interfering with the rights of some third party who might seek an injunction preventing continued use of the software. The client will also be worried about the fact that some of the software development company's staff will have gained a detailed insight into his business. The law of copyright and, to some extent, the law of confidence will give some protection to the software development company should the programs or the ideas contained therein be copied or plagiarised, but problems of proof and evidence make it desirable to place a contractual duty on the client to prevent copying or unauthorised disclosure of methods. This duty will run in parallel to any duties imposed by intellectual property law, but the contractual approach will be useful because it will draw the client's attention to the existence of these rights and the importance of making his employees aware of them and the consequences of infringement.

The client's employees may make, surreptitiously, copies of the programs and pass these on to others. If the software development company discovers these copies, it has remedies available under copyright law to prevent the use of these copies by the recipients and their further transmission to others, but it might be difficult to prove that the copies originated from the client. A unique serial or code number could be embedded in the programs identifying the software as being that given to the client and if the client is made aware of this and the consequences he may be more careful. The contract may state that the licence is to be terminated forthwith should copies of the programs find their way into the hands of third parties without the permission of the software development company. This will not preclude the software development company from seeking remedies for infringement of copyright - a fact which is often expressly stated in software licences.

On the subject of confidentiality, the client will want a term included strengthening and extending the common law duty of confidence. He will want to prevent the software development company's employees divulging details of his business methods and techniques and other confidential information such as client accounts, debtors and creditors. It is inevitable, if the contract is for a substantial amount of work, that the employees of the software development company and any freelance staff they use will be exposed to confidential information. Without such a term in the contract, the client may be lacking legal recourse, especially if the confidential nature of materials involved is not otherwise made clear. The software development company, too, may have worries about confidentiality; it may have developed special techniques for writing and testing software which the client's staff might see when the software is installed and tested. A contractual term imposing a two-way duty in respect of confidentiality should be included in the contract.

Warranties and Indemnities

It is usual for a licence agreement to contain a section headed 'Warranties and Indemnities'. Warranties normally found include those relating to the fact that the software development company warrants that it has the right to grant the rights to client provided for by the agreement and that the client will have 'quiet enjoyment' of the software and the client's use of it will be unaffected by any third party rights. Where, instead of licensing the right to use the software, the agreement is one under which the title to the copyright (ownership), is transferred (that is, an assignment of copyright), the Law of Property Act 1925 used to contain a form of words which would automatically include such rights in or over land, it also had some impact on other forms of property transactions). The person granting the rights would use the term 'As beneficial owner'. Now, as a result of the Law of Property (Miscellaneous Provisions) Act 1994, the phrase used is 'With full title guarantee'. This automatically implies covenants to the effect that the person making the assignment has the right to do so and that the property right transferred is free from all charges and encumbrances and all other rights exercisable by third parties (sections 2 and 3). Other warranties may be given which relate to the performances of the software and its freedom from major defects. This may be tied down to the specification.

Another aspect of intellectual property rights concerns the possibility that the software might infringe a third party's copyright or other right such as a patent or trade mark. Whether or not the infringement is deliberate will not usually be relevant. The client could have been using the software quite happily for a number of years when the software by some third party. That third party may then decide to pursue all the clients of the software development company who are using the infringing software and seek injunctions to prevent them continuing to use the software. Even if the client is not troubled in this way by the third party, the software development company will be prevented from continuing to support the software. It may be that the third party will be happy to allow the client to continue to use the software in return for a license fee. In any case, the client should satisfy himself that there is a term in the agreement with the software development company covering the infringement of intellectual property rights belonging to others. The term should give the client an indemnity against the event of legal action being taken against him as a result of the software infringing third party rights. The term should give the client an indemnity against the event of legal action being taken against him as a result of the software infringing third party rights. The term should be widely drafted so as to include all forms of intellectual property rights such as copyright, patents, designs and trade marks. The costs and implications of suddenly being unable to use an item of software might be quite enormous and it is likely that the software development company will hope to limit its liability under this head, perhaps to the amount of the licence fee. Any term dealing with indemnity against third party claims should allow the software development company a reasonable time to modify the software so that it no longer infringes the third party right, if that is a possibility without jeopardising the software's functionality.

Liability

Computer software is widely used to assist in the decision-making processes in business. A decision to engage upon a particular line of action may be based upon an interpretation of the results of running a computer program.

For example, a construction company might submit a bid for a motorway contract worth many millions of pounds; the bid total will have been calculated by estimators using computer software. If there is an error in the software, the total might be miscalculated, by say, £1 million this could mean that the company fails to secure the contract because their bid is to high or worse, still, they win the contract by too great a margin and make a substantial loss.

The software development company will be very keen to limit its liability if the software proves to be defective. The software development company will attempt to limit or exclude its liability for defects by the insertion of a suitably drafted exemption clause - for example, limiting its liability to the cost of replacing the software or remedying the defect. This is unsatisfactory from the client's point of view. Until recently, this way of dealing with liability has been very common but now must be reviewed in the light of recent court decisions such as those in *The Salvage Association* v *CAP Financial Services Ltd* [1995] FSR 654 and *St Albans City & District Council* v *International Computers Ltd* [1997] FSR 251. It is now clear that the controls over exclusion clauses in the Unfair Contract Terms Act 1977 will apply to most terms in software licences, the only major exception being those terms of dealing exclusively with the transfer or creation of intellectual property rights. Thus, section 2 of the Act applies to liability for negligence and section 3 controls attempts to exclude liability arising from the performance of the contract. In some cases, liability cannot be excluded or limited at all- for example, in the case of death or personal injury resulting from negligence. In most other cases, the exclusion or limitation of business liability depends upon the reasonableness of the appropriate term.

A software development company should take out

professional liability insurance to a reasonable level and limit its liability accordingly. Alternatively, the software development company could offer a minimum level of insurance and offer to increase this if the client is prepared to pay the additional premium. How successful this approach will be is difficult to predict but, above all, the software development company must make sure that its liability under the licence and its insurance are matched as far as it is possible to do this.

It should bed noted that a defect in software does not necessarily and inexorably lead to the conclusion that the software development company has been negligent or has failed to exercise reasonable care and skill. The problem may result from the client's use of the software and the question of how much control the software development company has over the use by the client may be a factor. For example, in the case of a spreadsheet a mistake may be the result of an incorrect formula entered by the client or the client may be using the spreadsheet software to make calculations requiring extreme mathematical precision. If the software development company has exercised the level of care and skill to be expected from responsible software development companies writing equivalent software, there should be no liability. If a financial loss arises because the software development company and the client have both been negligent, the amount of damages awarded will be reduced on the basis of contributory negligence.

Arbitration

It is prudent to include provision in the agreement for arbitration whereby a dispute between the parties will be referred to an arbitrator, an independent expert, who will rule on the dispute. Arbitration is a commonly used method of resolving disputes without having to go to the courts. The parties to the contract appoint in independent third party who will listen to both sides and then make a ruling. Arbitration is less formal than a court hearing, although the basic rules of evidence and procedure are adhered to, and it has the advantage that the arbitrator, unlike a judge, will be an export in the technical matters involved. In a dispute involving computer software, the arbitrator would be expected to have considerable knowledge of software engineering and be a leading member of the computer profession. Another advantage of arbitration over a normal court bearing is that arbitration should be, in principle, quicker and chapter, although this is not always so. Arbitration hearings can be fairly formal involving the calling of expert witnesses.

It is common for arbitration clauses to state that the arbitrator's decision shall be final and binding on the parties, and the courts will not interfere with an arbitrator's decision unless he has erred on a point of law. A court will usually accept the arbitrator's evaluation of the facts of the case as being conclusive. If the contract provides for arbitration, neither party will be able to take a short-cut to the courts because a judge will insist that the arbitration procedure is adhered to in the first instance. It must be stressed that the decision of an arbitrator, and any award(s) he makes, is binding upon the parties.

A disadvantage of arbitration is that the arbitrator might not have the depth of legal knowledge of a High Court judge and an arbitrator could be more likely to err on a point of law or procedure. For example, an arbitrator might admit evidence which should be inadmissible. Although a judge will not usually have the technical expertise of an arbitrator, judges by their training and experience have a knack of getting to the kernel of a dispute and are able to concentrate on the important issues without being sidetracked. It must be said, however, that, in practice, arbitration works extremely well and the standard of arbitrators, who belong to the Chartered Institute of Arbitrators, is very high. If an arbitration clause is included in the agreement, the machinery for selecting an arbitrator should also be dealt with, the usual practice being to appoint an arbitrator agreed upon by the parties or, failing such agreement, a person to be nominated by the British Computer Society which holds a register of suitably qualified arbitrators.

Alternative Dispute Resolution

Taking a dispute to the courts or submitting it to arbitration will plunge the parties into the adversarial contest fundamental to the English legal system. The outcome usually will be total success or failure; there are no halt measures even though the decision of the court may be based on the most slender weight in favour of one party on a balance of probabilities. Occasionally, a more attractive route may be that offered by Alternative Dispute Resolution (ADR) where a mediator is appointed to assist and encourage the parties in the negotiation of a settlement to their mutual satisfaction.

The mediator can take an active role and make suggestions for resolving the conflict. However, there is no legally binding obligation on the parties to continue with the process and they may abandon it at any time. The process itself is based on informality and consent. It is said to be a highly successful means of settling disputes with an estimated settlement rate of 90 per cent (Hayward, D, 'Compromising Positions', *Computing,* 8 June 1995, p 31). One technique which may be used is for both sides to make a presentation before senior members of the organisations who will then attempt to negotiate a settlement with the assistance of the mediator. It would be better if the negotiators were not directly involved in the matters leading to the dispute as they are likely to be more objective and more willing to compromise. The following example shows how ADR might present the best course of action.

Imagine that Pickwick Trading has asked Bardell Software to develop and deliver new accounting software. An appropriate contract was made and a detailed specification annexed to it. When the software was delivered it was found to be slightly slower than allowed by the benchmark tests in the specification. Additionally, one particular feature was missing in that the software would not produce annual VAT summary reports as detailed in the specification. The total price is £85 000, 10 per cent of which was payable upon commencement of the work. The time for delivery is six months.

Pickwick has refused to accept the program and has withheld the final payment of £76 500. Bardell presses for more time to add the VAT report and argues that the speed of the software is to close to that specified as to be of no consequence. The possible outcomes of resolving the dispute by litigation and ADR are discussed below.

Litigation

Bardell sues Pickwick for wrongful repudiation of the contract and seeks damages equivalent to the outstanding sum plus interest and other direct costs. Pickwick submits a defence and counterclaim based on the shortcomings of the program. Pickwick claims the return of the £8500 already paid plus £12500 in wasted management time, etc. At the court action, the judge holds that Bardell is guilty of a breach of condition and that Pickwick's repudiation was lawful. He awards Pickwick £21 000 plus costs, leaving Bardell to pick up the bill for £31 000 in legal costs also.

This result is unsatisfactory from the point of view of

both parties. At the end of it all, Pickwick does not have the program it wanted and will now have to engage another software development company. It may be another six months or so before the program is ready. This could seriously handicap Pickwick's business. Bardell is even less happy as six months' work has been wasted and it has a bill for £52 000. Bardell now thinks that it would have been better had it never heard of Pickwick - a view that is reciprocated by the latter.

Alternative Dispute Resolution

The contract between Pickwick and Bardell contains a term providing for ADR and a mediator is appointed. After only two days of negotiation the following settlement is reached:

* Bardell will be given one more month to complete the software so that it will be capable of producing the VAT report (Bardell has also agreed at no extra cost to alter a particular screen display because Pickwick has had second thoughts about it).
* Pickwick will be given a 5 per cent discount on the total price which it will put towards some additional memory for its computer which should increase its speed of operation.

Pickwick and Bardell will share the mediator's fee of £2500. It is left to the reader to reflect on which is the best solution.

Other ADR techniques are adjudication in which a neutral third party gives a non-binding ruling on the case or certain aspects of the case and expert appraisal in which a technical export assesses each of the parties' cases for the purpose of assisting negotiations.

Alternative Dispute Resolution is not always appropriate; indeed, it may only be a minority of disputes for which it represents a satisfactory method. There are some drawbacks. It is inappropriate where a point of law is involved, where the issues are very complex or where one party seeks an injunction or court declaration. Although any negotiations will have taken place without prejudice to either party's legal rights, there is danger that subsequent litigation could be influenced by what has been said in abortive negotiations. ADR allows the parties to gauge the strengths and weaknesses of each other's case and could even be used, cynically, as a prelude to litigation. It should be noted, however, that the court will not, under normal circumstances, allow evidence to be given of what has been admitted in negotiations which have been conducted 'without prejudice'. Another factor is that getting involved with ADR could compromise any insurance policy that might be relied upon to pay damages and costs awarded in any court action.

Any ADR clause in a contract must make it clear that anything admitted, said or done in connection with ADR is without prejudice to the legal rights of the parties. The clause should make provision for the appointment of a mediator (who should be skilled in resolving disputes by negotiation), payment, of his fees (usually these will be borne equally by the parties) and procedures to be adopted. The Centre for Dispute Resolution, at Princes House, 95 Gresham Street, London EC2V 7NA, provides information and advice about ADR procedures to be adopted.

The courts are becoming increasingly keen to encourage parties to consider alternative dispute resolution and a Practice Direction has been published to deal with the impact this may have on legal proceedings and directions given by the judge. See, for example, *Practice Statement*

(Commercial Cases: Alternative Dispute Resolution) [1994] WLR 14.

Other Terms

A contract for the writing or modification of software will undoubtedly contain other terms dealing wi the matters such as the training of the client's staff, termination of the licence and misrepresentation. It is also usual to include a term stating which is the applicable law ; this is essential where there is any doubt - for example, where a Scottish and English company are entering into a contract. Entire agreement clauses are common which attempt to limit the terms of the contract to those expressly contained within the formal agreement, thereby attempting to exclude any representations that may have been made in preliminary negotiations. Notwithstanding this, there may still be a remedy for misrepresentation should one party have entered into the contract on the basis of a promise by the other party which turns out to be untrue. Finally, the question of staff poaching is often addressed. This is where one party offers employment to an employee of the other party. The employees of each party will probably be in close contact for some time - for example, because the software is being developed at the client's premises - and this gives each party the opportunity to spot a 'star performer'. The client may have a vested interest in employing a key member of the software development company's staff who has intimate knowledge of the software written under the contract. Over a period of time, a software development company could find that it has a high turnover of staff. The usual means of countering this threat is for a clause stating that neither party will offer employment (or canvass with a view to offering employment) members of the other party's staff for a period of time, normally six months. In practical terms, there is little to be done beyond this, especially as such terms could be deeded to be in restraint of trade.

Consideration could be given to the use of standard from contracts such as those published by the Institute of Purchasing and Supply, at Easton House, Easton on the Hill, Stamford, Lincolnshire, PE9 3NZ. These contract forms have been developed to provide a fair balance between the parties' interests and incorporate a great deal of experience in this field. Standard form agreements exist for a variety of hardware and software contracts and can be adapted, if necessary, for a specific contract.

Independent Professional Supervision

In the case of large important contracts for writing software it may be advisable that the performance of the contract is overseen by a professional engineer who is a member of the British Computer Society. This person would be responsible for the following aspects:

* ensuring compliance with the specification;
* general supervision;
* determining whether the software is acceptable;
* certifying payments and completion;
* fixing rates for delays or extra work;
* authorising extensions of time for unavoidable delays or additional work; and
* acting as a first-stop informal mediator.

Although it is normal for such a person to be paid by the client, the contract should give certain powers to him as regards determination of the reciprocal rights and duties of the client and software development company. A chartered engineer will remain neutral as between the parties and will help the parties to resolve difficulties amicably and fairly, being particularly good at dealing with the day-to-day minor problems that are bound to occur. This will prevent small problems turning into full down disputes with the parties breathing fire at each other. This form of contract supervision has been used to great effect for well over 100 years in the construction industry. Should the engineer be unable to bring the parties to agreement concerning a serious difference, the parties could still have recourse to an independent arbitrator or alternative dispute resolution.

Is There a Contract?

It is not unusual for work to begin on a contract for the development of software before the precise details of the contract have been properly agreed and formalised. The modern pressures of business life may make it tempting to commence work before the 'legal stuff' has been sorted out but it is a temptation that should be avoided if at all possible. After committing resources or carrying out work, the other party may claim that there is not a contract. Even if it is accepted that there is a binding contract, there may be some uncertainty s to the precise terms of the contract and there is a limit to how much the courts may be willing to imply. uncertainty itself can be a factor in making a purported contract void and unenforceable.

The case of *Fraser Williams (Southern) Ltd* v *Prudential Holborn Ltd* (unreported) 22 July 1991 provides an example of the dangers and difficulties which might ensue if work begins before a contract is properly in place although in the event, it was held that there was a valid contract. The plaintiff submitted a proposal to the defendant to develop software. It was dated 3 March 1989 and was expressed as being 'subject to contract'. Two telephone calls from the defendant on 7 and 9 march 1989 confirmed that the plaintiff had got the job and a letter was sent from the plaintiff to the defendant on 10 March 1989 confirming this, though the letter showed that there were still some thing to be resolved, in particular how responsibilities would be shared between the plaintiff and an independent consultant engaged by the defendant in respect of the software. On 13 March 1989 the plaintiff commenced work and on 5 April it sent a draft contract to the plaintiff. Subsequently, the plaintiff raised three invoices which were paid by the defendant, but on 5 May 1989 the defendant informed the plaintiff that it was terminating the relationship and requested that the plaintiff vacate the defendant's premise immediately. The plaintiff complained in writing of the alleged breach of contract by the defendant but the correspondence remained unanswered until, on 27 November 1989, the defendant's solicitor wrote to the plaintiff asserting that there was no contract between them. It was argued that the letter of 10 March 1989 was merely a letter of intent and, even if it were an acceptance, there was still no contract as the plaintiff's offer was expressed to be subject to contract.

It was held that there was a binding contract. A number of factors were important, in particular:

* the plaintiff committed significant resources to the work and this was suggestive that there was a contract — it would hardly have done to otherwise.
* the proposal made it clear that the plaintiff required a contract to be in force before it commenced work.
* the phrase 'subject to contract' was of very limited effect - the proposal indicated that a contract could come into being in a number of ways by using terminology indicating the existence of a contract such as 'signing of the contract', 'signing the order' and placing a 'firm order'.
* the letter of 10 March 1989 was a clear acceptance

- it was not expressed as being a letter of intent nor was it stated to be 'subject to contract'.

* the issue of shared responsibilities yet to be resolved was deeded to be an administrative matter and did not detract from the contract being sufficiently certain to have effect.
* even if the letter of 10 march 1989 did not create a contact, the subsequent conduct of the parties was sufficient - the plaintiff did some work and the defendant paid for it, and at no time during this period did the defendant seek to redefine the functions of the plaintiff.

The dangers inherent in embarking on work without a formal contract in place are fairly obvious. In the above case, if the court had held otherwise, the software developer would have found it difficult to obtain any recompense for the work it carried out. One possibility is under a *quantum meruit* (see below). Another difficulty is determining the precise nature and scope of the contractual terms. If, eventually in the above case, an administrative decision was taken assigning responsibility between the software developer and the independent consultant, it could have been documental to the software developer. It could, for example, reduce the total job value for the software developer or increase the amount of work to be completed in an already tight timescale. However, where there is some uncertainty as to the precise terms of the contract, the terms implied by the Supply of Goods-and Services Act 1982 may save the contract and make it valid. Otherwise, if there is a previous course of dealing between the parties, that may provide some clue as to the precise scope of the parties' rights and obligations under the contract.

Where it turns out that there is no valid contract - for example, through a lack of certainty as to the terms of the contract - the software developer may be entitled to payment on the basis of the work he has done in pursuance of what he believed was a valid contract. The law will require that the defendant pays the plaintiff for the 'fruit of his labour'. This is what is termed a *qunatum meruit* (roughly translated - as much as he deserves). Of course, the defendant must have agreed to or at the very least acquiesced in the plaintiff carrying out the work. For example, if a software development company is appointed to write some software for a client but the purported contract between them is so vague and uncertain that it is ruled void, then if the software company has done satisfactory work for the client, it ought to be entitled to payment on the basis of a *quantum meruit*. Nevertheless, it is clearly preferable to have a valid and detailed contract containing all the necessary terms in writing and signed by both parties before the work commences. Writing computer software is sufficiently difficult and unpredictable without adding to the problems by having unsatisfactory legal provison for the work.

17 LICENCE AGREEMENTS FOR 'OFF-THE-SELF' SOFTWARE

This is software which is acquired as a ready-made package; it is mass-produced software usually obtained from a dealer and includes familiar packages such as word processing systems, spreadsheets and databases. It can be described as 'general purpose software.' It may be applications software (word processing, etc.), operating system software (for example, Windows or MS-DOS) or utility software such as disk management software, software for archiving files or anti-virus software. The contractual nature of transactions involving off-the-self software is not absolutely clear. Several possibilities exist:

- a licence agreement with the software publisher;
- a sale of goods contract with the dealer;
- a hybrid licence agreement/sale of goods contract with the software publisher (the dealer acting as the software publisher's agent)' or
- a *sui generis* form of contract.

Before looking further at these possibilities, it must be noted that it is the intangible rights which are dominant in the transaction — for example, the right to use the software. This right requires the licence of the copyright owner, otherwise the copyrights subsisting in the software (there are likely to be a number of copyright works) will be infringed. This is confirmed by section 16(2) of the Copyright Designs and Parents Act 1988 which states that the copyright in a work is infringed by a person who without the licence of the copyright owner does, or authorises another to do, any of the acts restricted by the copyright. As copying a work of copyright extends to making copies which are transient it is quite clear that simply operating or running software involves making copies, whether transient or not, and this must have the licence of the copyright owner. Of course, in most cases, the software will be copied from the disk or CD-ROM on which it was supplied to the hard disk of the computer of the person acquiring the software. Subsequent copies will be made when the software is used as it will be loaded into the volatile memory (RAM) of the computer.

This simple fact appears to have been overlooked by a number of persons who have considered the nature of a contract for the existence of off-the-self software. Another key fact is the method of delivery of the software. It may be handed over in a box which contains disks on a CD-ROM together with printed documentation such as a manual and licence agreement. Increasingly, these days, software may be delivered on-line, with no tangible items being delivered to the person acquiring a copy of the software. Where software is supplied on physical media, in some cases the licence agreement will be exposed on the outside of the package. This is the so-called 'shrink-wrap' licence. The idea is that it enables the person acquiring the software to inspect the terms before opening the package. This is usually backed by a statement to the effect that, if the person acquiring the software does not agree with the terms of the licence, he can return the package unopened to the dealer is recover his payment. Another technique is to have the disks or CD-ROM in a sealed package separate to the licence and with a statement that breaking the seal signifies acceptance of the terms of the licence agreement, again, usually backed by a promise that the software can be returned before the seal is broken and any payment refunded. In the case of software delivered on-line the person acquiring it will usually be required to signify his acceptance of the terms of the licence before the software can be 'downloaded.' Incidentally, the word 'download' has come in for judicial scrutiny and in *R* v *City of London Magistrates and the Director of the Serious Fraud office, ex parte Jeffrey Green* (1998) ITCLR 35, it was held that it meant 'transfer from one storage device or system to another, as in the *Concise Oxford Dictionary* which also suggests it applies especially in relation to it being done remotely.

Licence Agreement

Where no tangible items are transferred to the person acquiring the software — for example, where the software is downloaded for the Internet—the only contract is a licence agreement. This would also apply where software is specially written for a client and installed on the client's computer from the software development company's disks which are then retained by the latter. If the software is obtained remotely, it is likely that an opportunity will be given to read the licence agreement before the person wishing to obtain a copy of the software is committed to the transaction. Some software is available without cost over the Internet but it must be stressed that its copying and subsequent use must still be licensed by the copyright owner. Even with 'free' software, there are likely to be terms imposed on the person acquiring it controlling on limiting its subsequent use and copying. For example, it may state that the software is for personal and private use only and must not be further distributed or sold without the permission of the copyright owner. There may also be other rights in relation to the software such as the author's moral rights to be identified as such and to object to a derogatory treatment of the work (these rights do not apply to other items of software such as a database or document or image in digital form).

The licence agreement is likely to state what the applicable law is and, in many cases, it will be that of one of the United States of America such as California, New York or Florida. Where this is so, it should be noted that the copyright owner may still enforce his rights in the United Kingdom. The Copyright (Application to Other Countries) Order 1993, amended in 1994, extends the qualification provisions for United Kingdom copyright in the original works to persons and incorporated bodies for a considerable number of other countries. This is to give effect to the international conventions on copyright such as the Berne Copyright Convention. Thus an American company or citizen of the United States can bring an action for copyright infringement occurring within the jurisdiction of the United Kingdom.

As far as the licence agreement itself, this may be enforced subject to the rules of jurisdiction. The licence may state that not only is the licence subject to the law of a particular country or state but that it is also subject to the sole jurisdiction of that country or state. The rules of jurisdiction are complex and, in relation to bringing an action outside the European Economic Area, leave of the court is required before proceedings can be commenced. Within Europe, the Brussels and Lugano Conventions on jurisdiction and enforcement of judgments in civil matters apply.

The licence will often be of indefinite duration, with no fixed period being stated, although there may be some provision for termination, such as if the person acquiring it, the customer, contravenes some term in the licence agreement which is stated to terminate it. A term requiring the customer not to transfer the software to a third party could be an example. Strictly speaking, the licence cannot endure longer than the copyright in the software because, when the copyright expires the software effectively falls into the public domain and can be used freely without requiring permission. Some licence agreements allow the customer to terminate unilaterally simply by destroying all the copies of the programmes and documentation, although why he should want to do this is hard to understand. If he no longer requires the software, he may be able to transfer both it and the licence to a third party in return for a payment unless the licence agreement provides otherwise.

Sale of Goods Contract

A contract for the acquisition of computer software is unlikely to be regarded as a sale of goods contract, especially where he predominant purpose of the transaction is the acquisition of the software. It has also been noted that where the software is incorporated into a good such as a motor car and the predominant purpose is the acquisition of the good rather than the software, then it will be a sale of goods contract. Where off-he-self software is obtained, it cannot be a sale of goods contract because to so classify the contract is to trivialise the main purpose of the contract, being the right to use the software. To say it is a sale of goods contract on the basis that some tangible items are handed over is to defy logic and to completely ignore the fact that the use of software requires the licence of the copyright owner. Even so some writers (and some judges) seem unconvinced and prefer to rely on a familiar and tried and tested area of law to discuss or resolve actual or potential disputes. The convenience of this is that the Sale of Goods. Act 1979 implies important terms into sale of goods contracts which give the person acquiring the software some useful rights if it turns out to be defective in some way.

The perceived problem of taking a contract to acquire off-the-self software out of the sale of goods arena is not serious as the common law has long since been capable of implying appropriate terms into contracts — indeed, many of the terms implied by the Sale of Gods Act 1979 and the Supply of Goods and Services Act 1982 are derived from terms which were implied under common law. This was recognised by Sir Iain Glidewell in the Court of Appeal in *St Albans City and District Council* v. *International Computers Ltd.* [1997] FSR 251 where he implied a term into a contract for the transfer of a computer program that the program would be reasonably fit for its purpose, that is, for achieving its intended purpose .

Hybrid Contract

This is a possible scenario where the property in tangible items also passes to the person acquiring the software in addition to the right to use it, typically where a person goes into a retail computer shop and buys a software package. There may be two separate contracts: one between the person and the shop owner, being a sale of goods contract; and a licence between the person and the owner of the copyright subsisting in the software.

Consider a situation where George, who wishes to obtain a copy of the ABC spreadsheet software, goes to a computer software dealer, Acme Computers. George goes to Acme Computers and asks of a copy of the ABC spreadsheet software. He pays £200 and is given a sealed box. Inside the box is a CD-ROM on which the software is recorded, a manual and a licence agreement. There must be a contract between George and Acme Computers on the basis of normal sale of goods law. This will relate to the tangible items. Thus, if the CD-ROM is damaged and the software cannot be loaded onto George's computer because of this, he will have a remedy under section 14(2A) of the

Sale of Goods Act 1979 as the CD-ROM is not of satisfactory quality. He will be able to obtain a replacement from Acme Computers or he may return the whole package and obtain a refund of the price he paid.

As between George and the owners of the copyright subsisting in ABC, Lemming Software plc, George must have Lemming's licence to use the software. The problem is what the terms of that licence are. It could be that they are those printed on the licence agreement which came with the software but there may be some problems with this as George may not have seen the licence until after he brought the software. A basic rule of English contract law (and many other jurisdictions) is that it is not possible to unilaterally introduce new terms into a contract after it has been made. If the contract is made at the time George hands over the money in return for the box containing the software, then he will not have see the licence until it is too late.

Software publishers have tried various methods of giving their licence agreements the force of law. One technique used is to have the licence exposed on the outside of the package, the whole being wrapped in clear plastic, so that the licence may be inspected before the package is opened. This is the 'shrink-wrap' licence. Another technique used is for the licence to be printed on a sealed packet containing the disks or CD-ROM with a note to say that breaking the seal signifies acceptance of the terms of the licence. This is usually coupled with a promise that the customer can obtain a refund if he returns the software with the seal unbroken in the event of the customer being unwilling to accept the terms.

Both of the above approaches and variants of them are not without their difficulties as a means of incorporating the terms of the licence into the contract with the customer.

The opportunity to read the terms comes after the contract is made because, at the latest, this occurs when the package containing the software is handed over to the customer. In *Olley* v *Marlborough Court Ltd* [1949] 1 All ER 127, a husband and wife went to an hotel and paid for a room. Their room contained a notice excluding liability for articles lost or stolen unless handed to the manageress for safe custody. A fur coat belonging to the wife was stolen and the hotel sought to rely on the exclusion notice. It was held that the notice was not part of the contract which had been completed at the reception desk when the room had been paid for and the hotel was liable for the loss because of its negligence. There had been insufficient supervision at the reception desk and the thief was able to take the key to the room from behind the desk. However, there are two contrasting cases dealing with tickets: one for a railway excursion ticket, *Thompson* v *LMS Railway* [1930] 1 KB 41, and one involving a ticket given after hiring a deck chair, Chapelton v *Barry Urban District Council* [1940] 1 All ER 326. In the former the ticket contained a reference to the conditions in the company's timetable and was held to be validly incorporated into the contract whereas, in the latter case, the exclusion of liability on the reverse of the ticket was deemed to be ineffective as the ticket was considered to be a mere receipt.

The Court of Appeal has suggested that a particularly burdensome term on a delivery note would only be enforced if it had been specifically drawn to the attention of the other party (see *Interfoto Picture Library Ltd* v *Stiletto Visual Programmes Ltd* [1988] 1 All ER 348). Of course, if the term is in a document signed before or at the time the contract was made, the term will be binding on the party signing whether or not he has read it, providing that he has not been misled by the other party as to its effect. Therefore, to be absolutely sure that the terms in the licence are part of the contract the customer should be asked to sign the licence before the package is handed over. In many situations, however, this is impracticable—for example, where software is acquired by mail order.

If the terms do not become part of the contract by means of any of the ways discussed above, one way in which they might do is by virtue of a previous course of dealing—For example, where the customer previously has acquired software produced by the same software publisher. One final possibility is that the courts will imply appropriate terms based on what is reasonable in the circumstances and necessary to give the contract business efficacy. Custom may be very helpful in this respect and the courts would almost certainly look at what terms have become customary in the trade of software publishing.

A further but less likely possibility is that the Acme Computers acts as agent for Lemming Software and, as agent, makes a sale of goods contract and a licence agreement between George and Lemming.

Sui-Generis Contract

This is the fourth mechanism which might be possible and it has a lot to comment it. A Scots judge suggested that contracts for the acquisition of off-the-shelf software of the 'shrink-wrap' licence variety in *Beta Computers (Europe) Ltd* v *Adobe Systems (Europe) Ltd* [1976] FSR 367 were *sui generis.* Beta, the pursuers (plaintiffs), supplied Adobe, defenders (defendants), with computer software produced by Informix Software Inc, a third party. It was accepted that Informix owned the copyright subsisting in the software. It had been ordered by Adobe by telephone and was a standard upgrade package suitable for Adobe's computer. The software was delivered with a 'shrink-wrap' licence and the package bore the words 'Opening the Informix S.I.

Software package indicates your acceptance of these terms and conditions.'

Adobe claimed that it had the right to return the software without using it and that it had the right to reject it until such time as the package was opened, which it had not been. Beta sued for the price of the software.

Lord Penrose, in the Outer House of the Court of Session, in Edinburgh, reflected upon the legislative framework of the Copyright, Designs and Patents Act 1988 in the context of computer programs. He concluded that the supply of the medium on which the program is stored must be accompanied by an appropriate licence conferred directly or by implication from the acquisition of the software. An essential feature of the supply of off-the-shelf software is that the supplier undertakes to make available to the purchaser both the medium and the right of access and use of the software. In effect, the supplier undertakes that he has the right to communicate the benefit of the use of the software: in other words, that he transfers the benefit of the copyright owner's licence. Lord Penrose said:

> The supply of proprietary software for a price is a contract *sui generis* in [it is] unacceptable to analyse the transaction in this case as if it were two separate transactions relating to the same subject matter. There is but one contract....

The time such a contract is made is when the conditions imposed by the owner of the copyright were tendered to the purchaser of the software and accepted by the purchaser. Otherwise, there could be no *consensus ad idem* (agreement of the same thing) which is essential for a contract to exist. That being so the purchaser can reject the software at any time before acceptance by performing the stated act — in this case, opening the sealed package.

Lord Penrose said that if the contract was considered to be a sale of goods contract this would produce the odd result that the dominant characteristic of interest to the parties (the right to use the software) was subordinated to the medium by which it was transmitted to the users.

There is one problem with the decision which may prevent it being fully applicable in other jurisdictions. Scots law is based on Roman law, not common law, and it was held that the contract gave rights to the copyright owner as a third party. This is possible under the Scots law of contract but not under English law. However, an alternative way of looking at the transaction is that it does not give rights to the copyright owner. Conversely, it is the copyright owner who gives rights to the purchaser of the software. Where there are restrictions in the licence agreement, they simply constrain the rights given to the purchaser rather than giving rights to the copyright owner.

In the United Sates, there has been less difficulty with shrink-wrap licences. In the 7th Circuit Court of Appeals, shrink-wrap licences were held to be enforceable; terms did not have to be exposed on the outside of the package containing the software. It was sufficient if there was a notice to the effect that there was a licence agreement inside. Furthermore, the purchaser was entitled to a full refund if, after reading the licence, he did not agree with the terms and conditions (*The Times*, Interface Supplement,' 10 July 1996, p. 6).

Typical Terms in Licences for Off-the-shelf Software

Usually, licence agreements for off-the-shelf software are not very lengthy. The copyright owner will want to set out the conditions of use of the software and confirm the fact of copyright subsistence and the grant of a licence to the purchaser. The licence may include some warranties and will have to address the impact of the applicable law on the licence. It may also deal with upgrades, user support and termination. Typically, the use may be limited to a single computer or a stated number of computers or users. A term dealing with whether the software and licence can be transferred to another person is also common.

The Copyright, Designs and Patents Act 1988 makes void and unenforceable some terms in licence agreements which try to prohibit or restrict the permitted acts of decompilation of computer programs and making necessary back-up copies of computer programs. There some other controls which relate to databases. A form of words which might be used in a licence agreement to restrict decompilation to that permitted under the Act is 'You may not reverse engineer, decompile, disassemble or otherwise modify or alter the software except as provided for by section 50B of the Copyright, Designs and Patents Act 1988.'

The inclusion of warranties is not universal by any means and where they are given by the copyright owner, they are usually very limited. It may be that they are restricted to the return of the price paid for the software if it fails to perform substantially as stated in the documentation. We have seen that terms excluding or restricting liability for deffective software are strictly controlled by the Unfair Contract Terms Act 1977 in the context of bespoke software. However, it is possible that much greater restriction or even exclusion is possible with off-the-shelf software, bearing in mind, of course, that liability for death or personal injury caused by negligence cannot be excluded or restricted by a term in a contract or notice by virtue of section 2 of the Unfair Contract Terms Act 1977. In respect of other types of liability, it would seem reasonable that liability can be restricted or excluded.

The main reason is that the software is 'general purpose' and has not been written or a particular client's requirements. Furthermore, the company producing the software has no knowledge of the uses to which end users will put the software. If a person using spreadsheet software to perform some complex financial calculation makes a mistake, that is hardly the software company's fault. However, if there is an inherent defect in the software which is not obvious to a reasonable user, it is a moot point as to whether an exclusion clause would be effective. Until such time as exclusion clauses in of-the-shelf software licences come under judicial scrutiny, it is likely that no warranties will be given or, where they are, they will be limited to the price paid for the software.

If there are no warranties (whether the licence expressly states this or is silent on the point), would the courts be likely to imply any warranties? We have seen in the *St Albans* case that one judge thought an implied term of fitness for purpose would be appropriate. This would seem a sensible approach with off-the-self software, the purpose being that for which such software is usually obtained.

Finally, the licence is almost certain to contain an applicable law clause and, possibly, a term stating which courts are to have jurisdiction. A typical formula might be 'This licence agreement is governed by the laws of England and Wales and any dispute under it is subject to the sole and exclusive jurisdiction of the courts of England and Wales.'

Misrepresentation and Dealers' Promises

If we accept that a computer software dealer (or mail order supplier) acts as the agent of the copyright owner (usually the software publisher) in bringing about a licence between the software publisher and the customer this has certain legal implications. The dealer has the authority, express or implied, to bind the software publisher contractually and this should not lead to problems. He dealer may have misled the customer, however, about the nature and performance of the software; he may, deliberately or otherwise, have made false claims which have induced the customer to obtain the software. A licence agreement is likely to contain a term to the effect that the software company will not be bound by anything which the dealer says in the pre-contractual negotiations and that the licence itself contains the entire agreement between the parties to the exclusion of anything else. Entire agreement terms are subject to the reasonableness test as stated in section 11(1) of the Unfair Contract Terms Act 1977 by virtue of section 3 of the Misrepresentation Act 1967 (as inserted by section 8 of the former Act). In *Mackenzie Patten and Co* v *British Olivetti Ltd* (unreported) 11 January 1984, the buyer of computer hardware claimed, *inter alia,* that he had been induced into entering into the contract on the basis of a salesman's misrepresentation. However, the judge did not need to rule on whether an entire agreement clause in the contract was effective to remove any liability resulting from the misrepresentation as he found for the buyer on the basis of a collateral warranty (a term in a subsidiary contract inducing the party to enter into the main contract).

If the view is taken, contrary to *Adobe* v *Beta,* that a shrink-wrap licence is ineffective and a licence is implied, this could defeat the copyright owner's preferred choice of applicable law. Some licence agreements contain a term stating that the applicable law is other than English law. It is common to see licence agreements for software from the United States with the law of California or New York designated as the applicable law. If the licence supplied with the software an be disregarded and a licence is implied, that implied licence will most likely be subject to English law (or Scots law as the case may be). In any case the legal maxim *caveat emptor* (let the buyer beware) applies. The vast majority of mass-produced software is of a very high standard but, if the customer is uncertain, it is wise to check with some existing users of the software or in some of the many excellent computer journals and publications which carry out comparative tests on these software packages. It should be borne in mind, however, the sometimes magazines fail to be truly objective or my omit to test some particular software.

Back-up Copies of Programs

making a back-up copy of a computer program infringes copyright unless sits making is:

- permitted by the copyright owner;
- within the scope of an implied term; or
- necessary to the licensed use of the program.

Notwithstanding that there may be some doubt as to the contractual status of the licence agreement, as discussed above, it is sensible to check any provisions concerning back-up copies. If making a back-up copy is necessary to the licensed use of the program then section 50A of the Copyright, Designs and Patents Act 1988 states that any term in a licence agreement which attempts to take this right away is void and unenforceable at law. One way around this would be to prohibit the making of back-up copies while providing a service to replace the licensed copy of the program promptly, hereby making the need to take a back-up copy no longer necessary. Even so, it is unlikely that the word 'necessary' will be interpreted in a strict and narrow sense.

In practical terms, a sensible approach to back-up copies is required by both sides. Licenses should guard against the danger of danger of proliferation of back-up copies which can soon become working copies, exceeding the licensed use. If an organisation requires 12 working copies, it should obtain a licence to cover 12 users not a single-user licence. Users of software should develop a system of software audits to check and monitor the number of copies in use, and information and advice on how to implement software audits can be obtained from the Federation Against Software Theft (FAST). There are a number of other benefits. Regular auditing is part of good practice and quality management and will encourage a responsible attitude towards the use of software. During an audit, some employees might be found to be using old or defective versions of software and any pirated software brought into work by an employee may be discovered and dealt with. The implementation and enforcement of effective software audits also prevents the embarrassment of being raided by software copyright owners who have obtained an Anton Piller Order (now called a 'search order') giving them powers, accompanied by a solicitor, to enter and inspect the computer equipment and remove unauthorized copies of software to be used in evidence in copyright infringement actions.

Integration and Upgrades

A person acquiring software should always check how well, if at all, the software will integrate with other software and whether data can be easily transferred to and from the software. Will the software run satisfactorily on the customer's hardware? What is the position if the customer decides to upgrade his equipment or operating system software: will the software still be usable? What if a better version of the software is made available in due course:

can the customer trade in his old software or will he have to pay the full licence fee for the new version? These are the type of questions someone contemplating an off-the-shelf system should consider; even though some of the events described might seem unlikely at the time, they have a nasty habit of becoming relevant later and if a customer is in doubt it is better to err on the side of flexibility. The pace of development in the computer industry shows no signs of slowing down and, as more powerful hardware becomes available, existing software packages will be enhanced in a like fashion and new software applications which were hitherto impossible or impracticable will appear on the market.

Training and Support

Training is an aspect which is often overlooked. A computer dealer may offer training under a separate contract between himself and the customer. The quality of the training will obviously be important as will the provision of refresher courses. Many organisations have their own internal training and training videos can usefully supplement this but many organisations will need some external support. Most software publishers provide support, usually by telephone, and it is worth checking with existing users as to the effectiveness of the service. Many such support services leave much to be desired and there seems to be a general inability to deal with anything but the most obvious problems. A typically hard nut to crack is whether the fault is caused by a hardware defect or software fault. A computer dealer may be able to help but, in many cases, a user group may be of more assistance.

A final point concerns 'hotline' support. Will the dealer be prepared to provide an emergency call-out service if there is a problem related to the use of the software such as trying to interface a word processing package with a new printer? In a case like this, the software itself will not be at fault; it will be a matter of installing the software in the correct manner for the particular printer. A dealer will charge for this type of support and the rate he requires will depend, among other things, on the speed of call-out expected by the customer.

18 CONTRACT BETWEEN SOFTWARE AUTHOR AND PUBLISHER

Not all software is developed directly by companies marketing the software. A self-employed software author, being the owner of the copyright, may prefer to deal with a software publishing company, already well established, with a good reputation and a high volume of sales. This may prove to be the most satisfactory way of exploiting the software. The software author will therefore consider granting a licence to a software publishing company permitting the latter to market the product on the basis of agreed royalty payments. The licence is likely to be an exclusive licence, which means that the author will grant the publisher the sole rights to deal with the software.

An important side-effect of an exclusive licence is that the licensee, the software publishing company, will have rights under copyright law as if it owned the copyright itself; the software publisher can sue for infringement of copyright directly, usually by joining the author in the action. Thus, if Arnold grants an exclusive licence in respect of his new computer game to Boris, a software publisher, and the game is copied without permission by Carol, Boris can sue Carol after joining Arnold as co-claimant. Any award made by the court will be shared with Arnold, usually on the basis of his royalty. As far as Arnold is concerned, this is an excellent arrangement as he may not have the resources to mount an infringement action himself. The licence agreement between the author and publisher should make provision for legal action taken by the exclusive license. For example , it may specify that the licensee will pay all legal costs and pay the author's other expenses in addition to a share in any award of damages or account of profits based on the royalty rate in the agreement. The agreement should also lay down whether the licensee is bound to take action if called upon by the author to do so or whether the licensee has discretion to take action and/ or to make a settlement.

Rather than granting an exclusive licence, the author may assign the copy-right (that is, transfer the ownership of the copyright) to the publisher. In practical terms, there is little difference between an assignment and an exclusive licence although from the author's point of view an exclusive licence is preferable. If the publisher is granted an assignment of copyright and later reassigns that copyright to a third party, he author may have difficulty enforcing any obligations owed to him under the agreement. He will still be able to sue the first publisher but will not be able to take any action against and subsequent owner due to lack of privity of contract. Thus, if the first publishing company has ceased to exist—for example, because it has been wound up the author will not be able to take any action in respect of royalties now due or accruing in the future. If the author does assign copyright, he could consider including a term in the agreement to he effect that the benefit of the agreement cannot be subsequently assigned at all or only with his express written approval.

Payment

A very important provision in the agreement will concern payment: how it will be calculated and when it will become due. Usually, the software author will be paid on the basis of royalties; it may be a fixed sum for every unit sold or it may be expressed as a percentage of the price charged for the software. Less commonly, the author will be paid a lump sum for granting the exclusive licence, although this should be avoided unless there are special circumstances. The quantification of royalty payments must be precisely defined in the licence agreement. If royalties are based on the price of the software is this the retail price or the payment the software publisher receives form a dealer? The author should look at the agreement and ask questions such as, what happens if the software publisher does not try very hard to market the product? What if the software publisher suddenly decides to distribute the software at a cut price? How does the software author know that the sales figures disclosed by the publisher are correct? Has the author the right of access to the publisher's accounts and sales information? How frequently will payments be made and what is the position if the publisher is consistently late in making payment? What is the position in respect of 'returns'—for example, unsold software that has been returned by a dealer? What if the publisher decides to stop marketing the software package; does this terminate the agreement? Finally, an the author terminate the agreement and, if so, under what circumstances?

Training, Maintenance and Defects

Other matters that will require the attention of the author and publisher include questions of training and maintenance and who is responsible for doing this. If the author is to be responsible will he be paid anything for his work or is it included in the royalty payments? If the software publisher has to correct subsequent defects in the software, will the author be charged? Related to such questions is the need for the licence agreement to state clearly and precisely what the author has to provide and when he has to provide it.

Indemnity

The software publisher will expect to receive an indemnity form the author in case the software or any part of it turns out to infringe a third party's right, such as a copyright or trade mark. An indemnity clause should allow the author the opportunity to make the necessary modifications to the software to remove or substitute the offending part so that the software no longer infringes. The software publisher may wish to recoup the cost of distributing modified copies of the software to existing users and other associated costs form the author.

Some thought needs to be given to the extent of the indemnity required should it not be possible to modify the software so that it does not infringe the third party right. It is reasonable to expect the author to return all payments received under the agreement but is it reasonable to expect him to pay the whole of the software publisher's costs (including legal costs), expenses and lost profits? The relative economic strength and bargaining position of the author and publisher should be a factor, especially if the author is a self-employment individual working on his own with few resources. Whether the author can insure against such an eventuality is another factor. Indemnity clauses are subject to the test of reasonableness by section 4 of the Unfair Contract Terms Act 1977. Where the indemnity granted relates to an intellectual property right or interest however, paragraph 1(b) of Schedule 1 will apply nullifying the effect of section 4. Thus, if the author does not own the copyright he purports to grant a licence in respect of, any indemnity clause is not controlled by the Unfair Contract terms Act 1977 (it might be controlled in other ways) but, if he does own the copyright and the software displays some third party's trade mark on the screen thereby infringing it, it seems that section 4 will apply because that is outside paragraph 1(b).

An indemnity might also be sought by the publisher in respect of any defamatory statement contained within the software or if the software is otherwise illegal and the publisher is prevented form exploiting it or has to defend any legal action resulting form use of the software.

Confidentiality

The author should satisfy himself that the software publisher is fully aware of the confidential nature of elements of the software. The author may provide the publisher with the source code and the specification, including flow chart, for the software. The agreement should spell out the duty of confidentiality in respect of these materials, reinforcing the common law duty. If the author has access to the publisher's information about sales and marketing techniques, a reciprocal duty could be placed on the author.

Liability

The relationship between the author, publisher and ultimate customers is shown in Fig. 18.1.

The author grants an exclusive licence to the publisher giving the publisher the exclusive right to produce copies of the software and to market them. The publisher 'sells the software through a dealer, granting non-exclusive licences to the customers. The dealer is an agent whose role in this context is to act on behalf of the publisher to bring about the contract (the licence agreement) between the publisher and the customer subject to what has been said about the nature of such transactions. The dealer having brought this about then effectively drops out of the picture. The author and ultimate customers are not in a contractual relationship but the law of negligence operates without the need for a contract as long as there is a duty of care owed by one person to another. The author will therefore want to be protected against any claims for losses to ultimate customers caused by defects in the software. The publisher will probably protect himself by having a suitably drafted exclusion or limitation clause in his licence agreements with the customers. The author should ask the software publisher to draw up any such term in the licence agreement with the ultimate customers in language wide enough to give some protection to the author, bearing in mind the legal controls on exclusion clauses.

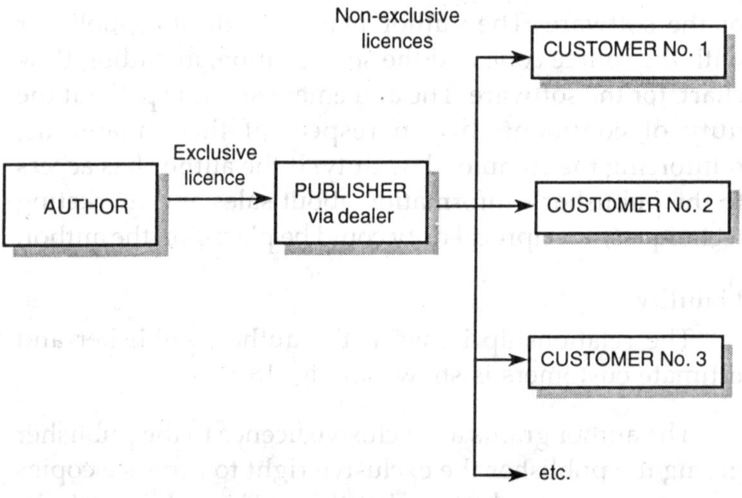

Fig. 18.1 Licence arrangement between author, publisher and customers.

Other terms will be relevant in these forms of agreements, dealing with matters such as definitions, items provided, specification, delivery, liquidated damages copyright and arbitration (or alternative dispute resolution).

Internet Service Providers and Defamation

Organisations providing Internet access to authors are potentially liable in a number of ways. Information placed on the Internet (or other electronic publishing medium) by an author may infringe copyright, be defamatory or include a negligent misstatement. The Internet service provider could find himself liable at law as publisher of the information — for example, by implicitly authorising infringement of copyright by persons who down load the information or as a publisher of defamatory material. (Note that Scots law on defamation is not identical to that in England and Wales.) The liability under copyright law is the context of electronic publishing.

Already, there have been a number of cases of defamation on the Internet. For example, in *Rindos* v *Hardwick* (unreported) 31 March 1994, the Western Australian Supreme Court found that a statement made by an academic which seriously denigrated another academic's competence and which also imputed misconduct on his part was defamatory and an aware of A$40000 in damages was made. In *Stratton Oakmont Inc* v *Prodigy Services Co* (unreported) 24 May 1995, the Supreme Court of the State of New York held that the defendant, a service provider, was the publisher of statements on its bulletin board and granted summary judgment against it in respect of libellous statements made on the bulletin board. In the United Kingdom, a lecturer accepted undisclosed damages in an out-of-court settlement for on-line statements that were potentially defamatory (Calow, D, 'Defamation on the Internet,' *Computer Law and Security Report* (1995) 11 (4), p. 199).

A publisher is likely to require a warranty form an author that the material concerned is not defamatory in any way. This applies as much to software as to written statements. The warranty may be backed by an indemnity so that, if the publisher is sued for defamation and has to pay £ 40000 in damages to the persons defamed, the publisher will be able to recover this from the author. It is important that authors check for the presence of such warranties and indemnities in the agreement as awards in defamation cases can be notoriously high. Defamation is something of a rarity in that it is a civil action in which a jury may be sworn in and, if this is the case it is the jury which decide whether defamation has been made out and, if so, the jury also decides the award. Under section 8 of the Defamation Act 1996, however, the judge may deal with the case summarily where it appears that the case is very clear cut—for example, where the plaintiff has no real chance of success.

One thing an author should be wary of is a term in the agreement which enables the publisher to settle a defamation action out of court at the publisher's discretion and still be able to recoup the money agreed in settlement form the author. There should be, at least, the insertion of the word 'reasonable'—for example, as in '... The reasonable exercise of the publisher's discretion.' The danger is, of course, that a publisher may be prepared to settle out of court simply to avoid the nuisance and publicity of a trial, safe in the knowledge that it will be able to recoup the settlement from the author.

There are two branches of defamation: libel and slander. Generally, libel relates to written statements whereas slander relates to the spoken word. The distinction is important because libel is actionable *per se*—that is, without proof of damage. Except in some cases, slander requires proof of damage. It appears that a defamatory image will be classed as libel rather than slander. In *Yousopouff* v *MGM Pictures Ltd* (1934) 50 TLR 581 the defendant made a film which suggested that the plaintiff was a Russian princess who had been 'ravished' or seduced by Rasputin. This was held to be libel, not slander.

Recently, an image taken form a computer game resulted

in a libel action in the House of Lord. In *Charleston* v *News Group Newspapers* [1995] 2 AC 65, a Sunday newspaper carried a photograph which had been taken from a pornographic computer game. It depicted a man and woman who appeared to be engaged in sexual intercourse or other sexual activity. Superimposed on the photographs were images of the heads of the plaintiffs, actors who played Harold and Madge Bishop in the television 'soap' *Neighbours.* The captions ran 'Strewth! What's Harold up to with our Madge?' and 'Porn Shoker for Neighbours Stars.' However, because the text underneath made it clear that the image had been produced as part of a pornographic computer game which had used the images of the plaintiffs without their permission, it was held not to be libellous. The low does not take account of 'a moron in a hurry'—that is, a careless reader who would not read such a 'disclaimer' and might not realise the true nature of the image is ignored in determining whether it is libellous.

The difficulty in which publishers of electronic media containing information and Internet Service Providers could find themselves in respect of defamatory material made available through their service has been eased somewhat by the defamation Act 1996. Before looking at the defence available to publishers and Internet Service Providers, the basic requirements for defamation are set out briefly.

Basics of Defamation

A defamatory statement is one which, when published, tends to lower a person in the esteem of right-thinking members of society generally; or which attends to make them shun or avoid that person. The statement does not have to allege some moral turpitude or wrong doing on the part of the claimant (plaintiff) and it can be defamation to allege insanity or being the victim of a crime such as rape.

It is common to see disclaimers as to the character portrayed in a film. It is dangerous to publish something containing, for example a fictional character with a name that might be the same as a real person. In *Hulton and Co.* v *Jones* [1910] AC 20, an article was published by the defendant which was alleged by the defendant to be fictitious. It contained defamatory statements about one 'Artemus Jones,' a churchwarden form Peckham. However, and unfortunately for the defendant, by coincidence there was a person with that name who happened to be a barrister living in North Wales. He successfully sued for libel. It was thought that some of his friends and acquaintances might think the article referred to him.

Publication is required and it must be to at least one person other than the plaintiff. It may be by means of words, pictures, visual images, gestures or any other method of signifying meaning. The defendant must either publish the material himself or be responsible for publication. Every repetition of a defamatory publication is a fresh publication and actionable. Thus, if defamatory material is placed on the Internet, every time it is accessed and read by someone, this constitutes a separate defamation. The potential is that thousands or even millions of causes of action could accrue in respect of placing defamatory material in, say, a Web page. Also, a reasonably foreseeable repetition of a publication by a third party will also bring liability. In *Slipper* v *British Broadcasting Corp* ([1991] 1QB 283, which concerned a film broadcast by the defendant, the claims made by the plaintiff included damages for reviews of the film in the press. The Court of Appeal refused to strike out these additional claims. In respect of republication it was held that this could be a *novus actus interveniens* (a new act breaking the chain of causation) if it was unauthorised. However, where reasonably foreseeable the chain of causation was not broken.

There are a umber of defences to a defamation action including fair comment, justification (that is, that the statement is true), an offer to make amends and privilege. The publisher's defence is described below.

Publisher's Defence

Prior to the passing of the Defamation Act 1996, the Lord Chancellor's Department specifically looked at this problem. The 1996 Act has, therefore a specific defence in which a person can show that he had no responsibility for the publication. The defence came into force on 4 September 1996. Under section 1, the defence applies if a person shows that:

- he was not the author, editor or publisher of the statement complained of,
- he took reasonable care in relation to its publication, and
- he did not know, and had no reason to believe that what he did caused or contributed to the publication of a defamatory statement.

Under section 1(3) of the Defamation Act 1996, a number of persons are not to be considered authors, editors or publishers if only involved:

(a) in printing, producing, distributing or selling material containing the statement;

(b) in processing, making copies of, distributing, exhibiting or selling a film or sound recording containing the statement;

(c) in processing, making copies of, distributing or selling electronic medium in or on which the statement is recorded or in operating or providing any equipment, system or service by means of which the statement is retrieved copied, distributed or made available in electronic form;

(d) as the broadcaster of a live programme containing the statement in circumstances in which he has no effective control over the maker of the statement;

(e) as the operator or provider of access to a communications system by means of which the statement is transmitted or made available, by a person over whom he has no effective control.

It can be seen that (c) above applies in relation to publishers of computer software on disk or CD-ROM and (e) applies particularly to Internet Service Providers. In other cases, the court may use the above provisions by way of analogy in deciding whether a person is considered to be an author, editor or publisher.

Under section 1(4), employees or agents are in the same position as their employer or principal to the extent that they are responsible for the content of the statement or the decision to publish it.

To determine whether a person took reasonable care, under section 1(5), regard is to be had to:

(a) the extent of his responsibility for the content of the statement or the decision to publish it,

(b) the nature of the circumstances of the publication, and

(c) the previous conduct or character of the author, editor or publisher.

Thus, where an author or publisher has been in trouble before in relation to defamatory material, that is a factor in determining whether he took reasonable care. In other words a previous history of publishing defamatory material requires the person responsible to exercise greater care to prevent it happening again. This could apply, for example, where a publisher of computer games has previously published games including libellous statements.

The section 1 defence may be vulnerable once an Internet Service Provider has been informed that material which contains a statement alleged to be defamatory has been placed on the Service Providers' server and it is not removed immediately. In *Godfrey* v *Demon Internet Ltd, The Times*, 20 April 1999, a subscriber to an Internet Service Provider, the defendant, made material available through the defendant's service which was alleged by the plaintiff to be defamatory of him. The plaintiff brought the present action to strike out part of the defence as disclosing no sustainable defence to a libel action, based on the publication of the material by the defendant. After the plaintiff informed the defendant of his allegation that the material was defamatory, the defendant did not remove the material (although, eventually, it did so).

It was held that the defence did not apply in this case as at common law, once the defendant became aware that the material contained defamatory statements it could no longer satisfy two of the requirements in section 1(1) — that is, that reasonable care had been taken in the publication and that the defendant had no knowledge or reason to believe that he caused or contributed to the publication of the defamatory statement. Mr. Justice Morland pointed out that section 17 of the Defamation Act 1996 states that 'publication' and 'publish' have the meaning they have generally for the law of defamation but 'publisher' is specially defined in section 1. He did accept, however, that the defendant was not a commercial publisher for the purposes of section 1(2), being a person whose business is issuing material to the public, or a section of the public, who issues material containing the statement in the course of that business. Unfortunately for the defendant, for the section 1(1) defence to apply all three requirements must be satisfied. The defendant's argument that it had played a passive role was not accepted and the judge thought the situation analogous to that of a bookseller who sold a book containing defamatory material.

The significance of this case is that the special defence may be quite limited in is scope. If a person alleges that defamatory material has been placed on the Service Provider's server, it may no longer be safe to rely on the defence and the Service Provider's ought to consider removing the material immediately. This is quite important as each time an individual accesses the material there will be a fresh libel. Whether a Service Provider has no reason to believe that he causes or contributes to the publication must be an objective test based on the reasonable person having knowledge of the facts known to the Service Provider and which must be coloured by the allegation of defamation.

Consider a situation where an Internet Service Provider is informed by someone that a statement defamatory of him has been placed on the Service Provider's server. If the material is not removed immediately, the issue for the court may become one simply relating to the general law of defamation. If the statement is held by the court to have a defamatory meaning, it is highly unlikely that the section 1 defence can apply. For example, if the matter is being decided by a jury and it finds the statement defamatory, it will almost certainly consider that, after being informed of the allegation of defamation, the Service Provider did indeed 'have reason to believe.' The same probably applies where there is no jury and the case is heard before a judge alone. On the other hand, if the finding is that the statement is not defamatory, that is an end to the matter. Thus, the section 1 defence is likely to be relevant only up to such time as an Internet Service Provider has been informed of the allegation. If that is so, Internet Service Providers would be well advised to remove the material immediately. However, if they respond in that way, that makes freedom of information vulnerable to persons who simply do not like what is said about them over the Internet without the statements necessarily being defamatory. Given the sensitivity of the issue and the potential of numerous actions for defamation, Internet Service Providers are likely to play safe if there is any possibility that the statement complained of may be defamatory.

19 HARDWARE CONRACTS

Computer hardware may be purchase outright or hired. Much of what has already been discussed in relation to computer software contracts, in particular contracts for the writing or modification of software, will apply to contracts for the acquisition of hardware. Very often, the purchase of or hire of computer equipment will include software, such as operating system software, computer programming languages, utility programs or applications programmes. These items of software usually will be subject to collateral licence agreements.

Computer software is important; the choice of the software best suited to the client's requirements in critical and when it comes to setting up a computer system in a company or business that has not used computers before or where a change in computer equipment is contemplated, the decisions regarding the selection of software are of primary importance. The secondary decision should then be to determine the type of computer equipment which will be most suitable for running this software, not forgetting other important considerations such as future growth, the impact of the computing operations and the future of the software packages and computer equipment. Will the company manufacturing the computer to develop and support it in the longer term? Is it an industry standard with a wide range of available software?

If the client already has some computer equipment and software, this will influence any decisions about obtaining new hardware. Compatibility with the existing equipment will be important and some compromises may have to be made. The aim should be that in three or five years' time the decision will still seem to have been a good choice. Long-term planning is essential, not only in terms of computer equipment but also taking into account the client's business strategy and plans for development and how these will prescribe and influence its computer needs.

Performance

The performance software is directly related to the computer's performance. The speed of operation of the computer will be very important and a contract for the purchase or hire of computer equipment should make reference to this. Information about processing speeds, storage capacities, data transfer and networking capabilities will be paramount. The purchaser must satisfy himself as to the performance of the equipment, bearing in mind the environment in which the equipment will be working.

Simple benchmark speed tests may not provide a very good picture of the computer's performance if it will be used to carry out many different tasks at the same time, with multiple concurrent access to data files. The client should think about the operating system and whether it is a common one able to run a large variety of applications programes. Similar considerations apply to networking hardware and software. Another point which might be relevant is whether there are any limitations on the number of data files the computer will permit to be in use at the same time.

Representations and Collateral Warranties

A salesperson will usually extol the virtues of the equipment he is trying to sell and he will try to convince the would-be purchaser that it is everything he needs; in other words, it is the answer to a maiden's prayer. If the equipment turns out to be totally unsuited to the client's needs, the supplier will probably point to a term in the contract of sale which states that the printed agreement represents the entire agreement between the parties and nothing said or done in preliminary negotiations is part of the contract. This poly may not always work, as the case below demonstrates.

In *Machanzie Patten and Co. v. British Olivetti Ltd.* (unreported) 11 January 1984, the plaintiff was a firm of solicitors which wanted a computer to handle its accounts and the defendant company was approached by the plaintiff with this in mind. Following negotiations with the defendant's salesman, the plaintiff agreed to obtain one of the defendant''s computers under a leasing agreement with a third party. The computer proved totally unsuitable for the plaintiff's needs and the plaintiff's staff were incapable of using the computer effectively even and the plaintiff's staff were incapable of using the computer effectively even following training by the defendant. After hearing expert evidence, the judge decided that the computer was obsolete and not suitable for the defendant's requirements. Indeed, as the plaintiff firm was a small one, it was questionable whether a computer was needed at all. (Things are much different now; even the smallest firm needs computer technology and, preferably, also access to the Internet).

The judge held that the plaintiff had relied on the salesman's statements when entering the leasing agreement. The statements were a collateral warranty and, as they were not true, there was a breach of this warranty. There was an 'entire agreement' clause in the contract but his was held to be ineffective as it was stated in terms of a contract of sale and, in fact, the contract entered into by the plaintiff was a leasing contract. No sale to the plaintiff took place or was contemplated (the plaintiff could not afford to buy the computer outright). The contract contained an exclusion clause but the judge held that the defendant had failed to prove that it was reasonable, applying the test in section 11 of the Unfair Contract Terms Act 1977. The judge awarded the plaintiff the sum of £16204 which comprised £2661 for payments made under the lease agreement, £12692 for payments owing under the agreement and £851 interest. A further claim for wasted time in meetings and the like of £1200 was dismissed by the judge as being too vague and too remote.

If the entire agreement clause held been found to be effective to exclude the salesman's statements, the plaintiff would probably have had a remedy under section 2 of the Misrepresentation Act 1967, any attempt to exclude liability being subject to the reasonableness test in the Unfair Contract Terms Act 1977. Hence, suppliers of computer equipment should make every effort to ensure that the would-be purchaser is fully aware of the equipment's capabilities and limitations. The purchaser would be wise to seek independent advice and the supplier, if there is any doubt about the suitability of a particular piece of equipment, would be wise to suggest that such independent advice is sought. In particular, it is unwise to attempt to sell obsolete or unsuitable equipment to a solicitor, although, in the above case, it appears that the solicitor signed the agreement without first reading it thoroughly!

Maintenance and Upgrades

The contract should state exactly who does what in terms of installation and initial testing. Once the equipment is installed, how well will the supplier support it? Maintenance will probably be provided for by a separate contract, renewable annually, and the client should check this contract to see what it has to say on the point of speed of response to a breakdown. If repairs have to be made to the computer equipment, does the client have to pay for parts or labour or both and is there a minimum call-out charge? The maintenance contract may provide for the loan of alternative equipment while repairs are carried out and if it does not so provide, it could be worth asking why not. The client should also check whether third party maintenance is a possibility.

Sooner or later the computer equipment will become obsolete as faster, more powerful equipment is continually being developed. This can have one of two consequences. First, the new equipment is better in so many respects and so different that there is no possibility of upgrading the old equipment to the new standards. It is then a matter of making do, standing by the existing equipment, consolidating it and adding improvements when they become available with a view to reviewing the situation in a year or two, when the quality and performance of the new equipment has been fully tested by others. The general acceptance of equipment among the computer world is very important. Sometimes, a new computer will catch on and sell in volume and this will then encourage the leading software companies to produce appropriate software for the new machine, making it an even more attractive proposition. Once a new computer attracts the attention of the software companies it is well on its way to becoming established. It is very tempting to stay with the market leaders when buying computer equipment. As the old adage used to go, 'No one was ever fired for buying IBM!'

A second consequence of the announcement of new,

improved equipment is that it may be possible to upgrade the existing equipment to those standards, and the new equipment may be in the form of an upgrade. When buying computer equipment, it is worthwhile finding out what the manufacturer's attitude is to his existing customers regarding upgrades or new equipment. Will the improved equipment be sympathetically priced as far as existing customers are concerned? Will a generous trade-in be allowed on the old equipment or is there a good second-hand market for the manufacturer's equipment? Does the manufacturer have a history of upwardly compatible machines or does he bring out new equipment that is totally unlike the old equipment? Does he change operating systems continually? Ideally, the manufacturer should have a policy of building on his past products. It must be borne in mind that there is a dichotomy here for manufacturers. A manufacturer will want to attract new customers and, to do this, the equipments must be up to date and make use of the latest technological developments. On the other hand, the manufacturer will owe a moral duty to his loyal customers to maintain some degree of compatibility. The history of computing is one of change and abandoning out-of-date equipment and the person or company considering purchasing a computer or other computer equipment would do well to bear this in mind. There is little that can be done contractually, apart from insisting that the supplier (it will be the supplier and not the manufacturer who will be a party to the contract unless the supplier and manufacturer are one and the same) will continue to support the equipment for a reasonable period of time, regardless of whether it is later withdrawn from the market place.

If the equipment is hired, problems of obsolescence are less important providing the hirer is not committing himself to an unduly long period of hire. Hiring is often referred to as leasing; there is no particular significance in this because a lease contract and a contract of hire are basically the same thing. The duration of the agreement will be important as will be the presence of any term in the agreement concerning termination and the relevant circumstances. If a much better piece of equipment is suddenly available, the hirer may wish to terminate the agreement quickly so that he can avail himself of the new equipment. The company hiring the equipment out will obviously want some form of compensation should the hirer want to return the computer equipment before the normal time and this requires a sensible compromise.

Legal Controls

Statutory safeguards are more in evidence when it comes to hardware contracts. For example, the Sale of Goods Act 1979 will apply because a computer or other related equipment comes within the meaning of 'goods'; a computer is a personal chattel. This means that the important terms such as compliance with description and meeting the requirement of satisfactory quality will be implied into a contract to purchase a computer. Certain terms implied by the Sale of Goods Act 1979 are implied into all contracts of sale while others only apply where the seller sells in the course of business. Compliance with description is an example of the former while satisfactory quality is an example of the latter. Most of the contracts under consideration in this book will be in the course of business. Similar terms will be implied into hire contracts by the Supply of Goods and Services Act 1982. These implied terms can be excluded or limited in the case of a non-consumer sale but only in so far as the exemption clauses purporting to do this meet the requirement of reasonableness as provided for by the Unfair Contract Terms Act 1977, section 5 to 7.

The fact that the hardware is sold complete with software does not prevent the contract from being a sale of goods contract. For example, in the Australian case of *Toby Constructions Products Pty Ltd* v *Computer Bar Sales Pty Ltd.* (1983) 50 ALR 684, the Supreme Court of New South Wales held that the sale of a computer system comprising both hardware and software, was a sale of goods contract. The contract was primarily one for equipment as the hardware cost was A$12230 and the software cost was A$2160. This logic was approved of by *Scott Baker J in St. Albans City and District Council* v *International Computer Ltd.* [1995] FSR 686. Looking at the primary objective of the contract is a sensible approach. After all, the purchaser of a defective washing machine would be surprised to find that the Sale of Goods Act did not apply, even if the defect was traced to the programme controlling the washing cycle. Where the balance between hardware and software is more even, however, it is better to make two separate contracts so that the application of statutory controls is predictable.

A final point to consider is that there is a possibility that the computer hardware or the software sold with it infringes some intellectual property right. The hardware itself could infringe a patent, design or trade mark while the software might infringe a copyright or trade mark. The client should make sure that the contract contains a term indemnifying him in case this should happen. If the contract is governed by the Sale of Goods Act 1979, however, there will be remedies available to the buyer if he is prevented from using or hindered in his use of the equipment because it infringes another person's rights. By section 12(1), there is an implied condition that the seller has the right to sell the goods and, by section 12(2), there is an implied warranty that the buyer will enjoy 'quiet possession' of the goods.

Section 6 of the Unfair Contract Terms Act 1977 provides that section 12 of the Sale of Goods Act 1979 cannot be excluded or restricted by reference to any contractual term. If a company buys a computer and, at the time of the sale, the computer infringes a trade mark or patent, then the seller is in breach of section 12(1) of the Sale of Goods Act 1979. Because this is a condition, the buyer can repudiate the contract and claim back the purchase price, plus damages for any consequential losses he has suffered (provided they are not too remote). In *Niblett Ltd.* v *Confectioners' Materials Co Ltd* [1921] 3 KB 387, it was held that because goods, when sold, infringed a trade mark, this entitled the buyer to repudiate the contract. In Scotland the question is whether the breach is a material one.

It may happen that equipment does not infringe a patent when it is sold but does infringe a patent soon afterwards, perhaps because at the time of sale a patent application, made by a third party, was being processed. When the patent is granted, the third party may commence an infringement action against the buyer of the equipment. This occurred in a case involving road marking machines, *Microbeads AC* v *Vinhurst Road Markings* [1975] 1 WLR 218, where it was held that:

— there was not a breach of section 12(1) because, at the time of the sale, the seller had every right to sell (the patent could not be enforced at that time);

and

— the seller was in breach of section 12(2) the implied warranty as to quiet possession, and was liable to the buyer in damages.

There always a danger that computer equipment or equipment or software will infringe a third party's rights (even if it is inadvertent) because of the rapid development of new hardware and software. The remedies in section 12 of the Sale of Gods Act 1979 are useful but it is advisable to make specific contractual provision for the eventuality. For example, in a situation like that in the *Microbeads* case, the buyer may prefer to be able to repudiate the contract rather than being limited to damages only. However, there is a defence to a patent infringement action if a person, in good faith, does the act or makes effective and serious preparations to do the act before the patent's priority date (see Patents Act 1977, section 64).

Tenders

An organisation wishing to obtain computer equipment (the client) may ask a number of suppliers or manufacturers to submit tenders. Each of the companies submitting tenders will be asked for their price to supply the equipment described in a detailed specification. In this way, the bids can be compared on a like for like basis and, usually, the one submitting the lowest bid will be awarded the contract to supply equipment complying with the specification. Letting contracts by means of a tendering process is very common and public authorities and many large private organisations make use of this process. In some cases, the organisation will have no other option as it will be laid down in the constitution or articles of association. In some cases, it may be imposed from elsewhere—for example, where the contract value exceeds a particular value, it will have to be open to tenders because of government or European Community regulations.

The contractual status of a tender is that a company submitting a tender is making an offer which can be rejected or accepted by the client as he thinks fit. Indeed, the client can choose not to accept any unless, for example, he has bound himself to accept the lowest. Consequently, the company submitting a tender bears the cost involved in its preparation such as determining which equipment is suitable and calculating the total price. If the hardware is complex, this cost can be considerable. The use of tendering as a means of letting contracts is very common in the construction industry. The convention that the person submitting the tender bears the costs of preparation of the tender is deeply ingrained; that it also applies in the context of computer contracts was emphatically stated in *Comyn Ching Ltd* v *Radius plc* (unreported) 17 March 1997, which concerned a tender for the supply of computer equipment and software. The judge cited a passage from *Keating on Building Contracts*, 6th edn (a leading practitioner text), to the effect that the contractor preparing a tender may incur considerable cost in doing so but there is no implication that he will be paid for this work. Indeed, '...he undertakes this work as a gamble and its cost ... he hopes will be met out of the profits of such contracts as are made as a result of tenders which prove to be successful!' The judge went on to say 'I see no difference in principle between a building contract and a computer contract.'

Tenders can be requested from a selected list of companies or open tendering can be used—that is, where anyone who wishes may submit a bid. Select list tendering is more usual nowadays and has the advantage that only those companies perceived as being competent are invited to submit bids. However, this may again be subject to rules imposed by government or through the European Community.

The tender process is broadly as follows:

1. A detailed specification is drawn up detailing the functional and performance requirements.
2. If it is to be a select list tender, that list is drawn up and those on it are asked if they are interested

in submitting tenders. If open tendering is to be used, an advertisement will be placed in an appropriate newspaper or journal or other publication (for example, the *Official Journal of the European Communities).*

3. To each tenderer, a set of tender documents will be sent comprising the specification (including any drawings and schedules), a form of agreement (so that the tenderer can see what the contractual obligations will be) and, in some cases, a bill of quantities in which the tendering company can write prices or a schedule of rates to be completed or a simple form on which the overall price can be written. The bill, schedule or form will contain a reference to the other documents.
4. A period of time will be allowed and a deadline will be stated for return of the tenders in sealed envelopes—for example 'no later than noon on 28 February 2000.' Tenders received after this deadline must be rejected (to prevent the possibility of corruption).
5. The sealed tenders will be opened after the deadline. This may be before a senior officer and chairman of the appropriate committee in the case of a public authority. Any arithmetic will be checked carefully. (Mistakes can cause all sorts of problems if not picked up and dealt with. If there is a mistake it is usual practice to ask the company submitting that particular tender whether it wishes to stand by its mistake or withdraw the tender).
6. A letter of acceptance will be sent to the successful company (usually that submitting the lowest bid) and a contract will be executed, typically under seal, as per the original form of agreement.

Tenders can be seen as a very fair means of letting contracts and the system has evolved as a way of reducing the possibility of bribery and corruption. However, tendering is not without difficulties. The client has to make sure that the tender documents are of a high quality, accurately describe the desired equipment and its performance and provide fully for any eventuality. If there are any shortcomings, the successful company may use these as a basis of additional payments and extensions to the time for delivery. A major headache for the client is that the companies submitting tenders, or at least some of them, will wish to make changes to the specification or time for delivery, etc. If this is permitted, it makes comparison of the tenders more difficult. A usual means of trying to maintain some comparability is to ask any company which has expressed a wish to submit on a different basis to submit two tenders, one as per the original tender documents, the other on its preferred specification.

20 ELECTRONIC CONTRACTING

Information technology allows and encourages the conduct of many aspect of commercial activity by electronic means, at least in part. Forms of agreement and other contractual documents are likely to be created using a computer and may be transmitted in electronic form anywhere in the world. Standard forms and precedents used by solicitors to draw up agreements, such as a software licence or a will, are now published electronically. Typically a solicitor acting for a party to contract will load an appropriate form of agreement into his word processor, make any required modifications and additions, and then either print it out or transmit it to the other party's solicitor. A contractual offer may be made in this way and may be accepted electronically by the other party transmitting his acceptance of the terms of the agreement.

Many transactions are now effected electronically. For example, by the use of automated teller machines (ATMs or cash point dispensers outside banks) and electronic fund transfers (EFTs) transactions are made between financial institutions and even at the point of sale. A growing number of organisations exchange data electronically. For example, a large manufacturing company may order components automatically and electronically from its suppliers when stock levels reach a predetermined lower limit. Electronic data inter-change (EDI) has the potential to maximise efficiency by reducing repetition and delays, increasing accuracy and permitting the maintenance of minimum stock levels by placing orders for 'just-in-time' delivery. A large proportion of the information flows between organisations may be handled electronically, including quoting or submitting tenders for work ordering, scheduling, invoicing and accounting.

All of this sounds very good apart, perhaps, from concerns about security but, as expected, there are a number of legal consequences associated with electronic trading.

- The law requires that some contracts are in a particular form — for example, by deed or in writing.
- There may be doubts as to when the contract was made and, if the parties are in different countries, which country's law will apply to the contract.
- The evidential weight of electronic documents must be considered and assessed.

To take an example, imagine that Karen, who has a large footwear store in London wishes to buy 1000 pairs of shoes from Luigi in Milan. Both Karen and Luigi have computers and both use electronic mail. All the preliminary negotiations are carried out using electronic mail. Eventually, Karen transmits a contract for Luigi's approval on Monday at 10.00 am GMT. Later that day, at 2.00 pm GMT, Luigi sends a message to say that he accepts Karen's offer. However, Karen does not read that message until Wednesday as she has to make a trip to Scotland in the meantime. There is a term in the contract to the effect that Karen can terminate the contract if she fails to sell more than 50 pairs of shoes in any one week, returning the remaining stock to Luigi and paying only for those that she has sold. After four weeks, Karen has sold 250 pairs of shoes but 175 pairs were sold in the first week following an intensive advertising campaign. Sales have plummeted since and in the fourth week only 12 pairs were sold. Karen wishes to exercise her right to terminate the contract but the only evidence she has of the numbers sold each week is the record of sales on her computer, entered by her various shop assistants as and when they sold shoes.

The questions that arise in the above scenario related to the use of electronic contracting are:

- Is the contract valid—that is, did the electronically transmitted offer and acceptance create a biding contract? (If so, what would the position have been if Luigi, who did not receive confirmation until Wednesday, had sold the shoes to a third party on Tuesday?)
- If there is a valid contract, when was it made and it is subject to English or Italian law?
- Can a printout of the computer record of sales be used as evidence to prove that Karen sold insufficient numbers of shoes so allowing her to invoke the termination clause?

The three main issues relating to electronic contracting concern the legal formalities, the time and place that the contract was made and the admissibility of computer evidence in civil proceedings. These are considered below. At the end of the chapter, we will return to Karen and Luigi and advise them accordingly.

Legal Requirement as to Form

A contract may be made in a number of different forms. For example, a contract may be made by deed, made in writing, evidenced in writing or it may be oral, or it may be a combination of these. For example, section 4 of the Sale of Goods Act 1979 states that a contract of sale:

> ....may be made in writing (either with or without seal), or by word of mouth, or partly in writing and partly by word of mouth, or may be implied from the conduct of the parties.

An example of a contract implied from the conduct of the parties is given by the case of *Brogden* v *Metropolitan Rail Co* (1877) 2 App Cas 666 concerning a contract to supply coal. It was held that the conduct of the parties by dealing with each other in accordance with a draft contract could only be explained on the basis that they approved the draft contract and a binding contract came into existence, at the latest, when the plaintiff supplied the first order of coal placed by the defendant.

Although for some contracts the from used does not matter (as in a sale of goods contract above), occasionally the law requires that a particular from be used. Some contracts must be by deed, an example being a lease of real property Act 1925(. A deed is a written document that is signed, sealed and delivered and a contract made by deed is referred to as a contract under seal. This requirement can be traced back to the Statute of Frauds 1677 which was intended to prevent lack of documentation being used as a means of fraud. The formality associated with a deed demonstrates a clear intention to be bound and, therefore in terms of a contract, there is no requirement for consideration (for example, payment or goods) which is a normal prerequisite of legally binding contracts.

In recognition of the fact that some flexibility is now required and the traditional from of deed — originally written in beautiful cursive script on vellum with a wax seal attached (or more recently a red adhesive wafer) — is no longer relevant in today's society, the Law of Property (Miscellneous Provisions) Act 1989 abolishes some of the old rules that applied to some deeds. Now to qualify as a deed, the instrument must make it clear on its face that it is intended to be a deed (for example, by using a from of words making it clear that it is a deed) and it must be validly executed—for example, signed in the presence of witnesses and delivered (section 1(2) and (3)). The meaning of 'sign' includes making one's mark. It is possible that this could extend to a digital electronic representation of a signature and because of the other relaxations in the rules, there seems to be no reason why an electronic deed cannot be valid. Nevertheless, because there is still a degree of uncertainty, it would be wise to print out the deed on paper before it is signed before witnesses, although this would then require physical delivery, losing one of the advantages of using information technology.

Relatively few legal documents are required to be by deed. However, some must be in writing. For example, an assignment of a copyright must be in writing and signed by or on behalf of the assignor (section 90(3) of the Copyright, Designs and Patents Act 1988), and regulated consumer credit agreements must be in documentary from and signed (section 61 of the Consumer Credit Act 1974). The same applies to contracts for marine insurance, by section 22 of the Marine Insurance Act 1906, and contracts for the sale or other disposition of an interest in land, which must also incorporate all the terms expressly agreed by the parties (section 2(1) of the Law of Property (Miscellaneous Provisions) Act 1989). Yet other contracts must be evidenced in writing, an example being a contract of guarantee by section 4 of the Statute of Frauds 1677.

For contracts where writing is a requirement it is important to determine whether documents stored magnetically in digital from comply. Fortunately, Schedule 1 to the Interpretation Act 1978 contains the following definition:

> 'Writing includes typing, printing, lithography, photography and other modes of representing or reproducing words in a visible form, and expressions referring to writing are construed accordingly.

This would appear to include computer storage. Words stored in a computer may be reproduced on screen or printed on paper. In any case, it is unlikely that a judge would take a restrictive view of this, although the preceding words are somewhat narrow.

Where signatures are required, what has been said earlier in respect of deeds should still hold. The matter is not beyond doubt but there is no logical reason why a person's mark cannot be stored in digital from and affixed to a computer file electronically. The purpose of a signature is to identify the signatory's assent to the document or transaction. This can be done effectively by electronic means, particularly if a from of encryption is used. The stylised handwritten name signatures we are so familiar with are of relatively recent origin. Most of us now have one or more PIN numbers so that we can draw cash from the 'hole in the wall' without the need for any signature. However, use of such facilities is founded on a printed contract signed in the usual way!

If the formalities required by law are not complied with then, at law, the contract will be unenforceable. However, equity may still be available. For example, the party denying that there is a legally binding contract may be estopped from denying its existence and may have to perform his obligations nonetheless. This would be appropriate where that person had behaved in some dishonourable way in the knowledge that the other person was acting to his detriment in the belief that the contract would be binding.

When and Where is the Contract Made?

The ability to point to the exact time that a contract is made may be important in a number of cases. For example, a contract for the writing of a new item of software may require that the work is completed no later than three months from the date of creation of the contract. A contractual offer for the sale of computer equipment may be expressed as being open for acceptance for seven days only (though such an offer will be binding only if supported by consideration — for example, where the person to whom the offer has been made has paid a fee for the benefit of the 'option').

Most contracts contain a term, often at the end of the agreement, stating under which country's law the contract is to have effect. For example the agreement may state that 'this agreement is subject to the laws of England and Wales.' Where the contract is silent about the applicable law, however, pragmatic rules have been developed by the courts to determine this question. In the absence of any statement or indication to the contrary, the basic rule is that the applicable law is that of the country in which the contract is made. This is all well and good where the parties execute the contract in each other's presence but, where they are dealing at arm's length and are based in two different countries, the question becomes more difficult. This problem is not new to computer technology and also arises in connection with the post telephone, telex and the fax machine as means of communicating offer and acceptance.

The normal way that a contract is made is when an offer made by one party is accepted, unconditionally and on identical terms, by the other. The contract is made the instant that the person to whom the offer is made (the offeree) communicates his acceptance to the person making the offer (the offeror). The first the this rule ran into difficulties was in relation to the use of the postal system which, as a means of communication, inevitably results in a time lag between making the offer or the acceptance and its receipt by the other party. Typically, problems can arise where the person making an offer revokes that offer before receiving the other's acceptance. A revocation of an offer is effective when communicated to the offeree — that is, when it is actually received by him. If, in the meantime, he posts an acceptance of that offer there is likely to be a conflict.

In *Adams* v *Lindsell* (1818) 1 B and & 681, the plaintiff was a manufacturer of woollen items located in Bromsgrove. The defendant was a wool merchant in St. Ives now in Cambridgeshire, some distance away. The defendant wrote to the plaintiff making an offer to sell wool to the plaintiff requiring an answer in the course of the post. Due to the defendant's negligence the letter was delayed by three days but almost immediately upon receiving it, the plaintiff wrote back accepting the offer. In the meantime, not having received a reply by the date he expected, the defendant sold the wool to a third party. The plaintiff successfully sued for breach of contract as the court decided that the contract was made when the letter of acceptance was posted.

The exception to the general rule applies only where it is reasonable to expect communication of acceptance through the post — for example, where the offer is made through the post and there is no stipulation or a different form of communication (see *Byrne* v *Van Tienhoven* (1880) 5 CPD 344). The rule would not apply if the offeror required communication of acceptance by some other method—or example, by telephone or fax.

The postal rule is an exception and where the means of communication being used by the prospective parties is almost instantaneous, the general rule will prevail. Thus, in *Entores Ltd* v *Miles Far East Corp* [1955] 2 QB 327, where offer and acceptance were communicated by telex, it was held that the acceptance took effect not when it was transmitted from Amsterdam but when it was received in London and, accordingly, the contract was subject to English law rather than Dutch law. The House of Lords approved of this decision in *Brinkibon Ltd* v *Stahag Stahl und Stahlwarenhandelsgesellschaft mbH* [1983] 2 AC 34. In the case the plaintiff, an English company, wished to buy a quantity of steel from the defendant, an Austrian company. The plaintiff sent a telex from London to Vienna, accepting the defendant's offer but the steel was not delivered and the plaintiff claimed damages for breach of contract in England. The house of Lords confirmed that the contract was made in Austria and, therefore, outside the jurisdiction of the English courts. Where the method of communication of acceptance is instantaneous a contract is made when the acceptance is received by the offeror. (This case may have been decided differently had the Brussels Convention on jurisdiction and enforcement in Civil trials been applicable—an option is that a defendant can be issued in the state in which the breach of contract occurs).

The House of Lords went on the stress that this is not a universal rule and the circumstances of a particular case might result in a different outcome. There may be all sorts of variations—for example, where the transmission will be received outside office hours and it is expected that it will be read later or where it is sent to a third party's telex machine or to the agent of the of error. Lord Wilberforce said:

> No universal rule can cover all such cases; hey must be resolved by reference to the intention of the parties, by sound business practice and in some cases by a judgment where the risks should lie.

Where an offer and acceptance are to be communicated by electronic mail, the basic rule should prevail, that is, that the acceptance is effective when it is received. Confirmation of receipt and reading is available in electronic mail systems and should be used. Difficulties may arise where the message accepting the offer is not read immediately upon receipt, perhaps because it is received during the right (for example, where one party is in Hong Kong and the other is in England) or the person to whom the receipt is addressed is out of he office for some time. It makes sense in such situations for the parties to stipulate their own rules—or example, that the acceptance is not effective until such time as it is read by the offeror or acknowledged by him. Great care must be taken by any person who has made offers to a number of other persons in respect of the same subject matter. However, where a person wishing to sell an item of computer equipment, for example, places details on the Internet, this will not be deemed to be an offer as such. It is more akin to placing an advertisement in a magazine which is an invitation to treat — in other words, an invitation to others to make euphorias to buy the equipment. In *Partridge* v *Crittenden* [1968] 2 All ER 421, Partridge place an advertisement in the Cage and Aviary birds magazine for the sale of Bramblefinches at £1 5s each. He was prosecuted under Section 6(1) of the Protection of Birds Act 1954 for offering or sale a wild bird. His conviction was quashed — he had not offered the birds for sale because the placing of the advertisement was not an offer, merely an invitation to treat.

Bearing in mind the transnational nature of the Internet, any person making offers or advertising goods or services should include a message to the effect that all enquiries, negotiations, offers acceptances or transactions will be governed by English law unless some other specified legal system is preferred.

Evidential Status of Electronic Documents in Civil Trials

A court of law will only allow evidence to be placed before it if it is admissible in accordance with what generally can be put in evidence. This rule has all but disappeared but remnants of it still remain.

The courts have recognised that a rigid adherence to the best evidence rule is inappropriate in the contest of the accuracy with which copies of originals may now be made. Lord Justice Lloyd said in *R* v *Governor of Pentonville Prison, ex parte Osman* [1989] 3 All ER 701:

> We accept that it [the best evidence rule] served an important purpose in the days of parchment and quill pens. But, since the invention of carbon paper and, still more, the photocopier and telefacsimile machine, that purpose has largely gone.

A general exclusion on copies of original documents is no longer fitting. Indeed, in some cases a document may be unintelligible in its original form without its being converted and displayed on a screen or printed out—for example, in the case of a document stored digitally on a magnetic disk. However, the original must still be produced if it is available. This would not apply where the original had been destroyed or lost.

A long tradition in English law has been the importance of a person giving evidence of what he personally knows or has witness with his own eyes. The fact that a witness is confined to matters of which he has personal knowledge and can be examined and cross-examined on those matters is a central plank of the English law of evidence. Second-hand or third-hand evidence is by is nature very unreliable so much so that it was not allowed to be heard until recently.

There was a rule against admitting hearsay evidence in civil trials (the rule still exists in relation to criminal trials. Hearsay evidence is secondary evidence such as where a witness relates something that was told to him by another person but not directly seen or heard by the witness—for example, where Bill states that Jenny told him that she saw Paul trying to erase a computer program. The rule was quite strict and such evidence would not be admitted at all except in specific circumstances, some of which applied to information stored on computer. Section 5 of the Civil evidence Act 1968 allowed statements contained in documents produced by a computer to be admitted in civil trials as evidence of any fact stated therein if the evidence would have been admissible as direct oral evidence, but only subject to certain conditions. However, the Civil Evidence Act 1995 has effectively swept aside the old rule against hearsay evidence in civil cases. The relevant provisions came into force on 31 January 1997. The new law applies only in respect of cases where proceedings commenced before this date.

Hearsay evidence is now admissible under Section 1 of the Civil Evidence Act 1995 and is defined as a statement made otherwise than by a person giving oral evidence in the proceedings and includes hearsay evidence of whatever degree. There are certain safeguards as regards notice to be given to other parties.

Although hearsay evidence is now admissible, it may not be given much weight. For example, if it is a document stored on computer which has undergone many alterations that have not been properly recorded or logged, it may carry little weight. Under section 4 of the Act, the weight, if any, to be given to hearsay evidence depends on the circumstances and regard shall be had to whether:

- it would be reasonable and practicable to call the original maker of the statement as a witness,
- the original statement was made at the same time as the occurrence or existence of the matters stated,
- the evidence involves multiple hearsay,
- any person involved has any motive to conceal or misrepresent matters,
- the original statement was an edited account or made in collaboration with another for a particular purpose, and
- the circumstances in which the evidence is adduced as hearsay are such as to suggest an attempt to prevent proper evaluation of its weight.

Hearsay may carry little weight unless it would have been admissible under Part I of the Civil Evidence Act 1968, now repealed. Factors included:

- regularity—whether the computer was regularly used to store or process information, for the purposes of any activities regularly carried out, over a period which includes the time when the document was made,
- consistency—during the relevant period information of the kind contained in the document (or of a kind from which such information is

derived) was regularly supplied to the computer in the ordinary course of those activities,

- reliability —the computer was operating properly during the martial part of that period (or, if not, any malfunction or breakdown that occurred would not have affected the accuracy of the material contained in the document),
- orthodoxy—the information contained in the document reproduces or is derived from information supplied to the computer in the ordinary course of the activities regularly carried out over the period in question.

Where a number of computers had been used—for example, successively or in a network—all the computers involved were treated as a single computer in determining the purpose of the activities. A person wishing to proffer a computer statement as evidence had to provide a certificate identifying the relevant document and the manner in which it was produced and giving other particulars. The certificate was required to be signed by a person occupying a responsible position in relation to the operation of the relevant device or the management of the relevant activities. It did not matter if the information was supplied or produced without any human intervention by means of appropriate equipment. This covered the situation where a computer was set up to record information and produce documents automatically.

Although the hearsay rule has been relaxed, if not altogether scrapped, the fact that a number of factors determine the weight to be given to such evidence means that it may not always be very influential, if at all. The main advantage flowing from the 1995 Act is that the formal rules under the 1968 Act have gone to be replaced by a welcome degree of flexibility. It will still be important, however, to show that the computer was operating reliably at the time and there is nothing to indicate that the evidence is unreliable. Adherence to the relevant standards applying to security and good computer practice will help in this respect.

Distance Selling

Buying goods or services by means of the Internet poses particular dangers for consumers. Credit care fraud is one problem and another is that insufficient information may be provided by the seller. The very nature of the Internet may tempt individuals to buy on impulse without properly thinking through the implications of the obligations they are entering into. As a result of these and other dangers, there is a possibility that individual member states of the European Community may implement very restrictive legislation, while others might encourage contracting over the Internet leaving it largely unregulated. The Commission to the European Communities considered that distance selling, particularly in the light of the introduction of new technologies ought to be subject to regulation which is harmonised throughout the Community. Eventually a Directive was adopted by the European Parliament and the Council (Directive 97/7/EC on the protection of consumers in respect of distance contracts, OJ L 144, 4.6.1997, p. 19). It has a number of implications for contracting over the Internet and is due to be implemented by member states no later than 4 June 2000. The main provisions of the Directive are described below.

Definitions and Exemptions

A distance contract is one concerning goods or services between a supplier and a consumer under an organised distance sales or service provision scheme run by the supplier who, for the purposes of the contract, makes exclusive use of one or more means of distance communication up to and including the moment the contract is concluded. Thus, right up to and including the time the contract is made, all negotiations and contracts must be by distance communication which includes electronic mail, videotext, videophone, television, radio and fax machines as well as more traditional forms of distance selling such as by post, catalogue and advertising in the press with an order form. The list is not exhaustive and is intended to be indicative only.

A consumer is an individual who does not make the contract in the course of his trade, business or profession and a supplier is a person (an individual or legal person such as company) who makes the contract in a commercial or professional capacity. An operator of a means of communication is a public or private provider of a method of distance communication to suppliers. This will include, for example, Internet Service Providers, commercial television and radio bodies and postal authorities.

The Directive does not apply to some contracts including certain contracts relating to financial services, automatic vending machines, in relation to land and auction sales. Also exempted are contracts concluded with telecommunications operators through the use of public telecommunications systems. The provisions in the Directive which apply to the giving of information, the right of withdrawal and the obligation to execute an order within 30 days do not apply to certain contracts for the supply of perishables and for the provision of accommodation, transport, catering or leisure.

Provision of Information

Certain information must be provide to the consumer before the contract is concluded. This is set out in Article 4 of the Directive and includes information about the identity of the supplier, the main characteristics of the goods or services, the price, delivery costs, payment details and existence of the right of withdrawal. It must be provided in a clear and comprehensible manner, having regard to the principles of good faith in commercial transactions. Where the telephone is used, the supplier must make his identity known at the beginning of any telephone conversation with the supplier. As regards the Internet or electronic mail, the provision of prior information should not be onerous and can be easily incorporated into the supplier's Website or e-mail message.

Article 5 requires that written confirmation must be provided (or confirmation in another durable medium—for example, this might be by downloading a computer file) of much of the information mentioned above. This must be provided in good time. The right of withdrawal must be mentioned as must be the geographical address of the supplier to which the consumer may address complaints. Further information such as that relating to after-sales service and the effect of cancelling the contract must also be given. These provisions do not apply, however, to services performed through the use of means of distance communication where supplied on only one occasion and invoiced by the operator of the means of distance communication, although the geographical address must be divulged nonetheless.

Other Aspect

There is a right of withdrawal under Article 6 but this is limited. Bearing in mind the ease with which computer software, video and sound recordings may be duplicated, the right may not be exercised unless otherwise agreed and does not apply in respect of the provision of services after performance has commenced, the supply of personalised goods and the like, and the supply of audio and video recordings and computer software. Other things are included such as periodicals and magazines.

The basic rule is that orders must be executed within 30 days, subject to a refund if the supplier is unable to deliver within that time because of the unavailability of goods and services, though the provision of equivalent goods or services is possible if the consumer was informed of this possibility.

There are provisions dealing with credit card fraud, a major concern when making transactions over the Internet. A consumer will have a right to request payment be cancelled where fraudulent use has been made of his credit card in a distance selling contract and, if this occurs, a right to be recredited with the sums paid or to have them returned. Inertia selling is also controlled although law in the United Kingdom already deals with this under the Unsolicited Goods and Services Act 1971 and makes this form of selling a criminal offence.

Further provisions relate to the requirement that a supplier must have the prior consent of the consumer to distance communication by automatic calling systems and fax machines and other forms of distance communication may be used only where there is no clear objection by the consumer. Does this mean that, before too long, we will have an E-mail Preference System?

The rights provided to consumers will be protected by judicial and administrative remedies and the rights cannot be waived nor compromised by a choice of law clause where he applicable law is that of a country outside the European Community. Member states may adopt a higher level of protection and may, in particular, prohibit the marketing of certain goods or services such as medicinal products. Furthermore, member states are required to inform consumers of these rights. As is becoming usual in consumer protection legislation, the burden of proof will lie with the supplier in most case.

Summary

The law has developed to take account of the use of information technology in commercial activity and, on a number of occasions, judges have had to deal with modern modes of information transmission such as telex, facsimile machines and computers. As has been shown, there are still some grey areas and those wishing to make full use of new technology to conduct their business must be aware of these areas and make appropriate provision. The strictness of the old rules relating to deeds and written documents has been mollified to some extent but the day has not yet arrived when writs can be served by electronic mail. In *Hastie and Jenkerson* v. *McMahon* (unreported) 3 April 1990, the Court of Appeal accepted that some documents could be validly served by fax. In this case a list of documents was required to be identified by court order and served by the plaintiff to an action on the defendant. All that was required was a legible copy of the document in question placed in the possession of the party on whom it was served and the fax machine achieve this. However, this does not apply to documents which must be served personally or documents initiating legal proceedings, such as a writ.

To conclude this chapter, it will be useful if we return to consider the position of Karen and Luigi and their contract for shoes. First, is there a valid contract? Karen appears to have made a clear offer by sending a copy of the contract for approval and Luigi has indicated his acceptance of its terms. If the transmission of the contract and Luigi's acceptance have been accurate, there should be a legally binding contract providing all the other requirements are met (for example, that the offer and acceptance were unconditional and that there was clear mutual agreement (*consensus ad idem*).

The next question to determine is the time that the contract was made. It would seem reasonable to expect that the acceptance became effective when it was first read by Karen on Wednesday, on the basis of the *Brinkibon* case—that is, when it was first communicated to Karne. *Brinkibon* is also authority for the contract being made in England and, providing there was no term in the contract to the contrary, the contract will be subject to English law.

INDEX

T

U

V

W

□□□